PLEASE RETURN THIS BOOK

Constance J. Wilson

TOWARD
THE
PH.D.
FOR
DOGS

TOWARD THE PH.D FOR DOGS

Obedience Training from Novice Through Utility

Robert J. Martin
and
Napoleon A. Chagnon

Harcourt Brace Jovanovich
New York and London

This book is respectfully dedicated to
Utility Dogs and their handlers,
and to our own dear companions,
Martin's Baron Friskiblitz, U.D. (1963–1974)
and
Gustav von Arborstadt, U.D. (1972–   )

Book design by Ulrich Ruchti

Printed in the United States of America

Library of Congress Cataloging in Publication Data

Martin, Robert J
  Toward the Ph.D. for Dogs.

  Includes index.
  1. Dogs—Training—Handbooks, manuals, etc.
I. Chagnon, Napoleon A., 1938–   joint author.
II. Title.
SF431.M45   636.7'08'8   74-33669
ISBN 0-15-190911-3

First edition
B C D E

CONTENTS

Note. We have indicated the page where each exercise is introduced; most of the exercises are modified in subsequent weeks. The breakdown in the Contents can thus serve as a guide for those who have difficulties in later weeks and must revert to earlier training lessons. Each week of training begins with an outline of the schedule for that week.

INTRODUCTION

Any dog more than six months old, even old dogs, can be trained by the methods in this book. An obedient dog may not always be a thing of beauty, but he certainly is a joy forever. Nothing is more impressive and satisfying to animal lovers than to watch an alert, sensitive, and intelligent animal express his acquired skills enthusiastically, smartly, and precisely on a verbal or hand signal from his master. And nothing is more disheartening than to watch an intelligent animal slink, with his tail between his legs, this way or that, as his uninformed master repeatedly barks seething commands at him, an animal who would probably risk his life to save the hand that is raised to beat him.

The difference between the two situations is merely one of intelligent training. Ardent trainers, we are well aware of the limits and abilities of dogs—and of the immense satisfaction that comes from training and owning a happy, healthy, and skillful animal—and so abhor the kinds of techniques used by both professional and amateur trainers that can lead to injury of the animal or the breaking of his "spirit." There seems to be a general sentiment in our society that dogs, being dumb brutes, must be trained with their brutishness uppermost in mind. Some popular training techniques emphasize such things as beating a dog into submission, kicking him, throwing hard metal objects at him, slapping him in the face with a newspaper, jabbering and shouting at him, slamming him on the floor, et cetera. Other training techniques go to the opposite extreme: beg him to perform, they urge, reward him lavishly with food, never scold or correct him—love will work a miracle. This kind of training is predicated on the opposite—and anthropocentric—assumption about dog nature: that dogs are human.

Dogs are neither dumb brutes nor sublime quadrupedal primates; they are very intelligent animals that, like all animals, respond to correction and praise, to negative sanctions and positive. It is not possible to train a dog without both, but it is not necessary to become excessive in either.

If you want to turn your pet into a happy, obedient dog, you can do one of several things. You can send him away for several weeks to a "canine college" for some very expensive and inadequate training, thereby engaging in what Thorstein Veblen puckishly called conspicuous consumption: afterward, you can tell your friends that your dog has been professionally trained . . . as they nervously edge into a corner to avoid having gigantic paw marks impressed upon their monogrammed, custom-made shirts. And all this for several hundred dollars.

Or you can enter a community-sponsored, inexpensive group class at the local YMCA and, with forty other people and their dogs, spend ten frustrating weeks learning what you should have learned in two days—from an instructor who took the course himself for the first time ten weeks before! If you last out *that* ten-week course, often called "Sub-Novice," you can move on to the next ten-week course for more of the same.

Or if you are lucky enough to have in your area a competent trainer who is familiar with and participates in all the obedience trials—from Novice through Utility—you can take an authoritative training course from him.

Or you can train your dog yourself, using a book. This one. It is written for people who do not have a very good chance of finding a trainer with an obedience course effective enough to get them into and successfully through any American Kennel Club (AKC) obedience trial. The ideal solution, of course, would be to combine the training of an experienced teacher with the lessons outlined in this book. Still, this book can stand alone. If you follow it carefully, you can train your dog and enter your first show in twelve weeks. (We even tell you how to obtain information about upcoming shows in your area and how to enter them.)

One of the two purposes of this book is to put forth a humane and efficient program for teaching a dog the most fundamental and practical skills of obedience, such as how to behave when his master is shopping, going for walks, driving, entertaining, and so on. If you follow the methods described, you will soon be able to go to the supermarket, tell your dog to lie down outside, and then go shopping. He will be there when you come out, waiting patiently. Or, if you let him out the back door to run in the yard and he begins to wander beyond it, you can bring him back with one command; he will be sitting at your feet, waiting for the next command, tail wagging.

The second objective is to help handlers prepare their dogs for competition in AKC shows and to provide a rigorous, systematic schedule leading to three of the AKC obedience titles. This is a book that you can carry in your hip pocket, so to speak, right up to the ring.

Thus, though we describe the techniques with an eye toward effective handling in an AKC obedience show, the training is the same for house pet and competition-quality obedience dog alike. Whether you are shooting at a modest goal, like being able to control your dog at home or in the street, or the more ambitious one of training him to be a Utility Dog Tracker (U.D.T.), the methods are the same in their broad principles. Obedience is obedience is obedience. The rigor we emphasize in the training, the precision and definitiveness we emphasize in command and performance, will ensure a better dog, a dog that will enthusiastically sit or stay when told to do so, whether in front of a supermarket door or in a crowded show ring under the glare of lights and the appraising eyes of a judge.

The only distinction between the two goals rests on the owner's interest and the dog's official or unofficial pedigree. All dogs can be taught to perform the exercises in this book, whatever their breed or pedigree. However, only purebred dogs can be shown in AKC competition.* In some respects this is lamentable; as distinct from conformation shows (breed), where a dog is judged on his looks, AKC obedience trials are run so that the dog's *learned skills* and *abilities* are judged, and the judging is objective: the dog either does the required exercise prop-

* (New York: Howell Book House, 1972), p. 521.

erly, or he does not. Thus, the dog is judged on skills learned, not inherited, and the precision with which he executes them. It is therefore unfortunate that nonregisterable dogs cannot compete for obedience degrees. But this is the rule, and should be considered at the outset of training: if you are interested enough in obedience training to want to compete, then your dog must be a registered purebred of a breed officially recognized by the AKC. The alternative, itself meritorious, is to be satisfied with your dog's ability whether he is of degree standards or not.

As enthusiasts of obedience competition, we encourage all of you who use this book to go on to competition if you have registered dogs. Your dog does not have to be particularly beautiful to earn obedience degrees, but he must be thoroughly trained. If you are partial to the democratic notion that the greatest good is that which is earned, you will enjoy AKC obedience trials. There, the people who handle the dogs are usually the people who trained them, folks like us. While you are there, take a look at the breed rings, where most of the dogs are handled by people who do not own them. It is unlikely that you will be able to secure your dog's breed championship unless you pay a professional handler, handsomely—some people go so far as to invest many thousands of dollars in handling, boarding, and transportation fees to get their dogs through a championship in the breed ring.

Obedience, however, is learning, and a dog's pedigree and looks are less important than his abilities. Genetics teaches us that hybridization increases viability, survivability, and vigor—and perhaps intelligence. Thus the most hybrid of mutts may be more capable of learning and performing than the greatest scion of a registered breed.

This is not to say that a pedigreed dog is likely to be stupid. In any population, human or canine, there is a range of intelligence, a mean intelligence with variation around it. All dogs, sometimes in spite of their breeding, are intelligent and therefore trainable. There is variation both within a breed and among breeds. For instance, some schnauzers are smarter than others, and schnauzers as a group are more trainable than some breeds and less trainable than others. But the smartest dog of the most trainable breed would, given the wrong kind of training, run a poor second to the least smart but properly trained dog of the most untrainable breed. There are two components to demonstrated ability: the genetic component and the socially acquired, or learned, component. With proper training, the genetic component can be brought to its maximum potential. Left untrained, it lies dormant, unexpressed. Thus, when you see a dog skillfully executing some command, you shouldn't think "What a smart dog!" but rather, "What a well-educated dog!" If you see a dog slinking around avoiding people and other dogs, you should think of a disadvantaged, maladjusted person who has been kicked around by society, for whatever biological component there is in this kind of behavior has been modified and intensified by experience.

In these times of rising crime rates and accompanying insecurity, many people are obtaining and, even worse, trying to train their own "attack" dogs—in utter ignorance of the amount of effort and training it takes to make a dog reliable and predictable. The going rate for a trained attack dog is anywhere from $2,000 to $5,000, and most of them are virtually uncontrollable, having been taught only to be indiscriminately fierce. Some are trained to bite and maim until the victim stops twitching. Such dogs cannot be handled by their owners, indeed are dangerous even to them.

We train attack dogs—mostly shepherds—but *not* to be attack or guard dogs *until* they have mastered what is in this book. And by the time they are ready for that kind of training, they could qualify as AKC Utility Dogs. First we teach them basic obedience—to be reliable and keenly aware of the single command. A properly trained attack dog is not noticeably different from any other well trained dog: attack is to him a command to execute a particular exercise efficiently, stop when commanded, and return for praise. It is done without much passion and wholly without anger. It is, simply, an exercise, like heeling or fetching a dumbbell.

We frequently demonstrate these kinds of dogs in front of children. The children can put their heads, hands, arms, or legs into the dog's mouth with impunity, box his ears, tease him, step on his tail. The dog will wince occasionally but will not bite. However, one command can alert him, and one command can stop him (he can, so to speak, be stopped in mid-air)—but only if he is well trained in basic obedience.

If you have an attack dog and he does not behave this way, he is a potential menace to you, your family, and your friends. If your dog cannot perform the material in chapters I and II, it would be both foolish and dangerous to try to train him for attack from one of the several available manuals. Most dogs will bite when they feel like it, but a properly trained attack dog will bite *only* on command. And, most important, *stop biting* on command.

Most people do not need, and furthermore should not have, a dog that will attack. What they really want is a dog that will harass a would-be intruder. A dog that makes a good deal of noise is usually sufficient to turn back unwanted company; most "professional" burglars insist on absolute silence in their work.

The obedience exercises and training procedures in this book constitute the basic preparation for training dogs in other, more specialized skills, not only attacking but also such tasks as finding a lost child by tracking, or locating explosives or weapons in connection with airport, state, or national security. If your dog can learn what is in this book, he can easily move on to more specialized training. But each skill builds upon and is an extension of an earlier one. The exercises are simple at first and may sometimes seem meaningless (to humans), but they are all important. You cannot start somewhere in the middle and work up. You must start at the beginning, at chapter I, whether you want your dog simply to stay put while you shop, or whether you expect him to track a lost child in Yellowstone National Park, find a bomb in someone's luggage, or roll over and play dead on command. In dog training there are no short cuts and no gimmicks that work. It takes time, patience, and a combination of two simple sanctions: correction for improper behavior and praise for proper behavior. Charlatans will try to convince you that expensive and elaborate instruments are necessary, but these are, in the final analysis, irrelevant ploys. All that is needed for the basic training is a choke-chain collar, a leather lead, a few pieces of guide rope, and an understanding of the difference between proper behavior and improper behavior. Firmness in correction, sincerity in praise, and the ability to maneuver diligently on your own two feet are what you, as the handler, have to learn to master as you train your dog.

In chapters II and III you will need special objects but not necessarily for teaching your dog obedience; they are mostly the objects you will be training your dog to fetch, find, or jump over. Thus they are necessary only if you wish to compete in the AKC obedience trials at a more advanced level, or if you want your dog to learn how to track, to find objects with your or other people's scent on them, or to find people.

Training your dog is like giving him a college education, and this book will enable you to have your own backyard university. The first degree a person earns in college is a bachelor's. In dogdom, in AKC trials, it is the Companion Dog (C.D.) degree.* People sometimes go on to earn a master's degree; in dogdom the equivalent is the Companion Dog Excellent (C.D.X.) degree. Like its human counterpart, it is a bit more advanced and more difficult, and few dogs go on to earn it (see chapter III, Week 1, for statistics). And last and most difficult of all, for people, is the doctor of philosophy (Ph.D.) degree; for dogs, it is the Utility Dog (U.D.) degree. Just as very few people earn the Ph.D., very few dogs earn the U.D. Some dogs go on to earn another degree, or title, the Tracking dog certificate; they bear after their name the initials U.D.T., meaning that they have both the Utility Dog degree and the Tracking degree, which is relatively easy to earn (some dogs earn it before finishing the U.D., although a dog that has a U.D. can usually earn the Tracking degree very easily).

We assumed, in writing the more advanced chapters, that the dog being trained was a bit on the recalcitrant side. Or, to put it another way, we did not assume that you had the most trainable dog in the world. If your dog is especially precocious, you can dispense with much of the aid the guide ropes provide and modify the techniques to fit your dog's ability. Too many books, however, give too little space to the dog that *resists* learning an exercise. We made the assumption that all dogs would resist some particular exercise and described all the training techniques accordingly. Our experience has been that sooner or later a dog suffers a slump.

We would also like to comment on our usage of pronouns in the text. If you look through a judging program for an AKC dog show, you will find the statement " 'Dog' means either sex." And so when you see the word "he" in this book, it means "he *or* she," unless the context clearly specifies the sex of the particular individual (dog, trainer, judge,

---

* Where we use the phrase "obedience degree" (to emphasize the analogy we wish to make with human higher education), the correct phrase would be "obedience title." Thus, a dog earns the C.D. title, not the C.D. degree, et cetera.

stewards, et cetera). We apologize in advance to any of our female colleagues who feel slighted.

What are obedience training and competition all about? Why do we and countless others get excited and enthusiastic about them? These are perhaps personal questions. Competition in AKC obedience trials is one of the most democratic sports in the country. It is open to all dogs and people, irrespective of size, shape, amount of musculature, age, sex, color, political persuasion, and social class. It is an athletic event of sorts, but one in which cunning, charm, ability, personality, and patience count more toward success than sheer strength or size. It is a skill in which your native abilities are limited only by the degree of success you have had in obtaining the respect and reciprocal co-operation and affection of your teammate—your dog.

Finally, whether or not you show your dog in AKC obedience trials, there is the fun of learning a skill and causing your dog to learn one. An alert, well-behaved dog is a pleasure to have around—a true companion, as the Novice title implies. Whether you are training your dog for competition in the obedience show ring or for companionship around the house, the methods are the same. One principle stands out in both cases; it is perhaps best stated in the American Kennel Club's *The Complete Dog Book* *:

> There is, however, one absolute requirement identical in ring and home—your dog must learn to obey you instantly, with one and only one command or order. The truest sign of the poorly trained dog is the repeated command or commands, quite generally given in a rising voice, and only reluctantly complied with by the dog.

Come, then, and experience some delightful moments with your dog. Training will be punctuated once in a while with frustration and good-natured chagrin, but, in the end, your dog will go get the proverbial newspaper and slippers for you and be much more fun to have around.

---

* See Chapter I, Week 10, for an explanation of how to obtain an Indefinite Listing Privilege for dogs that are purebred, but have no registration papers.

TOWARD THE PH.D. FOR DOGS

I
THE
NOVICE
EXERCISES

Toward the Bachelor's Degree:
Companion Dog

NOVICE WEEK 1

OUTLINE OF TRAINING SCHEDULE
Introduction to Collar and Lead
Basic Heeling
Corrections for Forging and Lagging
Automatic Sit

A few general comments are in order as we begin the formal training. Occasionally there will be exercises and procedures we will insist have to be done in a certain way, without deviation. We do not always explain why, largely for reasons of efficiency: these situations usually arise in the middle of something quite complicated, and to explain them in detail at that time would distract you from the specific lesson. In general, the form and rigor we insist upon are based on one fact: the training procedure you are learning is intimately related to a more advanced lesson, and the techniques we are urging you to follow are designed to preadapt you and your dog for the more advanced exercises.

We provide a schedule that is largely derived from the formal classes we give in obedience training. These classes meet once a week, for one hour. Each class has approximately ten to twelve people in it, and each person/dog team has about six minutes to work on an individual basis, in front of the others and the instructor during the hour. Handlers or dogs that are having particular difficulties either receive more individual attention during the regular class period or remain afterward for special instruction. The members of the class are then expected to practice a few minutes every day between meetings.

Obviously, in a book designed for teaching your dog at home, we cannot participate directly with you in your training program. We cannot see you and your dog work, diagnose your handling problems, or evaluate your dog's performance. One way we have tried to compensate for the disadvantages of communication by distance is to provide photographs that illustrate in detail how to effect particular handling techniques. Often we show an entire exercise as it should be executed in show circumstances. It should be relatively easy to train your dog on the individual exercises by first reading the text and then studying the photographs and captions. When you move out to your yard or basement, bring your text with you and quickly glance over the photographs before attempting to work your dog: the illustrations are an abbreviated version of the training methods and techniques. Indeed, they help tell a major part of the story.

Another way we have tried to offset the distance problem has to do with failure: most books tell you how to do something and assume that your dog will do it right away. Such an assumption is unwarranted. In this book you will find an explanation of what to do if the dog fails to perform as expected. Because we are constantly involved in competition and must have our own dogs in top-notch form, we are keenly aware of the myriad problems and how to overcome them. This we pass on to you as well.

The weekly schedules are designed in such a way that your dog could enter competition soon after the tenth week of training, assuming that you have given him a bit of public exposure toward the end of the course. Much depends on the rigor with which you keep to the schedule: two or three training sessions per day for about five minutes each session, unless otherwise specified. Each training session will incorporate exercises from previous weeks. Thus your dog will be perfecting old skills even as you introduce new ones.

Even if you are not interested in competition, the schedules we provide are desirable ones to follow. They are geared to the rate at which dogs can learn and master particular exercises, beginning slowly and then gradually accelerating. You may stretch the ten-week Novice schedule if you wish, but it is *not* advisable to jump ahead, skipping particular lessons merely because something more advanced is more attractive to you, or because Mitzi does not "like" heeling. Mitzi will not be able to handle anything reliably *beyond* heeling if she cannot master it first. Heeling teaches the dog something more than just walking beside a handler in the proper position. It teaches Mitzi that she *must* obey when commanded, and that she, not you, is wearing the choke-chain collar.

Basic Equipment and Terminology

Your dog's first lesson will be to learn about the choke-chain collar and lead. This is an important lesson and it should be brief—about two or three minutes. The objective is to get the dog to stay close to you without trying to move away when he is "on lead"; do not try to accomplish any more than that. But before we explain what the lesson entails, let us take a close look at the equipment and terminology we will use.

The Choke-Chain Collar   Get a good-quality choke-chain collar with close, *small* links that run freely through the rings. The size of the collar should be such that approximately two or three inches hang free when it is around the dog's neck. Choke-chain collars with large links tend to drag too much, catch on obstacles, and pull hair out of the dog's neck. Periodically, run the links through your fingers to see if the chrome has peeled or if there are any sharp metal bristles or protrusions.

The choke-chain collar is to be used *only* during training, or when you are able to see your dog. Never let the dog run loose with his choke-chain collar on, and never tie a rope to it and leave him alone that way. As its name suggests, *it can choke your dog—to death!* Get into the habit of removing the choke-chain collar if your dog is to be confined in the car, his kennel, or wherever he might accidentally catch the collar on something and hang himself. A good practice is to keep a leather collar (with tags attached showing identification, inoculation, and license) on your dog when you are not working with him. Put the choke-chain collar on only for the training.

5

The choke-chain collar has a running end and a stationary end. These are often referred to as the "live" and "dead" ends of the collar. As the names suggest, the ring through which the chain passes is stationary, or dead, and the ring that is able to move up and down is the running, or live, end. A good choke-chain collar will, if properly fitted to your dog's neck, automatically expand to its maximum diameter by gravity alone; that is, the weight of the ring at the running end will be sufficient to keep the collar open and loose.

It is important to put the collar on the dog with the running end in the position shown in figures I-1 and I-2. If it is upside down, it will not run smoothly and will tend to be tight because it cannot run through the dead ring. Your dog will learn to recognize the slight tinkle of the chain as you begin training and correcting; if the chain cannot run, it will not make this noise.

The Lead   It is important that the lead be six feet long, since the training will involve a number of exercises that assume a six-foot distance between the dog and handler. Ideally, the lead should be made of leather. Avoid chain or link leads; they are too heavy and are not approved for AKC competition. An obedient dog does not *need* a lead that is excessively heavy or thick. A good width for the lead is as follows: ⅝ inch (leather) for large dogs, including Saint Bernards, and ⅜ inch for dogs smaller than forty pounds. In training, both you and your dog could be injured with a heavy chain lead used improperly.

If a leather lead is not available, a nylon or other fabric lead can be used. As a last resort, a six-foot piece of clothesline rope with a swivel snap at one end and loop at the other can be substituted.

During most of the Novice exercises, the dog will be working "on lead," and you should have a light, comfortable lead that you can handle efficiently, one that does not distract or confuse the dog. It should be relaxed enough to apply very little pressure on the choke-chain collar—until a correction is made. The correct position for holding the lead is shown in figures I-3 through I-6. Note that it is held in the right hand and hangs loosely. These figures also demonstrate the proper heeling position, from which most of the exercises in this book are begun. Study the photographs carefully, for you will be instructed many times throughout these lessons to "put your dog into the proper heeling position."

Balance, Leverage, and Corrections   You, as the handler/trainer, will have to concentrate on two principles: *balance* and *leverage*. *Balance* refers both to the dog's balance and to your own. Your job will be to stay "on your toes" and continue maneuvering in such a way that when you apply a *correction* (described in a moment), you will effectively knock your dog temporarily off balance. This means that you will have to display a certain amount of finesse and agility to keep yourself in a position—and balanced—to correct effectively. *Leverage* means positioning yourself in such a way that, as you maneuver around with your dog on lead, you can apply a correction at the proper angle and with

I-1. The choke-chain collar should have small, tight links that are free of burrs or metal protrusions. The leather lead is attached to the "live," or running, end. This is called a "slip collar" in the *AKC Obedience Regulations*. (See chapter 2, section 17 of Appendix I.)

I-2. The collar opens to maximum diameter by the weight of the live ring alone—if the collar is placed on the dog as shown. A properly fitted collar will have two or three inches of extra length protruding when the collar is tightened around the dog's neck.

I–2

7

the requisite amount of force. In the early training you will often have to apply several corrections in rapid succession, so your maneuvering and positioning, as well as your timing, will have to be co-ordinated. It sounds rather complex when described in words, but it is actually quite simple—once you get the hang of it.

A *correction* is a sharp tug on the leather lead. It should be made only with sufficient force to knock the dog off balance temporarily, to spin him a bit so that he has to scramble to get his feet back underneath him. The correction should be very quick so that the dog knows it is being applied as a correction, not merely as a gradual tightening of the lead. It should *not,* however, be violently executed. The purpose of the correction is to inform the dog that *he is in the wrong position* and, as soon as he gets into the right position, the correction will stop. It follows that in order to do all of this properly, you must keep several things in mind, things that will, after a few practices, become fixed as habit in your mind and, more important, in your dog's.

Angle. Looking at the procedure from above, it is clear from geometric principles alone that you can apply the correction more effectively if you position yourself at the proper angle. Figures I-7 and I-8 show the improper and proper angles, respectively. The closer your lead is to 90° with respect to the dog's axis, the better leverage you will have and the more effective your correction will be. In most cases, you will not be anywhere near 90° when you correct your dog, but you should try to apply your correction with the ideal, or optimal, *angle* in mind.

Size of Dog. Since big dogs are somewhat more difficult to knock off balance than small dogs, the larger your dog, the more important it is to maneuver into such a position that the angle of your correction approximates 90°. While you will later be working and correcting with only your right hand holding the lead, it is appropriate—and sometimes necessary—for you to use both hands to correct the dog, especially a very large dog, during the introduction to the collar and lead. Even burly, strong people with recalcitrant dogs may initially have to use both hands for corrections. Remember, however, that the object is to get the dog to behave without having to apply corrections, so strive to get back to single-hand corrections as soon as possible.

The Surface on Which You Train. The more effectively you can unbalance the dog, the more alert and responsive he will be to any change in direction you make. It is easier to knock a dog off balance on a slippery surface than on one that affords him good, stable traction. Therefore, training for the first few weeks on a somewhat slippery surface, such as tile or, if you are working outdoors, worn concrete,* will enhance the effectiveness of your corrections and facilitate your mastery of the acrobatics you must execute to keep in proper position. You should wear crepe or regular rubber-soled shoes to maximize your traction and discourage the dog from relying on the sound of your feet to reveal your position to him. Avoid training on ground where the dog can dig in and resist your corrections. If it is possible for him to avoid the correction and

---

* Do not go to the extreme of selecting a surface that is *too* slippery. We find that worn concrete is the best surface.

I-3. The proper heeling position, side view. The dog's neck should be adjacent to the handler's left leg.

I-4. The proper heeling position, front view. Note that the leather lead should have a good deal of slack in it and that it is held with the right hand only.

I-5. The proper heeling position, oblique view. This is the minimum amount of slack in the leather lead.

I–6

I-6. The proper heeling position, top view. Note that the dog's axis is perfectly parallel to the handler's. Both have an identical "direction of march."

I–9

I-7. An unfavorable angle between the dog's axis and the leather lead. A much larger expenditure of energy is required to knock the dog off balance from this poor position. The dog can easily resist a correction made from this angle.

I-8. A favorable angle between the dog's axis and the leather lead; a correction here would require minimum effort to achieve maximum effect and knock the dog off balance momentarily.

I-9. A straight-line correction: avoid doing this. Note how successfully the dog resists the correction by digging in—and he is learning that a correction can be resisted.

being knocked off balance, he will attempt to do so; he must be convinced that he *cannot* resist the correction. This is an important point, and will come up again later: you must always be in a position to enforce any command by correcting the dog if he fails to respond. He must learn from the outset that he will be corrected if he performs incorrectly and that the correction is irresistible. Some dogs will react to a new or strange surface by lying down, crouching, or tiptoeing as if they were walking on eggs. If your dog has never before been on a surface as smooth as the one you plan to train on, allow him some exploration time on that surface first so he can build up his confidence.

Balance and leverage are important principles to keep in mind throughout this course. Effective, painless correction depends on how well you master your own maneuverability and keep yourself in a position to apply a correction quickly and efficiently. The better your angle, the more effectively you can make a correction with minimal effort on your part, and minimal discomfort to the dog.

Straight-Line Corrections. One kind of error new handlers commonly fall into is the tendency to make a straight-line correction, to pull—or try to pull—a dog in a straight line to correct him. When pulled in that fashion, most dogs will automatically resist by digging in and crouching—and, in most cases, resist successfully. Figure I-9 shows what happens when a straight-line correction is made. Avoid this by quickly moving yourself into position to correct from the proper angle, an angle that enables you to knock the dog off balance.

Praise. The obverse of a correction is praise, or reward. The most effective and appreciated praise is your indication that you are pleased with your dog's performance. He will work enthusiastically for that pat on the head, that happy-voiced "Good dog!," that pleasurable sense that you are delighted with his good behavior. Inject some happiness into your verbal praise when the dog has successfully and proficiently completed an exercise; rub his head or neck and pat him affectionately. *Do not use food as a reward.* It is much less effective than your genuine approval and will lead to extreme unreliability in a pinch. In addition, anybody can interfere with your dog's obedience if food is used as a reward—your dog might, to give an exaggerated example, change directions in mid-heeling and walk away at heel with some popcorn-munching stranger passing by in the opposite direction.

Finally, one must be aware of individual differences in dog temperament. Some dogs are more sensitive than others, and some are able to sustain greater amounts of correction than others. It is necessary to use both correction and praise to train your dog, but we want you to be aware of the fact that you must work out the appropriate combination that keeps your dog alert, aware of his obligations, and happy to learn new exercises.

Introduction to Collar and Lead

With this brief background you are ready to introduce your dog to the collar and lead. In brief, your dog's formal training in obedience begins here. Your training also begins here: get into the habit of allowing your   11

I-10. To introduce your dog to the collar and lead, form a loop in the collar by allowing the chain to drop through one of the rings. Then attach the swivel of the lead to the ring, which can move back and forth when the chain passes through the other ring.

I-11. Slip the chain over the dog's head with the lead attached to the "live" end of the collar.

dog to relieve himself before you train. You should have a signal to indicate to him that he is not expected to work. We use the word "okay," which releases the dog from a command and permits him to go out to the end of the lead, either to relieve himself or just as a break from work.

Form a loop in your choke-chain collar and snap the swivel of your leather lead to the running end of the dog's choke-chain collar, as shown in figure I-10; place the collar on the dog's head, as shown in figure I-11.

Your first lesson will be to keep silent. Most people, without realizing it, speak and jabber to their dogs. If you have that habit, stop it. It is unnecessary, and will lead to disqualification in an obedience trial for those of you who continue on to competition. Most important, our method of training is predicated on a schedule and philosophy in which the dog will obey a *single* command, whether it is given verbally or by hand signal; to achieve that level of proficiency, you must remain silent while you are working the exercises. If your dog has got into the habit of hearing you jabber when you are neither commanding nor praising, it will be difficult for both of you to follow our training procedure. Within a few days of training, your dog will be straining to hear your lovely voice, so do not use it unnecessarily.

Your dog is now wearing the choke-chain collar. Remember, you should put this collar on him only while you are working with him. From this point on, we will assume that you know that while you are training, your dog is on one kind of collar: the choke-chain collar. We will refer to it hereafter as simply the "collar."

You should start your exercise on a smooth surface, one that your dog has had a chance to explore and on which he feels confident.

Begin with the dog somewhere near you and let him wander out toward the end of the six-foot lead, as in figure I-12. When he gets there, make a very sharp correction at the proper angle: a sudden tug on the lead that spins him off balance, toward you (fig. I-13). Pay no attention to him—do not look at him—just pretend that nothing happened. Let him wander out again to the end of the leather lead. This time, adjust yourself in such a way that when he reaches the end of it (fig. I-14), your next correction spins him in toward your left side (fig. I-15). You should be making the corrections with your right hand only if your dog is small; if he is big, it is appropriate and reasonable to apply the correction with both hands—especially if *you* are small. An effective correction at this stage would be to spin the dog completely around, so that when he regains his balance he is moving in the opposite direction from his initial position. If his lead is adjusted up toward his head—high on his neck as in figure I-16—a very small correction should cause him to spin that much, if your surface is linoleum or tile. On concrete or asphalt, a slightly more rigorous correction would be necessary. Thus, if you are squeamish about applying a meaningful, smart correction, the onus of selecting the most effective surface falls on you. It takes less force to roll a marble across a smooth table than it does to roll it across a crushed-stone driveway. Similarly, it takes less 13

I-12. To introduce your dog to the collar and lead, allow him to wander out to the end of the lead, and try to adjust yourself in such a way that, when you make your first correction, you do so at a desirable angle. (Note: For photographic purposes, the introduction to the collar and lead is shown outdoors, on a lawn. The proper training surface at this stage in your dog's training should be tile, linoleum, hardwood flooring, worn concrete, or asphalt.)

I-13. Your first correction should be made with just enough force to spin the dog off balance, toward you. Say nothing, and act as if nothing had happened. The dog will begin to think that he is bringing the corrections on himself by being in the wrong place.

I-14. Most dogs will be puzzled by the first correction you make (fig. I-13) and ignore it. Soon they wander out to the end of the lead again. Adjust your position to correct at an advantageous angle: when the dog is about like this, apply a sharp tug on the lead to spin him toward you, knocking him off balance.

I-15. The dog has been spun off balance a second time and begins to realize that there is something about his position with respect to you that is causing the peculiar discomfort.

I-16. If you adjust your dog's collar high up on his neck, your corrections can be made more efficiently and humanely —it takes much less force to make a proper correction when the collar is close to the dog's head.

effort to correct effectively on a smooth surface than on a rough one, such as your lawn (see the explanatory note on fig. I-12).

Let your dog wander out to the end of the lead again if he is inclined to do so. Stay in position to face the dog; as he reaches the end of the lead, make sure you are at an advantageous angle and again correct with a smart tug on the lead, spinning the dog off balance and in toward your left side.* You want him, eventually, to remain at your left side—the proper heeling side. As soon as he catches on to the fact that whenever he gets beyond a certain point he will be knocked off balance toward your left side, he will begin to come in to your left side and remain there, somewhat confused about what is going on, but at least very much aware that he is, by being in that position, avoiding the peculiar sensation of being off balance (see figs. I-17–I-25). To keep yourself facing the dog, you will have to move definitely and swiftly, even walking backward at times, actually tempting the dog into getting a bit too far away and sustaining a correction. Each time the dog tries to get out to the end of the lead, apply a correction with just sufficient force to spin him around and in to your left side. As he comes in, praise him verbally as you walk away in a straight line. He may then try to do

* Some dogs will attempt to bite their handler, although this is very rare. To protect yourself from a bite, if your dog is predisposed to try it, make certain that you have control over the leather lead. Simply lift the dog up off the ground by the lead, allowing only his hind feet to touch. Keep him in that position for a while—until he struggles a bit to get back down. He cannot move from that uncomfortable position unless you relax the lead. He will soon learn not to try to nip you.

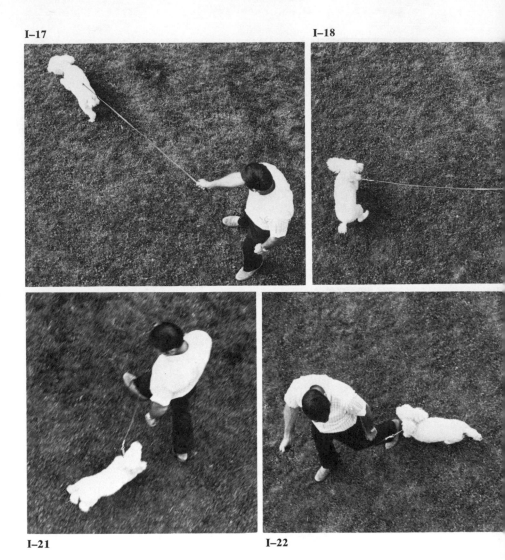

one of several things. If he bears off to your left, step in the opposite direction to help him get to the end of the lead more quickly, make another correction in to your left side, and then walk away so as to keep the dog on your left. If he tries to cross to the right in front of you, step backward and slightly to the left, exposing the left side of your body to him and correct again, spinning him toward you. If he tries to go around behind you, turn quickly so as to keep your left side exposed to him, and correct again, spinning him toward you. In short, wherever he goes, keep your left side toward him, knocking him off balance every time he tries to move away from your left side. Each time you make a correction, go forward in such a way that the dog is at your left side; sometimes you may have to go to the left, sometimes the right, sometimes even backward—but keep him on your left side, and keep him spinning in to you after each correction. It is important to move away after each correction; if he fails to come with you, he will get another

I–23   I–24   I–25

I-17–25: Teaching Your Dog the Basics of Heeling.
Examine the sequence of illustrations. Try to keep
moving in a counterclockwise direction, correcting the
dog in to your left side as you move. Remain silent and
keep moving, adjusting your position so that your angle
of correction is advantageous. You may have to move
to the left, the right, or backward to keep in an advantageous position. Help the dog keep to your left by
exposing your left side to him as you correct him in to
you. After about sixty seconds of this, the exercise
should end. By that time, most dogs will be scrambling
to keep close to you and at your left side.

correction—one that again brings him in to your left side. Try to maneuver yourself in such a way that the dog is not only on your left side, but perpendicular to the axis of your leather lead. You might have to move quickly to maintain that relationship.

Another way of putting it is, *help* the dog remain at your left after you give a correction. Do not rely on the correction to bring him in to your left side, but position yourself in such a way that when he regains his balance he will be at your left and in motion as you walk in a straight line; as soon as he attempts to move out of this position, turn your left side toward him and correct him in to you with a tug on the lead. Make it clear to him that if he comes in to your left side and remains close to you, he can avoid the tug on his lead and receive, as a bonus, a "Good dog!" verbal assurance as you move off again.

The first lesson is taxing on both dog and handler. The handler must scramble and pirouette to keep in an advantageous position; the dog will soon learn that he must do the same to keep up and avoid a correction. Make the corrections in such a way that he is always brought in to your left side. Generally, it is more convenient to move in a counterclockwise direction as you teach him the fundamentals of heeling.

The description of this routine may seem complex and lengthy, but the lesson should last only a few seconds—not more than a minute. If your dog is normal, and if you apply the corrections silently and effectively, the dog will be coming in to you and trying to remain close to your left side. The moment he begins to do this, give him verbal praise and encouragement, but keep in motion to make sure he is scrambling to keep on your left-hand side, close to your leg.

When he is clearly trying to do that, and has his attention undividedly focused on you, allow him to come up to your left leg as you keep moving, and then come to a halt. As you do, pull up on the leather lead with your right hand and push down on his rump with your left hand (fig. I-26). Do not say a word. Make certain that you pull up on the lead directly over the dog's head and push firmly down on his rump. When he is sitting, give him a good deal of verbal praise and love him up. The lesson is over.

Again, and this point cannot be stated too strongly: do *not* give your dog food as a reward. This means that you must adjust your training and feeding schedules in such a way that you do not feed him for at least half an hour after your training sessions. The object is to get the dog to work for praise alone; the best dogs are those that would seem to do anything to please their handlers. In fact, a pat on the head and "Good boy!" is more pleasurable to a normal dog than a piece of meat is.

From this point on, you should sharply distinguish your training from your mere walking. An important lesson will be to make the dog aware that when he is on the leather lead and choke-chain collar, he is subject to your commands. You should show him that there is a time for freedom on the work collar and a time for work. One lesson the importance of which cannot be overstressed has to do with his natural calls. Before you work him, let him relieve himself. Get him

I-26. End every heeling practice with an enforced sit like this: as you come to a halt with the dog at your left side, quickly pull up on the lead with your right hand and push down on the dog's rump with your left. Do it swiftly— after a few days the dog will try to beat you to it and come to an immediate sit whenever you halt. Give praise only after the dog has come to a sit.

to do it *on lead,* and permit him to do it only after you say "Okay!" The "Okay!" should be used to tell the dog that he is no longer supposed to be heeling or working, but is free to go out to the end of the lead to relieve himself. After he has done so, give him a reassuring "Good boy!" Under no circumstances should you allow him to relieve himself while you are training; if he must go, quickly take him out of the training area and give him the "Okay" release command. We will explain later why you cannot allow the dog to relieve himself during an obedience exercise. For the moment, get into the habit of allowing the dog to answer nature's call while he is released ("Okay!") from a work command and before the work actually starts. Needless to say, you should familiarize yourself with the local rules about allowing your dog to relieve himself; each community has its own.

Let us end with a speculative view of what the dog has just been through. Although we cannot pretend to know what a dog "thinks" while he is being trained, our experience has been that a dog seems to dislike being off balance *per se* and will attempt to avoid it. Thus the correction to put him off balance need not and should not be painful. Another thing we have learned is that the dog does not associate the correction with the handler *if* the correction is made silently and without passion, but seems rather to "blame" himself for being in the wrong place or wrong configuration; he seems to think that he did it to himself and therefore must change his behavior to avoid it in the future. The fact that you, the handler, are strangely silent and unconcerned strengthens his conviction. It is clear to him that he does not cause himself the inconvenience and discomfort of being spun off balance if he adjusts his position in such a way that he is always on   19 your left and close to your leg. Your happiness at seeing him there, as evinced by your verbal and other praise, reinforces the knowledge that he is acquiring. With this twofold benefit of avoiding discomfort and gaining praise, he will *love* being there and will be delighted to remain there.

The dog's first lesson should not last longer than a minute or so. He will be virtually wrung out after that. You will notice that he will sleep heavily that night. He has, after all, been forced to think for an intensely long period of time, to concentrate on something that is new, even revolutionary in his life. And yours.

It is perfectly all right for your dog to sniff around at bushes and trees when he is on the "Okay" release command. From now on, however, you will be giving him the command "Heel!" to begin work, and after this command you should not allow any sniffing. If he tries to sniff at dogs or where dogs once were, or tries to move away from you to sniff, give him a sharp correction and get him back into the working position. The reason for this, too, will be explained later.

The introduction to the collar and lead *could* be accomplished in two or three sessions (two days of training). Some dogs might be a bit slower than others in learning, and some handlers might be less effective than others—a slow dog and novice handler might have to spend the first week perfecting the routine. Average conditions are assumed— normal dogs and normal novice handlers—in the schedule for Novice training.

Basic Heeling

The second day of training begins the heeling exercises. You should try to work twice with your dog on the second day: once in the morning and once in the later afternoon or evening. Each session should last from three to five minutes—but no longer than five minutes.

What you do on the second day will be repeated for the next several days; normally, the basic heeling exercises can be taught in a few weeks of working twice a day for three to five minutes in each training session.

A number of heeling terms have precise meanings, especially in AKC competitions; they should be fully understood and memorized.

The Heeling Position After the second day, your training routines will all begin from the proper heeling position. The dog should be sitting at your left side, with his bottom squarely on the ground and *not* slouched over on one hip. He should be about the width of a shoe from you, not touching your leg or leaning on it. Put him into this position by pulling up on the lead with your right hand and pushing down on his rump with your left. You should be free to move away in a straight line without touching the dog. The lead should be hanging loosely, forming a definite loop under his neck but not touching the ground; it should *not* be taut. The dog's neck should be adjacent to your left leg. If he is large, the mid-point of his neck will be adjacent to your thigh; if he is small, it will be adjacent to your calf. Examine figures

I-3 through I-6 above, and reread this paragraph with the illustrations and captions in mind. It will pay off later.

The Right Turn A right turn is executed when the dog is at your left side and both of you are walking in a straight line. You make a right turn by pivoting on the ball of your right foot and turning 90° without pausing or changing your speed. The lead should always remain loose during turns, and the dog should hustle to keep in the proper position, next to your left leg, but not touching it. As you turn, the dog will have to speed up and, when you resume a straight-line march, he will slow down to your speed. We will explain in a moment how to get your dog to do the right turn properly.

The About Turn An about turn is always made to the right. As in the right turn, you pivot on the ball of your right foot, turning 180° instead of just 90°. You should, after the turn, be walking back along your original line of march. You might want to practice on a straight line, *without* the dog, to make sure you can do it smoothly; many people, when attempting to concentrate on several things at once, concentrate too hard on some things and botch up the obvious ones—like turning in the wrong direction when given the command "About Turn!" by the AKC judge or trainer, or turning 210° instead of 180°. Again, the dog will have to speed up to keep his position near your left leg.

The Left Turn You will not use the left turn during the first week of training; your dog is not ready for it and you could set the training back a week by attempting it before the dog has mastered the right turn and about turn. It is, however, logical to describe it in this section and explain later how to do it properly. The left turn is executed while both dog and handler are walking at a normal pace in a straight line. The handler pivots on his left foot and turns 90° to the left. The dog will have to slow down and he must not touch the handler's leg.

The Automatic Sit The dog should come to a sit in the correct heeling position, without any vocal command, as soon as the handler comes to a complete stop.

Timed Corrections This is not an AKC term, as most of the other terms are; we use it in our training classes to mean a sequence of appropriate corrections that knock the dog off balance, first to the right and then to the left, in a zigzag fashion. Timed corrections reinforce appropriate behavior in the dog; they are applied in the manner described until the dog seems eager to do what is expected of him. Normally, two or three rapid corrections are sufficient to show the dog the most desirable thing to do; then they are stopped so that the dog can show that he will do what is expected of him.

Begin the first lesson of the second day by brushing up on the collar and lead exercise with your dog, making sure that he keeps within the length of the lead. As soon as he starts responding and comes toward you, begin walking in a straight line and make a right turn. The dog must learn that unless he turns to keep up with you he will be corrected. Be silent as you make your correction; be matter-of-fact. It is actually advantageous if he fails to keep up or to turn, not 21

I–27

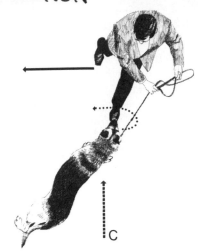

C

B

I-27. Correction sequence for a dog that lags.

A. The dog falls behind the handler—he lags. If you catch him in this position, take a quick wide step off to the right, turning to face the dog as you step.

B. Knock the dog off balance, as indicated by the arrow.

C. While the dog is still off balance from the first correction, quickly make a second correction in the direction indicated by the dotted arrow near the dog's head.

D. Note that you are now heeling in a new direction, 90° from your initial direction of march. The dog is back in the proper position, with his neck adjacent to your left leg. Praise him when he gets back to this position.

A

D

I-28. Correction sequence for a dog that forges.

A. The dog is too far ahead of the handler—he is forging.

B. Stop and take a long step backward, correcting the dog back toward you, as indicated by the dotted arrow along the lead. This correction should be firm enough to spin the dog completely around to face you.

C. While the dog is still off balance, apply another quick correction in the opposite direction, as indicated by the dotted arrow along the lead.

D. As the dog moves past you, apply the final correction as indicated by the dotted arrow near the lead, knocking the dog off balance and toward your new direction of march.

E. As soon as you make the last correction, turn your body so that the dog is again at your left side and in the proper heeling position.

F. Come to an immediate halt when the dog is in the proper position and enforce his sit. Praise him at this point. Pause a moment in the normal heeling position, and then give the command "Heel!" and continue working.

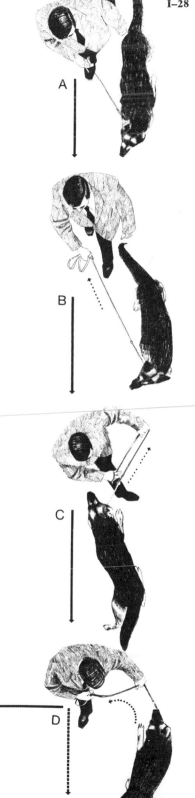

F   E   D

because handlers should delight in correcting their dogs whenever possible, but because there is nothing like a mistake to teach a dog the desired behavior. Indeed, there is more cause to worry if he makes *no* mistakes and seems to learn everything flawlessly. Few dogs do, in fact, learn things "flawlessly"; sooner or later, they fail to do something they have performed perfectly all along—more often than not, it happens in a show! One of the most common remarks one hears from handlers whose dogs have just disqualified in a show is "I can't understand it! He never louses up that exercise at home!" The fact is that had the dog loused it up at home once or twice, he would be much less likely to do so in a show.

If the dog does make mistakes during the initial heeling exercises, do not be too harsh on him. Be patient, but be persistent. Keep moving, walking backward if necessary, applying timed corrections to keep the dog off balance until he is scrambling again to catch up to you; then turn and walk a few steps in a straight line before making another right turn. If he lags on the right turn and does not keep up, correct again. If he begins trying to catch up, stop correcting him and give him lots of praise: hug him and talk to him. You should be able to get him to make both right and about turns on the second day.

Corrections for Forging and Lagging

Keep in mind that the correct position for the dog during heeling is next to your left side, with his neck adjacent to your left leg. If he is too far ahead, he is *forging;* if he is too far behind, he is *lagging.* Both are relatively simple to correct if you catch them early enough; the longer the dog is permitted to forge or lag in training, the more fixed the mistake becomes. If you do not correct it, he simply thinks that it is what you *want* him to do: you are, in effect, *training* him to do it.

Although it is important to keep the lead in your right hand while heeling, it is sometimes necessary when correcting for forging and lagging to use both hands (figs. I-27–28), to achieve the most effective angle of correction and to apply additional force.

Lagging Figure I-27 shows the proper sequence for correcting a lagger. Do not make a straight-line pull, and do not change your normal pace and adapt to the dog's. Start the correction by making the dog hustle to keep up with you, as you did when you introduced him to the collar and lead in the first lesson.

Time the second correction in such a way that it is made before the dog has completely regained his balance from the first; this will make him hustle to catch up and heel properly. If he persists in lagging, go into the correction sequence a second time. Remain silent and act as if nothing had happened; if he hustles to catch up, praise him, but continue heeling.

Most lagging is merely a product of daydreaming on the part of the dog and is easily remedied in a single correction sequence. However, it is important to correct even the slightest lagging in Week 1;

if you allow it to continue, you will encourage the dog to daydream and be a sloppy worker.

Forging This is also easily corrected, essentially by coming to a stop and rapidly backing up, applying a series of short, timed corrections to get the dog back to you. The penultimate correction (marked *C* in fig. I-28) should bring the dog toward you; as you make him pass you (going in the opposite direction of your line of march), apply a final correction to make him turn about to *your* direction of march; then immediately make him sit (see Teaching the Automatic Sit). Figure I-28 shows how this is done. After two or three times, the dog will be conditioned to pay more attention to your line of march.

Automatic Sit

Assuming that the dog is heeling properly and keeps at your left side when you walk in a straight line, does not lag or forge, and hustles to keep up as you make right turns and about turns, you are both ready to learn the automatic sit. This exercise can usually be introduced by the third day of training, though of course a lot depends on the dog, the handler, and the amount of time spent during the first two days of training. If you have ended each day's training by forcing your dog into the sit (fig. I-26), the automatic sit should be easy for him to master.

Heel forward with your dog, walking in a perfectly straight line. Keep the leather lead in your right hand and allow your left hand to swing freely at your side as you walk. Have the slack adjusted in the lead in such a way that you can, as required, pull up on the dog's lead

I–29

I-29. Teaching the automatic sit. After heeling in a straight line, come to a halt; as you do, pull up on the lead with your right hand and push down on the dog's rump with your left hand. Do not say a word as you force the dog into the sit.

I-30. The first verbal command: "Heel!" Start from the normal heeling position. Simultaneously step off with your left foot and give the command, using the dog's name: "Nemo. Heel!"

and apply tension. Come to a halt and, as you do, pull up on the lead with your right hand, squat down, bending to the left with your waist and knees, and push down on the dog's rump with your left hand (fig. I-29). Do not give a vocal command; do not say a word. When he sits, praise him by rubbing his head or patting his shoulder or whatever you do when you are conveying affection. After a few sessions, your dog will be going into the sit position whenever you halt. It is important that he be conditioned to sit perfectly squarely. One way to achieve this is to use your left foot as a guide: when he begins to sit automatically after you halt, put your left leg back as a guide for the dog—it will keep him from sitting with his butt twisted around behind you.

At this point we move into more complicated handling techniques. You are now ready to give your first verbal command: "Heel!" While the dog is sitting in the correct heeling position at your left side, say his name and then "Heel!" As you say it, step forward with your *left* foot and walk in a straight line (fig. I-30). It is important to step off with your left foot, *for that, too, is a signal to the dog.* Later, you will use your right foot for a signal with precisely the opposite meaning: "remain sitting."

If the dog hesitates when you give the command "Heel!" and continues to sit there, step off smartly to the right so that you can apply a correction from an advantageous angle. Take a few steps and then make him sit.

Start again from the proper heeling position, with the dog sitting at your left. Give his name and the command "Heel!," and step off with your left foot. Walk in a straight line for a few steps and then, saying nothing, come to a halt, pull up on the leather lead with your right hand, and push down on his rump with your left hand, this time a little more quickly than before. Praise him for sitting, but not until he sits squarely, with his bottom on the ground. Stand back up to the heeling position after praising the dog, and, giving the verbal command again, heel forward. After three or four such exercises, the dog should automatically come to a sit when you stop. Do not praise him for this, since it is the standard position for him when he is not executing another exercise.

A word of caution is in order about the tone of your voice in this and in all subsequent vocal commands. Do not shout or sound upset when you give a verbal command. Your tone of voice is *not* the cue for the dog. Give the command in a normal tone of voice, but loud enough so that the dog can hear it clearly. Under no circumstances are you to give the command more than once. If he fails to respond to the first command, heel forward without a word and correct him as described above. He must learn early in the training that he has to obey a *single* command or else be corrected. Therefore, never give him a command unless you can *enforce* it. During the training on lead this will be easy to follow, but later, when you are working off lead, you will not always be in a position to correct the dog if he fails to obey on a single command. So make certain that you give only *one* command while he is working on lead, and enforce it if he disobeys.

This covers all that you can comfortably teach your dog in the first week. If you work twice a day, for a few minutes each time, by the end of one week your dog will be heeling smartly at your side and coming to automatic sits when you stop. Moreover, he will be hustling to keep up with you as you make right turns and about turns. In total, it will be about one hour of your time and you will have achieved about as much with your dog as many canine colleges do in several weeks—for several hundred dollars.

You have established a set of *principles* on which you and your dog can now build as the exercises become more complex and intricate. Fundamental among these is the fact that your command *must* be obeyed; if it is not, a correction follows. If it *is* obeyed, praise and encouragement follow. If you have trained properly and have used correction and praise judiciously, your dog will be, by the end of the first week, working *more to please you* than to avoid the correction.

NOVICE WEEK 2

OUTLINE OF TRAINING SCHEDULE
Old Exercises (Practice these first each session.)

Basic Heeling
    Right Turn
    About Turn
    Automatic Sit
    Corrections for Forging and Lagging (if necessary)
New Exercises
    Left Turn
    Heeling at Different Speeds
    Figure 8
    Corrections for Heeling Errors
Suggested Length of Practice Session: 5–8 minutes, twice daily

Left Turn

Start this exercise from the correct heeling position and step off on your left foot, giving the dog's name and the command "Heel!" Walk several steps forward, making sure that you have slack in your lead and that the lead is in your right hand. The turn is executed by pivoting on the ball of your left foot 90° to the left.

As you make the left turn for the first time, your dog is likely to bump into your leg. This is *interference with the handler.* You should anticipate this: just before making the turn, take up a little of the slack in the lead with your right hand and, as you turn, pull the dog's head toward your left leg, while simultaneously bumping his shoulder with the inside of your right leg (figs. I-31–32). The pull across your body is made the instant your left foot touches the ground. To emphasize that he should stay in close to you but should not touch you, make the first bump on his shoulder sharp and unequivocal so that the next time you turn left he will keep his eye on your legs and remain away from them. As soon as he does a left turn properly—slows down his pace so as not to touch you, and makes the turn with you, keeping in position—give him praise and encouragement. To keep him alert, mix left turns, right turns, and about turns randomly, praising him for doing each one properly. If you practice too much on one exercise, he will begin to anticipate your slightest move and get out of position. It is a good practice during the first and second week of training *not* to walk in a straight line very far, but to keep turning and changing directions, mixing up the turns and giving praise and correction as needed. This will achieve two things: reduce the probability of lagging and forging during heeling, and keep him constantly alert for your next move. Fundamentals. You are working on the exercises that build blue-ribbon-quality competitors. Do not think that because they are so basic they are less valuable. They are what will distinguish you and your dog from those who also ran—but did not place.

Heeling at Different Speeds

Your dog now knows the following exercises from Week 1: (1) heeling at your left; (2) automatic sit when you halt; (3) right turns and

I-31. The first time you make a left turn, anticipate that the dog will bump into your left leg. Begin the correction the instant that your left foot touches the ground.

I-32. When the dog bumps your leg, he is interfering with his handler. Pull him in to your right leg with the lead and bump him on the shoulder with your right knee as you do. This will convince him that he must be close to you, but not too close. Note that the handler and dog are heeling around a low obstacle —a milk bottle.

about turns; and, from the first day of the second week, (4) the left turn.

Now you are going to work on his heeling *speed* and make him keep at your side no matter what pace you take. It is important that your change of pace be obvious and detectable by both your dog and other people who may be watching—and judging—you. Therefore, when you walk a normal pace and want to do a slow heel, be sure your change of pace is definite and noticeable; similarly, when you go from a normal pace to a fast heel, you should actually begin to trot. The most common practice in shows is for a judge to make you go into both slow and fast heels from a normal pace, but you should be prepared to go from any pace to any other. It is also possible for a judge to give a halt command (and your dog must then do the automatic sit) from a fast, normal, or slow pace.

There really is no new procedure involved in teaching the fast and slow heeling; your dog, because of the way you introduced him to the collar and lead, and because of the nature of the corrections you have been giving him during the first week, will already be alert for any move that you make when you heel. This includes any change in your pace. To teach the slow and fast heeling, you merely heel and go through the turn sequences at random, changing your pace from normal to either slow or fast as you come out of the turns, and going back into a normal pace before making another turn. If you have followed the sequence of teaching the exercises so far, your dog should do the slow and fast heeling without any trouble. The kinds of errors dogs make are likely to be lagging and forging, and we have already shown how to correct for those.* To practice the heeling and turns, do the following exercises:

1. Start from the heeling position with your dog sitting.
2. Give the command "Heel!" step off with your left foot, and heel away at a normal pace.
3. Make a left turn, and, as you complete the turn, slow down momentarily and walk very slowly for a few steps before resuming a normal pace.
4. Walk at a normal pace for a few more steps, make a right turn and then, as you complete it, go into a trot. Go four or five steps before resuming the normal pace. Then halt and wait for the dog to sit automatically before giving praise.

Alternate your turns in such a way that the dog does not begin to think that slow heeling always comes after a left turn and fast heeling after a right turn; mix up the exercises so that there is no fixed pattern relating a particular turn to a particular heeling speed.

It is often helpful to have a friend or relative give you the verbal commands.† This is not necessary, but it will improve your technique

---

* The kind of error the handlers make is to try to adjust to the dog's speed so as to keep the dog in the proper position. This is a very serious error. The *dog* has the collar on, not the handler, and the dog must always be made to adjust to the handler's speed, *not* vice versa.

† Forward! Slow! Normal! Fast! Normal! Right Turn! Left Turn!

as a handler and preadapt you to keeping alert for a judge's command. It is also good experience for the dog to be exposed to other people and other dogs; it reinforces his obligation to remain alert for *your* commands. Such exposure will at first cause him to be distracted— and to make a mistake. This is valuable, for the correction that follows will remind him that he is still at work for you and on a command. Only if he is trained in this fashion will you be able to walk confidently in crowds or near other animals and expect your dog to remain at your side, heeling properly or staying in whatever position you command him to take. If you fail to correct him now, you cannot expect him to obey predictably in a pinch later; obeying on a single command could even save his life—as when he bolts suddenly away from you to chase another animal and runs toward a busy street. If your dog has been properly trained during the heeling exercises, he can be given a single command to lie down and he will stop—in mid-chase—and lie down. But he will *never* do it unless you reinforce your commands during the Novice exercises you are learning right now.

Figure 8

The figure 8 heeling exercise may seem silly, but it serves to sharpen up your dog's heeling skills and keep him constantly alert for changes in your speed and direction. It also reinforces the fact that you have him *under your control.* Indeed, it reinforces everything you and the dog have learned up to this point, for it involves right and left turns, automatic sits, and slow, fast, and normal heeling. By the end of the ten-week course, you will be going through the figure 8 at a constant pace, as in a show, but your dog will be hustling to keep at your side on the outside turns and slowing down to adjust to your speed on the inside turns.

The figure 8, in short, is an extension of and improvement upon the skills you should have acquired in the first ten days of your training. Begin doing the figure 8 early in the second week; this will also improve his skill in the left turn.

Start the training by placing two fairly large objects, such as trash cans, or sticking broomsticks into the ground in a vertical position. Set them no more than about five or six feet apart—the idea is for you and the dog to be constantly turning as you are learning the exercise. After a few weeks of practice, you can begin to increase the distance, up to eight feet, while introducing objects of ever smaller size, down to a milk bottle. After your dog has mastered the figure 8, he does not have to see the objects, since he will be turning in response to your position, speed, and direction, whatever the size of the objects that you walk around. In a show, the "objects" will be people, standing motionless eight feet apart.

Figures I-33 through I-37 show the series of positions in which you will be heeling as you and the dog do the figure 8.* The objective

* Note that the illustrations show the dog *off* lead; you, of course, will be doing the training on lead. The figure 8 is done off lead in more advanced competition (see chap. II).

I-33–37: Teaching the Figure 8. **I-33.** Use two people, two trash cans, or two broomsticks stuck in the ground for the posts of your figure 8. Start with the dog centered between the posts in the normal heeling position. Here, the handler will go to the right, as indicated by the dotted lines, but it is also permissible to start to the left. The radius points would be where the two people are standing.

I-34. As you approach the first post of the figure 8, pick up speed to encourage the dog to move faster around the turn. After a few weeks of practice, your dog will hustle on the outside turns while you walk at a normal pace.

I-35. Note that the dog is still in the proper heeling position as the handler rounds the turn and begins to heel toward the opposite post of the figure 8.

I-36. As you round this turn, slow your pace so that the dog must slow his. In time, the dog will slow down naturally while you maintain a normal pace.

I-37. Come to a halt somewhere midway between the two posts of the figure 8. Your dog should sit automatically—and straight. In Novice competition, the judge will tell you to halt when you are about at this position.

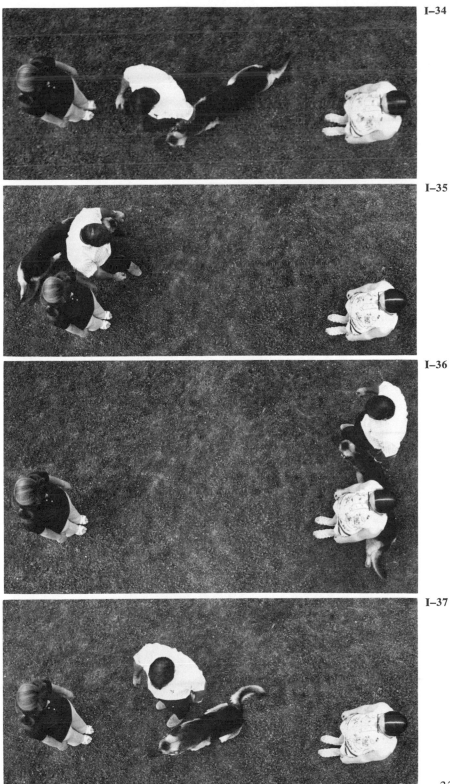

is to keep the dog at the same position as he would be in if you were heeling in a straight line, that is, at your left side and with his shoulder adjacent to your left leg. If you turn in a circle to the left, you must walk a longer distance than the dog walks to make the same turn: he is on your inside, and therefore closer to the radius point. Similarly, if you turn in a circle to the right, the dog, being on the outside and farther away from the radius point, must travel farther to make the turn. Thus, on turns where he is on the inside, he will have to *slow down* to keep in position next to your leg, and on turns where he is on the outside, he will have to *speed up* to maintain that position. Figure I-33 shows what we mean by radius point; it is as if both you and the dog were tied to a string that is fixed to the ground where the people are standing and must keep it taut as you walk in a circle around the point where the imaginary string is fixed.

Teaching the figure 8 heeling exercise requires somewhat different procedures from those you will go through later. First, the two objects are *closer* together so that you and the dog do not walk in a straight line between them. Second, you change your speed as you walk, moving slowly on the turns where the dog is between you and the object, and quickly when you are between the dog and the object as you turn around the latter.

Begin the figure 8 exercise with the dog in sitting position, facing the objects and close to them (fig. I-33). The *dog,* you should note, is centered between the objects, since it is *he* who does the exercise and

I–38

I-38. To correct a dog that leans on your leg during sits, pull the lead across your body and bump the dog on the shoulder with your left leg.

is judged for *his* performance. You may begin the figure 8 in either direction, as is the case in AKC shows.

Give the command "Heel!" and step forward with your left foot, turning in whatever direction you choose. Let us assume you turn right the first time. You should pass close by the object and, since the dog is on the outside in this turn and must speed up to stay in position, *you* should speed up to remind him. At first, you might want to keep a little distance between you and the object on this turn so as to have time to do a conspicuous fast heel around it. As you finish the turn, return to a normal pace, and then slow down as you make a left turn around the other object; this time your dog will be *between* you and the object (fig. I-36). Continue at a slow pace until you have made this turn, resume normal pace between the objects, and then pick up speed as you go around the other object a second time. When you complete this turn, slow down to normal and come to a halt midway between the objects (fig. I-37). Praise your dog if he comes to an automatic sit; correct him if he does not.

Heel away giving a verbal signal and the proper foot forward, and do another turn around both objects, coming to a halt in the middle again. The next time you do the figure 8, make your initial turn around the *other* object so the dog does not begin to think that the first turn is always in the same direction. As he becomes more proficient at the figure 8, make your halts more random—stop in the middle of a turn. But before you randomize your halts, make sure the dog has caught on to the fundamental point of the exercise: *he must speed up on outside turns and slow down on inside turns.*

The corrections for lagging and forging are all that you need to know for the most common errors that the dog will make during the figure 8. If he lags on the outside turns, correct with a smart tug; you will very likely be at a good angle, since you are already turning away from him. He will usually try to catch up, so that you need not interrupt the figure 8 training. If he persists in lagging, move away from the figure 8 objects and do similar turns in an open area, one that permits you to maneuver around without running into anything. Make the necessary corrections there until the dog is hustling again, and return to the figure 8. By this time you should be working twice a day with your dog, for five to eight minutes each session.

The figure 8 is often ignored or not practiced much. People who think that it is unimportant usually end up with very sloppy heelers—dogs that lag, forge, and interfere—and themselves become, in undesirable compensation, sloppy handlers, adjusting their pace to fit their dog's or holding too tight a lead. We cannot emphasize strongly enough that the figure 8 is an important and creative exercise, and that it helps to develop a smart, alertly heeling dog. The figure 8 completes the list of heeling exercises for Novice training and, incidentally, contains most of the elements of the heeling exercises in the more advanced obedience courses. Your dog will be proficient at the heeling exercises in the more advanced work only if you practice the figure 8 as described in this chapter; it is fundamental to later work. At this point, accept nothing short of perfection.

Go through all the heeling exercises every day during the entire week of training; these include the turns, the automatic sit, the various speeds at which you walk, and the figure 8.

Corrections for Heeling Errors

There are several kinds of errors that dogs will make in heeling exercises. We have described the two most common, forging and lagging. Three more deserve mention at this juncture:

     Interference with Handler

     Drifting to the Left

     Leaning on the Handler's Leg while in Sitting Position

Interference with Handler   This common heeling error occurs when the dog bumps into the handler or brushes alongside his leg while heeling. The correction is to pull the dog's head in to your left knee with the lead, bumping him smartly and simultaneously on the shoulder with the inside of your right leg; the dog *must* be both pulled and bumped simultaneously to remind him that he must remain close, but not too close, to your leg. A simple bump with your leg would make him shy away (figs. I-31 and I-32 show the proper correction).

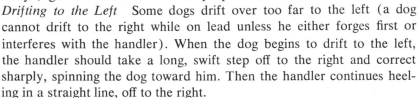

Drifting to the Left   Some dogs drift over too far to the left (a dog cannot drift to the right while on lead unless he either forges first or interferes with the handler). When the dog begins to drift to the left, the handler should take a long, swift step off to the right and correct sharply, spinning the dog toward him. Then the handler continues heeling in a straight line, off to the right.

Leaning on the Handler's Leg while in Sitting Position   Some dogs like to lean on the handler's leg while they are sitting. This can and must be corrected, using a technique similar to the one for correcting a dog that interferes with the handler: pull the dog smartly into the *outside* of the left leg with the collar and lead, and bump his shoulder with your left leg (fig. I-38). Note that you correct a *moving* dog with your right leg, but a *sitting* dog with your left leg.

NOVICE WEEK 3

OUTLINE OF TRAINING SCHEDULE
Old Exercises
    Basic Heeling
        Right Turn
        About Turn
        Left Turn
        All Speeds and Halts

        Automatic Sit

Figure 8
Corrections for Forging, Lagging, Interference, Leaning and Drifting to the Left
New Exercises
Sit-Stay and Return
Handling Precision
Suggested Length of Practice Session: 5–10 minutes, twice daily

Sit-Stay and Return

These two exercises will be taught simultaneously. The object of the first is to get your dog to remain in a sitting position while you leave him and walk away. The object of the second is to condition him to remain sitting while you walk back to him, cross around behind him, and return to the proper heeling position. He must not move when you complete the return, so you will actually add a *third* exercise to the sequence—a heel forward two steps—to condition the dog that he must remain sitting until another command and exercise have been completed.

Remember how you always began the heeling by stepping forward on your left foot first? Now you are going to step forward with your *right* foot first—it is part of the signal to the dog that he should stay, not heel forward. You are also going to learn your first hand signal, and it would be well to practice it a few times before giving it to the dog. The hand signal for stay is done with your *right* hand (figs. I-39 and I-40 show how to transfer the lead from your right hand to your left). Stick your right arm straight out, away from your body, keeping the palm of your hand open (see figs. I-41 and I-42). Swing your arm around, keeping it horizontal to the ground, as if you were going to slap the dog on the face with an open palm; it is important that your swing be smooth and that the dog can see it coming toward his face. You do *not* touch the dog as your palm comes up to his nose: you stop short. Your swing, we emphasize, should be wide and exaggerated at first so the dog can see it clearly as your arm comes around your body toward his face.

You will also give the verbal command "Stay!" without the dog's name. (Remember that in the command "Heel!" you gave the dog's name first, then the command.)

Begin with the dog at your left side, sitting squarely, in the proper heeling position. Simultaneously give the hand signal and the verbal command "Stay!" and step off on your right foot, turning in front of the dog and coming to a stand directly in front of him (examine figs. I-39–43). The dog must remain sitting. If he tries to move, pull up slightly on the leather lead; if he tries to stand, push down on his rump while pulling up on the lead (fig. I-44). Stand there motionless and silent for a few moments. It is important to reinforce this new position, since in a later exercise the dog will be expected to come to you and go into it. He should be squarely facing you, sitting straight; you should be close enough to him that you can touch his head without leaning forward to 37

I-39–43: Teaching the Sit-Stay. **I-39.** Begin from the normal heeling position. Transfer the leather lead from your right hand to your left hand so that your right hand is free to give the hand signal for stay.

I-40. Your right hand is now free to begin the hand signal for stay.

I-41. Simultaneously: give the hand signal, step off with your right foot first, give the verbal command "Stay!"

I-42. Make your hand signal conspicuously visible to the dog. It should be a smooth, sweeping motion that stops just short of his face. Turn immediately in front of your dog by pivoting on your right foot.

I-43. Stand in front of your dog in this position. Study the position carefully, for it will be used in other exercises. If the dog tries to lie down or move, pull up firmly on the lead and make him maintain the position until you give him another command.

return to the normal heeling position (with the dog on your left), pause a moment and then give the command: "Baron, heel!" Take two steps forward and halt, quickly enforcing the sit so that the dog associates the praise that follows with the stay exercise, not with the automatic sit.

I-44. To enforce the sit when the dog is in front of you, pull up on the lead and push down on the dog's rump.

I-45. Teaching the return. Walk around the dog to the right, holding the leather lead over his head. Make sure the lead is slack. When you

I-46. Correcting your dog with a bop on the nose. Grasp your dog's nose in such a way that it does not protrude beyond your hand. Then smack *your hand* firmly with your palm. This motion reinforces the stay command.

reach it. In the advanced training the dog will be bringing you an object in his mouth, and you will have to remove it without stretching your body forward, so study the dog and handler positions in the photographs, especially figure I-43, with care.

After standing there for a few minutes, slowly lift up the lead with your left hand, passing it over his head with ever so little tension on it, and step around him slowly to the right. Keep the lead under very slight tension as you walk around him (fig. I-45), taking it back into your right hand as you come up alongside him to return to the normal heeling position. Stop at the proper heeling position for a few seconds, then give the following command: "Emerson, Heel!" (use *your* dog's name; "Emerson" is not part of the exercise). Walk forward, this time with your *left* foot first, and stop after two paces, *quickly* enforcing the sit by pulling up on his lead with your right hand and pushing down on his rump with your left hand. At that point, give him praise. *You* must make the dog go into the sit, even though he will now do it automatically; this is to keep his mind on the new exercise—the stay—and to associate the praise with that, not with the automatic sit.

While in the sit-stay position, the dog should not move a muscle. If he tries to stand, lie down, or walk away, make a correction by holding the leather lead close to the swivel and correcting the dog quickly around in a complete circle, which is 360° of unlikable off-balance time for him; as you bring him back to the proper sitting position, cup your left hand over his nose in such a way that he can see over it, then bop your left hand with the open palm of your right hand. Do it smartly—you are hitting only yourself, but a minor shock will be felt by the dog. The twisting motion reminds him of his mistake, and the bop reinforces the hand signal for stay because it is done with the same motion. He will remember it better the next time. Figure I-46 illustrates this correction.

Handling Precision

Begin to concentrate this week on the precision of your handling techniques, particularly the smoothness with which you step away on either your left foot or your right and the association of your foot motions with the right-hand and verbal commands. Work on your hand signal to make it smooth and visible to the dog, not an up-and-down chop, since it will later replace the vocal signal entirely. Finally, as you practice the heeling and the turns, make sure that your lead always has the proper amount of slack and that you do not accidentally put tension on it when you make the outside turns. Your left hand should not be touching the lead during the heeling.

Work also on sharpening up your dog's heeling by keeping an eye open for bad habits he might be falling into—drifting, forging, lagging, interference—and make sure he is always in a straight position when he sits. If he is sitting for more than a few minutes at your side and tries to lie down, correct him to make him stay in the alert sitting position. It will pay off in the later exercises.

NOVICE WEEK 4

OUTLINE OF TRAINING SCHEDULE
Old Exercises (Practice these first each session.)
    Basic Heeling (all turns, all speeds, halts, automatic sit)
    Figure 8
    Corrections for Forging, Lagging, Interference, Leaning, and Drift-
       ing to the Left
    Sit-Stay and Return
    Handling Precision (Avoid tautness in your lead.)
Modification of Old Exercise
    Long Sit (Sit-Stay)—1 minute at a 6-foot distance—and Return
New Exercise
    Long Down
Suggested Length of Practice Session: 10 minutes, twice daily

Long Sit (Sit-Stay) and Return

This week is devoted to increasing both time and distance during the sit-stay exercise. What we are preparing the dog to do is called the "long sit" by the AKC; since we are now going to increase our time, we will hereafter also refer to this exercise as the long sit. In competition, the dog will be expected to sit, off lead, for a full minute while you are standing, facing him, across the width of the ring.* In addition, your dog will be sitting with anywhere from six to fifteen other dogs, all lined up and all expected to remain motionless during the long sit.

Last week you taught your dog to remain sitting while you stood in front of him, holding his lead. He continued to sit while you returned to him by passing around behind him; then you paused, and gave the command "Heel!" for the two-steps-forward termination of the exercise. Practice this routine for the first day of this week, enforcing his automatic sit so that he associates the praise with the long sit.

This week, on the second repetition of this exercise, go out the full six-foot distance. When you give the dog the signal for stay† (simultaneously by hand, verbally and by stepping off with your right foot), keep your hand in front of the dog's face for a longer period of time, holding it there as you slowly back away from him, playing out slack in the lead. Carefully and slowly, allow your right arm to drop back down to your side and away from the dog until there is a comfortable amount of slack in the lead. You should be nearly six feet away from

---

* You should begin to concentrate on keeping your hands in a natural position, that is, at your sides. Under the 1975 rules, you will be penalized a "substantial deduction" if your hands are not kept at your sides in some of the exercises. In brief, learn to keep your hands at your sides for all the exercises—it really looks better as a handling technique anyway (see fig. I-76).

† Remember not to use your dog's name as part of the command "Stay!" This holds for all the stay commands in subsequent weeks *and* in competition.

him. Avoid putting any pressure on the leather lead, since this is a signal for come, and the purpose of the exercise is to keep the dog sitting at a distance from you.

If the dog remains motionless while you stand there a few seconds, return to him cautiously, handling the lead with both hands, as you did the previous week: walk around behind the dog, keeping the lead suspended over his head, and come to a smooth halt in the normal heeling position. The lead should now be back in your right hand and have slack in it. Pause a moment and give the command "Heel!," taking two steps forward and enforcing the automatic sit when you halt. Praise the dog for mastering this step in the training for the long sit.

If the dog moves, lies down, stands up, creeps forward, or slouches over while you are standing in front of him, quickly move in and correct him as you did the previous week. When he is back in the proper sitting position, bop his nose and then carefully back out to the six-foot distance again. Do not give any verbal reprimands; remain perfectly silent as you make the necessary correction.

Your second training session for the day should include a repetition of the above sequence. This time, stand in front of him for an additional three or four seconds before returning.

On the second day of this week's training on the long sit, you will add a degree of professionalism to your handling. When you begin the exercise, concentrate on your handling technique: Step off on your right foot after giving the proper signals to the dog, but this time do *not* back away as you move out to the six-foot distance. Instead, walk away slowly, as if the dog were heeling next to you (see figs. I-47–49). When you get out nearly to the end of the lead, turn around to face the dog, pivoting on your left foot, that is, counterclockwise. Make sure there is slack in the lead as you stand facing the dog. If your dog is going to make a mistake, it will be when you walk nonchalantly away from him without a lengthy hand signal for him to remain sitting. If he breaks, quickly return to him and correct him 360°, as in the previous week, bopping him on the nose after you have put him back in the proper sitting position. Go back out silently to the six-foot distance and stand there, facing him. This time, stand there for a full sixty seconds. It may seem like an eternity to you, but the dog can do it.

We must enter a warning here, since you will be practicing the long sit for longish periods of time for the remainder of the course. Dogs seem to have very sensitive biological clocks built into them. If you practice the long sit for exactly sixty seconds each time you train, your dog will tend to become fidgety as soon as the sixty seconds have expired, and might begin wiggling and worrying about why you have not returned to him. It is therefore necessary to vary the length of the long sit as you practice. Alternate your time between forty-five and seventy-five seconds, but do it randomly. In an AKC trial, the time could vary by that amount, and you do not want to have to worry about your dog's patience should the exercise take seventy-five seconds.

On the third day and successive days of training for the long sit this week, increase the distance at which the dog does the long sit. If your 43

I-47. In the sit-stay, begin adding a degree of professionalism to your handling: do not back away after giving the command "Stay!," but step off in a straight line and walk out to the end of the lead before turning to face the dog.

I-48. The first time you walk out to the end of the lead in the sit-stay, you might want to keep your eye on the dog as you do so—and quickly correct him if he moves forward. Hereafter, you will not look back as you leave the dog and go out to the end of the lead—or the opposite side of the ring.

I-49. Make sure there is a good deal of slack in your lead as you face the dog. Remain standing there a full 60 seconds the first time you go to the end of the lead. Be careful when you return around behind the dog— do not accidentally put any pressure on the lead and thus cause him to move. Pause a few seconds after your return to the proper heeling position, and then heel forward two steps to end the sit-stay and return exercise.

dog does the exercise consistently from the six-foot distance, he will be able to do it from twenty feet as well. Put him in the normal heeling position. Let the leather lead drop to the floor in front of the dog. Give the appropriate signals and leave him, walking out to about twenty feet (seven or eight paces) before turning to face him. Do not back off; simply walk away nonchalantly without looking back at the dog. (You can be penalized in an AKC trial for backing away from your dog during this—and other—exercises.)

Remain at the twenty-foot distance for the full sixty seconds the first time you do this exercise. The lead is still attached to the dog's collar, reminding him that he is in a correctable position. If he moves, quickly go back and correct as described above.

When you return to your dog this time, do not pick up the lead before taking the two steps forward and do not enforce the automatic sit; allow him to do it himself. He should have enough experience from the heeling work you are doing to come to a sit after you have taken your two steps forward to terminate this exercise. From now on, delay your praise until the dog has done the entire exercise, and come to a square sit. Be sure that his sit is perfectly straight before giving the praise.

Practice the long sit for the remainder of the week at the full

twenty-foot distance, remembering to alternate your times between forty-five and seventy-five seconds.

Long Down

This is an exercise in which your dog lies down while you walk away from him, off lead, as far as you wish. He will remain in the down position until you give him another command. In a Novice show, the long-down exercise requires that you "down" and leave your dog, walk across the width of the show ring, turn to face him, and remain motionless for three minutes. However, since the long down is an exercise also found in more advanced obedience competition, we will teach you and your dog to build up gradually, during your Novice training, to the conditions required in the more advanced exercise: five minutes of long down with the handler—you—out of the dog's sight. Thus, during the fourth week of your Novice training, you will actually be preparing your dog to do somewhat more than is required to qualify in the Novice long down.

In Novice AKC obedience trials, you may say your dog's name before the command "Down!," and you should use his name now as you introduce the exercise: it will immediately cue your dog to listen for 45

I–54   I–55

I-50–57: Teaching the Long Down. Begin from the proper heeling position. **I-50.** Drop your right knee to the ground and put your left against the dog's side. Keep the lead in your right hand, adjusted with only enough slack to permit you to reach the dog's right ankle, and put your left arm around the dog's back ready to grasp his left ankle.

I-51. Simultaneously: give the command "Down!," pull the dog's feet forward (*not* toward you), and push against his side with your left knee to roll him onto his side in a comfortable position.

I-52. If the dog is particularly large and you cannot get your left arm around his back to grasp his left ankle, reach under his neck with your left hand. You can increase your leverage by using your left elbow as a fulcrum as you pull the dog's feet forward.

I-53. Pull the dog's legs out to the front, and roll his back end over with your left knee. This will condition the dog to "down" parallel to your line of march.

I-54. When you put your dog into the down position, try to condition him to roll over on one hip so that he will be comfortable and relaxed during a long down.

I-55. A dog that assumes this down position will fidget and be uncomfortable if expected to remain there for any length of time. He is likely to become so uncomfortable that he will break his position.

I-56. When your dog is in the down position, gradually relax your grasp on his legs and make sure he is rolled over on one hip.

I-57. Come to your feet and pause a moment. Then drop the lead on the ground near the dog, give the proper stay command, and leave the dog.

a command—he will hear his name and expect something to follow. Later, we will gradually "wean" you from using the dog's name. There is a very practical reason for this. Imagine an emergency situation where the dog is in danger if he continues to run in a particular direction— across a busy street, for example. You lose too much valuable time by giving the dog's name and then the command; you want him to drop to the down position as soon as he hears the single word.

Finally, you are going to learn gradually to put your dog into the down position with a single command without having to move your body. You will be able to stand perfectly motionless and simply say "Down!"—and the dog should drop where he is standing. During the fourth week you will, of course, have to bend over and assist your dog by pushing some parts of him and pulling others, but eventually he will quickly go into the down on a single verbal command.

Teaching the Long Down   The long down requires that the dog lie down parallel to you. To teach him to do this, you have to pull his forelegs out from underneath him and push him off balance with your knee, literally causing him to fall down. You must kneel with your right knee on the floor and your left knee pressed against the dog's shoulder. The only tricky part is to be in a position to pull the dog's front legs gently out from underneath him while kneeling at his side and pushing against him with your left knee.

Here is the sequence. Start from the proper heeling position. Give him the command "Down!," remembering to precede it with his name. As you give the command, take up enough slack in the lead so that you can reach his front leg with your right hand and still hang on to the lead (fig. I-50). You should be in a kneeling position close to the dog's side, with your right knee on the floor and your left knee touching the dog's shoulder. Grab the dog's right leg near the paw with your right hand (fig. I-51). Note that you still have the lead in your right hand. If you have a very large dog, reach under his chest (fig. I-52) and grab his left leg near his paw. Pull the dog's forelegs forward while simultaneously pushing against his shoulder with your left knee (fig. I-53). It is important to pull the dog's legs out toward the front, not in toward you; if done correctly, your pull will cause him to "down" in a position parallel to you, not crooked. If the dog is small, use the calf of your leg instead of your knee to push him. Ideally, you want the dog to roll over on one hip and lie down in a relaxed position (fig. I-54). He will be more comfortable if he is lying that way and less tempted to get up; if he remains squarely on both haunches (as in fig. I-55), he is actually in a less comfortable position and therefore more likely to move.

When the dog is in the down position, rise slowly to your feet and stand still (figs. I-56–57). After a few moments, drop the lead to the ground in front of the dog, give the command "Stay!," walk away (right foot forward on the first step) about twenty or thirty feet, and turn to face the dog. Remain there at least three minutes, but vary your time on each practice exercise.

If the dog breaks from the down position or creeps forward, walk quickly (do not run) to him. Take the lead in both hands, quickly turn him around 360°, and put him back in the original down position—but do not give him a verbal command while you do this. The 360° turn in effect knocks him off balance. Remember to bop his nose after he is in the down position. Do *not* repeat the commands ("Down!" or "Stay!") when you make the correction.

Some dogs are more active than others and break from the down or creep forward if the handler moves as far as twenty or thirty feet away. It will be necessary to work with such dogs by remaining within the length of the six-foot lead until the dog overcomes this.

This completes the exercise introduced in Week 4. After two or three training sessions in Week 4, the dog will gradually begin to understand the verbal command "Down!" Later we will tell you when to begin working this exercise on a verbal command only.

NOVICE WEEK 5

OUTLINE OF TRAINING SCHEDULE
Old Exercises (Practice these first each day, twice daily.)
  Basic Heeling (all turns, all speeds, halts, automatic sits)
  Figure 8
  Corrections for Forging, Lagging, Interference, Leaning, and Drifting to the Left
  Long Sit
  Long Down
  Handling Precision (Avoid tautness in your lead and do not give the dog's name as part of the command "Stay!")
Modification of Old Exercises
  Long Sit: Thirty-foot distance
  Long Down: Greater speed in downing the dog
New Exercise
  Finish
Suggested Length of Practice Session: 10 minutes, twice daily

Long Sit Modified

This week's training will bring you to the point of AKC regulations for this exercise: you will do the exercise with the dog off lead and go to a thirty-foot distance. As a training aid, you will need a short knotted cord; figures I-58 and I-59 show how to make a suitable short lead from a piece of ordinary rope.

Put the knotted cord and leather lead on the live ring of the dog's   49 choke-chain collar as you begin the training sessions this week. This will accustom the dog to wearing the knotted cord. Keep the cord attached during the heeling routines. It will serve, when the leather lead is removed, as a convenient handle with which to apply a correction.

The first practice session for the long sit should be done with the lead attached to the dog's collar, but lying on the floor in front of him. Give the appropriate signals for stay and walk out to thirty feet before turning to face him. Remain there sixty seconds and return to the dog. When you give the command "Heel!" and take the two steps forward to terminate the exercise, do not use the lead; make sure you have positioned it on the floor in front of the dog in such a way that he does not have to trip over it as he heels two steps forward and comes to a sit.

If he performs this well, you are now ready to remove the leather lead. Unsnap it, wrap it up, and toss it on the floor behind the dog as you begin the exercise. Reach down and make a reassuring adjustment to the dog's collar, putting the knotted rope in a position that will enable you to grab it conveniently in case you must return to make a correction. This little diversion will also remind the dog that he still has some sort of handle attached to his collar and can be corrected. Give the proper stay commands and walk out the full thirty-foot distance. You know the rest of the routine by this time.

Do not attempt this exercise outdoors in an unfenced area if your dog is still unreliable off lead. Try it first in an area where you can regain control over the dog if he decides to bolt away (see Week 10 for what to do if he does).

Long Down Modified

In Week 4 you taught your dog the command "Down!" but you had to assist him into position by pulling his legs out from underneath him. Now we are going to eliminate this portion of the exercise and substitute a simpler enforcing mechanism to get the dog to go down on command.

Start with the dog in the proper heeling position. Move your right hand down the lead and grasp it somewhere near the swivel snap, simultaneously bending down, ready to kneel on your right knee and put your left knee (or calf if it is a small dog) against the dog's shoulder. Put your left hand on the dog, as in figure I-60, and go into the kneeling position, at the same time snapping the lead toward you and down with your right hand as you push the dog off balance away from you with your left, rolling him over on his hip into the down position. Stand up slowly, pause for a moment, give the command "Stay!" and walk twenty or thirty feet away, as in Week 4. Remain there at least three minutes—perhaps even four minutes so that your dog will become conditioned to remaining in the down position for *any* length of time, and not get edgy when he thinks the three minutes have elapsed. Repeat this exercise every day, gradually speeding up your routine so that the dog learns that "Down!" means go down *immediately*.

Finish

50 The *finish* begins with the dog facing you, at your feet, sitting squarely

I-60

I-58. Cut a length of highly flexible cord or rope and tie both ends together in this fashion. Pass the loop of the cord through the live ring on the dog's collar. Adjust the length, if necessary, by tying an extra knot in the end.

I-59. After passing the loop of the cord through the live end of the collar, pass the knot through the loop of the cord and tighten it. The cord should hang down two or three inches. The dog should grow accustomed to wearing it as he does all the exercises.

I-60. In order to get your dog quickly into the down position, put your left hand on his withers and push smartly as you simultaneously pull on the lead in the opposite direction. The command "Down!" should be given at the instant you begin the exercise so that the dog associates the command with the sudden push-pull that knocks him off balance and rolls him onto one hip. 51

I-61–64: An Acceptable Type of Finish. The dog begins the finish on the command "Heel!" by passing to the handler's right, then behind him, ending at the normal heeling position. We feel that a dog is more likely to be distracted by activities around him in this type of finish, since he is momentarily out of sight and "on his own." Accordingly, we do not use this type of finish.

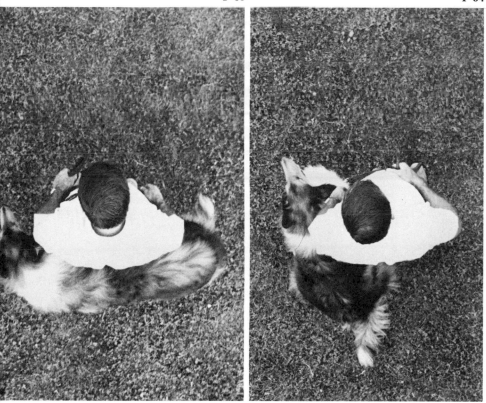

(fig. I-61). From this position he is to come to your left side—and into the proper heeling position—on a single command: "Heel!" There are *two* acceptable ways to finish. One is for the dog to rise up on your command "Heel!," walk around your right leg, then cross behind you and come to a sit alongside your left leg, in the proper heeling position (see figs. I-61–64). In this type of finish he is momentarily out of your vision and more likely to be distracted by events or people around you. For this reason we prefer the second type of finish—the type known in dog-training circles as the "military" finish. His vision is more restricted because he keeps his head toward your leg most of the time.

The military finish begins with the dog sitting in front of you. On your command "Heel!" he gets up, turns toward your left leg, passes by it, turns, and sits at your left side parallel to your direction of march (see figs. I-65–67).

Teaching the Finish In Week 3 you put your dog into a sit-stay position, in part to condition him to remain alert and motionless as you stood in front of him. Thus he is already prepared for the position from which you begin the finish.

I-65–67: The Type of Finish We Prefer. The dog begins from the position shown in figure I-65. On the command "Heel!" he passes to the left of the handler and at the same time begins his turn. He terminates in the normal heeling position. The dog is never out of sight, and he turns with his head facing your leg, which reduces the possibility of his being distracted.

Begin the exercise with your dog in the proper heeling position, sitting at your left side. Simultaneously give the command "Stay!," step off on your right foot, give the hand signal for stay, and turn to face your dog, standing squarely in front of him so that his head is within one foot of your body. Pause there momentarily and mentally prepare for the next portion of the exercise: you will run your left hand down the leather lead nearly to the swivel snap. (Do not grasp the swivel snap—it has a tendency to open easily under accidental pressure.) Essentially, teaching the finish involves pulling the dog slightly to the left, to take him off balance, and toward you as you step back with your left foot, and then turning the dog's body back to your direction of march and stepping forward. Your left hand will describe a counterclockwise arc which will be followed by the dog's nose.

Enough mental preparation for the finish. Now, run your hand down the leather lead and grasp it near the swivel-snap end, close to the dog's neck (fig. I-68). Make sure the choke-chain collar is up near the dog's head—this will maximize your leverage, allowing you to use a minimum amount of force. Say the dog's name and the command "Heel!," simultaneously stepping back a very long step with your left foot (fig. I-69), while keeping your right foot firmly planted on the ground, and firmly tugging the dog's head slightly to the outside and then toward your extended left leg (fig. I-70). Be sure to try to make an arc with your left hand as you do this. As the dog moves past you and begins to come in somewhat, and is therefore off balance, let go of the lead with your left hand and move your left foot forward, stepping away as if you were heeling off. The dog will be somewhat behind you at this point. Heel forward two steps and immediately come to a stop, enforcing the automatic sit, and give him praise (figs. I-71–72). It is important for you to make the dog go into the sit, even though by this time he can already do it, to make him associate your praise with the finish, not the automatic sit.

This is to be practiced every day for at least one week. Some dogs might be a bit confused when required to go through the exercise, and will be a little stubborn at first. If the dog is small, the stubbornness is not so much of a problem, because the handler can easily enforce the exercise without unusual stress and strain to himself. A large stubborn dog is more of a problem. It is important at the outset to maximize your leverage advantage by making sure that his collar is up close to his head and that you grasp the leather lead very close to the swivel snap. You might have to make the initial correction with both hands near the snap in order to knock the dog off balance as you step back on your left foot. Finally, it is very important that you step back a *long* step to get the dog a good distance away from where he was sitting when you initiated the exercise. The dog should come into the sit position in a smooth manner, and this is possible only if he moves past you a good body length or so. Some dogs, once they get past the handler's leg, are tempted just to keep on going, as if they were off lead. This is why you must make the second correction to knock the dog off balance and toward you as you step forward two or three steps.

I-68–72: Teaching the Finish.

I-68. Begin with the dog on lead, sitting squarely in front of you. Reach down and grasp the lead near the swivel snap. Simultaneously give the command "Heel!," step back with your left foot, and make a sharp tug on the lead to the left and back, describing an arc with this motion.

I-69. Make your step back long enough so that you can maximize your leverage and move the dog past you. Your right foot should remain firmly planted.

I-70. When the dog has passed you, correct him back in the opposite direction, in to your leg and forward. Your arm motion continues to describe an arc. This same motion is a hand

56

signal for the dog to finish, and will be used later with the dog completely off lead.

I-71. When the dog has turned back to your direction of march, step forward with your left foot, correcting the dog ahead if necessary.

I-72. When the dog has come back to the proper heeling position, quickly force him into a sit—even though he does the automatic sit.

NOVICE WEEK 6

OUTLINE OF TRAINING SCHEDULE

Old Exercises (Practice these first each day, twice daily.)

    Basic Heeling (all turns, all speeds, halts, automatic sit)

    Corrections for Forging, Lagging, Interference, Leaning, and Drift-
ing to the Left

    Figure 8

    Long Sit

    Long Down

    Handling Precision

Modification of Old Exercises

    Long Down: Stepping on the lead

    Finish: Correcting anticipation and eliminating the forward motion

New Exercise

    Recall

Suggested Length of Practice Session: 12–15 minutes, twice daily

Long Down Modified

By now your dog should be associating the command "Down!" with
going into the down position. If he begins to go down voluntarily as
soon as the command is given, he has made the association between
the command and the desired position. If he does not show any indication of voluntarily going into the down position on command,
continue working on the methods described in Week 5 to get him into
the down position. Eventually he will voluntarily go down as soon as
he hears "Down!"

    Once the dog has made the association and starts to go down on
command, proceed as follows. Begin with the dog in the proper heeling
position. Take the lead into your right hand, but leave a slight amount of
slack in it (see figs. I-73–76). Give the command "Down!" and simultaneously step on the lead with your left foot with enough force to
pull the dog's head toward the ground, hanging on to the lead in such
a way that the dog's head moves, not your hands. You should still be
using the dog's name with "Down!" at this point; midway through
Week 6, and subsequently, you will stop using the dog's name and
simply say "Down!"

    Continue enforcing the down command by stepping on the lead
until the dog voluntarily goes into the down position on the first verbal
command. Some dogs will hesitate to go down until they see the handler's left leg start to move. If your dog starts to hesitate in this fashion,
you must step on the lead quickly enough to cause a sharp snap; the
dog will attempt to avoid this and will voluntarily go down as soon as
he hears the verbal command.

    When your dog is in the down position, pause for a few moments;

then give the command "Heel!," take two steps forward, stop, and praise him.

Finish Modified

All during Week 5 you practiced getting the dog to finish on lead; you enforced it by taking a long step back with your left leg. By this time the dog should be anticipating your heel command when he is sitting in front of you: as you say "Heel!" he should be starting to move in the proper direction. The anticipation is a good sign that he understands the exercise, but it is also a potential flaw. He must not finish until the verbal command is given. If he is starting to do so, you will have to correct him at this point to prevent it from becoming a habit.

The proper correction is to grasp the lead near the swivel snap with both hands and apply a steady upward pressure so as to make the dog uncomfortable; hold the pressure until the dog settles back into the sitting position. If he is sitting straight, you can proceed with the command "Heel!" and finish as you did the previous week. If he settles back and is sitting crooked, step backward and, maintaining a small amount of upward pressure, make the dog settle into a sit that is perfectly straight, facing you. Then you can proceed with the finish exercise.

Now, if the dog understands that he should not go into the finish until the verbal heel command has been given, we are prepared to modify the training somewhat—approaching what we want the dog to do ultimately—by eliminating a portion of the exercise: this week do not step forward during the finish. Do everything precisely as in Week 5 up to the point when the dog turns toward you; then merely bring your left foot up to your right foot and immediately put the dog into the sit, enforcing it so as to remind him that the praise that follows is for the finish, not the sit.

This is how you practice the finish in Week 6. Begin from the proper heeling position. Give the stay command verbally, with your hand, and with your right foot forward; turn and face the dog, pausing before going into the finish. Say his name and then "Heel!" and, as you take a long step back with your left leg, describe the arc with your left hand grasping the lead near the swivel-snap end. Now, as the dog comes past you and begins to turn, merely bring your left foot *up to* your right foot and put him into the enforced sit, *without* taking two steps forward. Praise him.

As you practice during the sixth week, concentrate on two things: (1) deliberately describing the arc with your left hand, and (2) increasing your speed. During Week 5, the dog was literally shown what to do and has associated the finish with the motion of your left hand as it makes the arc. We want him to remember that motion. Speed is now an important consideration; he must do the finish without dragging or wandering, so make certain that he does it rapidly when you say "Heel!" Gradually work up to a fairly fast pace so that the dog jumps when he hears the command, and goes into the finish smartly and enthusiastically.

Recall

The *recall* is one of the more practical AKC obedience exercises: the dog comes to you on a single command, no matter what he is doing, and sits squarely in front of you—close enough for you to touch his nose without having to reach out too far (figs. I-77–81).

The dog has already learned the portion of the exercise that involves sitting before you while you taught him the components of the long sit. If your dog cannot do the long sit (sit-stay and return as we described it during the initial training), then he cannot possibly begin the recall exercise. Thus, before you attempt to teach the recall, practice the long sit and make whatever corrections are necessary to ensure that he remains in the sitting position when you are at some distance from him.

During the first week of training on this exercise you will need only your leather lead. The following week, however, you will have to use a long rope; its thickness should be governed by your dog's weight. We find that quarter-inch braided nylon is the best material for training because it does not stretch excessively, coils up easily, and is very strong. A fifty-foot coil would be the best length to purchase if you plan to continue your training beyond the Novice exercises, since it is essential in teaching the Open exercises. But if you do not intend to

I-73. Put your dog into the normal heeling position and adjust the slack in your lead so that you can conveniently step into the loop near the dog's collar.

I-74. Simultaneously give the command "Down!" and step smartly and quickly on the lead, making sure that the downward thrust of your foot pushes the dog's head down and does not merely jerk the other end of the lead out of your hand.

I-75. Your foot should go all the way down to the ground and remain on the lead until the dog has settled into the down position.

I-76. Pause a few moments with the dog in the down position. Then give the command "Heel!," take two steps forward, halt, and praise your dog.

I–78   I–79

I-77. Begin the recall exercise from the normal heeling position. Give the dog the stay command, both verbally and with the hand signal, and walk away from him about 40 feet without looking back. Turn and face the dog.

I-78. When you give the command "Come!," the dog should come to you in a straight line, moving swiftly and enthusiastically. Note that the handler's hands are hanging naturally at his sides. The 1975 *American Kennel Club Obedience Regulations* requires this; the

handler must not have his hands folded, in front of his body.

I-79. The dog comes to an automatic sit at your feet when he reaches you. He must neither touch you nor stop short of you.

I-80. When you give the command "Heel!," the dog goes into the finish: rising from his sit, he moves into the proper heeling position at your left side.

I-81. The dog should sit squarely after executing his finish and wait for you to give him the next command.

continue training beyond Novice, a thirty-foot piece of clothesline will be suitable. Avoid plastic-coated wire-core clothesline; it is too inflexible. If you elect to purchase nylon rope, most hardware or building-supply stores stock it in bulk rolls or in pre-cut coils of fifty or one hundred feet; boat marinas are also good sources, but they tend to charge more than hardware stores do. You might also purchase a swivel snap for the rope.

The recall exercise is fairly complicated. We advise you to read through it several times before attempting to teach your dog the basic components. Study the illustrations and legends thoroughly as well; this will contribute to the smoothness of your handling techniques.

One of the most important aspects of the recall exercise is the dog's angle of approach once you call him: he must come in a straight line to you—not veer off or approach you in a zigzag fashion. The straighter your dog comes to you on the command "Come!," the higher the probability that his sit will be perfectly straight. In a show ring, you and your dog will be positioned at opposite ends of the length of the ring, and the most direct route between you will be a perfectly straight line. Your training and practice sessions should duplicate that situation. Since you have probably been correcting your dog for crooked sits, there is no need to tempt him into one as you teach him a new exercise. Make it simple for the dog: call him to you in a straight line.

Finally, the demeanor and enthusiasm with which the dog comes to you are an important consideration. A dog that sulks and walks very slowly to you is not performing adequately. He should move swiftly and happily as soon as you call him. Swiftness, of course, is partially a function of the dog's breed and size. Some dogs, such as shepherds, have a deceptive gait: they cover a great deal of ground in a few strides. Other breeds, especially smaller dogs, might have to scurry furiously to cover the same distance in that time. Encourage your dog to move swiftly to you by giving him extra praise for coming on command.

Teaching the Recall Begin your training with the dog in the proper heeling position, with the lead attached correctly. Leave your dog exactly as you did in the long sit exercise: give the verbal command "Stay!" as well as the hand signal, turn, and step off on your right foot (fig. I-82). Walk to the end of the lead before you turn to face the dog, being careful not to put any tension on the lead which would pull the dog accidentally off balance and start him into a forward motion. Remain standing and facing the dog for a few seconds with a good deal of slack in your lead (fig. I-83). Remember, you are now standing in the same position as you were when you taught your dog the long sit; to avoid any anticipation, be careful to vary the length of time that you remain standing in front of him. Initiate the recall by giving the dog's name and the command "Come!"; simultaneously begin taking long, smooth steps backward as you apply a light tug—*not* a violent pull—on his lead. You can begin your backward motion with either foot.

When the dog begins to move toward you, start gathering up the lead with both hands so that he closes the gap and catches up to you. As he comes in, prepare to stop, and apply an upward pull on the lead as you do; it is probably more convenient to pull up with your right hand, since you must also simultaneously push down on the dog's backside to enforce a sit (fig. I-84). This routine is essentially what you did when you taught the dog the automatic sit, but the angle is different: you are facing the dog as you enforce the sit. You must make the dog come to a perfectly straight sit when he reaches you, even if you must take an additional step backward to correct him into it. His final position should be immediately in front of you, close to your feet. At no time during this exercise are you to give the verbal sit command; the dog must sit automatically.

A few additional points are in order regarding the position of the dog as he comes to a sit. The dog is not permitted to bump into your legs as he comes to you, or paw at you as he sits or after. Finally, he must be close enough to you when he sits so that you can remove an object from his mouth without leaning forward; you may reach down, but you should not have to lean conspicuously forward and outward.

The most efficient way to get your dog to execute the recall properly is to make a simple but effective correction for any deviation from the correct routine. The necessary correction consists of making an upward pull on the leather lead with sufficient tension to raise the dog's body weight slightly off his forelegs, and taking a smooth step backward, bringing the dog in to you as you do. When the dog is sitting squarely relax the tension on the lead gradually. After he remains sitting a few seconds, praise him *gently* with a pat on the head and a few words of encouragement—lavish praise might excite him and cause him to break from the desired position. You do not want this to happen for two reasons: it will cause you to make another correction and unnecessarily generate resentment in the dog for the recall exercise; the recall is *always* followed by another exercise. For the moment, we will do a repetition of the exercise as the sequel to the recall. Without moving from your standing position, give the verbal and hand stay signals and pivot in place clockwise. Then walk to the end of the lead and turn to face the dog again. Repeat the recall in exactly the same way that you did the first time.

Note that you have given the stay command to the dog while you were facing him. This is the first time you have ever done this, so your dog might seem a bit puzzled. It might be a good idea to exaggerate the hand-signal portion of the command by keeping your palm in front of his face a bit longer than you would normally. Your dog may need a few repetitions of this exercise before he is confident of your expectations, but he will quickly come to realize that he can be given the stay command from *any* position. Do several repetitions of the recall in the above fashion, working backward in a straight line; each time the dog comes to you and sits squarely, give the stay command and repeat the exercise again.

If the dog anticipates the come command by starting toward you before you actually give it, start alternating the recall training with

I-82–84: Teaching the Recall. **I-82.**
Initially, the procedure resembles
what you did to teach the long sit.
Transfer the lead to your left hand,
give the stay command, and walk to
the end of the lead.

I-83. Be careful to avoid putting
tension on the lead. Stand there a few
seconds before giving the command:
"Baron, come!" As you give it, step
backward and gently tug the dog
toward you, taking up lead as the dog
closes the distance. When he reaches
you, make him sit squarely at your
feet—you might have to back up five
or six steps to ensure that he can.

I-84. When the dog reaches you,
quickly enforce his sit by pulling up
on the lead and pushing down on his
backside. Do *not* give a verbal sit
66 command.

the long-sit (sit-stay and return) exercise. That is, if he anticipates the recall, put him back into the sitting position, walk to the end of the lead, turn to face him, and pause a moment before you walk back to do the return portion. After you have returned to the dog, end the exercise by giving the command "Heel!," taking two steps forward, and enforcing his automatic sit. By randomly mixing up the recall and the long-sit exercises, you will not be allowing the dog to anticipate which one you are doing; he will have to remain sitting until a command or your movement tells him which one you want done.

We have consistently emphasized that the proper way of making corrections with the leather lead is without any straight-line pulls. The recall exercise is one in which you must work a little harder to avoid a straight-line correction. When you are at the end of the lead, facing the dog, you should begin your pull by extending the lead out to one side as you apply the slight tug to get the dog moving toward you. Your previous corrections have knocked the dog off balance, so the position of the lead slightly out from your body will remind him that the pull could knock him off balance should he refuse to come to you on the first gentle tug. If he does refuse to come after the first tug, move in close to him so you can improve the angle with which you apply the correction and more easily knock him off balance. When he begins moving toward you, start your backward motion, bringing the dog in to you as you take up slack lead.

It is important to repeat the recall exercise several times in suc-   67 cession each day this week. Work in a straight line for the several repetitions, and end your recall training by doing a long sit to reinforce the fact that the dog can be expected to do one of several exercises when you are at a distance from and facing him. This will also remind the dog that the recall is always followed by some additional exercise.

NOVICE WEEK 7

OUTLINE OF TRAINING SCHEDULE
Old Exercises (Practice these first each day, twice daily.)
    Basic Heeling (all turns, all speeds, halts, automatic sit)
    Corrections for Forging, Lagging, Interference, Leaning, and Drifting to the Left
    Figure 8
    Long Sit
    Long Down
    Handling Precision
    Recall
Modification of Old Exercises
    Testing the Hand Signal for Stay
    Finish: Both feet stationary
    Recall: The lead off, the rope on, the distance increased
New Exercises
    Stand for Examination
Suggested Length of Practice Session: 15 minutes, twice daily

Testing the Hand Signal for Stay
All during the practices up to now you have been giving the dog a triple stay signal: verbal command, hand signal, and foot signal (stepping off on your right foot). At this point, it is advisable to see how well your dog has associated all three signals with "stay" and whether or not he will stay when the vocal command is eliminated. You should try to get your dog to stay by giving only the hand signal and stepping off on your right foot, pivoting clockwise, and walking completely around him. In a show this would be a perfectly normal activity; in the group exercises (long sit and long down), you must put your lead and your armband on the ground behind your dog while he remains in a sitting or lying position.

    If you have consistently given all three commands during the training, your dog should remain sitting with just the hand signal. If he moves, reinforce the signal with a correction (pulling upward on the lead) and a verbal command, but try to wean him off the verbal command from this point on; give the hand signal alone on some of your commands, and give the verbal and hand signals on others; at the end of ten weeks, he will stay with just the hand signal. You may use both simultaneously in an AKC Novice obedience trial, but later, in advanced work, you will have to make the dog stay with a hand signal alone.

Finish Further Modified

During Week 6 we introduced the finish modification that eliminated the handler's forward motion to get the dog into the proper heeling position. By now the dog should be doing the finish without much physical assistance from you. He should be very much aware that the arc that your left hand describes involves a correction. If the dog does not willingly go into the finish at this time and you are still applying corrections, you should revert to the early training described in Week 5. It is better to make the dog learn it properly at this point than to try to add refinements to a poor foundation.

We are now prepared to modify the finish by eliminating the backward step with the left leg, continuing, however, to make the exaggerated arc with the left arm.

Begin the finish practice session from the proper heeling position; give the stay command and stand in front of your dog, facing him. Pause to make certain that he will not automatically finish—he must wait for the command "Heel!" Take the lead near the dog's collar with your left hand, and give the command "Heel!" as you begin to make the arc. This time do not move your left foot; keep it firmly planted. Be sure that the dog has enough slack in the lead to execute the finish—that is, do not grasp the lead too near the swivel snap. The first time you do this, the dog might be confused; he thinks that your moving left leg is part of the trick, and since you have not moved it, he might not move either. In this case, take up the lead with both hands, grasping it near the swivel snap, and, without moving your left leg, give the command "Heel!," apply enough force to the lead to get him moving into the finish, and release your left hand from the lead to give him slack to complete the arc; be sure to move your arm through the desired arc as if you were still holding on to the lead. By the end of the week your dog should go smoothly into the finish as soon as he hears the command "Heel!" and sees your left hand, on the lead, moving in an arc.

Recall Modified

You will need the fifty-foot (or thirty-foot) rope this week to modify the recall exercise and more closely approximate the ultimate goal of calling the dog to you from a great distance. We suggest that you dye the clothesline or nylon rope a dark color after the first or second day of training this week; dogs are color-blind, so any dark color will make the rope blend in with the grass in your training area. If you have a swivel snap, attach it to one end of the rope for convenience in fastening and removing the rope from your dog's collar. You could simply tie the rope to the live end of the dog's collar, but since you will be 69 putting it on and taking it off regularly during the training, a swivel snap will be a timesaving convenience.

Lay the rope out on the ground the first day of practice; it will serve only as a guide for the dog while you work on the leather lead. Do a series of recalls along the rope, beginning at the swivel-snap end, using the leather lead as you did in Week 6. The rope should define the center line of your practice route as you work. When you approach the end of the rope and have only enough room for one more repetition, terminate the sequence with a long sit (sit-stay and return). After you return to the dog, give the verbal command and take two steps forward before halting. If the dog does his automatic sit properly, give him a good bit of praise. Then heel back to the swivel-snap end of the rope and put the dog into the proper heeling position, looking down the length of the clothesline. The rope will be the center line of his direction of march. Unsnap his leather lead and fasten the swivel of the clothesline to his collar. Put the leather lead in your pocket, on the ground, or anywhere outside the dog's vision except in your hand. Give the triple stay command as before (right foot forward, hand signal, verbal command, all simultaneously) and walk to the end of the rope without looking back. Turn and face the dog (fig. I-85). He will probably assume that you are doing the sit-stay, since he has never done the recall at such a great distance. If you have practiced consistently, your command "Come!" should now be effective. Give his name and the command "Come!" He will most likely come to you, dragging the rope along with him (fig. I-86). As he approaches you, be prepared to grab the rope near his collar if he looks about ready to overshoot you or not sit. If he comes and sits straight, walk around behind him and come up into the proper heeling position, pause, and heel forward two steps. Then give him a bundle of praise. You will eventually be combining the recall exercise with the finish. For the time being they are treated as two separate exercises to prevent the dog's anticipating the heel or finish command.

If he fails to come on the first command, simply bend over, pick up the rope, and give it a gentle tug. Do not give a second vocal command when you do this. Most dogs need only this gentle reminder to come and will then complete the exercise.

If the dog fails to come with the gentle tug on the line, do not give another tug; walk back to the dog, snap the leather lead back on his collar, remove the rope, and resume the training as in Week 6: start the recall work over again until the dog learns the command "Come!" Then move on to the rope modification just described. If the dog cannot do it with the rope on his collar, he will not do it off lead.

The next practice session should be conducted in the same fashion, except that you begin with the rope attached to the dog right away. After two days of work, the dog should be confident and come on the first command. It is then time to dye the rope (green, blue, purple, black —any dark color that will blend with the grass).

Practice the remainder of the week with the dog on the rope. Be sure to lay the rope out in different areas of your yard each day you

I-85. Lay out your rope and use it as a guideline as you practice the recall on the leather lead. Then put your dog into the normal heeling position at the swivel-snap end of the rope and attach the rope to his collar as you remove the leather lead. Give the proper triple stay command and walk to the end of the rope. Stand facing your dog a few moments, then give the command "Baron, come!"

I-86. The dog will be able to return to you with the rope attached to his collar. Be prepared, as he reaches you, to enforce a perfectly straight sit, using the rope as your lead.

71

I-87–91: Teaching the Stand for Examination. **I-87.** As you come out of an about turn, drop your left hand down and cup the palm of it around the dog's nose, applying a little pressure on the lead to pull the dog's nose into your palm.

I-88. Give the command "Stand!" as soon as your hand touches the dog's nose, and continue moving, slowly, steadying the dog with your left hand. Note that the pull on the lead is horizontal—an upward pull has been used during training to cause the dog to sit.

I-89. Come to a halt, gradually relax your left hand, and slowly drop it down to your side. Say nothing, but be prepared to correct if the dog tries to sit, walk, or lie down.

I-90. Some dogs are fidgety. If yours is, use both hands to steady him into a relaxed stand.

I-91. When the dog is standing motionless, you should do the same. It is a good idea, as you teach your dog the stand, to keep the lead in your hand in case a correction is required.

72

train so that the dog learns that he can be recalled from any position. Finally, do not attempt to do the exercise off lead at this juncture. Most dogs will in fact come to their masters when called; that is a fairly natural thing. However, what we are working toward is a dog that will come to the handler on a single command—swiftly and in a straight line —and then sit squarely in front of his handler's legs awaiting a second command. If the dog is not on lead while he is learning this, the handler cannot effectively correct any errors the dog might make.

Stand for Examination

One of the Novice exercises requires that you stand your dog so that the judge can examine him. The *stand for examination* is not an exercise in which you want your dog to assume a picture-book show pose. He will be judged on his ability to stand motionless, not on how good he looks while he stands motionless, so make sure you stand him in a comfortable position. You are allowed, in the *AKC Obedience Regulations* and in AKC shows, to "pose" your dog, which means that you can physically touch him to adjust his feet so that they are directly underneath him. However, once you give the dog the command "Stay!," you cannot touch him again until after the exercise is completed.

Teaching the Stand for Examination   When the dog has learned this exercise, he will come to a motionless stand on a single hand signal, with his legs squarely underneath his body, and then, on your stay command, continue to stand there, perfectly motionless, after you walk away. In a show, the judge will approach the dog and feel him from head to tail; the dog must not growl, show his teeth, shy away, or move his feet. He can, however, move his head, lick the judge, and wag his tail.

The exercise is begun on lead. Start with the dog in the proper heeling position. Heel forward and make an about turn so as to have the dog slightly behind you as you make the first attempt to stand him. As you come out of the turn, drop your left hand down to his nose, cup the palm of your hand around it (fig. I-87), and say "Stand!" Put a little tension on the lead to direct his nose into your cupped hand. Continue moving forward slowly and then gradually turn around counterclockwise (fig. I-88) and come to a slow halt with your left hand still cupped around the dog's nose (fig. I-89). Then, remove your hand slowly from the dog's nose and assume a normal posture two or three feet from him (fig. I-91). If he tries to sit down at this point, move quickly, without saying a word: take him by the collar with your right hand and lift his rear up with your left, putting pressure on his belly just inside his leg with your thumb—this is kind of ticklish for him and he will respond readily.

If your dog wiggles his head a good deal when you try to cup your left hand around his nose, use your right hand as well—but make sure your left hand gets around his nose first (fig. I-90).

During the first week of teaching the stand, use the vocal stand command in order to communicate to the dog that something new is going on—he does not know what the word means, but he will expect

I-92. When you return around your dog, be careful not to put any tension on the lead. Your dog must remain motionless, even after you have returned and are standing with the dog at your left.

something to follow. At the end of the first week of practicing the stand you will drop the verbal command and never use it again—not even in the advanced exercises later in the book. Therefore, take advantage of this and, if necessary, give a second verbal stand command as you teach the exercise—but no more than two, and *never* after the command "Stay!" has been given when the dog is standing. Later, we will describe how to enforce the stand, if the dog is recalcitrant, without repeating the verbal command.

Assume that the dog is standing and you have managed to get a foot away from him without his going into a sit. Give the stay command vocally and with a hand signal, making sure the dog sees the hand signal; note that you are standing in front of him, facing him when you give the hand signal. The first time you perform the stand exercise, pause there some fifteen or twenty seconds after the stay command has been given, and then return around behind your dog, just as you did when you taught him the long-sit exercise. You must be very careful not to apply any upward pressure on the lead during your return, so give it a great deal of slack (fig. I-92). Any upward pressure on your lead will make the dog sit. Incidentally, your dog is not permitted to move from the stand position until you give another command, such as "Heel!" Therefore, when you have returned around him and come to a halt next to him, he should remain motionless, standing. Pause there a   75

I-93. Slip your hand under the rings of the collar in this fashion; your correction should be made without a tightened collar.

I-94. Lift the dog slightly off the ground by pulling up on the collar and lifting up with your left arm under his belly.

I-95. Make your correction quickly and sharply: push the dog's rump one way and pull his head the other, then quickly reverse the directions of these motions.

few seconds, then give the command "Heel!" and, stepping off with your left foot, heel forward two steps, come to a halt, and enforce the automatic sit, even though he can do it.

Ironic as it may seem, you have just taught your dog to stand when you come to a halt; prior to this he automatically sat. There are several reasons for his not sitting the first time: First, he heard a new command, "Stand!" Second, you did not come to a halt while he was at your side —you did it as you came out of an about turn. Third, you reinforced the stand by cupping your hand around his nose and holding it. This was all very strange to the dog—your position, your command, and halting while facing him.

You should practice the stand all week with the idea of gradually increasing two things: first, the distance between you and your dog as he stands, until you get out near the end of the six-foot lead (you must be very careful, as you get to the end of the lead, not to put any pressure on it—it will cause the dog either to sit or to come forward); and second, the length of time that the dog stands motionless—it should be about thirty seconds by the end of the week's practice sessions. That will be sufficient to enable him to pass the AKC examination procedure successfully.

Corrections for Failure to Stand   Some dogs find the stand exercise a little difficult to master; others break by sitting or lying down. The proper correction to keep the dog in the stand position is to return to him, gather up the choke-chain collar in your right hand (fig. I-93), and slip your left hand underneath the dog's belly, near his hind legs (fig. I-94). Note that the choke-chain collar is held firmly in your right hand in such a way that it cannot move through the loop. When you have got into this position, lift the dog up off the ground slightly and correct in a push-pull fashion—pull his head toward you with your right hand and push his rump away, then quickly reverse the directions (fig. I-95). You have to use the sideways correction, because a pull down on his lead by this time means "down" and a pull up on the lead means "sit." A sideways correction will mean "stand still, dummy." After a couple of rapid corrections of this kind, set the dog down on the ground and, to reinforce the command, bop him on the nose. Then move out in front of him while he stands.

This is all that you need to know during the week to teach your dog the proper stand. By the end of the week he will begin to associate your left hand with the stand.

NOVICE WEEK 8

OUTLINE OF TRAINING SCHEDULE
Old Exercises (Practice these exercises first each day, twice daily.)
    Basic Heeling (all turns, all speeds, halts, automatic sits)

Corrections for Forging, Lagging, Interference, Leaning, and Drifting to the Left

Figure 8

Long Sit (minimum of 2 minutes, but vary the time each practice)

Long Down (minimum of 4 minutes, but vary the time each practice)

Handling Precision (Remember that you should not use the dog's name as part of stay commands; avoid backing away from your dog when you leave him in the recall, stand, long sit, and long down.)

Recall

Modification of Old Exercises

Finish: The handler remaining motionless, the dog doing all the moving

Recall: Off lead for the first time; recall combined with finish

Stand for Examination: Elimination of the verbal stand command; getting dog to stand without your turning toward him

New Exercise

Examination (Have a member of your family or a friend examine your dog while he is in the stand.)

Suggested Length of Practice Sessions: 15 minutes, twice daily

Finish Further Modified

At the beginning of Week 8 try to get an idea of the dog's general knowledge by diagnosing his abilities—how well has he learned what you have taught him thus far?

Place the dog in the proper position to execute the finish. Give the command "Heel!" but do not move your body at all. Merely hold on to the lead with your right hand, keeping your left hand at your side. On hearing the command the dog should go into the finish, make a smooth arc, and come into a smooth sit by your left side. If he does not do this, determine what portion of the finish he has not done properly and review the appropriate material in Weeks 5 through 7, bringing him up to the point where he will do the finish well on a single verbal command. From now on, you will not enforce the automatic sit: praise him for the entire finish, including the sit portion, which he should do automatically. If the dog does the finish properly, as described in this paragraph, do not treat it as a separate exercise any more; it will be combined with the recall.

A note about enthusiasm. Some dogs become so fond of the finish exercise that they can hardly wait to do it. They sit there, waiting for the command, and as soon as it is given, they literally jump up into the air, turn in flight, and land next to the handler's left leg, grinning all over themselves. Our shepherd, Baron (U.D.), was one such dog. He was so much the envy of some handlers for the enthusiasm and precision of his leap into the finish position that one of them, privately, tried to get his dog to emulate Baron. He figured that to get the dog to leap into the air, there must be something worth leaping for. Accordingly, and with defensible logic, he decided that a juicy hotdog would do the trick. So he put one in his mouth to entice his shepherd to jump up during the finish, grab the hotdog, and end up in the proper sitting position. We saw him, shortly after he had begun his practice, wearing a conspicuous bandage on his nose. When we asked what happened, he good-naturedly confessed the hotdog story—his dog had missed the wiener on one of his jumps, but he got his handler's nose instead!

The finish in combination with the recall, to be discussed in a moment, will now be done *off* lead—the ultimate test of how well both of you have practiced and learned it.

Recall Modified and Combined with Finish

The recall will be done completely off lead this week, though the knotted short rope will still be attached to the dog's collar in case a correction must be made. Also the recall will be combined with the finish for the first time.

Lay the long clothesline out on the ground as you did in Week 7 and do one recall with it attached to the dog's collar. If the dog does it correctly, return to the proper heeling position by walking around behind him, pausing, and heeling forward two steps; when he sits, praise him. Now, heel him back to the swivel end of the line, but this time *unsnap* the clothesline and quietly put it on the ground. He will think he is still hooked to the clothesline. Give the command "Stay!" and walk to the end of the clothesline—that is, about forty feet—making sure that the rope is between your feet and serves as a straight guide for the dog. Say his name and then "Come!," and be prepared to correct a crooked sit with the knotted cord attached to his collar.

After the dog reaches you and is sitting expectantly in front of you, give the command "Heel!" Be prepared to see a puzzled look on his face—he has never done the finish in combination with the recall before. He will very likely hesitate; if so, reach down and take the short rope as if you were going to correct him. The slightest movement of your hand should be sufficient to make him go into the finish; if he does not, enforce the finish with the short piece of rope and repeat the entire exercise from the long distance.

You might wonder why we have waited so long to combine the finish with the recall, since in a show they are always combined. The reason has to do with eliminating a very common and difficult-to-correct habit that dogs are prey to: they begin to think that the finish is just part of the recall exercise and, when they come to their handlers, simply screech to a halt, pause, and automatically go into the finish without waiting for a command. You have trained your dog in such a way as to reinforce the fact that the recall and finish are two *different* exercises. By periodically doing a return after the recall, you have consistently encouraged the dog to wait for the command that follows his recall; if the command had always been "Heel!" he would be, by this point in his training, anticipating it and, more than likely, going right into the finish just to please you.

Stand for Examination Modified

If the dog has learned how to stand motionless during the previous week of practice, you can advance to the following modifications: drop the verbal command and use only a hand signal; do not face the dog when standing him, but do it from his side; allow strangers to examine the dog while he is standing. The dog will continue to work on lead during this week.

For the first two days of this week, you will concentrate on getting the dog to stand on hand signal alone. Then you will have to recruit some help from a family member, who will examine the dog. Throughout the week you will train the dog to expect a stand signal during any heeling exercise, not just when you are facing him.

Modifying the Command Begin the first practice session of Week 8 for the stand by heeling the dog through an about turn. As you come out of the turn, resume a straight-line heeling march for a few steps and, as you come to your halt, give the hand stand signal (not the verbal signal this time): put your left palm in front of the dog's face. Make certain he sees it before you drop your hand back to your side, but do not leave your hand there too long. The dog should, if you practiced the stand last week, come to a perfect stand. If he does, do not praise him yet. Merely give the command "Heel!" again and continue in a straight line for a few more steps before giving a second hand stand signal. The extra effort involved in teaching your dog now to stand on hand signal alone is insignificant considering the time that it saves you later and the trouble it saves you during Novice trials; while all about you must wrestle their dogs into position, you simply give a hand signal and he stands. You might occasionally have to adjust one of his feet slightly, but by doing sequences of stands on hand signal, the dog learns to go into a comfortable standing position automatically, and if you keep him standing thirty seconds or longer at a time, he will *try* to stand comfortably the first time.

Work for two days doing the sequences of stands on hand signal. Gradually shorten the duration of your hand signal by reducing the time that your hand is in front of the dog's face. If you have a particularly short dog, you trained all during the seventh week by bending over to give the hand signal. Now you will gradually work toward giving the stand signal without bending at all.

If the dog fails entirely to stand on your hand signal, drop back to Week 7 and start the stand exercise from scratch. This time, emphasize the movement of your left hand toward the dog's muzzle as you start to cup his nose in initiating the stand.

A Typical Stand for Examination and the Examination About the third day of this week you should have a family member or friend examine your dog while he stands. It is a good idea to introduce your

I-96. The stand for examination. You should be about six feet away from your dog. Practice this week on lead, and have a friend or family member conduct the examination while you hold the lead and keep your distance of six feet.

dog to the examination procedure by starting off with someone with whom he is acquainted.

Heel your dog into an about turn, and put him into a stand by using a hand signal only. Try to do it so that you stand your dog approximately six feet from and facing your assistant. Give the dog the command "Stay!," step off on your right foot, walk toward the end of the lead, and turn to face the dog (fig. I-96). The examiner then approaches the dog with his left hand offered to him for sniffing; as he walks past the dog, he brushes his hand along the length of the dog from head to rump and circles around behind him before coming back to where you are standing.* Both of you should remain motionless facing the dog for a few seconds. Then you return slowly to the dog, circle around behind him, and come to a halt in proper heeling position; the dog should continue to stand. Pause there a moment and then, using the dog's name, give the command "Heel!," take two steps forward, and halt. The dog should sit automatically, at which time you praise him.

Later, after the dog has grown accustomed to the examination, you can have strangers touch him all over, rub him, et cetera. It takes time to build up to this, and such rigorous examinations are not part of the Novice requirements—but they are part of more advanced obedience exercises.

When you leave your dog in the stand position to go to the end of the lead, make certain that you do not look back at him or back away from him.

At the end of this week's training and practice, your dog should do, tolerably well, all but one of the obedience exercises required to earn qualifying scores in any AKC-sanctioned obedience trial. The remainder of the material in this chapter is geared toward a training schedule that will maximize your chances to score high, win the shows, and earn the C.D. degree in three straight trials. Our students regularly achieve these distinctions by following the training procedures we have described here.

* See figure I-99 (Week 9) for an illustration of the stand for examination in an actual AKC obedience trial.

NOVICE WEEK 9

OUTLINE OF TRAINING SCHEDULE

Note. Practice the old exercises in the order given on the morning of the first day of the week only. Thereafter, follow the text.

Old Exercises (Practice these first on the first day only.)

> Basic Heeling (all turns, all speeds, halts, automatic sit)
>
> Corrections for Forging, Lagging, Interference, Leaning, and Drifting to the Left
>
> Figure 8
>
> Long Sit (minimum of 2 minutes, but vary the time each practice)
>
> Long Down (minimum of 4 minutes, but vary the time each practice)
>
> Handling Precision: Avoid body English on the recall and finish, and backing away after the stay commands; do not use your dog's name as part of the stay command; avoid tautness in the lead while heeling.
>
> Recall
>
> Stand for Examination

New Exercises

> Simulating Show Conditions

Suggested Length of Practice Session: 10 minutes in morning; 15 minutes in practice ring, afternoon

Simulating Show Conditions

This week you will conduct a fairly severe, but enjoyable test for your dog. You will see how both of you respond under simulated show conditions and, incidentally, take a major step forward in your preparation for competition at the AKC obedience trials. You will need the help of a friend or family member during some of your practice sessions this week. Ideally, you should go through the show routine once a day, but since you will need an assistant, that may not be practicable. At least three such sessions would be a minimum acceptable number for this week. We suggest that you do your early-morning training alone, without the aid of your friend, and reserve the afternoon training for the simulated show conditions. This will enable you to spot the flaws in your dog's behavior and straighten them out by the time your more formal practice comes up.

We find that our own students are much more relaxed and confident at actual shows when they have had an opportunity to train under simulated show conditions; they make fewer handler's errors in the show ring and exhibit an enviable degree of professionalism.

You will need a few pieces of equipment to make your simulated show ring: about a hundred and fifty feet of old clothesline or heavy cord to define the boundaries of your practice show ring, and old broomsticks, rake handles, or sticks to use as corners. You can simply take some of your household or garden tools and, mophead and all, stick them into the ground according to the plan shown in figure I-97. If you plan to continue into advanced training, described in chapters II and III, you might purchase the entire amount of rope required for a practice ring at this stage of your training. You can use the same size practice ring throughout all the exercises detailed in the more advanced chapters.

Your assistant should read the material for this week of training or else spend a few minutes before the practice sessions being briefed by you on what to do and when to do it. (It would be very helpful to have a friend who is also training a dog and is approximately at this stage of training; or, ideally, to be in a group class that is using this book as the text. The instructor would then act as the judge during the practice under simulated show circumstances.) The actual show commands that the assistant will, as judge, be giving you are listed at the beginning of each exercise; your assistant can simply read them off, at the appropriate time, as you handle your dog through the routines. Even if you have no assistant this week you can still do the exercises by yourself, but less effectively.

This week pretend that you are at an actual AKC obedience trial. Although this is just a practice run, you can expect a show to be very much like what you will go through this week and next in your final training. As you practice the exercises, concentrate on the technique, the commands, the do's and don't's of handling.

Set up your practice ring with dimensions about like those given in figure I-97. The ring can be as small as 30 feet by 40 feet in an AKC show; for practice, you can approximate either set of dimensions. The ropes that you tie at the corners will sag in the middle, so be sure to tie them high enough that they do not at any point sag lower than your knee. All rings will have an entry, as shown, and all handlers and dogs *must* enter and leave the ring through that entry. A dog is not permitted to leave the ring during the exercises, unless excused by the judge. This happens, for example, if you arrive at the show and your female dog comes into season that day; her scent would wreak havoc among the male dogs. Another possible reason for being excused is obvious signs of sickness or lameness in the dog. If your dog develops a limp just before the show, you can expect that the judge will carefully scrutinize him before permitting him to do the exercises. More than likely, the judge will not permit you to show him.

Before entering your practice ring, make sure you exercise your dog and allow him to relieve himself. He should not do it in the ring. If you are at an indoor show, your dog would be disqualified immediately.* If you are competing in an outdoor show, he would be disqualified if he relieved himself during an exercise, but not if he did so between exercises. Our philosophy is that the dog should be given the

---

* We are using the word "disqualify" in the popular sense. Actually, we should be saying "nonqualifying performance," since "disqualify" has a technical meaning in AKC shows having to do with gross behavior on the part of the handler/dog team.

opportunity to relieve himself before the show, in the designated area. You have, of course, been training your dog for the past eight weeks to answer his natural calls only when you give him the release command "Okay!"

Examine the diagram of the practice ring again. Note that there is a judge's table near the entry. You do not have to provide one when you train this week and next, but when you go to a show, report to that table as soon as you arrive, pick up your numbered armband, and watch a few of the contestants. The judge will give *you* the same routine on the heeling exercises (though it is possible for the judge to put left turns before right turns or vice versa, so long as he gives you all of the turns and halts). You will also find two stewards at the judge's table. They will be the posts of the Figure 8 exercise and will assist the judge in the Long Sit and Long Down.

The photographs used to illustrate this week's training were taken at actual shows. You will note an obvious similarity between them and what you and your dog are doing.

Assuming that early in the day you have worked your dog through all of the Novice exercises he knows, and that you feel his performance warrants proceeding under simulated show conditions, set up your ring and instruct your assistant. Attach the short knotted cord to the dog's collar and keep it on him throughout the practice.

Putting Exercises in Proper Show Sequence   The first group of exercises that you will do will be the *individual exercises,* during which you and your dog will be the only contestants in the ring. They include, in the order in which you must do them, the following:

1. Heel on Leash (including the Figure 8)
2. Stand for Examination
3. Heel Free
4. Recall

Your practice this week will not include the Heel Free (Heel off Leash). That will be saved for Week 10.

The second set of exercises you and your dog must do will be the *group exercises:* the Long Sit and the Long Down, in that order. There will be other dogs and contestants in the ring with you at this time—a minimum of six pairs of handlers and dogs, a maximum of fifteen. This week, to simulate show conditions, leave the ring with your dog at the end of the Recall exercise and take a break for a few minutes before going back in for the Long Sit and the Long Down.

Position your assistant in the ring near the spot where the judge's table would be. Heel up to the entrance on lead and come to a halt. Stand there until your assistant indicates that you may enter the ring. He or she should say something like "Dog number 87. Step in, please." Heel into the ring and come to a halt just inside the entrance. Your dog should go into an automatic sit. In a show, no corrections are permitted either in the ring or on the grounds where the show is being held; that

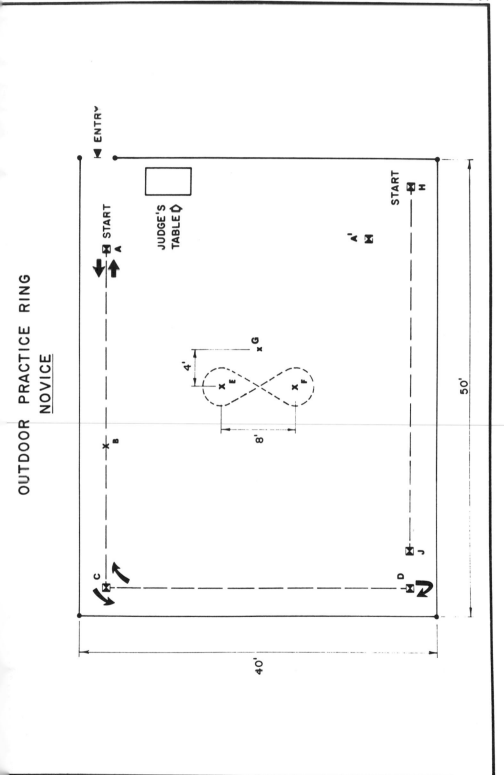

OUTDOOR PRACTICE RING

NOVICE

is considered training your dog in the show area.* For this week of practice, however, you will make whatever corrections are required as you go through your sequences, even for minor errors, such as crooked sits. Next week, you should cut down on your corrections for the minor errors in the practice ring and work a bit harder on the weak exercises after your complete practice session is over.

Your assistant should ask you if you have any questions before starting the exercises. At this time, a judge would explain to you how he might conduct the heeling routine or ask if you have watched other contestants go through the routine. In general, the judge tries to put you at ease, perhaps even make humorous comments. As a handler, he or she knows that you are probably scared out of your wits as you begin competition in Novice A Class since, by definition, you have never taken a dog through a C.D. degree (or else you would be showing in Novice B Class).

Heel on Leash. Your assistant should now tell you where to begin the first exercise, Heel on Leash. For this week, assume that it will be at the point on figure I-97 marked "Start, A."† You should heel your dog over to that spot, facing the end of the ring—point C. Put your dog into a straight sit when you get there, physically adjusting him into it if necessary. In Novice competition, you can straighten your dog up by grasping his collar and gently guiding him into the proper position before the exercise starts. The judge, your assistant in this case, then asks, "Are you ready?" The judging begins at the instant you answer yes. So, before you answer affirmatively, make sure your dog is sitting squarely and you have slack in your lead. If you and your dog are not ready, simply say no and adjust whatever has to be adjusted. When you are ready, you should be in a relaxed, normal stance. Have the lead in your right hand at about waist level and face straight ahead, with your left hand at your side. Figures I-3 through I-6 of Week 1 show what your stance should be as you begin the exercise.

JUDGE'S COMMANDS TO YOU FOR HEEL ON LEASH
1. Forward
2. Halt
3. Forward
4. Right turn
5. Left turn
6. About turn
7. Slow
8. Normal
9. Fast
10. Normal
11. Halt
12. Exercise finished

* For conditions under which specific corrections can be made on a show ground area, see chapter 2, section 26 of Appendix I.

† It could begin at point A′ of figure I-97, in which case a slightly different turn sequence would be required. We have not drawn in a heeling route from that point.

Your assistant should give you these commands as you execute the Heel on Leash according to the suggested pattern on figure I-97. After the halt commands, you must logically be given another "Forward!" to get you and the dog into motion. Your only utterances during the exercise will be the heel commands: one as you start, and one as you start from the first halt the judge asks you to make. Some judges will make you halt more than once. However, the second halt is usually followed by "Exercise finished!"

Study the heeling route on figure I-97 with your assistant. At point B you should make a halt. At point C, a left turn. About three or four paces into the route between C and D, do a slow for about half of the distance to D, and then, on your assistant's command "Normal!," heel at a normal pace to point D. Your assistant should then give you an "About turn!" as you approach point D. Again, about three or four paces into the route back to point C, the assistant should say "Fast!" and, about two-thirds of the way back, "Normal!" At point C, your assistant should say "Right turn!" and then, somewhere between point C and point A, preferably closer to point A, "Halt!" After the dog has come to a sit, the assistant should say, "Exercise finished!" You can then praise your dog by patting him on the head and talking to him. Remember, up until that point you can utter nothing but the appropriate heel commands (your dog's name, followed *immediately* by "Heel!"). When you go from normal to slow to fast, and back to normal again, your pace should change clearly and obviously, not just to a slightly slower or slightly faster than normal. Your normal pace should be the pace you would use if you had no dog at your side. Make your turns smoothly—the smoother they are, the better your dog will look, since he can adjust to *your* pace without your tightening the lead.

During your heeling practice this week pay careful attention to your own movements, not just the dog's. Increase the precision of your handling techniques and try to rid yourself of any poor habits you might have fallen into, such as mumbling to your dog, adjusting your pace to fit his, or putting tautness in the lead, especially on right and about turns. You should make your halts gradual by walking a step or two after hearing the command "Halt!" If you stop too suddenly, your dog, caught unaware, might overshoot and sit too far ahead of you—and *you* would be the cause of the poor sit.

Occasionally your assistant (and judges) will make a blunder on one of the commands; for instance, ask you to make a left turn into the boundary of the ring, or fail to give you a turn command as you come up to the end of the ring. If this happens, come to a halt and wait for the next command. In many shows the background noise interferes with the judge's commands. If you do not clearly hear the command, come to a halt and tell the judge. You will not be penalized for this. Normally he will move closer to you or speak a bit louder. If you have a hearing problem, tell the judge as you enter the ring, when he asks you if you have any questions; explain your problem and ask him to speak louder. (Figs. I-98 and I-99 show a typical Heel on Leash exercise in Novice A.)

This ends the first part of your Heel on Leash practice and pre-

I-98. A young handler performing the Heel on Leash exercise while AKC Judge Norman F. Wurtz inspects the performance carefully. Note the proper amount of slack in the lead and the dog's perfect position. The judge's table is immediately behind Judge Wurtz.

I-99. After Judge Wurtz declares the exercise finished, the handler praises his Brittany spaniel. The judge notes the handler's score on his Worksheet for the Heel on Leash exercise before informing the handler that the Figure 8 exercise will begin.

adapts you for your first competitive situation. Next week, you will go for perfection and will not correct your dog during the practice sessions in the simulated show ring.

The Figure 8. The second part of the Heel on Leash exercise is the Figure 8. Two stewards will move to the center of the ring at this time. You should anticipate that this will be next and move your dog over to the area of the ring where you see the stewards standing, which will most often be the middle of the Novice ring (see fig. I-97). In moving your dog over to the Figure 8 area, you may guide him gently with your leash, but you may not physically touch him or push and shove him into a more acceptable position. You may even give multiple commands to get the dog into a straighter position, or pat your leg to encourage him to move over toward you—but you must not touch him, except by guiding him while holding on to his collar.

The Figure 8 exercise in Novice is on leash. You should position yourself about four feet away from the stewards (milk bottles, trash cans, et cetera, will work for practice sessions), who will be standing about eight feet apart, facing each other, at points E and F on figure I-97. Make sure your dog is lined up in such a way that he faces the stewards and is about midway between them. The exercise begins from the normal heeling position, so make certain your dog is straight and you have slack in your lead when you respond "Yes!" to the judge's "Are you ready?" Most judges will explain to you that you may turn in

either direction when they give the command "Forward!" If the judge does not explain this, just assume it to be true.

JUDGE'S COMMANDS TO YOU FOR FIGURE 8

1. Forward
2. Halt
3. Forward
4. Halt
5. Exercise finished

Your only utterances will be the heel commands to your dog: once at the beginning of the exercise, and once after your first halt—when the judge again says, "Forward!" A typical Figure 8 pattern would be as follows—practice it all week: On the judge's "Forward!," give your dog's name and the command "Heel!," stepping toward the area between the stewards. Turn gradually to the right and heel around the steward at E on figure I-97, following a path similar to that shown by the dotted lines. Normally in Novice, the judge will tell you to halt when you are about halfway between the stewards, so expect to hear "Halt!" soon after circling the first steward. Do not anticipate it by slowing down; you will be able to make a gradual stop as soon as the command "Halt!" has been given. You are not being judged for the location you halt in, but, rather, for the precision of the dog's sit and heeling behavior. Remain motionless until the judge gives you another "Forward!" Then give your dog's name and the command "Heel!," and proceed with the Fig- 89

I-100. The Figure 8. Dan Barker, one of our students, heels his shepherd, Bup, around the stewards, Mr. and Mrs. Les Talley, Jr., while Judge Norman F. Wurtz observes. Dan took Highest Scoring Dog in Trial in this show with a score of 199.

I-101. The Stand for Examination in Novice competition. The handler, after leaving his dog, walks the six feet to the judge, turns, and faces his dog. The judge then conducts the examination while the dog remains motionless, undisturbed by being so near a complete stranger.

I-102. Dan Barker and his shepherd, Bup, about to begin the Heel Free exercise. Note the perfect sit of the dog as the judge asks, "Are you ready?" Note also the entrance of the ring immediately behind Judge Wurtz, and compare with point A on figure I-97.

90

ure 8, following a path similar to that indicated by the dotted lines on figure I-97. Your pace at this point should be constant. Do not slow down on the inside turns or speed up on the outside turns as you did during the early weeks of your training; that would be considered "adjusting your pace," and would be penalized. You can expect the judge to allow you to heel around the two stewards one full circuit this time, but be prepared to come to a gradual halt at any time. Usually, when your dog has completed his sit after the judge's second halt command, the judge will tell you that the exercise is finished. If your dog fails to sit when you stop do not give a second command.*

When you hear "Exercise finished!," the stewards will return to the judge's table. For your practice, you can either leave the trash cans standing there or remove them, whichever is easier. They will not be in the way for the rest of the practice session if left there. Praise your dog for his performance in the Figure 8 and, as you do, unsnap the lead from his collar: the Stand for Examination follows, and it is done off lead in a show. (Fig. I-100 shows a Figure 8 exercise in Novice A.)

The Stand for Examination. If your dog is steady and reliable at this stage, you can do the Stand for Examination off lead. If you have any doubts, practice the remainder of the week on lead, but go through the examination procedure as you have done in your practice sessions in recent weeks. In our regular classes we conduct the Stand for Examination on lead during Week 9.

The Stand for Examination takes place in the same area as the Figure 8 exercise. Usually, after declaring the Figure 8 exercise finished, the judge will immediately say, "Stand your dog for examination!" Some judges will add "Leave him when you are ready" or "Take a reasonable amount of time." This means that you must remove his lead and hand it over to the judge (or steward) and put your dog into the Stand. You may heel around in a circle, give the hand signal for stand, and then check the dog's feet to see that they are squarely beneath him. If they are not, adjust them. Your dog should be put into the Stand approximately six feet from the judge, facing him. When your dog is standing satisfactorily, give the command "Stay!" (*without* using the dog's name), walk to the judge's side, turn, and face the dog. We repeat: *walk* away—do not back away—and do not look back as you leave the dog. Never give the command until you are ready to walk away, for as soon as you say "Stay!," the judging begins. This means that if you touch your dog to adjust him further, or utter another word, you are disqualified. The command may be given verbally with the simultaneous hand signal, exactly as you have been practicing it during this course.

* The general policy of the AKC for double signals matches our opinion: a dog should obey on a single command. Technically, however, a dog can be given a second heeling command and still earn a qualifying score in Novice. The penalty for a second heeling command will be a "substantial" deduction of points—five to ten, depending on the judge. Thus, while heeling in a Novice show, it would be both permissible and desirable to give your dog a second "Heel!" if, for example, he wandered away from you and started to leave the ring. The training procedures we are developing, however, are such that your dog should be highly reliable by the time he gets into the show ring and not require a second command. 91

When you are at your assistant's (the judge's) side, he will walk toward the dog, pass along the dog's side while feeling him from head to tail, and return to his initial position. In most Novice trials, the judge will simply brush his hand along the top of the dog's back as he passes by in both directions. When the judge has returned to you, he will say, "Back to your dog!" Do not move until you hear this command. Then walk calmly to your dog, pass around behind him and come to a halt with the dog on your left side. Remain silent and motionless in that position. When the judge says, "Exercise finished!," give your dog's name and the command "Heel!," taking two steps forward. Your dog must remain standing until the judge declares the exercise finished. The reason you have been adding the two steps forward during your practice is to condition the dog to the fact that another exercise follows, that he is not free to break his stand until you give the command "Heel!" You are not, incidentally, judged for the two-step-forward routine. When the exercise is finished, you may praise your dog. Figure I-101 shows a Stand for Examination in an actual show.

Heel Free. The next exercise in a show would be the Heel Free, which is, except for the absence of the lead, identical to the Heel on Leash. We will not do the Heel Free this week. For purposes of practice, however, it would be prudent to go through the routine on lead again at this point in the training session, to condition both you and your dog to the show sequence and to fix the pattern more firmly in your mind. Have your assistant give the same commands as were given for the Heel on Leash. In a show, when your dog will be *off* lead, you may guide him over to the "Start, A" position of figure I-97 by holding his collar while heeling with him. Figure I-102 shows a Heel Free exercise about to begin.

The Recall. When the Heel Free exercise is finished, praise your dog and expect to hear the judge tell you to bring your dog over to a new position. You may guide the dog to that new position by holding on to his collar and heeling with him. Normally the Recall exercise is conducted along one of the long sides of the ring, indicated in figure I-97 by points H and J. The exercise could start from either point. Let us assume that you begin at point J. Put your dog into the normal heeling position there, facing point H. Make certain his sit is straight before you tell the judge that you are ready.

JUDGE'S COMMANDS TO YOU FOR RECALL
1. Leave your dog
2. Call your dog
3. Finish
4. Exercise finished

Your assistant should be prepared to move over behind the dog as soon as the dog begins to return to you so that he will be able to evaluate the straightness of the dog's sit. The best place for him would be near you, at a slight angle, so that he can also see if the dog bumps you when he comes in to sit or brushes your leg when he makes his finish.

After you have indicated to your assistant that you are ready (by answering affirmatively to his query "Are you Ready?"), stand motionless facing point H of figure I-97. After a brief pause, your assistant should tell you to "Leave your dog!" When you hear this command, give the stay command by simultaneously using the hand signal and the verbal "Stay!" Step off with your right foot first, without looking at the dog or backing away, and walk calmly to point H at the opposite end of the ring. When you get there, turn around and face the dog, standing in a normal posture with your hands at your sides. Wait for the assistant's next command: "Call your dog!" Give the dog's name and the command "Come!" Be careful when you give your command that you do not lean forward or engage in any body English—a handler's error that is easy to commit when you are under the strain of simulated or actual show conditions. Try to remain motionless when you give the verbal command to your dog—concentrate on it beforehand. Make certain your dog can hear your command.

Your dog should come to you quickly, in a straight line, and sit squarely at your feet. He should not bump your legs when he reaches you, or stop short. You should be able to touch his head when he is sitting in front of you. If you see, this week, that he is coming in crooked or is overshooting you, be prepared to grab the knotted cord on his collar and correct him smartly into the proper position.

Remain motionless and silent while the dog is sitting at your feet. On your assistant's next command, "Finish!," give your dog's name and the command "Heel!" Again, avoid body English. When the dog has come to a sit, the assistant should say, "Exercise finished!" Praise your dog, take him by the collar, and heel with him out of the ring, collecting your leash from one of the stewards at the judge's table as you go by. Put your dog back on leash as soon as possible, in the ring if convenient. You cannot have your dog off leash at a show; there will be officials in the crowd to reprimand you if you do. (Figure I-103 shows a Recall in an actual show.)

This ends the individual exercises for Novice. In a show, the next contestant will be waiting at the entrance and will be invited into the ring as soon as you leave it. You may have quite a long wait before you re-enter the ring for the group exercises, the Long Sit and the Long Down. The judge must not have more than fifteen handlers and dogs in the ring at one time for the group exercises. Some judges will call all of the first fifteen contestants back for the group exercises as soon as they have finished judging them in the individual exercises, but others will judge all of the entrants—perhaps as many as sixty or seventy—individually before doing any of the group exercises.

In practice this week, give your dog a few minutes to relax before doing the Long Sit and the Long Down.

The Long Sit. Pay attention at a show to the judge's pattern of doing the Long Sit and Long Down. In fact, when you enter the ring for the individual exercises you can ask him if he plans to do the group exercises at the end or after each group of fifteen. See Appendix III for the Judge's Worksheet, used in scoring the Long Sit and Long Down (scores are transferred to Worksheets for individual dogs). Study it carefully to see exactly what the judge looks for.

JUDGE'S COMMANDS TO YOU FOR LONG SIT
1. Sit your dogs
2. Leave your dogs
3. Back to your dogs
4. Exercise finished

Either a steward or someone on the public address system will announce that the group exercises (the Long Sit and Long Down) are "beginning for Novice A contestants numbers 5, 6, 7, 8, 10, 11, 15 . . . at ring number 7." When you hear it, put your numbered armband back on your left arm and heel your dog over to the area near the ring entrance. There, one of the stewards will line you up according to your catalogue (armband) number—lowest number entering the ring first. You are not being judged at this point, so try to keep your dog relaxed. You might put him into the down position if you have to wait for any length of time. Often there will be Novice A contestants showing their dogs in the breed ring, and occasionally the judge will wait for them to finish. On the other hand, he may allow them to complete the group exercises with a different group, out of their catalogue order. With as many as sixty contestants in large shows, there will be four different groups going through the Long Sit and Long Down before the judging of Novice is finished.

A word on protocol and regulations is in order at this point. If your dog happened to disqualify in one of the individual exercises, you are still *obliged* to complete the group exercises. If you do not, you may hear from the AKC. This is a reasonable and prudent rule: a minimum of six dogs must participate in a show before any one of them earns a "leg" toward the C.D. degree. It would be a shame if there were only six entries in the Novice class and one of them failed to return for the group exercises. In short, if you show up at a dog show you have entered, you *must* show your dog in all of the events he is scheduled to enter unless dismissed by a judge or a veterinarian. You cannot chicken out. Your entry form is often collected when you leave the show, so officials know that you appeared there, and you cannot leave the show *with a dog* unless you have an entry form for him. So do *not* bring two dogs to the show if only one is entered.

After all of the contestants have appeared and are in proper position outside the ring, a steward will lead them into the ring and position them, dogs on lead, along the side of the ring the judge has elected to use. It will be either between points C and A or points J and H of figure I-97. The dogs and handlers will line up facing the opposition side of the ring. Do not take your lead off the dog until everybody is in proper position, since you most often have to shift around or squeeze closer together to make space for others. Most judges will tell the contestants to "prepare your dogs for the one-minute sit." This means that the exercise will begin soon; take your armband off, remove the lead, coil

I-103. The Recall in Novice competition. Note that this Recall was performed right down the center of the ring. The judge carefully inspects the dog's sit before telling the handler to finish.

it up, and place it inside your armband. Then step behind your dog and place the armband on the ground in such a way that the judge can see your number to score your dog on the exercise. Return to your dog's side and check to make sure he is sitting comfortably, and not on an anthill or thorn bed. The judge will then check his watch and inspect the line to make sure everybody is ready. He will then say, "Leave your dogs!" Give the stay command, verbally and by hand, and walk away. Do not give the dog's name as part of the command.

In your practice this week, work toward a two-minute Long Sit. In a show, some judges will give you "traveling time"—that is, they will tell you to go back to your dog before the full minute is up, allowing your walking time to count as part of the one-minute sit. Other judges will make the dogs sit a full minute before ordering you back to them.

You should not move or talk to the other handlers while you stand at the opposite end of the ring. You cannot smoke; you remain motionless. When the time is up, your assistant should say, "Back to your dogs!" Walk back at a normal pace, passing to the right of your dog, around behind him, and coming to a halt at the proper heeling position. Remain standing there until the assistant says, "Exercise finished." Give the command "Heel!" and take two steps forward before halting, then praise your dog after he sits automatically. Take him by the collar and lead him back to the original position, in front of your armband and lead, and resume the normal heeling position again. The Long Down will begin immediately. (Figure I-104 shows a Long Sit in Novice A at an actual show.)

The Long Down. Practice the Long Down this week, in your simulated ring, so that your dog will remain down for between four and five

95

I-104. The Long Sit at an indoor show. Note that one of the dogs (extreme right) has broken from the Long Sit and is standing. He will not qualify and will not take a leg in this show.

minutes—vary the time. If he tries to break, quickly return to him and correct with the 360° spin and the bop on the nose.

JUDGE'S COMMANDS TO YOU FOR LONG DOWN
1. Down your dogs
2. Leave your dogs
3. Back to your dogs
4. Exercise finished

The judge will either tell the contestants to prepare their dogs for the Long Down, or announce that the three-minute Long Down will follow. Make sure your dog is sitting squarely and will not have to lie on an uncomfortable spot. The judge will then give the command "Down your dogs!" You may not touch your dog, but you may repeat the command "Down!" if your dog fails to go down the first time you say it. Do not use his name in this command. From this point on, the exercise is just like the Long Sit. At the end of this exercise, your dog is through showing in the Novice class. Put his lead back on him and walk out of the ring. (Fig. I-105 shows a Long Down in Novice A at an actual show.)

In a show, you will not know what score you and your dog earned until all the dogs in that class are through. The judge will add up the points for each contestant and call back into the ring all the qualifying dogs (dogs that have succeeded in earning a leg toward their degree). The four dogs scoring highest in the class will be awarded first, second, third, and fourth places, respectively, when all of the qualifying dogs have lined up in the ring. In some cases, there will have to be a tie-breaking runoff between dogs with identical scores to see which dog takes the higher place. This will be explained in Week 10.

I-105. The Long Down in an indoor show. Note the obedience rings for other classes in the background.

The Importance of Corrections at This Point in Training

During Week 9 you will be able to see clearly the areas in which your dog's obedience work is deficient. At this point he should have been exposed to all the exercises in the Novice obedience class except the Heel Free. While we have emphasized in the above description, perhaps a bit too strongly, the ideal circumstances in the simulated show ring, you should have firmly fixed in your mind that your dog *must* be corrected at this stage. In the practice ring this week, interrupt your exercise if the dog lags, forges, interferes, et cetera. Concentrate on his precision now, and demand high-caliber performance. By the end of Week 9 you should be able to go through the entire show sequence as described above, without interrupting to correct for a minor error (for instance, a slightly crooked sit). In fact, in your last practice session of the week you should do just that: pretend that you are in an actual show ring and do not correct for minor errors. If the dog does less than perfectly in an exercise, work on that exercise after you finish the show sequence. However, if the dog makes a serious error—such as failing to come on the Recall—you should correct immediately.

Relapses

Some dogs will occasionally suffer a relapse during their training: suddenly stop doing an exercise that they had fully mastered before. This often happens when the handler has been somewhat excessive in his corrections or has been working the dog too long. The best remedy for this is a day off and a quiet stroll with the dog, during which he can relax and enjoy your company without having to work for approval. We have emphasized that your corrections should be dispassionate and your approval genuine. Dogs know when you are upset and angry, and they

97

do not particularly like working with you if you are crabby and hostile. Be a good sport; firmness is not synonymous with harshness. Obedience work should be challenging and interesting for both you and your dog. Do not let it become a frustration and annoyance. You want a happy, enthusiastic dog when the training is over, and only your attitude and handling can create that condition.

Finally, some dogs will suffer relapses for no explicable reason. Be patient. Go back to the point in the training where the dog can perform the exercise. Occasionally you will have to build his confidence back up slowly.

NOVICE WEEK 10

OUTLINE OF TRAINING SCHEDULE
Note. Use this schedule also in the weeks immediately prior to showing your dog.
Old Exercises (Practice these first, in show sequence and using an assistant as judge.)
    Novice
        Individual
            Heel on Leash and Figure 8
            Stand for Examination (off leash)
            Heel Free (after first day, off leash)
            Recall
        Group
            Long Sit (exposing dog to other dogs)
            Long Down (exposing dog to other dogs)
Modification of Old Exercises
    Correcting Dog Unmanageable Off Lead
    Foot-guide Modification to Condition Dog to Sit Perfectly
    Practicing in New Areas (Move practice ring to parks, golf courses, neighbor's yard.)
New Exercises
    Heel Free
    Errors in Handling (Familiarize yourself with Judge's Worksheet.)
    Practice for Runoff
What You Should Know About Entering a Show
How to Go to a Show

Heel Free

This week we will add the final ingredient to the Novice exercises: the
Heel Free. If you have made the corrections for forging, lagging, drift-

ing to the left, and interference during your basic heeling practice in this course, your dog should Heel Free without any trouble. We have urged you to keep him on lead until this point to condition him indelibly to remaining in the proper heeling position. Now we must test the results of our training and dedication to the practice schedule.

Begin your training this week in your customary working area, with the knotted cord attached to the dog's collar. Go through the complete sequence of exercises in proper show order. After finishing the Long Down, give your dog a break for a few minutes and then heel with him on lead to reinforce the fact that you have gone back to work again.

Come to a halt. When he sits squarely, reach down and unsnap the lead and put it in your pocket. Give him the command "Heel!" and step off, as if he were still attached to the lead. If he hesitates, reach down and give a reassuring tug on the knotted cord, which you have previously placed on the top of his back for convenience in correction. Heel a few steps forward and come to a gradual halt. If he goes into the automatic sit, give him a good deal of praise and repeat the exercise again, taking only a few steps before halting. If he is performing as expected, and remains in the proper heeling position, lengthen your distance between start and halt to about twenty or thirty feet, giving him praise for his good behavior—which includes automatic, square sits. The next time you give the heel command, make a left turn soon after you are in motion. If he maintains the proper heeling position, go through all the turns, all the speeds, and do several more halts. He deserves an enormous amount of praise if he does everything properly.

If the dog does not respond as expected and tries to wander away, quickly put him back on lead and correct him. Heel with him on lead for a while and then unsnap it again. Repeat the off-lead heeling, coming to a halt after a few steps. Each time he makes a mistake, correct him. If the mistake is slight, you can use the short cord to correct. If his mistakes are more serious—such as wandering two or three feet away —quickly put the lead back on and correct him. Most dogs, after a few such corrections, will be aware that the Heel Free is like the Heel on Leash, and will come around to the proper behavior. Be patient with a recalcitrant dog; do not lose your temper or correct too severely. Some dogs need more experience at Heel on Leash before they perform the Heel Free well. If you have such a dog, expect to spend a few more days on leash. Practice the remainder of the week as described, but do the Heel Free portion of the work on leash.

Correcting Dog Unmanageable Off Lead It is highly unlikely that, after ten weeks of obedience training, your dog will be unmanageable when you take him off lead. He has been conditioned to obey on a single command throughout the training and, if he is a normal dog, will do so even when he is off lead. Still, there are a few exceptions; a small number of dogs will attempt to run away from their handlers when taken off lead, or will not come promptly on the first command.

If you have developed the proper balance of praise for good work and correction for sloppy work, your dog should be, at this point, an enthusiastic, happy worker. However, some handlers let their emotions get in the way and make their corrections with severity, conveying a mood that may cause their dogs to become unmanageable. Dispassionate correction and genuine praise and affection should keep your dog in high spirits and well behaved.

Then there are the genuine mischievous imps—those carefree, happy-go-lucky dogs that slobber all over you, wag their tails, do the on-lead heeling perfectly and, the moment they are taken off lead, bound gleefully away, smelling and sniffing at random, chasing butterflies, and periodically glancing back at the handler—all the time wagging their tails vigorously. There is great hope for such dogs.

If you suspect, or know from recent experience, that you will have difficulty recalling your dog when he is off lead, try to find a fairly large, enclosed area within which you can recapture the dog if he decides to bolt away. A tennis court would be ideal. You can condition your dog to come to you in such an area by allowing him, when heeling off lead, to drag his lead along behind him. If he decides to leave you and smell some flowers at the back of the court, you can bring him under control fairly readily. Never chase him; rather walk calmly toward him, after giving him a chance to come back to you of his own accord. Running toward the dog will only make matters more difficult. You should not repeat the command to come or plead with the dog to return. When he bolts away from you, give his name and the command "Come!" Remain standing to see if he will make any effort to return to you. If he does not, walk calmly toward him and try to pick up the end of his lead. When you have the lead in your hand, say nothing, but walk him back to the place from which he broke, keeping a goodly amount of tension on his collar—enough to make his front feet come slightly off the ground. This is quite uncomfortable for the dog, and he will no doubt wish to avoid it in the future. Do it dispassionately.

When you have returned to your initial place, give him another chance at the Heel Free, again allowing his lead to drag along behind him. Go through the turns and speeds as if you were on lead. If he breaks again, repeat the correction as described.

If the dog is particularly recalcitrant, use a long piece of rope as a lead, and let him heel with that dragging behind him. The long rope will enable you to recover him more quickly and convince him that he is still, even at a considerable distance, in a correctable position.

A few days of this should work. Move him to an unfenced area when he is responding properly and will both heel off leash and come when called.

Foot-guide Modification If your dog heels properly off leash, begin working for perfection. Try to catch any lagging or forging at this point by appropriate tugs on the knotted cord. Work on his sits during both the Heel Free and Heel on Leash. If the dog tends to sit with his bottom around behind you, use your left foot as a guide when you come to a halt: immediately after halting, stick your left foot behind you so that

the dog must sit with his bottom farther away from what he previously

I-106. Perfecting the dog's sit. To condition your dog to sit perfectly straight, train from this point on by using your left foot as a guide to the dog. When you come to a halt, stick your left leg behind you. The dog will begin to assume that it is there all the time and sit perfectly parallel to your direction of march. Caution: Do not let this become an unconscious habit on your part —you would fail to qualify in a show if you did this.

thought was a good place (fig. I-106). After a few such halts, the dog will begin to sit more squarely. If he sits with his bottom too far in the opposite direction, take a long step to the right side and correct him smartly in to you by pulling his head into your left leg while simultaneously bumping his shoulder or chest with the outside of your leg. If the dog comes to a sit too far behind you, take a step ahead and to the right and correct the dog into the proper position; that is, treat it as lagging and correct for it as such. Finally, if the dog sits too far ahead of you, take a long step backward, and correct him into the proper position, enforcing his sit when he is where you want him.

After the first day of training this week, you will be doing the Heel off Leash as a regular component of your workout in the practice ring. As in Week 9, try to work once a day in the practice ring, with an assistant to help you by giving you the proper judge's commands. Make whatever corrections are required while you are in the practice ring, but at the end of the week do a trial run by going through the show sequence as you would be expected to do under AKC regulations. If the dog makes only minor errors in the practice obedience trial, do not correct them at the time, but work on them immediately after the termination of the complete sequence. Correct immediately if the errors are substantial ones—such as failing to sit, or wandering away.

Practicing in New Areas

You should attempt to give your dog exposure to new surroundings at this stage in his preparation. He should be exposed to new places and 101 people, new smells and surroundings. There are two ways to do this. First, take him to busy shopping centers or places where there are large crowds of people who are strangers to him. You can do the basic heeling (all speeds and all turns) in a supermarket parking lot, as well as the Recall—provided the automobile traffic is not hazardous and your dog is reliable off lead. Second, set up your practice ring in new areas, such as golf courses or parks. Train fairly early in the morning in these areas, when they are usually empty: Few people will complain about a well-trained dog going through his obedience routines, but there will always be some who will resent it. You could also train in an obliging neighbor's yard, or in the yard of a friend who is also training a dog. The main objective is to give your dog experience at working in strange surroundings.

Dog shows can be held indoors or outdoors, and either kind of show has its peculiar distractions and discomforts. Try to give your dog some exposure to less than ideal circumstances. Indoor shows are often very noisy, so work in areas that provide noise distractions, especially on the off-lead exercises. Outdoor shows are subject to inclement weather. Unappealing as it may sound, you should work your dog in the rain occasionally.

An important kind of exposure for your dog is association with other dogs. Before entering your dog in competition, practice the Long Sit and Long Down in a practice ring with other dogs. In an actual show, your dog will be exposed, off lead, to dogs he has never seen before, and unless he has had an opportunity to work under such conditions, the temptation to get up and sniff around might be overwhelming. If your dog does break from his Long Sit in a show, one of the stewards or the judge will quietly move in to the dog and take him away, usually "downing" him in front of the other dogs. You should remain standing where you are if this happens. When the judge orders you back to your dog, walk over to your dog and stand there until the exercise is finished, keeping him under control so that he will not encourage other dogs to break from their position. Then put him back in line with the others, and proceed with the Long Down.

Errors in Handling

We have emphasized handling precision all during this course. Perhaps the most effective way of illustrating the importance of handling is to show you the mysterious paper on which the judge is busily jotting things down as the handlers go through their exercises: figure I-107 is the "Obedience Judge's Worksheet" for Novice competition.

The first thing you should note is the significance of the heeling exercises in terms of points: a perfect score for Novice is 200 points, and the Heel on Leash and Heel Free are together worth 80 points. It should be clear to you now why we emphasized the importance of correcting your dog's sloppy heeling. The second thing to keep in mind is that, in order to qualify in the trial, your dog must qualify in each exercise as well. That is, you must obtain at least 170 points, and you may not have a score of 50 per cent or less in any one exercise. (The same

OBEDIENCE JUDGE'S WORKSHEET

For Judge's Use ONLY – Not to be distributed or shown to exhibitors

DATE . . . .   NOVICE......CLASS   DOG No. . . . . . .

SHOW . . . .   (A or B)   BREED. . . . .

| EXERCISE | NON QUALIFYING | | QUALIFYING | | Maximum Points | Points Lost | NET SCORE |
	ZERO	LESS THAN 50%	SUBSTANTIAL	MINOR			
HEEL ON LEASH AND FIGURE 8	Unmanageable ...... ☐ Unqualified heeling.. ☐	Handler continually adapts pace to dog.. ☐ Constant tugging on leash or guiding.... ☐	Heeling / Fig 8 ☐ ... Improper heel position .... ☐ ☐ ☐ ... Occasional tight leash .... ☐ ☐ ☐ ... Forging .. ☐ Crowding handler, ☐ ☐ ☐ ... Lagging .. ☐ Sniffing .... ☐ ☐ ☐ ... Extra command to heel .... ☐ ☐ ☐ ... Heeling wide ☐ Turns ☐ Abouts ☐ ☐ ... No change of pace ☐ Fast ☐ Slow ☐ ☐ ... No sits............. Poor sits ☐ ☐ ☐ ... Lack of naturalness smoothness ☐ ☐		**40**		
STAND FOR EXAMINATION	Sits before or during examination .... ☐ Growls or snaps .... ☐	Moves away before or during examination .... ☐ Shows shyness or resentment .... ☐	☐ ... Resistance to handler posing .... ☐ ☐ ... Extra command to stay .... ☐ ☐ ... Moving slightly during exam .... ☐ ☐ ... Moving after examination .... ☐ ☐ ... Sits as handler returns .... ☐ ☐ ... Lack of naturalness smoothness ..... ☐		**30**		
HEEL OFF LEASH	Unmanageable ...... ☐ Unqualified heeling.. ☐	Handler continually adapts pace to dog .... ☐ Leaving handler ..... ☐	☐ ... Improper heel position .... ☐ ☐ ... Forging .... ☐ Crowding handler ☐ ☐ ... Lagging .... ☐ Sniffing .... ☐ ☐ ... Extra command to heel ☐ ... No change of pace ☐ Fast ☐ Slow ☐ ... No sits .... Poor sits ☐ ☐ ... Lack of naturalness smoothness ... ☐		**40**		
RECALL	Didn't come on first command or signal .... ☐	Extra command or signal to stay ..... ☐ Moved from position . ☐ Anticipated recall command .... ☐ Sat out of reach..... ☐ Leaving handler ..... ☐	☐ Stood or lay down Touched handler ☐ ☐ Slow response Sat between feet ☐ ☐ No sit Poor sit ☐ ☐ No finish Poor finish ☐ ☐ Extra command to Lack of naturalness finish or smoothness ☐		**30**		
			MAX. SUB-TOTAL		**140**		
LONG SIT (1 Minute)	Did not remain in place .... ☐ Goes to another dog............. ☐	Stood or lay down before handler returns . ☐ Repeated whines or barks .... ☐	☐ Forcing into position ☐ Minor move before handler returns ☐ Minor whine or bark	Stood or lay down after handler returns to heel position .... ☐	**30**		
LONG DOWN (3 Minutes)	Did not remain in place .... ☐ Goes to another dog............. ☐	Sat or stood before handler returns..... ☐ Repeated whines or barks .... ☐	☐ Forcing into position ☐ Minor move before handler returns ☐ Minor whine or bark	Sat or stood after handler returns to heel position .... ☐	**30**		
			MAX. POINTS ➡		**200**		

☐ H. Disciplining ☐ Shows fear ☐ Fouling ring ☐ Disqualified ☐ Expelled ☐ Excused   Less Penalty for Unusual Behavior ➡

EXPLANATION OF PENALTY   TOTAL NET SCORE ➡

standards apply in Open and Utility trials.) This means that it is possible for you to get a perfect score in all of the exercises but one and be disqualified. For example, you can go into the Long Sit and Long Down with a perfect score; if your dog gets up in the Long Down or lies down in the Long Sit, you do not qualify—even though your total may be 170 points. Examine carefully the kinds of errors associated with non-qualifying performance for all of the exercises, and note how important handling errors are.

While there is a high degree of objectivity in judging obedience performance, judges have varying interpretations of "substantial" and "minor" point deductions; some are more severe than others and will deduct many points for errors that others would penalize only slightly. Judge A might think that your dog returned to you too slowly on the Recall and deduct ten points, while Judge B, in your next show, might take off just one point. You will notice this after you show your dog a few times. Generally, a minor deduction consists of half a point or a whole point; a substantial deduction is anywhere from five to ten points.

During the time you practice immediately prior to entering a show, review the information on the Obedience Judge's Worksheet and study the kinds of infractions you, as handler, might make. You *must* also read the *AKC Obedience Regulations* (see Appendix I and read the "Agreement" Statement in fig. I-109). It will improve your handling by keeping you aware of the types of errors you might possibly make.

Practice for Runoff

In Novice, a runoff is a competitive Heel off Leash for two dogs with identical final scores; each tries to break the tie and take the higher place. A runoff is held only for dogs whose scores put them in contention for the top four places. The dog that performs the exercise most proficiently and wins the higher place has a "+" added to his score.

For example, assume that the top-scoring dogs have earned the following total points:

Dog 51: 198½
Dog 3: 198
Dog 8: 197½
Dog 47: 197½

A runoff must be held to see whether Dog 8 or Dog 47 will take third place. Before announcing the final results, the judge will call the two dogs and their handlers back into the ring and explain that they have identical scores and will have a runoff to break the tie. The handlers will be instructed to put their dogs in the proper heeling position, off lead, somewhere near one end of the ring, side by side. The judge will then give the heeling commands. The first dog to make an error or perform less precisely than the other loses. This could even happen immediately after the affirmative reply to "Are you ready?": if one of the handlers does not sit his dog squarely, the other dog wins.

Obviously you must find a dog-training colleague to do a runoff under show conditions. Since the runoff will be a Heel off Leash, practice in such a way that your dog moves forward smartly when you give the command "Heel!" If, as the Novice judging comes to a close, you suspect that your dog will be in a runoff, try to get him into an alert condition before going into the ring. If he has been lying down relaxing for an hour, do not simply bring him to his feet and heel him into the ring. Talk it up with him, rub his belly, get him a bit excited and alert. You might find that a slightly happier tone of voice will make him move a bit more precisely, or a slightly livelier stride in the heeling might make him look perkier. This might make the difference between first place and second for you.

There is also the distinction Highest Scoring Dog in Trial, which is awarded, simply, to the dog with the highest number of points in the obedience trial (for regular classes only). Since their exercises are somewhat easier, Novice class dogs frequently earn this distinction, which usually brings a handsome trophy and a moderate cash award (anywhere from ten dollars to fifty). If your dog has tied another for first place and loses the runoff, he may thus lose the Highest Scoring Dog in Trial award as well—another reason for taking the runoff seriously.

Finally, if Novice dogs are in competition with Open and Utility dogs for the Highest Scoring Dog award, the runoff will still be Heel off Leash. Unless your advanced competitor has been keeping up with his Novice work, you have the advantage.

What You Should Know About Entering a Show

This course has been geared to prepare you and your dog for competition in AKC-sanctioned obedience trials. By Week 10 you should have come to some kind of conclusion about whether you wish to show your dog in competition and work toward the C.D. degree. Many people who set about to train their dogs in basic obedience have no intention whatsoever of entering a show, but, after going through a training program such as the one described here, become bitten by the urge to try it—just once. Or, they may attend a show and see other dogs, less competent than their own, working in the Novice ring—and winning first place. The most practical thing you can do at this juncture in your training is attend an AKC-sanctioned obedience trial or match and observe the Novice A dogs in action. If there is a kennel club in your area, find out if there are any shows or matches scheduled for the immediate future.

Dogs That Can Be Shown in AKC Obedience Trials   Your dog must be an American Kennel Club registrable breed in order to compete for the C.D. degree at dog shows, since it is the AKC that awards the degree. If you know your dog is a registered dog of a breed recognized by the AKC, you may enter him in a competition that leads to a degree. Check your dog's registration papers and make certain they are in order. Figure I-108 shows an official entry form for a dog show. Slightly below the middle of the form, on the left side, you will find a box requiring one of several possible numbers. Your registration papers will give you either the dog's AKC registration number or his litter registration number. You must put one of these numbers on the entry form when you   105

OFFICIAL AMERICAN KENNEL CLUB ENTRY FORM

S A M P L E

This space would contain the following information:

1. *Name of Club that Sponsors the Show.*
2. *Location of Show.*
3. *Closing date for entries.*
4. *Where to send this application form.*
5. *To whom check should be made out.*
6. *Amount of entry fee.*

I ENCLOSE $ _____ for entry fees.

● **IMPORTANT—Read Carefully Instructions on Reverse Side Before Filling Out**

Breed	Variety See Instruction #1, reverse side (if any)	Sex
German Shepherd		*Male*

DOG Show Class	See Instruction #2, reverse side (Give age, color or weight if class divided)	Obedience Trial Class
		Novice A

If dog is entered for Best of Breed (Variety) Competition—see Instruction #3 reverse side — CHECK THIS BOX ☐	Additional Classes

If entry of dog is to be made in Jr. Showmanship as well as in one of the above competitions, check this box, and fill in data on reverse side. ☐

If for Jr. Showmanship only then check THIS box, and fill in data on reverse side. ☐

Name of Actual Owner(s)	See Instruction #4, reverse side
	Napoleon A. Chagnon

Name of Licensed Handler (if any) [_____ handler] ●

Full Name of Dog *Gustav von Arborstadt*

Insert one of the following: AKC Reg. # *WC 297633* AKC Litter # I.L.P. # Foreign Reg. # & Country	Date of Birth *3/30/72*	Place of Birth ☒ U.S.A. ☐ Canada ☐ Foreign Do not print the above in catalog

Breeder. *Carlene F. Chagnon*

Sire *August of Krisselhof*

Dam *Sudenfeld's Parma*

Owner's Name *Napoleon A. Chagnon* (Please print)

Owner's Address *etc.*

City _____ State _____ Zip Code _____

I CERTIFY that I am the actual owner of this dog, or that I am the duly authorized agent of the actual owner whose name I have entered above. In consideration of the acceptance of this entry, I (we) agree to abide by the rules and regulations of The American Kennel Club in effect at the time of this show or obedience trial, and by any additional rules and regulations appearing in the premium list for this show or obedience trial or both, and further agree to be bound by the "Agreement" printed on the reverse side of this entry form. I (we) certify and represent that the dog entered is not a hazard to persons or other dogs. This entry is submitted for acceptance on the foregoing representation and agreement.

SIGNATURE of owner or his agent ● duly authorized to make this entry _____ *(Very important to sign this)*

I-108. Those of you who co-own a dog must bear in mind that if either of you shows *any* dog in Novice A competition and takes that dog through a C.D. degree, then the other co-owner will be obliged to show any future dog in Novice B (*not* Novice A), whether or not he or she has shown a dog in competition before. Two of our students co-owned their two dogs; the send it to the proper official, usually a show superintendent. Either one is sufficient. Those with foreign-born dogs use the bottom line in the box.

The "I.L.P."—Indefinite Listing Privilege—is for those of you who got an obviously purebred dog at the local S.P.C.A. and have no registration papers for him. You can obtain an Indefinite Listing Privilege for him by writing to the American Kennel Club (51 Madison Avenue, New York, New York 10010) and asking for the appropriate forms and instructions.

If you have some doubt about what your dog's breed is, ask a knowledgeable vet if he can identify him, or consult the authoritative AKC *Complete Dog Book*. It contains photographs of all the registered breeds.

Different Kinds of Dog Shows A *breed* show is one in which dogs are exhibited and judged for their approximation to breed standards—how they "look." This book did not prepare you for that kind of show. An *obedience trial* is a show in which dogs are judged for their ability to do the exercises they are commanded to do. This book does prepare you to enter that kind of show. Most often an obedience trial is held in conjunction with a breed show, but a few obedience trials are held as separate events. A *field trial* is a show for hunting dogs—again, this book does not prepare you for that kind of show. Thus, before you try to enter your dog in a show, make sure it includes an obedience trial. We will explain how to do this later.

There are also *specialty* shows and *all-breed* shows, with or without obedience trials. For example, there might be a German Shepherd Specialty Show *and* Obedience Trial, sponsored by a local German shepherd club. This means that only German shepherds are eligible to enter the show—including its obedience-trial component. Specialty shows can be held for any breed, and may or may not include an obedience trial.

To complicate the situation further, there are *matches* and *shows*. A match is a dog show in which all competition is for the fun of it; the qualifying dogs may win prizes and distinction, but no official credit toward a degree. It is rather like an exhibition baseball game, which does not count on the record for the pennant race. Some matches are "AKC-sponsored"—meaning that the initiators of the match have the approval of the American Kennel Club to hold the show; before a local kennel club can obtain an AKC license to hold a point show, it must go through a period of observation by AKC officials that includes the

husband trained the first one and went through the C.D. degree with it. The wife then trained the second dog and had two legs toward the C.D. degree, she thought, in Novice A competition. She learned from the AKC that neither leg counted, since she was obliged to show in Novice B because she co-owned a dog that held the C.D. degree.

sponsoring of several kinds of matches. These matches are judged by very competent people. Other kinds of matches might be held by just about anybody—fun matches. A group of local enthusiasts might get together and have a fun match to raise money for a worthy cause. In some cases, the judging at these is quite arbitrary and prejudicial; in other cases, it might be quite competent. Do not be upset if you enter a match and receive a lower score than someone whose dog obviously did not do as well as yours, and do not take a high score in a fun match too seriously, either.

If you plan to enter your dog in a show and want to have his performance count officially toward an obedience degree, then enter him in one of the following kinds of shows: (1) all-breed dog show and obedience trial by an AKC-licensed kennel club; (2) obedience trial by an AKC-licensed kennel club; (3) specialty show and obedience trial for your dog's breed by an AKC-licensed kennel club.

We have mentioned that dog shows can be held indoors or outdoors. Some indoor shows are *benched*. This means that your dog will be assigned a cubicle, or bench, somewhere in the show building; you must keep him there except when you are showing him. Benched shows are usually large and attract many spectators, who want to inspect as many particular breeds as they can. Your dog will have a bench number, and people will be able to come and see him. If you have a Doberman pinscher, he will be benched among all the other Dobermans in the show—including those that are being shown in the breed ring; if you have a poodle, you will be benched among all the poodles, and so on.

Since people pay money to see the dogs at a benched show, the dogs should be kept at the show until closing time. If you show your dog in the morning, and the show is officially over at 5:00 P.M., you must spend the rest of the day at your bench with your dog—even though you finished your class at noon. You may not leave the show with your dog without surrendering your entry form, and the officials at the door may report people who leave early to the show officials. They cannot keep you at the show against your will, of course, but if you leave before the official time, you will very likely disappoint some of the paying spectators who cannot see *your* dog. So you should not plan to go to a benched show if you have to leave before closing time, unless you have a friend who can remain with your dog for you.

An *unbenched* show is one in which you may keep your dog at any convenient place, either within the building or in the show area outside. You may leave the show after you have completed your class; if your dog stands a chance of winning the Highest Scoring Dog in Trial award, you should stick around to collect the prize: only in some cases will they mail it to you.

How to Obtain an Entry Form An entry form is referred to as a "premium list" by most people in the dog-show world. Technically, the premium list is a small booklet that describes the content of the show, gives the names of the judges for each class, lists the prizes, and specifies the ground rules. It normally contains two official entry forms. To

AGREEMENT

I (we) acknowledge that the "Rules Applying to Registration and Dog Shows" and, if this entry is for an obedience trial, the "Obedience Regulations," have been made available to me (us), and that I am (we are) familiar with their contents. I (we) agree that the club holding this show or obedience trial has the right to refuse this entry for cause which the club shall deem to be sufficient. In consideration of the acceptance of this entry and of the holding of the show or obedience trial and of the opportunity to have the dog judged and to win prize money, ribbons, or trophies, I (we) agree to hold this club, its members, directors, governors, officers, agents, superintendents or show secretary, and any employees of the aforementioned parties, harmless from any claim for loss or injury which may be alleged to have been caused directly or indirectly to any person or thing by the act of this dog while in or upon the show or obedience trial premises or grounds or near any entrance thereto, and I (we) personally assume all responsibility and liability for any such claim; and I (we) further agree to hold the aforementioned parties harmless from any claim for loss of this dog by disappearance, theft, death or otherwise, and from any claim for damage or injury to the dog, whether such loss, disappearance, theft, damage, or injury, be caused or alleged to be caused by the negligence of the club or any of the parties aforementioned, or by the negligence of any other person, or any other cause or causes.

INSTRUCTIONS

1. (Variety) If you are entering a dog of a breed in which there are varieties for show purposes, please designate the particular variety you are entering, i. e., Cocker Spaniel (solid color black, ASCOB, parti-color), Beagles (not exceeding 13 in.; over 13 in. but not exceeding 15 in.), Dachshunds (longhaired, smooth, wirehaired), Collies (rough, smooth), Bull Terriers (colored, white), Fox Terriers (smooth, wire), Manchester Terriers (standard, toy), Chihuahuas (smooth coat, long coat), English Toy Spaniels (King Charles and Ruby, Blenheim and Prince Charles), Poodles (toy, miniature, standard).

2. (Dog Show Class) Consult the classification in this premium list. If the dog show class in which you are entering your dog is divided, then, in addition to designating the class, specify the particular division of the class in which you are entering your dog, i. e., age division, color division, weight division.

3. The following categories of dogs may be entered and shown in Best of Breed competition: Dogs that are Champions of Record and dogs which, according to their owners' records, have completed the requirements for a championship, but whose championships are unconfirmed. The showing of unconfirmed Champions in Best of Breed competition is limited to a period of 90 days from the date of the show where the dog completed the requirements for a championship.

4. A dog must be entered in the name of the person who actually owned it at the time entries for a show closed. If a registered dog has been acquired by a new owner it must be entered in the name of its new owner in any show for which entries closed after the date of acquirement, regardless of whether the new owner has received the registration certificate indicating that the dog is recorded in his name. State on entry form whether transfer application has been mailed to A.K.C. (For complete rule refer to Chapter 16, Section 3.)

JUNIOR SHOWMANSHIP — If the dog identified on the front of this entry form is entered in Junior Showmanship, please give the following information:

CLASS SEE DESCRIPTION OF JUNIOR SHOWMANSHIP CLASSES IN THIS PREMIUM LIST.

NAME OF JUNIOR HANDLER	DATE OF BIRTH

ADDRESS

CITY	STATE	ZIP CODE

If Junior Handler is not the owner of the dog identified on the face of this form, what is the relationship of the Junior Handler to the owner?

I-109. Reverse side of the entry form. If you make a copy of an entry form, be certain to reproduce both sides, staple them together, and send both to the proper show official.

enter your dog in a show, you simply fill out one entry form, sign it, and mail it to the place designated on the form itself, along with your check for the entry fee, which varies from show to show (between seven and twelve dollars; it goes up every year). Entry forms are dated, and your letter must reach the appropriate address on or before a date specified in the premium list; otherwise your money and form are returned to you. This date is about two weeks before the show.

A sample entry form, taken from a premium list, is given in figure I-108. Note that there is a space provided for "Obedience Trial Class"; you would put "Novice A" in that space, and fill in the appropriate blanks. The back of the form (fig. I-109) describes the nature of the agreement you enter into when you sign your name. This must accompany your application if you photographically reproduce someone else's entry form. It is acceptable to duplicate the front and back of the entry form, staple them together, and send them in that way. Sending a copy of only the front page is unacceptable.

There are several ways to obtain premium lists for dog shows. The most efficient way to go about entering a dog show would be to get a current issue of one of the popular dog magazines that list upcoming AKC shows and indicate which ones include an obedience trial. Three such useful, monthly publications (which can be purchased at many pet stores) are *Dog World* (10060 West Roosevelt Road, Westchester, Ill. 60153), *Off-Lead* (8140 Coronado Lane, Rome, N.Y. 13440), and *Front and Finish* (P.O. Box 333, Galesburg, Ill. 61401).

The American Kennel Club's *AKC Gazette* is an extremely useful publication—available by subscription only—containing complete information about past and future shows.

With a copy of one of these publications, you will be able to find almost all of the upcoming shows and matches in your area. When you have decided that you want to enter a number of specific shows, write to the trial secretary of the club that is sponsoring each, or to the superintendent of the dog show company that is conducting the show for the specific kennel club. There are some dozen companies in the United States licensed by the AKC to provide the tents, equipment, premium lists, et cetera, for most of the dog shows held. A list of these companies and their superintendents is given in Appendix II.

Hence the second way to obtain premium lists: you could write to the show superintendents who conduct shows in your particular area and ask for premium lists for upcoming shows. This is less efficient, since you depend more on blind chance than intelligent planning. A local kennel club might put on its own show right next door, and you might miss it because the company that sent you the premium lists is not handling it. Your best course of action would be to obtain a complete list of upcoming shows and write for premium lists for only those you might wish to enter.

Most shows are held on weekends. With a complete list, you can intelligently plan an enjoyable weekend and enter your dog in two shows that are being held within a few miles of each other. If you have friends who also show their dogs, you can share transportation.

To earn the C.D. degree, you must show your dog in a minimum of three different shows under three different judges. Therefore, if you plan to enter several shows in rapid succession, make certain that you check the premium list carefully to determine whether the Novice A judge is different for each show. If you desperately want to attend a particular show, but the Novice A judge is the same one under whom you have shown before or plan to show under soon, check the judging program for Novice B. You may enter Novice B instead, but be prepared to compete against experienced handlers (AKC judges and owners or handlers of any dogs that have earned the C.D. degree), who *must* show in this class. The competition is of course tougher than in Novice A, even though the exercises and judging procedures are identical. After your dog earns the C.D. degree and you train another dog, *you* must show the second dog in Novice B.

Once you have decided on what show or shows you wish to enter, fill in the entry form and send it in, along with your check for the entry fee. You can expect to receive the entry form back in the mail about five to seven days before the show, along with a brief résumé listing the number of entries in each class, directions on how to get to the show area, and a list of motels that will accept dogs.

Inspecting your returned entry form, you will find that you and your dog have been assigned a number. That number will be on your armband and listed in the catalogue, both of which you obtain at the show. If you examine the show resume, you will get a good idea of the ring your class (Novice A) will show in, and how many dogs are ahead of you and behind you in the sequence. The information might be: "Ring No. 6. 18 Novice A dogs (0035, 0036, 0185 through 0200). 9:00 A.M." If you are number 0185, you are the third contestant.

Be sure to take your entry form with you to the show; you might have to do a great deal of explaining in order to leave the show without it—you could be mistaken for a dog thief hustling someone's pet away.

Qualifications for Companion Dog Degree   As we said before, to earn the C.D. degree, your dog must qualify in three shows under three different judges. You are eligible at this point to compete only in the Novice (A or B) class. A qualifying score, as we have mentioned above, consists of earning a minimum total of 170 points, with more than 50 per cent earned in each of the exercises listed on the Obedience Judge's Worksheet (fig. I-107). If you qualify in your first show, you have earned one leg toward the C.D. degree. Your second qualifying show will be the second leg toward the degree, and so on. To earn the degree, you must have three legs—three qualifying scores in three shows. Our students regularly earn three straight legs in three shows, but occasionally they slip up and have to show an extra time or two. There is no limit to the number of times you may show your dog to earn the C.D. degree, but if you do not finish three legs in five shows, you and your dog had better go back to basic training and brush up on the exercises he fails. The two most common reasons for failing a show are handlers' errors and dogs breaking on the Long Sit or Long Down. 111

We expect that you will do very well in competition but suggest that you enter no more than three shows at first. You might want to enter a fourth show as a backup, in the event that you or your dog botch one of the first three. (Remember that, because of space limitations, some shows restrict the number of entries—for example, if the club that sponsors the show plans to use a relatively small area, it has to limit the number of contestants. If you want to compete in such a show, mail your entry form in as soon as possible. Acceptance is on a first-come first-served basis.) You must stop showing in Novice as soon as you complete three legs toward the C.D. degree, but if your backup show follows your third show by a week or two, go ahead and show your dog in that one as well. It will take at least that long for the AKC to process the records of your first three shows and mail your C.D. degree to you.

While there are no degrees between the C.D. (Novice) and C.D.X. (Open), there is the AKC-recognized class Graduate Novice. It is a combination of Novice and Open exercises, and permits you to give your dog show experience before he is ready for Open competition. The exercises for Graduate Novice are listed in Appendix III. This class is only rarely included in obedience trials, since no degree is associated with it, but it is often included in matches.

How to Go to a Show

Many of our students are anxious about what to expect at a real dog show, and how to go about preparing themselves and their dogs for the big event. We will end this chapter with some helpful suggestions.

• Make sure you arrive at the show on time. If your class starts at 9:00 A.M., be there at that time to check in at the proper ring, pick up your armband, and observe the other contestants. Until recently it was possible to arrive just before your turn. This has been abused by many handlers, so to avoid embarrassing reprimands from the judge—and possible disqualification—arrive early, well before your catalogue number.

• When you arrive at the show, there will be attendants at the parking lot to show you where to park. They will usually be selling catalogues for the show. Purchase one, since it will contain the final program. You will receive, with your returned entry form, a pass into the show area for one person. If you have additional people with you, they will have to pay a small entry fee.

• The night before the show, you might give your dog a dry shampoo or wash him if he is unacceptably grubby. Even though he is not being judged for his beauty, you do not want a disheveled dog. Do not change your dog's diet the night before the show, save for cutting back slightly on the amount of food you give him. A sudden change in diet could bring on a case of diarrhea in the show ring. You should also bring along a container of water and a small bowl for your dog, since a sudden change in drinking water could also produce diarrhea.

At most shows you will find dog-food company displays where you can obtain a free meal for your dog—they often have a tubful of already mixed food available for the contestants' dogs, as well as disposable bowls to hold it. Still, it is a good idea to bring your dog's regular fare along. Don't feed him until after he finishes his performance.

● Pack a lunch for yourself and your human companions. There are usually concession stands where you can purchase food and beverages, but they are often crowded. If it is an outdoor show, you might want to take along some folding chairs. Take a few large towels if the weather is expected to be hot; you can wet them down and place them on your dog to keep him comfortable. Many shows are held in areas where there is no relief from the blistering sun, and an overheated dog does not perform well.

● Necessary and/or useful items to have along include the following:

Your entry form

Your dog's collar and lead—no tags are permitted on the collar

A can of flea and tick spray and a *tube* of insect repellent; if there are biting bugs in the show area, put some of the insect repellent around your dog's eyes and ears so he will not be pestered during the Long Sit and Long Down. The flea spray should repel the beasties that other dogs might have brought into the area.

A roll of paper towels, in case your dog gets carsick en route

A brush or comb for your dog

● When you arrive at the show area, a number of regulations automatically go into effect. Some of the more important ones are:

You must have your dog on lead at all times

You may not train your dog or practice anywhere in the show area

You may not go into an empty ring to walk your dog around it "to see what it is like"

You must not correct your dog harshly. If your dog starts sniffing around, do not make a blatant correction; just get him back to you and under control.

● Take the dog to the designated exercise areas to permit him to relieve himself. Indoor shows invariably provide such areas, one for female dogs and one for male. Find out where these are, and allow your dog a chance to answer nature's calls shortly before it is his turn to enter the ring. Some outdoor shows also provide restricted areas, but most permit you to exercise your dog at any convenient place away from the main run of traffic.

A word of caution if you go to a large show, especially an all-breed: watch where you are walking, or you might have an unpleasant surprise. Not all dogs have been conditioned as well as yours to relieve themselves only after the command "Okay!" has been given, and large shows get pretty messy.

Final Hints on Showing Your Dog This chapter has prepared you and your dog to compete effectively in the Novice class at AKC obedience trials. If you have a normal dog whom you have trained regularly, following the procedures we have outlined, he should have no difficulty   113

I-110. We practice what we preach—and winning is
fun. Here the senior author accepts the prize for
Highest Scoring Dog in Trial. Reefer's score of 199½
in Novice B earned him first place in that class, Highest
Scoring German Shepherd in Trial, and Highest Scoring
Working Dog in Trial. Sherry Kline, one of our students, looks on. Her sheltie tied for Second Highest
Scoring Dog in Trial but lost the runoff and had to
settle for Third Highest Scoring Dog in Trial, first place
in Novice A, and Highest Scoring Shetland Sheepdog.
The junior author's shepherd took first place in Util-
ity A in the same trial, and Second Highest Scoring
German Shepherd in Trial.

qualifying in Novice A competition twelve weeks after your first lesson.
The only thing we cannot provide is exposure to other dogs, an important ingredient in the final weeks of preparation. That *you* must
provide.

You should be aware of your dog's ability and have confidence in him by the time you go into the show ring. But watch out for silly mistakes that you, as handler, might make—mistakes that could lead to disqualification. The simulated show conditions we described in Week 9 and urged you to follow for Week 10 and beyond should have helped prepare you for the ring and fixed the proper pattern into your memory. Still, there are unexpected quirks. A common error that overanxious handlers make is a double command. Try to concentrate on not doing this as you perform the exercises. Watch the contestants who show their dogs before your turn comes up.

Some dogs will lag or wander in the Heel Free exercise or fail to come immediately on the Recall. Do not give another command to the dog in the ring for the Recall if this should happen to you, although a second command in the heeling exercise is permissible (but would lose you points). Some dogs hesitate on the command "Come!" They sit there a moment, and then decide to come after all. If you prematurely repeat the command, you have automatically disqualified. A particularly gracious judge might give you a chance to call the dog again, as when an unusually loud noise has perhaps prevented his hearing you. When in doubt, do not give your dog another command. Let the judge instruct you if your dog seems to have botched something.

But your dog has been well prepared and will do the exercises well. You will be delighted to hear your number called off after the judge has totaled up all the points, for it means that you have qualified. If you take first place, you stand a good chance to win Highest Scoring Dog in Trial, since scores in Novice A tend to be high as compared with scores in the more advanced obedience classes. It is not unusual for the first-place dog in Novice A to have close to 200 points—a perfect score. The qualifying dogs and handlers are all called back into the ring at the end of the Novice judging and are usually awarded an official qualifying ribbon (green). As the ribbon is presented, the judge informs you of your final score.

Dogs who place are usually awarded more substantial prizes and ribbons of various colors representing the place they achieved. (A description of the official ribbons is given in Appendix I, the *AKC Obedience Regulations.*)

Each show has special prizes. Check the list of prizes offered to see if your dog has won any of them. Often they are awarded in the ring when the qualifying ribbons are passed out, but in some cases you must collect them from some official. For example, your dog might be the only Welsh corgi with a qualifying score in Novice A, and there might be a prize for Highest Scoring Welsh Corgi in Novice A.

Unless you have a perfect score, you might want to know what your dog lost points on. The judge must post the scores at the superintendent's desk as soon as the judging is over. Examine the final scores, and work a bit harder on the weak exercises in the practice sessions ahead.

While at your third dog show, look around at the concession stands for a wooden dumbbell that fits your dog. You will need it soon—for Open training.

II
THE
OPEN
EXERCISES

Toward the Master's Degree:
Companion Dog Excellent

OPEN WEEK 1

OUTLINE OF TRAINING SCHEDULE
Old Exercises
    Novice
        Review and practice all daily. After each daily workout, practice those in which dog is weak.
        Heeling: Concentrate on improving your handling techniques and precision at turning and halting.
New Exercises
    Advanced Heeling: Pivots and side steps
    Preparation for Long Sit and Long Down, Out of Sight
    Introduction to Drop on Recall: Perfecting the Novice straight recall
    Introduction to Dumbbell: Taking it, holding it, carrying it, releasing it
Suggested Length of Practice Session: 15 minutes, twice daily

Open obedience exercises are qualitatively more difficult than Novice exercises: a much more precise form of behavior is demanded from the dog, and the exercises are generally more complex. Still, if you have followed the Novice training regime carefully, you are much better prepared for Open training and competition than are people who followed other Novice training programs. This book preadapted you and your dog to the Open exercises from the outset, so that you enter "new turf" with background and experience that is not normally given in Novice courses. Many of your earlier training habits will carry over from Novice. For example, the two-steps-forward after completing an exercise is an invariable component of Open work: it conditions the dog to remain "on command" and therefore reduces the possibility that he will break prematurely from a position you have told him to take.

Some readers will begin their advanced obedience training after having used other training methods for the Novice exercises. We suggest that they read chapter I carefully, since some of the terminology and methods in chapter II carry over. Particularly important to understand is the fact that we do not give double commands, and that if the dog fails to do an exercise promptly on a single command, a correction (described in Week 1 of Novice) is called for. Also, we give affection and genuine praise as the sole reward to the dog for a job well done, not food. Finally, we keep our cool and do not get angry with ourselves or our dogs when we train.

Some of the exercises in this chapter are extremely useful, not to mention fun, for those of you who do not plan to compete in Open. The retrieving work and the jumping work are particularly useful, and the hand signals introduced here will give your pet an air of professionalism and dignity. Thus, while chapter II is oriented toward those who plan to show their dogs in obedience trials, the training and the experience are likewise useful to non-show enthusiasts. Where we assume that the handlers will be using regulation equipment (jumps, dumbbell), you can substitute appropriate around-the-house objects if you do not plan to go on to competition. You can teach a dog to jump over any kind of obstacle and retrieve anything that he can conveniently carry—even the proverbial newspaper and slippers.

At the end of successful competition in Novice, your dog earned the C.D.—the Companion Dog degree. The Open exercises will lead to the C.D.X. degree—Companion Dog Excellent. The exercises in Open are partly an extension of and improvement on exercises you learned in Novice, and partly new ones—particularly jumping and retrieving.

How do you know that your dog is ready for Open exercises? Those who do not care to enter competition—perhaps because they do not have a registered or registrable dog (required for Novice competition as well)—can test themselves as outlined in Week 10 of chapter I. For those who are show minded and have shown their dogs in Novice, the best test is whether your dog has earned the C.D. degree. We must point out that it is not a good idea to try to teach your dog some of the exercises in this chapter until he has earned the C.D. degree. This course depends on a step-by-step preparation for each successive exercise. As with humans, who do not jump from junior high school into college, dogs cannot jump from zero formal training into Open.

All during the training program in Open the dog will be on lead unless otherwise specified; the short rope (see figs. I-58–59) will be attached at all times, even while the dog is on the leather lead.

You will need some additional equipment during Open training. It would be a good idea to think now about purchasing or constructing two items in particular: a set of broad-jump hurdles and a high jump. (Appendix II lists the names and addresses of magazines that frequently advertise ready-made jumps; if you prefer to construct them yourself, see Appendix IV for the design.) Everything else you will need (except for the wooden dumbbell) should be available at any good hardware store.

One of the objectives during the early portion of Open training is to build up the dog's attention span from the relatively short periods of time required in Novice. By the mid-point of Open training, your dog should easily be able to endure the rigors of concentration that are *minimally* expected of accomplished Open competitors—and, by the end of the training, he should be able to concentrate long enough to meet the minimum requirements of Utility competition. Even if you do not go on to Utility (described in chapter III), your dog will be very stable in Open and extremely predictable. Because our Open dogs are of Utility caliber in concentration, our students have qualified in shows in which they might otherwise have disqualified. Chagnon's shepherd, Gus, was once pounced upon by a large, slobbering, hyper-affectionate setter who wanted to make love to him during the long sit, but Gus knew he was 119 not free to move from his position. The setter jumped on him, licked him, and humped all over him. Gus, stoically, if not irately, remained steadfast—much as he would have enjoyed devouring his liver-flecked conspecific—and *held* the sit. The stewards managed to remove the frisky setter. Gus qualified. In another show, Baron, Martin's shepherd, was assailed by a small, paranoiac spaniel who, recognizing in Baron a stalwart protectiveness, broke from his sit position, scurried over to Baron, sniffed him all over, and decided that Baron alone could afford the kind of protection he needed from the menacing beasts (Doberman pinschers) in the breed ring next door. He took up his long sit in a most defensible position: right underneath and between Baron's front legs. Baron did not flinch: a giant alter ego for an anxious but smaller colleague.

Concentration is a major goal. Your dog, now that he is entering graduate school, will be expected to perform more professionally.

Advanced Heeling

As in Novice, heeling is a significant component in the Open exercises leading to the C.D.X. degree. Throughout Open training we will concentrate on improving the dog's precision and skill at heeling. From this point on, your dog will be "distinguished" or "mediocre," depending on his precision. To win and place consistently in Open (and Utility), he must score above 195 points regularly; sloppy heeling can hold you back. It is unwise, therefore, to enter such tough competition until you have rid your dog of any bad heeling habits he has acquired.

All during the Open training you should religiously practice all heeling exercises. This includes varying the pace, making turns, halting, starting, and, in general, mixing up the routines to improve the dog's awareness, precision, and consistency. Do not hesitate to put the dog back on lead and correct smartly if he lags, forges, or drifts, because by this time he should be advanced enough in his skills to always maintain the desired heeling position. Remember, if you correct silently and without emotion, the dog will assume he did it to himself. In particular, you should modify the heeling routine in such a way that your dog will be able to halt from *any* speed. Most judges in Novice competition require that you come to a halt only from the normal heeling speed. In Open, the likelihood is greater that a judge will ask you to bring your dog to a halt while heeling in slow or fast tempo. *Most* judges will not ask contestants in Open competition to come to a halt from any speed other than normal—but some of them will. *All* of them *could*.

We are always ahead of ourselves—our horizon is a jump behind us at times. We are going to show you how to improve your dog's heeling ability in such a way that it will not only exceed the minimum standard of performance for Open, but will also qualify for the next and highest degree, the Utility Dog.

Side Step and Right Pivot   We will start the dog on lead and review the Novice heeling exercises to diagnose and correct any heeling deficiencies. The first complicated improvement—assuming that the dog can qualify in Novice heeling—is the *side-step* exercise, to see if the dog will automatically adjust himself into the correct heeling position (unless told to do something else, such as stay). The several side-step exercises you will teach your dog during this and subsequent weeks are absolutely essential; during Open competition you are not allowed to touch your dog's collar to adjust him into the proper heeling position as you begin each new exercise, so he must learn to assume the proper position himself. One of the Utility exercises (the *directed retrieve*) requires that your dog *pivot* (turn in place to keep at your side). Practicing this in early Open training preadapts your dog to several show circumstances and improves his general skills in heeling.

Heel the dog on lead and come to a complete halt. He should sit automatically. Then take a long, smooth step away and out to the side, and give the command "Heel!" (see figs. II-1–6). If the dog fails to move, correct by pulling him toward you sharply and, when he is close to you, pushing down on his rump to put him into the proper, straight heeling position. He may think you are a little nutty at first—he has never been expected to do this—but the whole point of the exercise is to get him to be aware constantly that he must get into the proper heeling position, whatever slight movement you make. To get him to do this, you should make clear, even exaggerated side steps during the initial weeks of training.

After he thoroughly understands that he must remain constantly in the proper heeling position, you are ready to introduce him to a further refinement: less obvious pivots that create an angle between your initial intended direction of march and his sitting position. He should learn to adjust his sitting position so that his direction of march is always parallel to yours. During the first week, concentrate on the side step and the slight pivot—but only *to the right*.

Preparation for Long Sit and Long Down, Out of Sight

In Novice training, the group exercises included a long sit for one minute and a long down for three minutes, with the handler only a few yards away and *within sight* of the dog. Open exercises for the long sit and long down are somewhat more rigorous: the sit is for three minutes and the down is for five, and in both cases the handlers all *leave the ring for the duration of the exercise* and cannot be seen by their dogs. In the first week of Open training you prepare for this by beginning to increase the duration of the sit and down until your dog can comfortably maintain them for the requisite time—with a *good margin* of safety. You will achieve the goal of a five-minute sit and eight-minute down—while you are out of sight—through a gradual, ever-accelerating training process.

During the first week of Open training, do the long sit and long down within the dog's sight. This will build his confidence and patience in sitting for a longer period of time; work toward about 3½ minutes for the long sit within sight and about 5½ minutes for the long down. *Do not neglect to train your dog on this exercise.* While it may seem 121

II-1–6: Teaching the Side Step to the Right. **II-1.** Begin with the dog in the proper heeling position.

II-2. Take a long step out to the side, away from your dog.

II-3. He might think you are a bit nutty at first, but he is out of position.

II-4. Make a firm correction by pulling the lead across your body to knock the dog off balance toward you.

II-5. When he comes toward you, immediately enforce his sit and pull his rump over toward you.

II-6. As you bring his rump over, make sure he sits parallel to you.

to be boring, it still *counts;* not doing well can disqualify a dog, even after a flawless performance in the individual exercises.

Introduction to Drop on Recall

One of the exercises that is carried over from Novice is the recall: the dog is positioned at the far end of the ring and, on the handler's command "Come!," moves at a brisk pace toward him. However, in the Open exercises, the dog must also be given a command to drop down to a lying position, where he must remain until called again.

This is the *drop on recall* exercise. Most dogs have a tendency to anticipate the drop portion of the recall by trotting slowly, sulking, or creeping until they get the drop command; this makes them look like sloppy workers and also loses points in competition. Therefore, we will not combine the drop portion of the exercise with the recall portion until somewhat later in training, but will instead continue to practice just the straight recall to give the dog more experience at running briskly toward you.

So, during the early training in Open, practice the straight recall daily and do not attempt to combine it with the drop until the dog can do each part unflinchingly—and *separately*. The drop procedure is taught as a completely separate and independent exercise in the second week.

During this week of recall training, gradually increase your distance from the dog to about fifty paces if he is sluggish and slow when he comes to you. The increased distance will encourage him to speed up. If your dog comes to you too quickly, work closer to him; you can then grab his rope lead if he overshoots you and correct him sharply back into a straight sit at your feet.

Introduction to Dumbbell

There are two exercises in Open competition that require the use of a wooden dumbbell: the *retrieve on flat* and the *retrieve over high jump*. For those who do not plan to go into Open competition but do want to train their dogs to retrieve a thrown object, a wooden dumbbell is still a useful and practical piece of equipment to purchase.* It is possible to teach the dog to retrieve any object, but, in our opinion, it is simpler and more practical to teach him to retrieve one that is manufactured and designed with a dog's mouth in mind. And who knows? Perhaps you might decide later to compete.

It is important to obtain a dumbbell that fits your dog. A dumbbell is made of hardwood, often maple, and is ideally of one-piece construction. It is a round bar with a square block of wood on each end (fig. II-7). When the dog picks up the bar, the two blocks of wood should protrude from either side of his mouth but should not stick out too far; nor should they be inside his mouth. Moreover, the dumbbell ends must be small enough so that they do not interfere with the dog's vision. Figure II-8 shows a number of dogs holding dumbbells in their mouths.

---

* See Week 10 of chapter I for addresses of magazines that advertise several brands of dumbbells for Open work. Also, concession stands at many of the larger dog shows sell dumbbells.

II-7. A properly chosen dumbbell should not interfere with the dog's vision. This is a good fit. The dumbbell should be painted a flat white so the dog can clearly see it (as should all jumps). Do not paint the bar of the dumbbell.

II-8. Note the difference in the size of the dogs and the corresponding difference in the size of their dumbbells.

Most dogs will readily fetch and retrieve objects for their masters; it is one of the more common forms of play in which humans and dogs engage. But that does not necessarily mean that your dog will easily and readily take to the dumbbell. Fetching the dumbbell is *not* a game; in fact, it is not recommended that you continue to play fetch games at this juncture unless you play according to the new rules. From this point on, 125 the dog will remain at the handler's side in the proper heeling position when the object is thrown, and he will *not* retrieve it until given a single command to do so. On the retrieve, the dog will run smoothly and directly to the object, pick it up, and carry it straight back to the handler without mouthing it unnecessarily, playing with it, tossing it up in the air, or letting it drop to the ground. The dog will come to his handler, sit squarely in front of him, and hold the object in his mouth, toward the handler, until commanded to release it into his hands. As in the recall, the dog will be in such a position that the handler does not have to bend over too far to comfortably remove the object from his mouth. Fetching, in short, is now a skill with definite and precise rules. Figures II-9 and II-10 show improper and proper positions for the dog after he returns with the dumbbell.

To introduce the dumbbell to your dog, you will familiarize him with it and teach him that he must carry it until commanded to release it. Thus you will teach him to take the dumbbell into his mouth and carry it during the heel-on-lead exercises, involving about a week of practice and exercise.

First, put the dog into the proper heeling position. Then take the lead in your left hand and the dumbbell in your right; apply a slight upward pressure on the lead while holding the bar of the dumbbell against the dog's front teeth. As you present the dumbbell in this fashion (fig. II-11), give the command "Take it!"—but without shouting or putting too much authority into your voice. This is a new exercise for the dog, and he will most likely resist. If he does, pinch the loose skin of his mouth against his teeth with the thumb and forefinger of your left hand to force him to open his mouth (fig. II-12). You can do this off lead (or with the lead lying on the ground) if you are sure your dog will not bolt away from you; otherwise, keep tension on the lead as you force the dog's mouth open with your left hand. When his mouth is open, place the bar of the dumbbell into it and relax the pressure on the lead slightly, giving him verbal, reassuring praise. Then give the command "Hold it!" and place your hands around his mouth in such a way that he cannot spit the dumbbell out (fig. II-13). Pause for several seconds, put your hand on one end of the dumbbell and grasp it, then give the command "Out!" and remove the dumbbell from the dog's mouth. If he releases the dumbbell on "Out!," praise him; if not (he has never heard it before), put your thumb in his mouth and over the top of the dumbbell bar, gently press up on the roof of his mouth with your thumbnail, and repeat the command "Out!" (fig. II-28). Praise him when he releases the dumbbell into your hand.*

Continue to practice this exercise every day the first week until the dog knows that he is supposed to take the dumbbell into his mouth at your "Take it!," continue to hold it at your "Hold it!," and release it *only* on your "Out!" After he has gone through this routine for a day or two from a sitting position, you can heel with him while he carries

* "Out!" is also a basic command and exercise in attack dog training; it means "stop biting."

II-9. An improper return with the dumbbell. The dog is too far away from the handler.

II-10. A proper return with the dumbbell. The handler does not have to lean forward to remove the dumbbell from the dog's mouth.

127

II–11

II–12

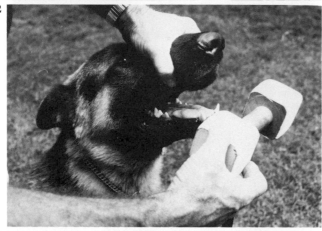

II–13

II-11–13: Teaching the Dog to Take the Dumbbell. **II-11.** Apply upward tension on the lead, place the dumbbell against the dog's teeth, and give the command "Take it!"

II-12. If the dog will not open his mouth to take the dumbbell, press the skin of his mouth against his gums and, when he opens it, place the dumbbell into his mouth. Give him praise for taking it.

II-13. When you have placed the dumbbell into the dog's mouth, put your hands around his mouth and give him the command "Hold it!"

II-14. When your dog has built up confidence at carrying the dumbbell, you can practice other exercises, such as the straight recall shown here, while the dog holds the dumbbell in his mouth. Most dogs can do this by the middle of the second week of taking the dumbbell.

the dumbbell firmly in his mouth. The first time you practice this, go just a few steps and halt. When he comes to an automatic sit, put your hand on the dumbbell, give the command "Out!," and praise him for releasing (and carrying) it. Always try to minimize the number of corrections that you give your dog as he learns something new. Practice heeling with the dumbbell a little each day, but do not make the dog carry it for the entire heeling exercise. If you make him carry the dumbbell too long too soon, he is likely to become bored and drop it after a few seconds. Gradually build up the time that he carries it, and never make him carry it an excessively long time—such as five or ten minutes.

Once he learns to carry the dumbbell reliably, you can build up his concentration and ability by combining it with another familiar exercise. Figure II-14 shows the junior author's Gus carrying the dumbbell while practicing a straight recall. It may take you a while to build up to this, however; many dogs require at least two weeks of training to develop enough confidence and skill to hold the dumbbell for more than a few seconds at a time.

OPEN WEEK 2

OUTLINE OF TRAINING SCHEDULE
Old Exercises
  Novice
    Review and practice all. Perfect those that the dog does not do
      perfectly. Do the figure 8 off lead as described below.
    Handling Technique (Improve precision and commands.)
  Open
    Advanced Heeling: Side step and right pivot
    Long Sit and Long Down: In sight first day (3½-minute sit,
      6½-minute down)
    Dumbbell: Taking, holding, releasing
Modification of Old Exercises
    Advanced Heeling: Pivot to the left, back step, figure 8 on lead
      and off
    Improving Dumbbell Work
New Exercises
    Drop at Random
    Group Examination
    Long Sit and Long Down, Out of Sight (2-minute sit, 4-minute
      down)
Suggested Length of Practice Session: 20 minutes, twice daily (long sit
    and long down begin to add more time)

Advanced Heeling Modified

This week during heeling practice you will concentrate on improving the
dog's awareness of your position; you will do pivots to the left and
back steps, encouraging the dog to correct automatically for the slightest
change in your position. This exercise is also preadaptive to Utility
work, where the dog *must* adjust to very slight pivots.

Pivot to the Left Begin by warming up, with general heel on lead
exercises, varying speeds and turns. At the last stop, pivot to the left
by stepping slightly ahead but out to the side of the dog a good distance
(see figs. II-15–17). Last week you merely side-stepped, and the dog
shuffled over toward you without having to turn his body. This week,
by stepping slightly to the front and turning a little, you have changed
your direction of march about 30°; the dog must not only shuffle over
toward you but also turn his body 30° to become parallel to your new
direction of march. You could just as easily do less exaggerated side-
stepping and turning, but your dog can see you better if you step slightly
out to the front; he has an additional visual cue that you are in a new
position. Gradually you can work the side step down until you merely
130   pivot in place, stepping neither to the side nor out to the front. For the

time being, however, exaggerate your movements so that the dog will be made aware of them.

Back Step Start with the dog in the proper heeling position. Take a long step back with your left foot (fig. II-18) and, as you do, correct the dog so that he backs up (fig. II-19) and comes into the proper heeling position; you must *enforce* the automatic sit by pulling up on the lead with your right hand and pushing down on his rump with your left (figs. II-20–21). Do a series of these each day until the dog needs no encouragement to jump quickly back and get into heeling position as soon as you move. If he fails to do so, continue to correct with a tug on the lead.

A common tendency in the Open heeling exercises—especially those where the dog is corrected *toward* the body of the handler, as in the side-step exercises—is for the dog to begin leaning against the handler's leg or stepping on his foot (or both, as in fig. II-22). This is because the correction unbalances the dog in the direction of the handler's leg. Leaning is a form of interference—the dog *touches* the handler—and should be discouraged. The correction is to bump the dog on the shoulder with your left leg while at the same time pulling the dog toward that leg with your right hand. The handler thus simultaneously pulls the dog *in to* the leg and bumps the dog away from it. Novice training included this correction, so the dog should respond to it. During the initial practice sessions, be sure to give your dog praise—even if he does lean —for moving to get into position as you pivot and change your direction of march.

Note: A dog that self-corrects (wiggles into a better position) *after* coming to a sit loses points; therefore, try to correct him smartly so that he sits properly on his first attempt and does not move until either corrected or commanded.

Figure 8 The pivot and side-step exercises should increase the dog's general awareness and skills in heeling work. After training on these, set up two obstacles and practice the figure 8 routine. In Open competition your dog's general performance in heeling will be expected to be much more precise than in Novice, so demand more exactness and co-ordination from him, especially on the outside turns and the sits; make sure he does not lag or sit crooked. Whenever he does sit poorly during the figure 8 exercise, you should practice the side step and pivot. This will give him an opportunity to practice his new adjusting mechanisms and will reinforce the fact that they can be demanded in any exercise from now on.

During the practice sessions this week, work on the figure 8 exercise both on lead and off, beginning each session with the dog on lead in the event that you have to correct by side-stepping or pivoting. After he seems to be keenly aware that the figure 8 is no longer the same kind of simple old thing, take him off lead but leave the short cord on his collar—and work a few circuits around your obstacles, paying careful attention to the dog's sits and his rate of speed as he rounds the

II-15–17: Pivot to the Left. **II-15.** Take a small step slightly forward and turn to the left about 30°.

II-16. Correct the dog over to you with the lead and be prepared to enforce his sit.

II-17. Make the dog sit perfectly parallel to your new direction of march. Begin to speed up your left pivots after the dog catches on.

turns. To avoid unnecessary duplication of practice and training, you can work this routine into your daily Novice review; this way the dog will gradually make the transition to show form (in Open competition, all the heeling exercises are off lead) and not be bored by exercises of which he already has command.

Improving Dumbbell Work

More is to be expected of both handler and dog during the second week of dumbbell work. First, all *repetitive* and *double* commands—"Take it!," "Hold it!," "Out!"—will be eliminated step by step; the hold-it command will be dropped altogether by the end of the week.

On the command "Take it!," the dog is to reach immediately for the dumbbell without hesitating even for a split second.

On the hold-it command, the dog is being "told" not to release the dumbbell, play with it, or drop it—until given another command.

On the command "Out!," the dog is to open his mouth fully so that the dumbbell can be gently lifted out; the handler must not have to pry his mouth open.

To encourage the dog to behave in this way on single commands you will probably have to correct him with the collar and lead. Examine figures II-23 through II-27 before training. At the beginning of Week 2 in Open, start the dumbbell practice by putting the dog in the proper

heeling position, with the lead in your left hand and the dumbbell in your right. Step off at an angle from the dog as you simultaneously apply slight pressure with the lead, give the verbal take-it command, and present the dumbbell to the dog (fig. II-23). This time, do not touch the dog's teeth with the dumbbell; hold it a few inches away from his face so he has to reach for it to take it. Keep the upward pressure on the lead as long as necessary to get the dog to part his teeth; then immediately release the pressure as you slip the dumbbell into his mouth. Heel away at a normal pace *without* giving the verbal hold-it command, and go through all the heeling speeds. If the dog drops the dumbbell, quickly come to a halt, pick it up, apply upward pressure on the lead, and insert the dumbbell without giving a second "Take it!" When he takes it, reinforce the fact that he has made an error by giving him a tap with the tips of your fingers under his chin (fig. II-27), and heel away again. If he drops it a second time, apply *firmer* upward pressure, put the dumbbell back into his mouth, and tap him a bit harder under the chin, but give no verbal command.

After you have gone through all the various speeds of heeling on lead, all the turns, and a few halts, come to a final halt. Place the lead in your left hand, put your right hand around the end of the dumbbell nearest you, and give the command "Out!" You will be surprised how well the dog will follow this command. Most dogs look forward to get- 133

II-18–21: Back Step. **II-18.** Begin from the proper heeling position and take a long step back on your left foot.

II-19. Correct the dog back to you with the lead—quickly.

II-20. When he is again turned around to the front, enforce a straight sit by getting his rump around to the proper position.

II-21. Make him sit fully upright and parallel to your line of march.

II-22. The advanced heeling exercises— pivots to the right and left—might cause your dog to begin leaning on your leg. If he does, simultaneously pull the dog toward you and bump his shoulder with the outside of your leg, as you did in

Novice training.

II-23–27: Correction Sequence If Dog Refuses to Take Dumbbell Instantly. **II-23.** Start from the proper heeling position and step out to the side of the dog before presenting the dumbbell. As you do, apply slight upward tension to the lead and give the command "Take it!" Keep the dumbbell out in front of his mouth so he has to reach for it.

II-24. If he refuses to take the dumbbell immediately, apply a firm correction toward the left to knock him off balance, but toward the dumbbell.

II-25. Hold the dumbbell out in front of him and back away, applying quick corrections to keep him moving toward it.

II-26. When he reaches out for it, let him take it, and give him a great deal of praise.

II-27. If he drops the dumbbell or spits it out, place it back in his mouth without giving a verbal command, and tap him under the chin wih your fingertips to remind him that he has made an error.

II–26

II–27

ting rid of the dumbbell—so much so that you have to work hard to keep them carrying it. A few dogs, however, will clamp down hard on the bar and refuse to release it on command. To effect an *immediate* release, place your thumb against the roof of the dog's mouth (fig. II-28) and give the command "Out!" again, applying pressure with your thumb until the dog releases the dumbbell. Then praise him.

At the end of the second week the dog is tested to see if he is capable of hanging on to the dumbbell for a full minute while you are at a distance from him. Thus, *for practice purposes only,* combine the Novice long-sit exercise with holding the dumbbell. Put the dog into the proper heeling position, give him the command "Take it!," and place the dumbbell in his mouth. When he has it, give him the command "Stay!," walk away, and go out about thirty or forty feet before turning to face him. Remain there a full minute before returning and finishing. After finishing, take two steps forward, give him the command "Out!," and take the dumbbell from him. Praise him. If he does this exercise without dropping the dumbbell, he is ready for more advanced work with it; if not, continue to work on the dumbbell exercises until he can do the one-minute sit while holding the dumbbell firmly in his mouth—without playing with it.*

Drop at Random

Because of your dog's Novice training, he is already able to go down on a verbal command: you have been using the command for the long down. Now we will see if the dog can associate the *exercise* down with the *word* "down" in other contexts. The test is simple to perform. Give him the release command "Okay!," either on or off lead, and let him wander a bit until his attention is not on you. When he least expects it, give him a sharp "Down!" Be prepared to enforce it by running in and "downing" him with his collar and your knee. Most dogs, however, will remember their Novice training and immediately go down. If your dog does, walk over to him and finish as in the Novice exercises: take two steps forward, *then* praise him. During this week, do not call the dog to you while he is in the down position.

This is the *drop at random.* It is geared to program your dog to go down on verbal command no matter what he is doing. He cannot anticipate the command, because he cannot associate it with any particular exercise. An important point: do not practice the random-down exercise too much. The dog could become very bored with it or begin to think he is being punished for something because you are constantly shouting "Down!" at him. Practice it sparingly, and always give very generous praise *after* the two steps forward to finish the exercise.

In competition, a dog must drop as soon as he is given the command to go down, whether the command is verbal ("Down!") or a hand signal (see later exercises). The dog must not creep forward and slink into the down position; rather, he must come to a rapid halt and drop. In recent shows the judging has become more and more critical on this

---

* A dog trained as we have described will probably not play with the dumbbell. However, if your dog does, correct him as you would for dropping it.

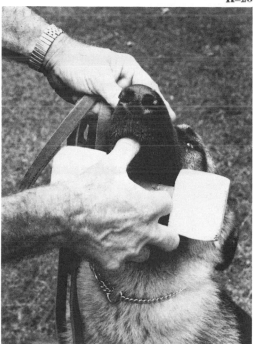

II-28. If the dog clamps down on the dumbbell and will not release it on command, press the back of your thumb against the roof of his mouth to encourage him to open up, giving the command "Out!" as you do. Then praise him.

exercise. Formerly, a judge would designate the spot on the floor where he wanted the dog to drop. Some dogs took so much time to go into their final down position that handlers were anticipating this and giving the down signal as soon as the dogs began the recall. Lately, however, such performance is being penalized heavily by some judges; the time and distance that the dog travels after he gets the signal to drop are being observed more and more carefully, as is the amount of creeping the dog does to reach the down position. The random-drop exercises condition the dog to drop immediately and without anticipating the signal.

Group Examination (Utility Stand)

The *group examination* is a Utility exercise, but we introduce it in Open training for one very simple reason. At the end of Novice, the dog still has the stand-for-examination exercise fresh in his mind, and it is very simple to carry this training over and expand on it in Open. Besides, you and your dog could be working in Utility within twelve weeks or so, and it is advantageous to enter the Utility training with some of the essential exercises learned and perfected.

The group examination, or stand exercise, is the only group exercise in Utility competition. The dogs are all brought back into the ring after their individual performances and put into the stand position, as in Novice, but they are all standing in the ring side by side. The handlers leave their dogs and go to the opposite side of the ring, and the judge examines each dog in turn. The examination may be more rigorous than it was in Novice, and the time that the dog is obliged to stand motionless is much longer—minimally, three minutes—but since the judge can conduct the examination very slowly, the stand might last up to five or six minutes, particularly if there are a large number of dogs to be examined (the AKC-defined maximum in a single group examination is fifteen dogs). The dog must gradually build up his patience and stamina so that he can stand motionless for upward of five minutes. He may turn his head and wag his tail, but he must not move his feet, sit, or lie down. He may not show any resentment when the judge approaches and examines him, but he may lick the judge and wag his tail. (A judge prefers that kind of dog to one that looks and acts a bit anxious.)

We teach our dogs to stand on hand signal, even though the AKC regulations for Utility group examination (stand) are such that you can, in fact, pose your dog into the stand position. In translation, this means that you may touch and adjust your dog to make his stand more comfortable. The reason we emphasize the hand signals is that another Utility exercise, the *hand signals,* requires that you put your dog into a stand position without touching him. Thus, by teaching the dog to stand on hand signal from the very beginning, we are in effect teaching several different and complex exercises at the same time. Figure II-29 shows a practice group-examination exercise.

Practice the stand for examination by doing it in two ways. First, initiate the stand from the normal heeling position with the dog sitting at your side. You can do this by giving the command "Heel!" and taking one step forward, simultaneously giving the hand signal for stand. The dog rises from the sitting position and goes immediately into a stand without taking more than a half step. Second, practice the stand while heeling at a normal speed as you come out of an about turn. As soon as the dog's new line of march becomes parallel with yours, stand him on hand signal. After he does that proficiently, vary the exercise by giving him the hand signal for stand out of the right turn, and by changing your pace from normal to slow or fast. This conditions him to be ready for your hand signal at any time and increases his general awareness. It also teaches him one of the more advanced lessons of Utility competition.

Long Sit and Long Down, Out of Sight

Your practice session the first day of this week is a continuation of the training described in Week 1: your objective is to increase the length of time that your dog will remain in the sit and down positions to about 4½ minutes for the long sit and 6½ minutes for the long down.

Your second practice session this week entails a major modification of these two exercises. Select a practice area in which you will be able to conceal yourself from the dog but still see him—an area with a hedgerow, large bush, or fence with slats would work very well. You must also be able to return to your dog quickly if he breaks from his position.

Put your dog into the sit position, with the lead attached to his

II-29. A group-exam-
ination practice. This
is a Utility exercise,
but we do it in Open
training while the
Novice stand for ex-
amination is still fresh
in the dog's experi-
ence. Thus, when the
dog enters Utility
after finishing Open,
he has mastered one
of the exercises.

collar. Give the verbal stay command and leave the dog. This time, hide behind your chosen obstacle while you wait out the long sit. Try to have the dog do the sit for two minutes and the long down for four the first time you do it out of sight. Be prepared to correct your dog for lying down on the sit or getting up from the down by returning quickly to him, taking his lead, and correcting as described in chapter I. Be sure to remain silent—do not give another command—and bop your dog on the nose as you leave him to complete the exercise (this rein-forces the "Stay!"). Go back out of sight.

After the first day, try to begin building up the length of time that you remain out of sight, but do it gradually. By the end of the week you should be able to do more than the AKC minimum of three minutes for the long sit and five minutes for the long down. Thereafter, vary the time at each practice session so your dog does not become fidgety when he thinks three or five minutes should be up.

OPEN WEEK 3

OUTLINE OF TRAINING SCHEDULE
Old Exercises (Practice these, in order given, before working on Modi-
    fications and New Exercise.)
    Novice
        Heel (off lead, with the short knotted cord)
        Figure 8 (off lead, with the short knotted cord)
        Straight Recall
    Open
        Advanced Heeling: Pivots to left and right; back steps   141

Dumbbell: Taking, holding, releasing; practice recall with dog holding and carrying dumbbell

Drop at Random (only as modified after first day)

Group Examination

Long Sit and Long Down, Out of Sight (vary between 3 and 4 minutes for sit, between 4 and 6 minutes for down)

Modification of Old Exercises

Drop at Random: Calling dog to you after he is down; finishing as in recall

Dumbbell: Getting dog to take it from any position

New Exercise

Introduction to the Broad Jump

Suggested Length of Practice Sessions: 20 minutes, twice daily

Drop at Random Modified

This week, modify the random drop by *calling the dog to you after he drops* instead of going to him. Work off lead, and finish as you did after a recall in Novice. This takes you one step closer to putting the drop and the recall together in the actual show sequence: the dog is coming to you from a down position for the first time. Be prepared to enforce the recall portion by correcting him into a straight sit, using the knotted rope lead he wears.

Further Improving Dumbbell Work

Concentrate during Week 3 on getting the dog to take the dumbbell eagerly and rapidly out of your hand, regardless of his position.

Begin from the normal heeling position, the lead in your left hand and the dumbbell in your right. Your left hand should be near the swivel snap, since you must be in a position to apply rapid tugs on the lead during this exercise. The remainder of the lead can be doubled in your hand. You should be standing slightly to the side of the dog (fig. II-30), with the choke chain adjusted high on his neck. This enables you to knock the dog off balance as the dumbbell exercise is performed.

To begin this exercise, simultaneously give the command "Take it!," step back with your right foot in a clockwise arc (see figs. II-30–33), and correct the dog toward you and the dumbbell, which should be about a foot away from his mouth. Continue to move in a clockwise arc so that your corrections will knock the dog off balance; simply backing away in a straight line would force you to make ineffective straight-line corrections. The object of this exercise is to make the dog work enthusiastically and rapidly to get the dumbbell, so make it a bit difficult for him. If he tries to take it right away, hold it back a bit farther so that he must reach out to get it. Once you are sure he is trying to get it, allow him to grab it and give him a good deal of verbal praise. Keep him in motion in the arc, however, so that he has every opportunity to spit the dumbbell out: only then can you be sure whether

II-30–33: Improving the Dumbbell. Start from the normal heeling position and step off to the side of the dog to present the dumbbell. Hold it about a foot from his mouth, give him the command "Take it!," and begin moving in a clockwise arc. You want him to ultimately take the dumbbell very rapidly. Keep far enough away from him that he has to reach for it; if he does not reach, give a quick correction toward the dumbbell, repeating the correction until he reaches out and grabs it.

143

or not he knows that he should carry it until commanded to give it up. If he spits the dumbbell out, correct as in Week 2 (and see figs. II-23–27); make him aware that he has made a serious blunder.

After a couple of days, the dog should be reaching for the dumbbell whenever he is in motion and it is out in front of him, as in figure II-34.

The remainder of the week should be devoted to getting the dog accustomed to taking the dumbbell from the floor. To achieve this, gradually lower the dumbbell each day as you move backward in a clockwise arc. By about the fifth day, let the dumbbell actually touch the floor—but keep moving it along with your right hand. Remember, the dog should be reaching for the dumbbell; if he hesitates, apply the short tug on the lead and, when he takes it, keep him moving while you praise him. Always give the command "Out!" when you remove the dumbbell from his mouth and praise him when he releases it.

Make no mistake about the necessity for correcting *often* and with sufficient force to make the dog understand what the dumbbell exercise is about. Most dogs (despite our notions of fetch games) balk at taking objects into their mouths *on command* and tend to spit them out whenever it is convenient. The only way to ensure consistent dumbbell work is to correct rapidly when the dog (1) hesitates to take the dumbbell, (2) drops it, or (3) fails to release it on "Out!" By the end of the week you will just about have terminated the work on the dumbbell in motion. During the next few weeks, the dog must learn to pick up a stationary dumbbell.

Introduction to the Broad Jump

In the *broad jump,* the dog is required to jump over a series of low obstacles, boards (see figs. II-35–40).* Generally he must jump twice the distance he clears in the *high jump,* which is 1½ times his height at the withers. (You will learn how to measure your dog in Week 4; for the time being, it is not necessary.) The exceptions to this are listed in Appendix I.

In Open competition, the broad jump is the last individual exercise, immediately following the retrieve over high jump. You heel your dog (without touching him) over to the area of the broad jump and stand about ten feet (but no less than 8) from the jump—with the dog at its center line (fig. II-35). A common tendency—and error—is for the handler to assume that *he* or *she* is the center of attention and should therefore line up on the center line. If the dog is too far to the left of the center line, he will most likely jump diagonally. The judge, after confirming that you and the dog are ready, will give you the command "Leave your dog!" You give the stay commands (fig. II-35) and walk over to the side of the broad jump, positioning yourself somewhere between the first and last hurdles with your toes about twenty-four inches from the edge of the jump (fig. II-36). The judge gives the command "Send your dog!," at which time you give a single vocal command: "Over!" The dog must clear the jump without touching any of the boards (figs. II-37–38). Pivot 90° to the right as the dog is in mid-air,

* Plans for building a set of jumps for this exercise appear in Appendix IV.

II-34. After a few days of work this week, your dog should be enthusiastically reaching out for the dumbbell while it is in motion.

and remain motionless while he lands, turns, and comes to you—as in the recall—without any further commands. He must come directly to you and sit squarely in front of you (fig. II-39). Then the judge will say "Finish!," at which you give the command "Heel!"; the dog finishes in the normal manner, coming to a straight sit at your left side without touching the jumps (fig. II-40).

This is a complicated exercise, with many separate parts. We find that modular training—that is, teaching one segment at a time, then putting the segments together in a single, smooth operation—is most effective.

First, the dog does the sit-stay exercise from Novice. Second, you leave him and assume a position *offset* from his direction of movement; he has never seen you in this peculiar position before. Third, he must jump an obstacle on a single command and then do another exercise *without* a command—that is, make a sharp turn and come in to you as in the Novice recall. Finally, he must execute a finish with an obstacle very close to him—and not touch it. Read the captions for the broad-jump photograph sequence carefully and with an eye toward conceiving of the broad jump as a set of separate exercises.

The major trick will be to get your dog to do the jump part of the exercise on a single "Over!" and clear the jump *down the center line* without touching any of the boards. It sounds simple, but it is quite complex. However, if your Novice training was up to snuff, you and your dog already know two-thirds of the exercise.

We have found that a good many dogs develop a dislike for this exercise, partly because some of it is redundant (the sit-stay and the finish) and partly because the offset position and the turn on a dime are difficult for the dog to master and require corrections from the handler to be achieved perfectly. Besides, the jump demands considerable effort in a short burst. What seems to happen to the dog is that he masters the new parts of the exercise at just about the time he has become bored with the exercise as a whole. And it is just at this point that the handler often makes a serious error in judgment by ceasing to practice the rou- 145

II–35

II–36

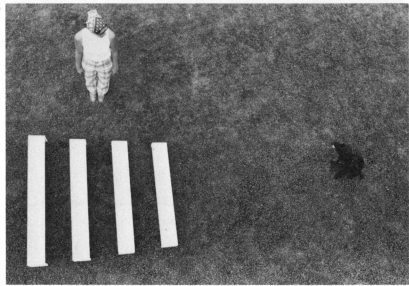

II–37

146

II-35–40: Broad Jump in Show Sequence. **II-35.** Center your dog down the middle of the jump, about ten feet from the first board. The judge will ask you if you are ready. If you are, he will instruct you to "leave your dog." Give the verbal and hand stay commands.

II-36. Walk over to the side of the jump and position yourself somewhere between the last and first boards, with your toes about two feet from the edge of the jump. The judge will then tell you to "send him," and you give the command "Over!"

II-37. The dog should jump right down the center line as soon as he hears your "Over!" He must not touch the boards.

II-38. While the dog is in flight, pivot in place to the right.

II-39. As soon as the dog lands, he turns and goes to you—without a command. Wait for the judge to say "Finish!"

II-40. You give the command "Heel!" and the dog finishes without touching the boards of the jump.

147

tine *in its entirety* because the dog seemingly understands the work and does it easily. The broad jump is complicated; a dog who shows early success is likely to begin forgetting parts of the routine and make errors unless he is obliged to practice the entire exercise daily. Do not confuse early success with mastery: a dog's command of the exercise is bound to be shallow for the first five or six weeks of training, and we urge you to follow carefully the training and practice schedule we describe, regardless of your dog's seeming control of the basic skills.

The First Day of the Broad Jump   The dog will be on lead for the first portion of the broad-jump training. You will need two of the hurdles, or boards, and the black-and-white-striped bar that you will be using in Utility; * all of these are described in Appendix IV. The dog will incidentally become used to jumping a suspended striped bar, something he will have to do in Utility training.

Mount the bar on the second hurdle by placing it on two pieces of scrap lumber that have been tacked to the sides of the hurdle (fig. II-41). Set the bar into the grooves of the upright pieces in such a way that it will easily fall if the dog touches it as he clears the obstacle.

The object of using the bar is to get the dog to jump in such a way that he gains height at the right phase of his jump; if the bar is put on a hurdle near the far end of the jump, the dog will probably reach the full height of his jump too late and will tend to clip the first board in order to maximize his height. If the bar is put on the first obstacle, the dog takes off, gains height too soon, and tends to clip the last hurdle as he comes down. Our experience has been that if the bar is put on the second obstacle, the dog achieves the proper jumping style and timing early in training: an efficient balance between his jump distance and maximum height as he goes over the boards. A good jumper will expend no more effort than is required to clear the jump at both ends, and will not gain too much elevation as he goes over.

Table 1 gives the relationship between the dog's jumping requirements in competition and the specific number of hurdles to be used, as well as the distance that the hurdles must be from each other. Each hurdle is numbered; the lowest is number 1 and the highest is number 4; in AKC competition, if your dog is expected to jump only three of the hurdles, you remove the highest one—number 4. For example, if your dog jumps twenty inches in the high jump, he must jump twice that, forty inches, in the broad jump. The table indicates that a forty-inch broad jump requires the use of three of the four hurdles; you remove the fourth hurdle and adjust the three remaining ones so that the front edge of Hurdle 1 and the back edge of Hurdle 3 are exactly forty inches apart. Hurdle 2 is adjusted in such a way that it is equidistant from the first and third. If you have a small dog—one that is required to jump between sixteen and twenty-eight inches—you need not use the bar as a guide to encourage the proper height; the dog should be able to clear the two boards without it.

* For those of you who do not intend to go on to Utility training, the handle of an old garden tool or broom, painted white, will work just as well.

TABLE 1

Determining the Number of Boards and the Distance Your Dog Must Jump in the Broad Jump

First, determine the height of your dog at the withers by measuring him in inches. Your dog must clear twice the distance in the broad jump that he jumps in the high jump, so you must first figure how high he must jump for the high jump—for most breeds, that will be 1½ times his height at the withers. (Appendix I, Chapter 4, Section 10 lists the dogs exempted from this rule.) The rules for calculating a dog's requirements are somewhat ambiguous. Most judges will avoid these ambiguities by giving your dog the benefit of a lower measurement. The following is a general guideline used by some AKC judges.

Height in Inches at the Withers	6	7	8	9	10	11	12	13	14	15	16	17	18	19	20	21	22	23	24
Distance Dog Must Jump	16	20	24	26	28	32	36	38	40	44	48	52	54	56	60	62	66	68	72
Number of Hurdles Dog Must Clear	2	2	2	2	2	3	3	3	3	3	3	4	4	4	4	4	4	4	4

Note. No dog is required to jump more than 72 inches.

149

Unless your dog is extremely small (a dachshund, for instance), set up hurdles 1 and 2 with about six inches of space between them (fig. II-42). Note that the bar is placed on hurdle 2.

Start with the dog in the heeling position with his axis centered with the center line of the jump (fig. II-42). Give the command "Heel!" and begin trotting toward the jump, slightly ahead of the dog and keeping a loose lead (fig. II-43). As you jump over the obstacle, the dog will be approaching a position to jump it; give the command "Over!" as he reaches the hurdle. Give an encouraging tug on your lead to pull him up and forward. When he lands, give him a great deal of praise for clearing the jump. Take him around to the starting position, come to a halt, and repeat the exercise. Always make certain that the *dog*, not you the handler, is centered. Make sure to praise the dog as soon as he lands; this reinforces the idea that the praise is for jumping the obstacle.

This is the routine that you will follow all during Week 3 of the Open exercises. You might have to go back to jumping *with* the dog in future weeks if he begins to *walk* over the hurdles. If this becomes necessary, make your encouraging corrections to "over" a bit more persuasive.

OPEN WEEK 4

OUTLINE OF TRAINING SCHEDULE
Old Exercises (Practice these, in order given, before working on Modifications and New Exercises.)
> Novice
>> Heel Free (on short knotted cord, carrying dumbbell)
>> Straight Recall (at great distances—over 50 feet)
> Open
>> Advanced Heeling: Pivots to right and left; back steps (short knotted cord only)
>> Drop at Random: Calling dog to you after he is down (as in Week 3)
>> Long Stand, or Utility Group Examination (3 minutes)
>> Long Sit and Long Down, Out of Sight (vary between 3 and 5 minutes for sit, between 5 and 7 for down). *Note.* Practice this after all individual exercises are over, including Modification and New Exercises.

Modification of Old Exercise
> Broad Jump: Adding a third obstacle and straddling the jump

New Exercises
> Introduction to Retrieve on Flat: Taking a stationary dumbbell
> Introduction to Retrieve over High Jump

Suggested Length of Practice Session: 20 minutes, once daily

Note. Because the more advanced practice sessions tend to take longer and dogs need less reinforcement at this stage, we restrict them to only one session a day. We have noticed that the dogs give a higher level of performance, are more enthusiastic, and learn more readily.

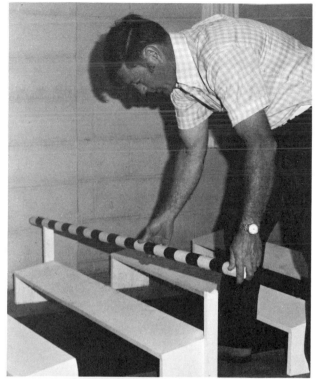

II-41. To help the dog develop the proper timing in his jumps, place a bar on the number-2 board. You can use the striped bar from the Utility bar jump or a garden-tool handle.

II-42–43: Day 1 of the Broad Jump. **II-42.** Start with the dog in the proper heeling position, on lead. Give the command "Heel!" and trot to the jump with the dog, clearing the two boards with him. As you begin the jump, give the command "Over!"

II-43. When you clear the jump, give the dog praise and return to the original position to repeat the exercise. As he is about to jump give an encouraging tug on your lead as you say "Over!"

Drop at Random

The practice for the random drop during the fourth week is identical to that of the previous week: the dog is given a "Down!" when he is not expecting it, and then recalled to the handler. Make sure not to over-exercise the dog on this, and be prepared to give a sharp and immediate correction if the dog does not go down immediately after hearing "Down!" Keep the knotted cord on his collar when you practice the random drop, and do not use your dog's name as part of the "Down!" command.

Introduction to Retrieve on Flat—Taking a Stationary Dumbbell

The practice work on the dumbbell is leading toward the AKC exercises *retrieve on flat and retrieve over high jump*—though of course it will also teach your dog to retrieve in general.

The retrieve on flat is executed as follows: You and your dog are at one end of the ring, somewhere near the center and facing the opposite end. The dog is sitting at your side in the normal heeling position, *off* lead (fig. II-44). You have the dumbbell in your right hand. The judge, after asking you if you are ready, gives you the command "Throw it!" Transfer the dumbbell to your left hand, give your dog the vocal and hand-signal stay commands, transfer the dumbbell back to your right hand, and throw it to the opposite end of the ring (fig. II-44–49). When the judge says "Send him!," you give your dog the command "Take it!" (fig. II-50). Your dog should bolt out smartly, run straight to the dumbbell, pick it up, and carry it directly and quickly back to you—without playing with it—coming to a halt and sitting directly in front of you (figs. II-50–54). At the judge's command "Take it!," reach out, put your hands on the ends of the dumbbell, and give the command "Out!" (fig. II-55). The dog should release the dumbbell into your hands and remain sitting until you are told by the judge to "finish," at which time you give the command "Heel!" The dog finishes as in the recall.

During this week your dog is going to take the dumbbell off the floor or ground at a short distance—about six feet. You will still be working on lead.

Begin with the dog in the proper heeling position. Allow the end of the lead to lie on the floor or double it up in your left hand. Take the swivel end in your left hand, near the dog's collar, making sure the choke-chain collar is adjusted up near the dog's head. Give no command, but simply step off in front of the dog and hold the dumbbell close to the floor in front of him and out as far as you can reach. He should not move from the sitting position—your hand on his lead near the collar should be sufficient to restrain him—until you give the command "Take it!" (fig. II-56). As you do, give a sharp snap on the lead to knock him off balance and start him in motion toward the dumbbell. Back up swiftly as he moves toward it, keeping the dumbbell in motion and out in front, moving swiftly in a clockwise arc (fig. II-57), and giving sharp tugs on the lead. When he makes a conspicuous effort to reach out and try to get the dumbbell (fig. II-58), allow him to take it into his mouth. This time, instead of keeping him moving and giving him praise while he carries the dumbbell, turn quickly toward the dog and come to a halt, facing him. Enforce the sit. The dog should now be sitting in front of you with the dumbbell in his mouth. Pause a moment to make sure he will hold on to it; then put your hands on the ends of the dumbbell and remove it from his mouth as you give the command "Out!" Pause a moment to see if he remains sitting, and then give the command "Heel!" When he finishes, give him praise.

When you are sure the dog understands that he is to move *swiftly* toward the dumbbell and *reach out* to take it on command, you can allow one end of the dumbbell to actually touch the floor—while keeping your fingers under the other end. The dumbbell should be kept moving. Your fingers under the dumbbell will encourage the dog to take it, but having one end of the dumbbell trail on the floor or ground will seem strange to him.

This is a critical step in the dumbbell work. Only after he confidently and enthusiastically takes the dumbbell while one end of it is on the training surface should you move on to the next step: allow the dumbbell to rest stationary on the floor or ground. Keep your hand near it to reassure the dog that this is still the same exercise—or one like it. But instead of moving the dumbbell this time, simply allow it to remain on the ground and give the command "Take it!," simultaneously snapping the dog's lead to get him in motion toward it (fig. II-59). He should take the dumbbell at this point. If he does, take his mind off it immediately by backing away in a different direction, bringing him in to you to make him sit facing you. Remove the dumbbell from his mouth as you simultaneously give the command "Out!," then go into the finish. Praise him after the finish.

If the dog does not take the stationary dumbbell, reach out and put your hand on the end of it and move it slightly away from him, simultaneously correcting him with short snaps on the lead until he is convinced that it is best to take the dumbbell. Work on this until he will take it while it is motionless.

Now we can move on to the next step. Begin with the dog in the heeling position, holding the lead in your left hand and the dumbbell in your right. Throw the dumbbell out in front of the dog about three or four feet. The instant that it hits the floor, give the command "Take it!" and set him in motion with a series of short, firm corrections that direct him to the dumbbell. If he takes it, turn swiftly to face him and back up, bringing him in to you. Stop and enforce his sit: he will be facing you with the dumbbell in his mouth. Remove it as you give the command "Out!," and make him finish before praising him. If he does not take it, put your hand on the dumbbell and set it in motion, correcting him with short snaps on the lead until he does pick it up. Then proceed into the finish as just described. If the dog takes the thrown dumbbell on your first command, you are on the road to the complete retrieve on flat exercise (figs. II-44–55). Concentrate the remainder of the week on 153

II-44–55: Retrieve on Flat. The exercise begins with the dog in the proper heeling position, off lead. The judge will ask you if you are ready (fig. II-44) and, if you reply affirmatively, will say "Throw it!" When he says this, transfer the dumbbell to your left hand (fig. II-45) and give your dog the verbal and hand-signal stay command (fig. II-46). Then transfer the dumbbell back to your right hand (fig. II-47) and throw it out toward the far end of the show ring (fig. II-48). Wait until the judge gives you the next command: "Send your dog!"

(fig. II-49). As soon as the judge gives you this
command, give your dog's name and the command
"Take it!" (fig. II-50). Your dog should *run* directly
to the dumbbell and pick it up. Some dogs circle the
dumbbell first and take it on their return (fig. II-51).
The dog should pick the dumbbell up by the bar (fig.
II-52) and return quickly to you (fig. II-53). When
he reaches you, he should sit perfectly squarely (fig.
II-54), holding the dumbbell toward you. Wait at this
time for the judge to give you the next instruction:
"Take it!" When you hear the judge's command, remove the dumbbell from the dog's mouth with both
hands (fig. II-55) while simultaneously saying "Out!"
Wait again for the judge's instruction: "Finish!" Give
the verbal (or hand-signal) heel command. The judge
will tell you, after your dog finishes: "Exercise finished."

II-56–58: Taking the Dumbbell off the Ground the First Time. **II-56.** Begin by holding the dumbbell low to the ground so that the dog must reach down and out to take it.

II-57. Continue to move in a clockwise arc, keeping the dog moving and the dumbbell low to the ground. Make him reach out to take it, and correct him if he fails to go for it on his own initiative.

II-58. The dog should make a conspicuous effort to reach out on his own initiative to take the dumbbell. When he does, allow him to grab it and quickly move in front of him. Remove the dumbbell from his mouth, pause a moment, and give the command "Heel!" When he has finished, hug him up—he has earned all the praise you can give and will very much appreciate it.

II-59. This is a critical step in the dumbbell work: the dog must take a dumbbell that is on the ground, stationary. He must do it unhesitatingly. As soon as you give the command "Take it!," snap his lead toward the dumbbell to encourage him to grab it up quickly. Then back away quickly, enforce his sit, and remove the dumbbell with the command "Out!" After he has finished, love him up.

 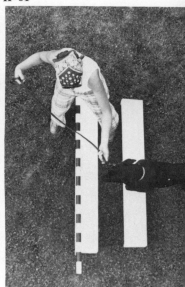

building his confidence if he takes it, encouraging him with both praise and correction if he does it haltingly.

Broad Jump Modified

Practice for the broad jump during this week will involve a number of modifications, though the dog will continue to jump on lead and over two obstacles (with the bar attached to the second one).

Put the dog in a sit-stay facing the jump, about ten feet from the first obstacle. Walk toward the jump, leaving slack in the lead, and go as far as you can toward the first hurdle, keeping as close to the middle as you can without blocking the dog's path down the center line of the jump. Give the command "Over!" as you hop or step over the hurdles. If the dog hesitates, give a slight tug on the lead to get him going. Praise him as soon as he has cleared the obstacles. This modification begins to condition the dog to work independently and to see you in a different position. Continue to practice it for two or three days.

During the last half of the week, if the dog has mastered this segment of the jumping routine, add another modification: some new handling techniques and a third hurdle. (Do not add a third hurdle, of course, if your dog is so small that he will only have to clear two in competition; refer to Table 1 to determine this.)

Change the routine by putting your dog in a sit-stay no more than about six feet from the first hurdle. Leave him, walk over to the jumps, and straddle the second hurdle (fig. II-60) somewhere near the center line. (You will be straddling the hurdle that has the bar on top of it.) Give the command "Over!" If the dog hesitates, apply a slight tug on the lead to get him in motion. As he approaches and jumps, step over the

160

II-60–63: Broad Jump Modified. **II-60.** Put the dog in a sit-stay no more than six feet from your intended position over the second hurdle. Straddle it and give the command "Over!"

II-61. As he reaches the first board, give an assist by tugging his lead forward and up.

II-62. After he lands, encourage him to come in to you with verbal praise. Next week you will begin to correct him into this position with a tug on the lead—to encourage him to make his turn sharp and inform him that he must come back to you without a command.

II-63. Correct him into a straight sit when he returns to you, and give him a good deal of praise before finishing. Do this exercise two or three times, and then add the third hurdle (if your dog must jump three hurdles).

second hurdle so as to be able to correct him back in to you. Examine the sequence in figures II-60 through II-63. The second time you do the exercise, add the third hurdle.

This routine should be followed every day for the remainder of the week, using three hurdles if your dog is of the size that requires three.

The reason that you stand in the midst of the hurdles, near the center line, is to condition your dog to jump *straight down the center line* of the obstacle. Many dogs disqualify in competition because they jump diagonally, clipping the last obstacle with their feet and landing out to the side of the hurdles—which means that they did not clear all the obstacles. By standing near the center line while you practice, you condition the dog to jump properly; later, you will have to stand *outside* the jumps and depend on this conditioning.

Toward the end of the week, begin to reduce the amount of praise you give the dog after he successfully completes the exercise; a pat on the head and a reassuring "Good dog!" should suffice. We will, in general, begin to cut down on praise as the dog becomes more proficient in his work. As your dog's level of competence begins to approach Utility standards, you must begin to reduce the opportunities for him to respond, jubilantly and tropismatically, to a bit of praise; in Utility competition, you will be penalized for a spontaneous outburst of frolic, since dogs are expected to be under constant control. An impromptu

162

II-64–67: Retrieve over High Jump. **II-64.** As soon as the judge tells you "Throw it!," give your dog the stay command and throw the dumbbell over the high jump. (Figs. II-44–55 show how to transfer the dumbbell from hand to hand before you actually throw it.) After it is thrown, wait for the next instruction from the judge.

II-65. When the judge tells you "Send your dog!," give him the command "Take it!" He should clear the jump, without touching the boards, down the center line and retrieve the dumbbell.

II-66. The dog must return over the jump without touching it, holding the dumbbell firmly in his mouth.

II-67. After clearing the jump on his return, the dog should come straight in to the handler and go into a sit, holding the dumbbell. Wait for the judge to give the next command: "Take it." On hearing this, remove the dumbbell from the dog's mouth with the command "Out!" and wait for the next instructions from the judge: "Finish" and "Exercise finished."

163

II-68. To measure your dog at the withers, find his shoulder blades, place a stick on them, parallel to the ground, and measure the distance from the ground to the stick. Then look up your dog's regulation jump height and distance in Tables 1 and 2. Make certain that your dog is not one of the exceptions to this (see Appendix I). It is important to practice measuring your dog with the help of a stranger. Some dogs resent being approached by individuals who are carrying sticks or other strange objects —even dogs that have had considerable experience in the Novice Stand for Examination. It would be a shame to discover this in a show ring. According to the 1975 *Obedience Regulations,* all dogs will be measured for the jumps unless they jump the maximum height.

celebration on the floor of the obedience ring before the appropriate time amounts to a loss of points. Celebration is fine, but overdoses of it must be deferred until you and the dog are out of the ring.*

Introduction to Retrieve over High Jump

The AKC regulation exercise *retrieve over high jump* (figs. II 64 67) involves throwing the dumbbell over the high jump and, on the judge's command, sending your dog to retrieve it.† The dog must jump the obstacle in both directions. You will teach him to jump the high jump *without* the dumbbell during the initial training period, and then add the dumbbell portion after the dog has mastered the jump *and* the retrieve on flat as separate exercises. You will, of course, need a practice high jump to train your dog to do this exercise. You will find a set of plans for building the wooden jumps in Appendix IV.

Ultimately, your dog will have to jump 1½ times his height at the withers (fig. II-68 shows how to measure him). Table 2 gives the correct high-jump heights for dogs of specific measurements. The height of the jump will, of course, vary with the breed of dog: a dachshund will not jump as high as a Great Dane. The minimum required height that any dog, irrespective of his breed, *must* jump is eight inches. The maximum height that any dog is required to jump, irrespective of his breed, is thirty-six inches. Thus, some very big dogs will have to jump as high as dogs quite a bit smaller. This mostly has to do with the weight and co-ordination of the excessively large breeds and the amount of shock their skeletal and muscular structure sustains when they land. For example, a Great Dane is not required to jump 1½ times his height at the withers, but a German shepherd is. This means that a particularly large Great Dane—thirty-four inches at the withers, for example—will have to jump only thirty-four inches, although a German shepherd of twenty-four inches will have to jump the full thirty-six inches. The several breeds that are *excepted* from the rule of 1½ times withers height are listed in Appendix I.

We will begin our training with just a single board, eight inches wide,‡ as the obstacle to clear, regardless of the dog's breed. This is the minimum that any dog will have to jump in an AKC obedience trial.

We start with so low an object because what you are going to teach your dog will not be the easiest exercise he has learned, and he needs encouragement, from the outset, to enjoy the jumping and feel confident at it. Also, the low obstacle will allow the dog to develop a sense of perception and timing: he will be able to concentrate on pacing himself as he approaches the jump and, as the obstacle is made higher, will be

* One of our students was penalized five points in an AKC Novice show for giving a normal amount of praise—the apassionate judge later told him he "fondled" his dog too much.
† The manner in which you transfer the dumbbell from one hand to the other for the retrieve over high jump is the same as for the retrieve on flat. Examine figures II-44 through II-47 again.
‡ Standard lumber, if you build your own jumps, come in 7½-inch widths. This is acceptable for training purposes.

TABLE 2

Determining the Height Your Dog Must
Jump in the High Jump

Determine the height of your dog in inches, measuring him at the withers (shown in fig. II-68). Most breeds must jump $1\frac{1}{2}$ times this measurement, but the widths of the boards in regulation jumps are always in even inches (from 2 to 8 inches). Usually the judge will make your dog jump the next lower height in even inches. The *AKC Regulations* list the dogs that must clear only their height at the withers (see Appendix I, Chapter 2, Section 10).

Height of Dog at Withers	6	7	8	9	10	11	12	13	14	15	16	17	18	19	20	21	22	23	24
Height he must clear	8	10	12	12	14	16	18	18	20	22	24	26	26	28	30	32	32	34	36

Note. No dog must jump higher than 36 inches.

II-69–70: Beginning the High-Jump Work. **II-69.** Run with the dog toward the jump and make him jump over a low obstacle. As you clear the eight-inch board, give the command "Over!" and tug on his lead.

II-70. Continue trotting in a clockwise pattern, as indicated by the dotted lines, and repeat the jump, as in figure II-69.

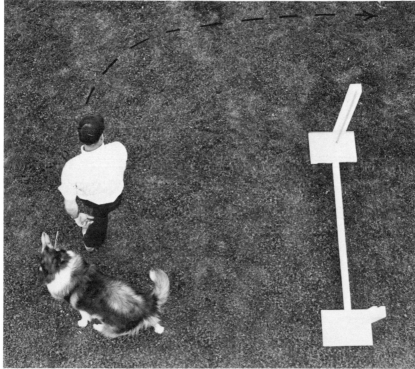

experienced enough to adjust his pace and timing accordingly. This is a *gradual* learning process; the best jumpers are those who pace themselves well and have developed their sense of timing over a longish period of experience.

Set up the eight-inch board in an area of the training ground where you can easily and comfortably run around either end of the jump. At first, *both* you and the dog will jump the obstacle. As the height gradually increases, *you* will start running past the jump instead of over it— but the dog will, of course, be expected to clear it.

The first week of training involves an on-lead exercise in which you and your dog run in an arc (figs. II-69–70). Leave a good deal of slack in the lead, but just as you and the dog jump the eight-inch board, give a slight tug and say "Over!" Some of the larger breeds will, of course, merely *step* over the board without jumping. If your dog does this, add another eight-inch board so that he *has to jump,* however effortlessly, to clear the obstacle. If he jumps and clears the obstacle, praise him while you continue trotting in the clockwise arc pattern shown in figure II-70, repeating the exercise two or three times. We are trying to accustom the dog to the command "Over!" as he approaches this new obstacle, "over" meaning that he has to jump. (The command "Over!" will not be used in the final retrieve-over-high-jump exercise, but it will be used later in the Utility directed-jumping exercises.) Since the obstacle is so low and the command is reinforced by a slight tug on the lead, the exercise is really not very difficult for the dog. Repeating it any more than five times a session would be tedious for him.

Practice the jumping for the remainder of the week, exactly as we have described it. This will gradually build up the dog's sense of timing and keep him happy. The harder part comes later; the more he can fix as habit during this week, the easier the work will be when it becomes rough sledding.

OPEN WEEK 5

OUTLINE OF TRAINING SCHEDULE
Old Exercises (practice these first)
    Novice (as modified to enhance Open training)
        Heel Free (on short knotted cord, carrying dumbbell)
        Straight Recall (It is important to practice this more than your
            regular amount this week as your dog learns the drop on
            recall.)
    Open
        Advanced Heeling: Pivots to right and left; back steps (on short
            knotted cord)
        Drop at Random
        Long Stand (3 to 4 minutes—vary the time each practice)

II-71–72: Hand Signal for Down. **II-71.** Raise your right hand in the air, smoothly, and bring it straight back down to your side. Do not let it remain above your head too long.

II-72. Your dog drops down in place on seeing the hand signal and waits for your next command.

II-73. Wrap your leather lead so that none of the metal is exposed. Then put it into an old white sock.

Long Sit and Long Down, Out of Sight (4 to 5 minutes for sit, 6 to 7 minutes for down). Practice these at the end of your daily training.

Modification of Open Exercises

Combining Drop with Recall and Beginning Hand Signal for Drop

Retrieve on Flat: Sending your dog for dumbbell at a distance

Broad Jump: Adding the correction to teach the turn and return

High Jump: Initiating the exercise from a normal heeling position

New Exercises

None

Suggested Length of Practice Session: 20 minutes, once daily

Combining Drop with Recall and Beginning Hand Signal for Drop

The random drop and the straight recall will be combined for the first time during this week of training. In addition, we will begin the training for dropping the dog on hand signal.

There are several acceptable ways to give a hand signal to "drop" your dog. We prefer a quick signal that involves the following motions: your right arm goes straight up into the air (figs. II-71–72) and comes straight back down to your side. The motion should be smooth and fairly rapid; it is made slightly off to the side so that the dog can see it more clearly and for a longer period of time (and also so that you do not jab yourself in the ribs with your elbow). Your hand should not remain above your head more than a split second.

To combine the drop hand signal with the verbal drop command and indelibly fix the association in your dog's mind, *throw* your lead at the dog. Anywhere in his general direction will suffice—you do not have to hit him with the lead. Before throwing the lead, be sure to prepare it in the following fashion: Take the metal end—the swivel snap —and wrap the leather around it to completely cover it and form a ball (fig. II-73). Then place the wrapped-up lead into a thick work sock made of white wool or cotton (white is much easier for the dog to see than dark leather or a dark sock). The object of the exercise is *not* to hit the dog, but to make him aware of the hand motion and the down command. The association is fixed more rapidly in his mind if he sees an object come sailing out of your hand when you give the vocal and hand-signal down commands simultaneously.

Do the drop on recall with the white sock the first time in the following way. Do several straight recalls with the white sock in your hand (from this point on you will practice the drop on recall only after doing one or two straight recalls, and the white-sock lead should remain in your hand during both exercises). Then do a drop on recall: call the dog to you and, when he has traveled a little more than half way to you, give a verbal down command while simultaneously raising the white-lead sock with your right arm and throwing it at him as you bring your

arm back down. It might be a good idea to practice the throwing part without the dog first, to develop your own skills. You do *not* have to throw it hard or hit the dog with it; although if it hits him it will not hurt him, since the metal part is not exposed.

Two points are in order here. First, do not overexercise your dog with the drop on recall, because he will begin anticipating the drop on *all* recalls, even the straight ones. Second, do not "drop" your dog in the same spot all the time. If you do not vary the drop spot, the dog will begin to think that when he reaches a particular spot he should drop automatically.

If you do more straight recalls than drops on recalls, your dog will look much sharper when you do the drops. So continue to practice the straight recall *as if* it were an Open exercise.

During the first week of practicing the drop on recall with the hand signal, you should reinforce the meaning of the hand signal by throwing the object at the dog every time you do the drop, simultaneously giving the verbal down command.

Retrieve on Flat with Rope Aid—Sending Dog for Dumbbell at a Distance

This week we will work for distance in the dumbbell work. We will have to use a rope for assistance to make the first step toward retrieving at a distance—the rope that you previously used to teach the recall. A pulley will be helpful for this exercise, but a smooth, small-diameter dowel or broom handle that will allow the rope to pass around it will work as well. You *will* need a pulley of the kind shown in figure II-74 in Utility training, so it might be practical to purchase one now. Most hardware stores have a variety of suitable pulleys. A tree would not do, since the bark would create too much friction. What you have to do is lay the rope out about twenty-five feet, pass it through the pulley, and bring the other end back to you so that both ends are at your feet. You will fasten one end on the dog's collar and pull on the other end to get him to move out toward the pulley. An excellent device is the screw-in type anchor (fig. II-74), to which you can attach the pulley.

Start with the dog in a sit-stay in the proper heeling position, but slightly askew of the rope so that the first pull you make on it will knock him off balance and set him in motion toward the pulley end (fig. II-75). This will eliminate any need for a harsher correction. Take up the loose end of the rope with your left hand, and throw the dumbbell out along the rope (fig. II-76). It should land just short of the pulley; as soon as it hits the ground, say "Take it!" and give a snap on the rope to set the dog in motion toward the dumbbell (fig. II-77). This will be the first time that the dog will actually leave you and go some distance away from you. If he takes the dumbbell, quickly call him as in the *recall* exercise and enforce a straight sit when he comes in to you with the dumbbell. Take it from him as you give the command "Out!" and praise him after he finishes. Figures II-76 through II-80 demonstrate the complete sequence.

If he does not go all the way out to the dumbbell, *make* him move out by pulling on the rope (or have an assistant do it). If he refuses to

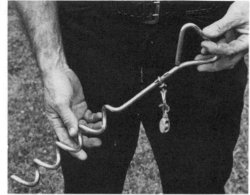

II-74. An auger-type anchor, which screws into the ground, and a pulley are useful aids for teaching the dog the retrieve-on-flat exercise.

II-75. Have the dog sit slightly askew of the rope so that your first correction can knock him slightly off balance and put him into forward motion toward the dumbbell.

II-76–80: Retrieving Dumbbell at a Distance. **II-76.** Throw the dumbbell out so that it lands short of the pulley anchor and near the rope.

II-77. Give the command "Take it!" as you simultaneously pull the rope. He will probably require no additional pull once he gets into motion, but if he does hesitate, run back with the rope to pull him all the way out to the dumbbell.

II-78. He should return immediately to you with the dumbbell firmly in his mouth. Encourage him with a verbal "Come!"

II-79. If he appears to be coming straight back to you, remain standing motionless. But if he acts as if he might overshoot you or stop short, be prepared to grab the rope and correct him into a straight sit in front of you.

II-80. Make him sit in front of you a moment before giving the command "Out!" Then, after you remove the dumbbell, finish and give him a great deal of praise.

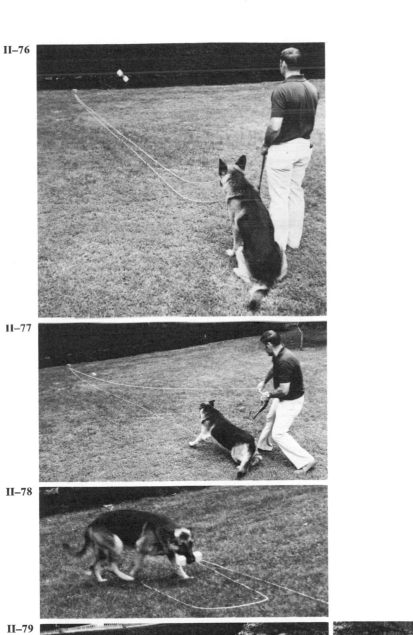

II-81. To get the dog to make a sharp turn when he lands, give a correction as soon as he lands and bring him quickly in to you, enforcing a straight sit. Praise him immediately and heel away without finishing.

go to the dumbbell, quickly run out, take up the rope near his collar, and apply short—but *not* straight-line—corrections that direct him to the dumbbell; you might also have to push the dumbbell with your right hand and set it in motion.

You should work on this part of the retrieve on flat until the dog does it enthusiastically and consistently. At this point, he will probably be anticipating the command "Take it!" by leaning forward from his heeling position as you throw the dumbbell and going after it without waiting for your verbal command. This is good now, since the *hardest* part of the exercise is to get him to go away from you enthusiastically. It is very easy to correct later for the anticipation; do not restrain the dog now. In fact, when he takes the dumbbell on command, you will be departing even more from the ultimate objective by giving him the command "Come!" to encourage him to return to you. The vocal command, of course, would not be permitted in a show, but it is practical and useful for training purposes. In the next week of training you will begin to correct for anticipating the command "Take it!" and eliminate the verbal come command. By that time the dog should have gained enough confidence in his ability to retrieve the dumbbell to appreciate the nature of the exercise and corrections.

Broad Jump Modified

This week you will introduce a new portion of the broad-jump exercise: after landing, the dog will be *expected* to turn and come to a sit in front of and facing you.

You will continue to work with three obstacles * as in the previous

* Or with two obstacles, if the dog is smaller

week, do everything on lead, and begin the jump portion by straddling the middle obstacle.

Put the dog in the sit-stay, leave him, and take up your straddle position at the jumps. Give the command "Over!" and step over the obstacle as the dog clears it. When the dog lands, and as soon as he has regained his footing and balance, give a slight tug on the lead to knock him off balance and toward you, and then take a step backward (fig. II-81). As you step back, pull the dog in to you as in the recall and put him into a square sit in front of you. As soon as he sits, give him a great deal of praise. Do not do the finish; merely heel away, and then do the exercise again.

Practice this modification for several days, or until the dog masters the turn at the end of the jump; that is, when, on regaining his balance after landing, he initiates the turn without any correction from you and moves in to you to take up a sitting position. Note that you must remain near the center line of the jump until the dog lands; then back away from the jump to correct for the turn and bring the dog to a sitting position. If you step away from the center line too soon—for instance, when the dog is still in the air—he will begin to take a short cut by jumping diagonally, knowing that he will eventually end up near your side of the hurdles anyway. Diagonal jumping must be discouraged.

High Jump Modified

This week you will eliminate running in an arc and will instead initiate the exercise from a normal heeling position. The dog, not the handler, will be centered with respect to the jump. You should both be about ten to fifteen feet away from the jump so that the dog can develop his pacing and timing as he approaches the jump. The jump should still have just the eight-inch board on it (unless your dog is very large, in which case there should be two eight-inch boards between the uprights).

Begin from the heeling position, with the dog on lead and centered. Give the command "Over!" and trot with him to and over the jump. This time do not assist the dog by giving a slight tug on the lead; let him jump it of his own accord. Run out in a straight line past the obstacle for another ten to fifteen feet, make an about turn, and, without giving any further command, trot back toward the jump and jump it again, from the opposite direction. When you have almost reached your initial starting point, slow down, quickly move around to the front of the dog by making a pivot turn on your left foot, and come to a halt with the dog facing you and sitting squarely at your feet. Enforce his sit and give him praise at this point; then finish. Figures II-82 through II-84 show the sequence for this part of the exercise.

This training sequence should be continued for two days to establish the pattern of the exercise in the dog's mind. After he seems to understand what is expected of him, add another eight-inch board to the jump—if *you* can comfortably clear this obstacle—and continue this pattern for the remainder of the week. The larger dogs will be jumping twenty-four inches when another eight-inch board is added. This can

II–82 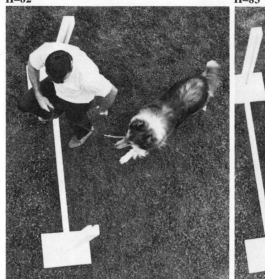 II–83

II–85

II-82–88: High Jump Modified, Week 5. **II-82.** Begin from the proper heeling position, with the dog centered. Trot to the jump and allow the dog to clear it. Continue running another ten feet, turn about, and trot back to clear the obstacle again, from the opposite direction.

II-83. As soon as you clear the jump the second time, quickly move out in front of your dog and continue to back up, pulling him into a straight sit, facing you.

II-84. Bring the dog into a perfectly straight sit and praise him before repeating the exercise.

II-85. The last day of this week modify your high-

II–86

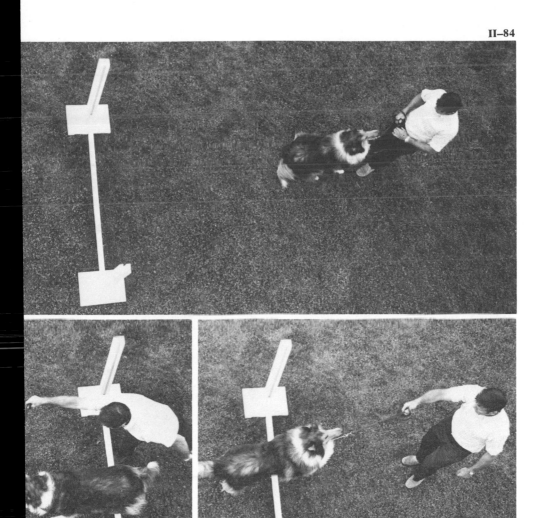

jump work by adding another board and beginning
the exercise six feet from the jump.

II-86. Give the command "Over!" and step toward the
jump, but let the dog go over it by himself. Give him
plenty of slack and remain standing close to the jump,
holding the lead over the obstacle.

II-87. When the dog regains his balance, apply a correction with just enough force to spin the dog back
toward you, giving him a second "Over!"

II-88. As he comes back over, put a little tension on the
lead to encourage him to come all the way back to you;
back up to give him room to land and come to a sit at
your feet.

177

become a bit difficult for some handlers, particularly short people or those of us who are out of condition. We urge handlers who cannot comfortably jump three eight-inch boards to add only a two-inch or four-inch board; the main object at this point is *not* to maximize the height of the jump.

As you practice this routine for the remainder of the week, keep in mind that the *pattern* is more important than the actual height jumped. The dog must become used to going over the jump in both directions, returning to you, and sitting automatically. He must never be permitted to go *around* the jump. By jumping *with* him, you do not even allow that as an alternative.

The last day of this week, practice the jump with two additional modifications. First, for those larger breeds that must jump fairly high obstacles, add another board. Second, stand close to the jump (fig. II-85) with the dog on the six-foot lead and give the command "Over!" Then step toward the jump (fig. II-86) but do not jump it yourself. Put plenty of slack in the lead, and let the dog clear it alone (fig. II-87). When he lands and begins his turn, apply tension to the leather lead and again give him the command "Over!," keeping slight tension on the leather lead as he comes back over (fig. II-88). Back up to allow him room to land in front of you; when he has gained his footing, put him immediately into a straight sit. Then do the finish and give him praise. This modification will preadapt him for the training in the following week, when he is expected to jump over the obstacle by himself and return to you, but from a greater distance and on a longer lead.

OPEN WEEK 6

OUTLINE OF TRAINING SCHEDULE
Old Exercises (Practice these, in order given, before working on Modifications.)
> Novice
>> Heel Free, Carrying Dumbbell (Keep the short knotted cord on the dog's collar for corrections.)
>> Straight Recall (Practice often as you develop your dog's skills in the drop on recall—the more straight recalls you do, the less your dog will anticipate a drop command.)
> Open
>> Advanced Heeling Routines: Figure 8 off lead; pivots to right and left; back steps. (Correct with short knotted cord for errors. In a show ring you cannot adjust your dog by touching his lead or his body.)
>> Drop at Random (Gradually reduce frequency until, by the end of the week, you are doing only one random drop per exercise or randomly between exercises. Always give lavish praise after a random drop.)

Long Stand (3 to 4 minutes, varying the time each practice)

Long Sit and Long Down, Out of Sight (about 5 minutes for sit, about 7 for down). Practice these after your daily training is completed.

Modification of Open Exercises

Drop on Recall: Reducing frequency of sock-wrapped lead enforcement of drop

Retrieve on Flat: Correcting for anticipation of "Take it!"; eliminating "Come!" when dog fetches dumbbell; eliminating lead (but not rope) when dog no longer anticipates "Take it!" and when he fetches enthusiastically

Broad Jump: Positioning yourself alongside obstacles for the "Over!"; adding all regulation jumps for your breed, but not the full jump distance; stepping into the jump as a guide when the dog jumps

High Jump: Adding height; over and back on long lead

New Exercises

None

Suggested Length of Practice Session: 20 minutes, once daily

Drop on Recall Modified

The practice for drop on recall during the sixth week is essentially the same as in Week 5. The only modification is that you will not throw the lead unless your dog still needs that reinforcement. By this time the motion of your hand should be sufficient, when given with the verbal signal, to cause him to drop instantly. Be careful, however, to add variation to the exercise: do *more* straight recalls than drops on recalls and, when you do "drop" the dog, make sure it is not always in the same spot.

You should be working about thirty to forty feet away from your dog. If he comes in to you slowly, increase the distance by another ten or fifteen feet and do proportionately more straight recalls. Remember, a desirable recall, whether straight or drop, is one in which the dog comes quickly to you as soon as he receives the command "Come!"

Retrieve on Flat Further Modified

Your dog must be doing the following in the retrieve on flat before you can make any additional changes in his dumbbell work: going out after the thrown dumbbell enthusiastically and quickly; picking it up without hesitation; returning straight to you with the dumbbell carried properly in his mouth, though he may still need additional encouragement, such as a come command; sitting in front of you, as in the recall, and releasing the dumbbell on "Out!"; and, finally, going into the heel position on command. If he performs all of these basic components of the retrieve on flat, you are ready to move into the final improvements of the exercise.

II-89. Correcting anticipation of "Take it!" after the dumbbell is thrown. Keep the leather lead on his collar when you throw the dumbbell. Pause a moment after the dumbbell lands. If the dog tries to lunge for it, correct with the leather lead and put him back into position. Remove the lead and then give him the command "Take it!"

For this week you will again attach the long rope to the running end of the dog's choke-chain collar. You will also leave the leather lead attached to his collar so that you can correct for anticipation of the command "Take it!"

Put the dog into the proper heeling position, facing the pulley end of the long rope. Take the leather lead *and* the free end of the rope in your left hand. The dog is, of course, in the proper heeling position at your left side (fig. II-89). Give the command "Stay!" and throw the dumbbell out, but be prepared to correct the dog this time with the leather lead should he bolt out after the dumbbell before he hears "Take it!" If he does, correct him sharply back into the sitting position without saying a word. When he calms down, unsnap his leather lead with your left hand and give him the command "Take it!" He is, of course, still fastened to the rope; if he fails to move on command, give a firm tug on the rope to set him in motion. (Figs. II-76–80 of Week 5 show the remainder of the sequence.) If you practiced properly during Week 5, he should go swiftly for the dumbbell and retrieve it.

This time do not give him a verbal come command if he picks up the dumbbell but hesitates on the return: instead, move swiftly out to him, take hold of the rope near his collar, and bring him back to your starting position with firm, but not sharp corrections that repeatedly knock him only slightly off balance. By this time the dog knows what the correction means, so it is not necessary to be at all severe—you do not want to distract him from hanging on to the dumbbell. As you back into your original position, make him sit squarely, give the command "Out!," remove the dumbbell from his mouth, and have him finish. Then praise him.

After a day or two of working on this modification of the exercise, the dog will still be eager to go out after the dumbbell but will be aware that a correction is inevitable if he anticipates the command "Take it!" Start to build up his patience by allowing the dumbbell to come to a stop and lie there a second or two before you give the command "Take it!" When he is reliable at this, you can make the next modification: remove the leather lead. When you heel up to the area from which you are going to begin the exercise, come to a halt, remove the lead, fasten the rope to his collar, and proceed with the exercise. Allow an interval of five or ten seconds from the time the dumbbell stops rolling to the time you say "Take it!" Similarly, build up the time that the dog is obliged to sit with the dumbbell in his mouth after he returns with it: work gradually on waiting at least ten seconds before giving the command "Out!"

In order to score high in Open, your dog must execute this exercise properly at every step of the sequence. While the exercise itself is not difficult, it does contain a large number of discrete components, which means that there are many opportunities for the dog to perform sloppily. You must be prepared to correct for anticipation, slowness or sluggishness in the retrieve and return, crooked sits or finishes, dropping the dumbbell, failing to release it on command, and playing with or excessively mouthing it.

Broad Jump Further Modified

This week we will introduce several modifications for the broad jump and rapidly approach the AKC regulation performance. First, instead of straddling the jumps after leaving your dog, you will stand outside   181 them with your toes about twenty-four inches away from the edge of the obstacles. Second, you will add a fourth jump if your dog is required to clear four hurdles for his regulation jump. We will not put the regulation distance into our training this week—the four jumps will continue to be close together. Your position will be about midway between the first and fourth jumps. If your dog jumps fewer than four boards, stand somewhere near the midpoint of the first and last jumps. Finally, you will replace the leather lead with about fifteen or twenty feet of rope. Instead of attaching this to the dog's collar, however, merely lay it down the center line of the jump as a guide. Only if he fails to move on command will you need to attach the rope to his collar, for purposes of correction. In most cases this will not be necessary.

Figures II-90 through II-94 show the training technique for this week; study them carefully. From your position at the side of the jump, you will step into the jump as the dog clears the obstacles. This reinforces the fact that he must continue to jump down the center line: if he does not, he will bump into you. Eventually you will remove this modification. For now, perform it randomly to keep the dog alert—he will never know when you might step into the jumps and provide an additional side obstacle. If the dog jumps diagonally and you are stepping into his flight path, use your right leg to bump him smartly on his shoulder as he passes. His velocity will be such that it will bend your leg, so he is not running into a fixed object. Finally, make the dog finish before you give him praise. That is, when he makes his turn and comes to you to sit, you will hesitate, give the command "Heel!," and praise him when he finishes. Note that you must be standing far enough away from the jumps to allow him to make a turn between you and the jumps, but you must not be more than two feet away from them.

To accustom the dog to a longer obstacle, you should straddle the jumps at least the first time you add the fourth hurdle. After the dog finishes, head back to the starting area, put him into the sit-stay position, and leave him. Walk over to the side of the jump. Your long rope lead should still be lying on the boards, marking the center line of the dog's flight path; the swivel-snap end of the rope should be on the ground, near the dog. Give his name and the command "Over!" As he approaches, step forward into the middle of the jumps with your right foot forward (fig. II-92). As the dog *passes you,* take a step back to your original position and turn right 90°, so that your body is parallel to the dog's flight path. He will be coming out of his turn at this point, and about to return to you. When he comes to a sitting position (correct him if he sits crooked), pause a moment (fig. II-93). He expects the praise here, but don't give it now. Instead, give the command "Heel!" When he comes to the heel position (fig. II-94), give him lots of praise. He will not even notice the jumps because he is focused on you and expecting the praise.

Adding Height to the High Jump

This week you will train your dog to go over the high jump and come back while on a long lead, as well as build up jump height. Your dog

182

should leave you on command and easily make the first jump, but you may need the long lead to correct him into jumping back over the hurdle to return (rather than going around it). The height of the jump will not necessarily be increased to maximum height, though, of course, for smaller dogs, what is added may in fact bring the jump to regulation height.

During the beginning of the week you might have to encourage your dog to jump by making a slight forward motion toward the high jump as you give the command "Over!," but by the end of the week you will drop this and use only the vocal command. Also during the early part of the week, you will concentrate on the dog's position when he has come back over the jump. You may have to back up to make certain that he comes in to you in a perfectly straight line and ends up in a square sitting position, facing you.

The exercise always begins with the dog, not the handler, centered with respect to the high jump. The desirable distance from the jump is eight feet, though after you become used to your dog's timing and how he lands after clearing the jump, you can make minor adjustments. You should begin concentrating on your skill at estimating distances.

On the last day of the previous week, you practiced the high jump with the dog on the leather lead to adapt him to jumping over the obstacle while you remained on one side of it. It is not wise to practice this particular exercise more than one or two days, since the dog can fall into the habit of making an abrupt turn as soon as he clears the jump in order to return *quickly* back over it—and thereby avoid any correction that he suspects might come.

This week you will again expect your dog to do the jump while you remain on the starting side of it eight to ten feet away. By keeping you on one side of the jump, this method requires your dog to do the work on command, as in AKC shows. However, for recalcitrant dogs a second method (figs. II-95–97) might be necessary: put the dog in a sit-stay and walk around to the opposite side of the obstacle. Drape the long lead—about thirty feet—gently over the high jump and, on the command "Over!," give it a gentle tug to get the dog moving toward you and the jump. Keep him fairly close to the jump to reduce his temptation to go *around* it. Use this alternative only for a day or two, until the dog is confident that he can make the jump by himself when he is on the opposite side and that he will be praised for it.

When he has this confidence, the first alternative—jumping both directions while on a long lead while you remain on the starting side—should then become the regular training exercise for the remainder of the week.

By the end of Week 6, your dog should be going over the high jump on a vocal command and returning back over to you. If he is confident on lead, you can introduce the following modification: put the dog in the sit-stay position, as if you were going to perform the jumping exercise. Remove the long lead from his collar and put on the short knotted rope. Leave the thirty-foot rope lead draped over the jump, as before. *He* still thinks he is on the long lead. Then give him the com- 183

II–90

II–91

II–92

II-90–94: Broad Jump Modifications, Week 6.
II-90. Use all of the boards that your dog's breed must jump, but do not put them at regulation distance yet. Drape the rope over the center line of the boards, but do not fasten it to the dog.

II-91. Leave your dog with the command "Stay!" and take up your position midway between the first and last boards, with your toes no more than twenty-four inches from the edge of the jump.

II-92. Give the command "Over!," and, as the dog begins his jump, step into the jump to encourage him to jump straight down the center line. When the dog passes you, step back and pivot to the right so that he can come in to you and sit.

II-93. Pause a moment while the dog is sitting squarely, and then give the command "Heel!" Make sure you are far enough away from the jumps so that he can finish, but not more than twenty-four inches away.

II-94. After he finishes, pause a moment, then take two steps forward to end the exercise. Give him lots of praise.

185

II-95–97: Alternative High Jump Return for Recalcitrant Dog. **II-95.** Put him in a sit-stay about ten feet from the jump with the rope attached to his collar, walk to the other side of the jump, and take up the rope to tug him toward you.

II-96. Give the command "Come!" and tug the rope to get him in motion toward the jump. The rope will also define the center line of the jump.

II-97. When he clears the jump, bring him in to a straight sit and praise him. Do not use this alternative for more than a day or two. When his confidence is built up, train as described in the text.

mand "Over!" On seeing the rope draped over the jump, he should follow it and clear it in both directions without another command. It is imperative that you not permit him to go *around* the jump, so do not introduce this modification until the dog is consistently clearing the jump, smoothly and gracefully, without balking on the return. That is, do not idly take him off lead just to "see if he will do it."

At the end of this week, pay attention to the dog's feet as he clears the jump—some dogs begin dragging their feet and "clipping" the jump with their hind feet. If your dog is doing this, remove one board from the jump to make it easier for him. You can correct for the clipping later; to do so now might confuse him and make him feel he is erring in the jumping and returning segments of the exercise.

OPEN WEEK 7

OUTLINE OF TRAINING SCHEDULE
Old Exercises
    Novice
        Heel Free, Carrying Dumbbell
        Straight Recall (interspersed with drops on recall)
    Open
        Advanced Heeling Routines: Figure 8 off lead; pivots to right and left; back steps
        Drop on Recall: Vocal down command only (See Modification of Open Exercises)
        Long Stand (3 to 4 minutes, varying the time each practice)
        Retrieve on Flat: Reverting to the long cord, but only as a guideline; it will complement the training in retrieve over high jump.
        Broad Jump (off lead and regulation standards)
        Long Sit and Long Down, Out of Sight (about 5 minutes for sit, 7 for down). Practice this as your last exercise each day.
Modification of Open Exercises
    Retrieve on Flat: Completely off lead, show standards
    Drop on Recall: Eliminating down hand signal. You will no longer give a double signal on this exercise. Vary the spot at which you give the command "Down!," and practice sparingly, mixing it with straight recalls.
    Broad Jump: Removing bar and guide rope; correcting for walking over jumps
    Retrieve over High Jump: Combining retrieve on flat with high jump
New Exercises
    None
Suggested Length of Practice Session: 20 minutes, once daily

Retrieve on Flat Modified

At this point you have a crucial decision to make. Many dogs appear to catch on quickly, and they convince their handlers that they know what the retrieve on flat is about. This often tempts the handler to take short cuts and shirk his training responsibility in some areas. At this stage in the retrieve on flat you could easily sustain a setback that would ultimately cost you weeks of additional training. If your dog does not clearly understand what is expected of him in this exercise, go back a week or two and make sure that he does *all* components consistently and well. Now you are going to move to the off-lead work, and it will not be possible to correct swiftly and precisely for errors. Thus an ill-prepared dog will be in serious difficulty: any bad habits that he is beginning to pick up will be magnified considerably. This includes "mouthing" the dumbbell.*

If your dog *is* ready for the seventh week, begin the practice for retrieve on flat by attaching a short knotted rope to the running end of his collar and heeling—off lead—into the practice area. You will perform the full retrieve on flat off lead. Leave the guide rope on the ground for security all during the week, but do not even pretend to attach it to your dog's collar; merely heel him up to the rope, halt, give the command "Stay!," and throw the dumbbell. Make sure your handling techniques are correct: transfer the dumbbell from one hand to the other, as described in figures II-44 through II-47, and pause for five to ten seconds before giving the command "Take it!" What your dog does then is largely a function of how well you have trained him in previous weeks; if you have followed our schedule and your dog is normal, he will execute the routine without difficulty and without hesitation, running directly to the dumbbell, picking it up, running back to you, and sitting squarely, waiting for your "Out!" and "Heel!" If he botches any part of it, go back to the relevant instructions in this text to refresh his memory.

You should begin examining your own performance now. There are a number of common errors that handlers make in this exercise, most of them involving body English during commands. The handler is expected, in an AKC show, to give all commands with only his lips ‡ moving. Many handlers tend to move their heads, hands, and arms, and bend at the knees to encourage their dogs to perform; often these extra movements are unconscious habits acquired during training. Again, the stay command is a golden opportunity to make errors: the handler must give it with either a vocal or a hand signal, or both, but the hand that signals *should not* be the one that has the dumbbell in it. So hold the dumbbell in your left hand and simultaneously give *both* the com-

* To cure a dog of excessive mouthing or chewing the dumbbell, replace the wooden dowel with a piece of aluminum tubing of the same diameter until he stops mouthing it.

‡ While it is permissible to give a hand signal to send the dog for the dumbbell, we do not encourage it, because it can lead to possible errors in Utility work, where the dog might either be tempted to jump an obstacle because a hand signal is associated with it or, on the "Go out!," veer over and jump the obstacle.

mand "Stay!" and the hand signal (with your *right* hand); *then* transfer the dumbbell into your right hand and throw it. Be very careful to make the signals simultaneously—any pause between them can lose you points and, if it is too long, disqualify you.

Practice the retrieve on flat every day this week as described above, concentrating on bringing your handling techniques up to show-perfection level as you do.

Drop on Recall Further Modified

This week's modification of the drop on recall is the removal of the hand-signal portion. In a show, you can use only one drop signal, *either* a hand signal *or* a verbal signal, *but never both.* Our reasons for teaching the two simultaneously are quite simple. First, the hand-signal portion of the training preadapts the dog for more advanced work in Utility. Second, and equally important, the dog learns to drop as soon as he receives the signal. On being given the vocal drop command, many dogs will slow their pace gradually before easing into a down position, which will lose them points in a show. With the rolled-up leather lead used as a "missile," the dog learns quickly to drop *as soon as the command is given.* Now, when the verbal portion is used alone, he should drop immediately and not creep several yards first. You can also imagine the usefulness of this exercise at home or on a walk: if the dog will drop unflinchingly and without hesitation as soon as he is given a command, you might sometime keep both him and yourself out of considerable difficulty, possibly danger—a potential dog fight or hazardous traffic.

Broad Jump Further Modified

By the end of this week your dog will be jumping pretty much as in AKC shows. On the first day, remove the bar on the second jump and the long rope you used as center line. During the week, gradually move the jumps out to their maximum show distance. Also, you should periodically stop taking your step into the jump, so that by the end of the week you are stepping in very irregularly.

Practice for this week is essentially the same as last week: Leave your dog about ten feet from the first obstacle with a stay command, with his body lined up with the center line of the jumps. After giving a "Stay!," go to the side of the jump and position yourself midway between the first and last obstacles. Make sure your toes are about two feet from the edge of the jumps. Pause there, look at your dog, and give his name and the command "Over!" Step into his flight path as he whizzes past, stopping *short* of the center line. As he lands and makes his turn, return to your position two feet from the edge of the jumps, and turn 90° to the right. Your dog should come to a straight sit. When he does, give the command "Heel!" and praise him after he finishes.

Some kinds of problems commonly develop at this juncture because of the greater distance between the jumps and the removal of the bar. Frequently dogs try to walk over the jumps by stepping on the boards or stepping in between them. If your dog begins to do this, re-

II-98–102: Broad Jump Modification, Week 7. **II-98.** Some dogs begin to walk over the jumps at some point in their training. To correct for this, put the dog on lead and begin from about ten feet away. Give the heel command, and run toward the jump, give the command "Over!" and a sharp tug on the lead to get him up in the air.

II-99. When the dog is jumping the boards with you and not walking over or around them, modify the training by running alongside the jump. Put him in the sit-stay and move off to the side with slack in the lead.

II-100. Say "Over!" and tug the dog toward the jump. As he approaches the first board, give a smart tug on the lead to encourage him to jump.

II-101. Continue to run past the jumps, allowing slack to develop in the lead.

II-102. As the dog lands, back away and bring him into a proper sit position alongside the jump. Praise him and then do the exercise again. When he is consistently jumping the boards, take him off lead and train as described in the text.

place the bar obstacle on the second jump with a piece of white clothes-line—it blends with the jumps in color, and encourages the dog to jump rather than walk. Make sure he is watching as you put the clothes-line on. It will make him aware that something peculiar is happening.

For recalcitrant dogs, as should be obvious by now, it might be necessary to be a bit more persuasive with your corrections, and to jump over or run along the obstacles with him as your persuasion is applied. You might have to remove a few of the jumps in order to clear the distance yourself. Figures II-98 through II-102 show this modi-fication.

High Jump Further Modified

During this week you will combine the retrieve portion of the retrieve over high jump with the jump portion, replacing the command "Over!" with "Take it!" At the same time you will continue to practice the re-trieve on flat, as a totally separate exercise.

Begin this week by removing all but one board from the high jump: only a single eight-inch board will be used. Lay the long rope out along the center line of the jump as a guide for the dog to follow (fig. II-103). He will have only the short knotted rope on his collar, in case you need to apply a correction. You will also use the long rope as a guide when you practice the retrieve on flat this week, so that the dog's association of the rope guide with the dumbbell will carry over to the retrieve over high jump when the two exercises are combined.

The purpose for removing all the boards except one is to allow the dog to concentrate on finding the dumbbell; the dumbbell should be plainly visible to him when you have thrown it over the high jump, and he will not have to worry about clearing so low a hurdle. He will, in effect, be doing the retrieve on flat—with a minor obstacle to clear. Next week, when he has caught on, you gradually add more boards until the transition to the retrieve over high jump is complete.

The first day you practice the retrieve with the high jump, try to maximize your dog's chances of doing everything properly. In other words, reduce to a minimum the number of opportunities he might have to make a choice. The major problems in this crucial step occur when the handler stands too far *back* from the jump or throws the dumbbell too far *past* the jump. Shorten your distance from the jump (which is reduced to a single eight-inch board), and throw the dumbbell just far enough past the jump for the dog to see it clearly and be able to execute a smooth pickup and turn to come back over. You might have to back up swiftly as the dog returns in order to give him plenty of room to come in to a straight sit in front of you.

Having the rope lead draped over the jump as a guide in both directions also reduces options for the dog. You, of course, must be a good enough thrower to have the dumbbell land somewhere near the rope so that the rope remains a guide. Poor throwers should practice a few times without the dog, trying to keep the dumbbell on center line and fairly close to the board. If the dumbbell takes a bad bounce and stops rolling too far to the left or right so that the dog can see it around

II-103. High jump modification, Week 7. Remove all but one board from the high jump and lay out the rope to define the center line. Throw the dumbbell out far enough so that the dog can see it, but not so far that he is tempted to run around the jump on his return. You should stand fairly close to the jump as you begin working with this modification.

the side of the jump, it is better to put the dog in a stay position and retrieve the dumbbell yourself. You will thus not even tempt the dog to go around the jump.

In AKC shows, as a matter of fact, the judge will sometimes ask the handler to keep his dog from retrieving a poorly located dumbbell and will go pick it up himself, carrying it over to the handler to throw again. In this event the handler is allowed to give the command "Stay!" again before throwing a second time—as if the exercise were beginning all over.

During the first few practice sessions this week, the dog should always be allowed to *see* the dumbbell when it comes to a halt on the opposite side of the high jump. By midweek the dog should be going consistently over the low obstacle, following the guide rope, and returning with the dumbbell (be sure to enforce straight returns). You can then begin to add more boards so that the dumbbell is increasingly difficult to see—and then finally out of sight completely. As you add height, you may also have to increase your distance from the jump so that, when he returns, the dog has room to come to a smooth sit in front of you with the dumbbell in his mouth, without bumping into your legs. Continue to toss the dumbbell fairly close to the guide rope.

Building up the height of the jump *gradually* reduces your dog's temptation to go around it. If you see that he is going to try to go around it—in either direction—do not allow him to complete the exercise. Run to him, take him by the short knotted cord, and bring him back to the starting point. Without giving him another command, run with him to the jump (holding on to the knotted cord), and make him go over it to retrieve the dumbbell. Let go of the rope as he jumps. If you have not

193

been able to catch up to him before he picks up the dumbbell, remove it from his mouth, throw it back on the ground, bring him back to the starting point and then make him go *over* the jump to get the dumbbell. It is useless to yell or scream at the dog if he makes a mistake, and doing so may cause him to run away from the exercise area entirely. Make this correction with a conspicuous degree of matter-of-factness— do not lose your cool!

OPEN WEEK 8

OUTLINE OF TRAINING SCHEDULE
Old Exercises
    Novice
        Straight Recall Combined with the Open Drop on Recall
    Open
        Practice all exercises in proper show sequence as described in text
Modification of Old Exercises
    Retrieve over High Jump: Regulation height; testing the dog's skills with poor throws; correcting a dog that clips the high jump
    Broad Jump: Regulation distance; correcting crooked sits when the dog returns to handler
    Practice all the Open exercises in show sequence to fix the pattern and begin approximating show conditions
New Exercises
    None. Your dog now knows all of the required exercises for successful competition in AKC obedience trials, Open class (A or B).
Suggested Length of Practice Session: 20 minutes, once daily

Regulation Height for Retrieve over High Jump
The objective during this week of training is to get the dog to clear the maximum (AKC-required) height in the retrieve over high jump without touching the jump with his feet or tail. If your dog clips the high jump, you will have to begin correcting him during this week, or clipping will become a habit. You will also remove the guide rope so that the dog must jump over the center line without a visual aid. Finally, you will put the dog to a severe test—entrap him by providing conditions under which he is very likely to be tempted into a mistake. This will serve to maximize his reliability under the most adverse conditions and fix the proper routine firmly into his behavior.

    At the end of last week, the dog was already jumping over an obstacle that interfered with his vision: he could not see the dumbbell

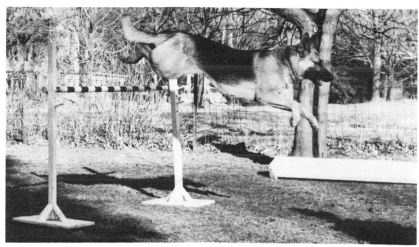

II-104. A dog that kicks his hind legs out and back when clearing the jump is using one strategy to avoid clipping.

II-105. A second strategy to avoid clipping is to tuck the hind legs up.

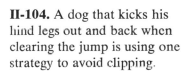

after it came to a halt. Now, you will merely add boards to the jump, making it AKC regulation height for your particular breed. When the dog begins jumping at regulation height, pay close attention to his feet and listen for any telltale tick of his toenails as he clears the jumps. You will not begin to correct your dog for clipping until the end of this week's practice. For now, if he clips the jump simply reduce its height by whatever amount is necessary to eliminate the problem—usually two inches will be enough, occasionally four.

When the dog is jumping maximum height during the practice sessions, avoid working him too hard and too repetitiously.*

During the first part of this week, give the dog every chance to do the exercise perfectly: throw the dumbbell so that it lands fairly close

* Take the dog to a veterinarian if he develops a limp at any time during his training.

to the jump and he does not have to look very long for it; try to keep it centered. Several days of practicing in these conditions will be sufficient to fix the total package of retrieve over high jump in the dog's mind. Be certain to make him come in straight on his return and give him praise only after he finishes.

By the end of the week the dog should be fairly consistent, and it is then that you put him to the test. Throw the dumbbell gradually farther from the jump to increase the distance that he must run back before clearing it on his return. Many dogs will try to run around the side of the jump when the distance is increased in this fashion. If your dog tries this, you must correct him firmly and rapidly, as described in Week 7. If your dog still persists in trying to go around the jump, you will have to step in closer to the jump and work with him from this position until he is consistently going over again. After correcting the dog in this fashion, you will have to hustle to get back and have the dog come in to you to sit with the dumbbell in his mouth.

Once your dog has passed this test, complicate the exercise by throwing the dumbbell off to one side, far enough so that the dog can clearly see it *around* the side of the jump. Give him the command "Take it!" and be prepared to correct him, either in the initial going out or in the return.

If your dog is strongly tempted to go around the jump when he can see the dumbbell from his sitting position, move up a bit closer to the jump so that it is literally staring him in the face and provides a counterbalancing temptation. Give him praise if he does the exercise properly, and keep on building up distance. As you continue to practice the retrieve over high jump, most of your throws should be to the center of the training area; give him bad throws only occasionally.

Clipping   This will not only lose points for your dog in competition; it could also cause him to injure himself accidentally, either by ripping a toenail off or by knocking the jump over and landing on it. In more advanced (Utility) work, the dog must jump a bar that is lightly balanced on two thin pegs; if he knocks the bar off, he is disqualified. Finally, clipping is just one step removed from using the jump as a springboard. Unless the dog is corrected, he will begin to use the top board for leverage and simply climb over the jump. Therefore you must correct for clipping as you continue practicing the retrieve over high jump.

Dogs who jump well do one of two things to avoid clipping: either kick their back legs up as they clear the jump or tuck their legs up close to their bellies as they clear (figs. II-104–105). In other words, dogs that customarily clip the jump are allowing their hind legs to dangle when they make their final spring to clear the jump.

We have found that dogs will learn to either tuck their hind legs up or kick them out if it is made uncomfortable for them to touch the board, if there is a weird noise or a strange sensation when they do so. To accomplish this, we use springy garden rakes (the leaf-rake variety) with long, flexible tines that ping when touched by the dog's feet (fig.

196

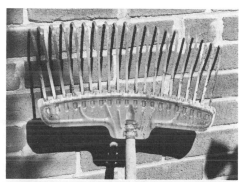

II-106. A cheap garden rake can be used to train the dog to stop clipping the jump.

II-107. Mount three of the rake heads on one of the eight-inch boards in such a way that about three or four inches of the tines stick up. Adjust the height of the jump so that the tops of the tines are at regulation height for your dog.

II-108. When the dog stops clipping the top of the jump, flip the board over so the tines are out of the way, but handy in the event that they are needed again.

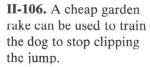

II–109

II–110

II–111

II-109. When the dog clips the tines, they will make a strange ping and provide no footing for him.

II-110. Soon the dog is jumping higher and keeping his rear feet from touching the tines. When he is doing this, flip the tines down by turning the board upside down and adjust the jump height back to regulation.

II-111. For additional safety and security, squirt a drop of silicon rubber on the tip of each tine. It is inadvisable to use lightweight portable jumps for your practice sessions. If your dog clipped and the jump were to tip over, as a lightweight jump might, and crash to the ground, the dog might develop a severe fear of the jump and refuse even to try to jump it when given the command. Should he accidentally knock over your regulation-weight jumps, it would be a good idea to place a few rocks on the base boards for greater stability.

II-106). The tines are metal, but rounded at the ends and bent over in the direction that the dog is to jump. Three of these rake heads are mounted on one of the eight-inch boards in such a way that at least three inches of the tines stick up over the top of the board—preferably more than that, because the more the tines stick up, the more flexible they are, and the smaller the opportunity for the dog to injure himself (also, the louder they ping when touched). Figure II-107 shows the arrangement of the rake tines on the board. They can be flipped over when not needed (fig. II-108) by merely inverting the board to which they are fastened. The wooden handles, incidentally, can be used as the posts for the figure-8 exercise when you work alone or as the corners for outdoor practice rings (simply pound them into the ground and tie string or light rope between them).

The first time the dog jumps the high jump and his feet touch the tines (fig. II-109), he will have an uncomfortable sensation, and the vibration they make when he touches them will produce a strange noise. After a few jumps, he will begin trying to avoid them as he clears, either by tucking his feet up close to his belly or by kicking them out and up (fig. II-110). After he has begun doing this, you might want to paint the tines a dark color, one that blends with the background of the training area (shrubs, grass), so that they are not easy for the dog to see. Later, simply flip the board that has the tines on it; they will be functionless in that position but handy if required again (fig. II-108). Should he resume clipping the jump, simply turn the board again and leave it until he learns to avoid dragging his hind legs. When you are working with the tines, adjust the height of your jump by eliminating boards.

Be sure to jump the dog first in the direction that the tines bend to avoid possible injury. Once he knows the tines are there, he will jump higher—and then you can jump him in both directions. Most dogs will clear the tines readily and easily, but some handlers might worry more than others about the remote possibility of injury. For more security and peace of mind, an additional precaution could be used: buy a tube of silicon-rubber sealer or silicon bathtub calking and put a drop of this on the end of each tine to make a soft, flexible ball (fig. II-111). The tines will still feel uncomfortable to the dog—they provide no footing or security to aid his jump—and make a weird noise, so he will still try to avoid them.

Broad Jump Further Modified

This week practice the broad jump as if you were in an AKC obedience trial. Consult Table 1 (Week 3) to determine the regulation distance your dog must jump and the number of boards he must clear, and set up the broad jump according to these specifications. The distance should be measured from the front of the first board to the back of the last board, with intermediate boards approximately equidistant from each other. Technically, you are permitted to stand anywhere between the first and last boards.

Concentrate this week on perfecting your handling in the broad

II-112. The junior author's Gus in a poor sit after clearing the broad jump. This can be corrected with the technique described in figures II-113–117 and in the text.

jump. Remember to position your dog no less than eight feet from the first obstacle and on the center line of the jump. Look him in the eye when you give the command "Over!," and do not put any body English into your command. When the dog is in the air, turn smoothly to the right, remaining within twenty-four inches from the edge of the jump as you do. Let the dog settle into his sit, pause a moment, then give the command "Heel!" Give him praise after he has finished, making sure he has sat squarely.

If your dog begins to cut corners, step into the jumps every once in a while to keep him honest—and down the center line.

Many dogs fail to sit squarely when they return to their handlers after clearing the jump, as the junior author's Gus in figure II-112. After clearing the jump in an AKC Open B trial, he made too wide a sweep to be able to come in straight—a tendency that heavier dogs are heir to, especially on indoor surfaces with poor traction.

You can improve the dog's turns and maximize the probability of a straight return by setting up a guide system along the side of the broad jump (see figs. II-113–117). Drive two stakes into the ground about twenty-four inches from the side of the jump, fastening a screw eye into each about one foot above ground level. Practice the broad jump with a conspicuous white rope stretched between the screw eyes. This will encourage the dog to make a sharper turn when he lands and come in to you straight.

After the dog has grown accustomed to jumping with the guide rope constraining the width of his return path, replace the rope with a heavy piece of nylon monofilament fishing line (about no. 20 test). Tie one end of the line to the screw eye on the far stake, and allow the other end to pass freely through the screw eye on the stake nearest you. Fasten a stick to the loose end of the nylon line so that you can conveniently grab it and lift it off the ground if the dog tries to cross it in making his turn. Running into an invisible monofilament line and hearing the snap as it is pulled taut will convince the dog that he cannot cross the barrier. After one or two attempts, he will begin to suspect that it is always there and will avoid wide turns.

The Proper Show Sequence

By this point in Open training, your dog knows all the basic exercises and is doing them all off lead. He may still be at the polishing-up stage in some of the exercises, but he should be doing all of them tolerably well—well enough to begin to practice them in the proper show sequence. Make whatever corrections are required as you practice this week, using whatever training aids (ropes, pulleys, et cetera) are necessary. After the practice sessions in show sequence, you should repeat those exercises in which your dog occasionally makes mistakes.

The proper sequence is

1. Heel Free. All speeds, all turns, plus two or more halts. Since each judge modifies the routine slightly, make sure that you mix up the turns randomly as you practice enough so that the dog does not automatically begin turning right when you pass a small maple sapling in the north corner of your back yard, for instance.

2. Figure 8. This is always the last heeling exercise.

3. Drop on Recall. This exercise is a potential point loser, even for the best of dogs. Make absolutely certain that your training routine (a) gives the dog more straight recalls than drops on recalls, which will help prevent his anticipating the drop, and (b) demands that he go down like a ton of bricks as soon as he is given the command (vocal *or* hand signal). This is accomplished by "dropping" him randomly; give the signal as soon as he takes off on some days, when he is almost to you at other times, and when he is midway in his return to you at still other times.

4. Retrieve on Flat. Continue to practice in such a way that the dumbbell lands in somewhat disadvantageous positions—off to the left or right. Make sure that you also vary the distance. It might be useful to put your dog to the test by throwing the dumbbell out increasingly long distances so that ultimately he is going out, say, twenty yards to retrieve it. If the dog plays with the dumbbell, mouths it excessively, or does not immediately pick it up, put him on lead and go back to short throws. If he still fails to pick it up immediately or if he begins to play with it, correct him smartly. The best performer is one who runs out quickly, picks the dumbbell up without sniffing around capriciously, and brings it quickly back without playing with it—in short, behaves as if the dumbbell were an important package he was sent for rather than a toy with which to amuse himself.

II-113–117: Correcting Wide Turns. **II-113.** Drive two stakes in the ground parallel to and twenty-four inches out from the line of the jumps. Stretch a white rope between the screw eyes in the stakes. (Note that the number-2 board has a white rope attached to it to encourage the dog to jump a bit higher.)

II-114. Give the command "Over!," and turn. After a few jumps the dog will begin to shorten his turn to come in straight.

II-115. Replace the white rope with a piece of heavy monofilament fishing line. Attach one end to the far stake and let the other end pass freely through the screw-eye near you. Tie the loose end to a small stick so you can conveniently pull it taut if the dog tries to cross the invisible line.

II–115

II-116. When the dog begins to come in straight, you can remove your stakes and train as before.

II-117. After a few jumps, the dog will assume that the monofilament line is always there, and will come in straight.

II–116

II–117

5. *Retrieve over High Jump*. If the dog is proficient, occasionally throw the dumbbell in such a way that he can see it around the side of the jump. Be quick to correct at any sign that he might try to go around the jump, and make certain that he continues to clear it down the center line in both directions. Vary the distance that you throw the dumbbell, getting him to be proficient at retrieving the object from as far as fifteen or twenty yards—and as close as a few feet away. In a show, especially an indoor show on a wooden or cement floor, you never know what kind of bounce you are going to get, so be sure to train your dog to expect all contingencies. However, keep working toward the ideal throw as well—the one that puts the dumbbell into a position that the dog likes and that suits his jumping pace. This is of course what you will strive for in an actual show. As in the retrieve on flat, your dog must be professional—it is an important package he is retrieving, not a toy.

6. *Broad Jump*. During your practice session, move the obstacles around in your training area so that the dog is used to seeing them in different positions, with respect to both the high jump and the boundaries of the training area. Do not let him get it into his head that the high jump and broad jump must be always located along the sides of the area, at maximum distance from each other. As a matter of fact, it might be a good idea to put them very close to each other as your dog masters the several exercises, and have him perform, for example, the retrieve on flat between the closely positioned obstacles; this will show you whether or not your dog knows the right exercise.

7. *Long Sit (Out of Sight)*. It is a good idea to give your dog a break for a few minutes between the last individual exercise (the broad jump) and the first group exercise, the Long Sit (Out of Sight). Rarely will your dog have to go immediately from his last individual exercise into the first group exercise. More often, you will have a boring wait of anywhere from half an hour to nearly two hours in big shows. Remember to tax your dog's patience, during practice and training; keep him sitting for longer than the minimum requirement of three minutes—work toward at least four. Try to put yourself into a position in which you can see your dog but he cannot see you and is not aware that you are watching him. Be prepared to go quickly back to correct him if he breaks position. You might have a friend or family member act as spy for you, relaying messages like "He went down" or "He's standing up." When working outside, make sure you do not sit your dog on top of an ant hill or briers. It is, in fact, a good idea to spray your dog with tick and flea spray before showing him in an AKC show, either indoors or outdoors; otherwise he might pick up some itchy parasites from another dog and be compelled to break his position. During the time of the year that flies and other buzzing insects might bother him, put a bit of stick insect repellent, such as 6-12 Brand, on his ears and around his eyes. Be careful not to get any into his eyes—avoid spray repellent for that reason.

8. *Long Down (Out of Sight)*. The hints we gave for the Long Sit also apply here. Build the dog up to at least six or seven minutes, and be careful about where you down him. A well-trained dog will hold

either the sit or the down for much longer than the AKC requirements; a poorly trained dog cannot be relied upon for even the minimum time. While this may seem to be a trivial exercise, it is in fact quite valuable and practical. Even the smartest individual performer will be unequivocally disqualified for breaking the Long Sit or the Long Down. It is not sufficient to have a dog that is good as an individual performer; he must be under control and under your command for the group exercises as well. See Appendix III for the Judge's Worksheet used in scoring the Long Sit and the Long Down.

After going through the above sequence daily, you will have noted the quality of your dog's performance in each of the separate exercises. If he goofed in some of them, work with him a few minutes after going through the show routine, but give him a break between the last exercise and the touch-up training. By the end of the week you will have the sequence down pat and should move from one exercise to the next without having to consult the text for the order. Remember, in an AKC Open class you cannot touch your dog's collar to *lead* him to the new area, as you were permitted to do in Novice, or physically adjust his position once there. You can, however, praise your dog by patting him—with moderation—after each exercise is declared finished.

OPEN WEEK 9

OUTLINE OF TRAINING SCHEDULE
Old Exercises
    Novice
        Straight Recall Combined with Open Drop on Recall
Modification of Open Exercises for Show Ring Practice
    Exposing Dog to New Training Areas and Adverse Conditions
        (Practice all exercises under simulated show conditions at least
            three times this week, in three different areas, with an assistant
            to act as judge. Correct immediately for major errors—wandering, failing to perform an exercise on one command—but
            not for minor ones—slightly crooked sit, et cetera.)
New Exercise
    Simulating Show Conditions
Suggested Length of Practice Session: 20 minutes daily

Exposing Dog to New Training Areas
Week 9 will be devoted mainly to reinforcing and perfecting your dog's training, and to conditioning him to go through the show routine in new   205

surroundings. As at the end of Novice training, you should engage a friend to act as judge. That is, you will have to practice with your dog in different training areas each practice session and simulate show conditions by having a second party give the commands. This will expose your dog to new sights, sounds, and odors, providing the kind of distractions you would encounter in an actual show. Ideally, you should work indoors in several different areas as well, but this is usually a bit more inconvenient than finding an available outside training area. If you have friends who train dogs in their basements or garages, perhaps you can arrange to alternate training areas so as to give everyone's dog exposure to new practice areas.

Outdoor shows provide the most diverse and trying conditions: rain, thunder, wind, excessive heat, blaring loudspeakers, active children, oestral dog odors, buzzing insects, rough ground surface, noise from other exhibitions or amusement parks nearby. . . . The American Kennel Club does *not* have the responsibility of ensuring that competitive dog shows be held in the most favorable circumstances. Local show committees pick their show sites for a number of reasons; often, if the show is a combined breed and obedience trial, little concern is shown for the obedience component of the show.

Indoor shows are not devoid of problems either, the major one being noise: while the dogs perform, blaring public address systems squeal and pop because they have not been adjusted properly; large pieces of equipment are banged around, and boards or props are dropped near the obedience ring. We once saw an akita who was earning a near-perfect score disqualify because some workers dropped a set of jumps just as his handler gave the command "Come!" for the recall: the dog did not hear the command because of the noise of the crash. On another occasion, Gus, the junior author's dog, disqualified in a Utility show because a loudspeaker, located immediately over his head, went on at precisely the moment the down hand signal was given. Gus jerked his head up to identify the noise and, of course, missed seeing the hand signal.

In both indoor and outdoor shows, your obedience ring may be adjacent to a ring where a breed show is being conducted. If your dog has to go near the edge of the ring while performing an exercise, half a dozen breed dogs may yap at him (something that obedience-trained dogs will not—or should not—do). Or, your dog might be in a sit-stay near the ring where breed dogs are being trotted in a circle; if he succumbs to the temptation to turn and watch them, he could easily miss a signal. Of course an adjacent obedience ring will also provide temptations and distractions. For example, your dog might hear a "Come!" or "Down!" from the next ring and forget that *he* is doing the Long Sit.

It should be clear that to maximize your dog's chances for success in competition, you must expose him to increasingly disadvantageous conditions during the final phase of training. Working him in new places will prepare him for the contingencies described above. There is, however, one problem that no amount of training will overcome: fleas and ticks. Remember to spray your dog with flea-and-tick compound immediately prior to entering a show area (an hour or two before his event is sufficient lead time).

Training in the rain is essential if you plan to show your dog in an area where rain is a common occurrence during the outdoor show season. Shows are not canceled because of rain; your dog must be trained to sustain the minor discomfort of sitting on wet ground for three minutes or working smartly in a drizzle. The senior author's shepherd, Baron, once competed in an outdoor show that was held on low-lying ground during a heavy downpour. Very few dogs qualified in that show, but Baron was among them—even though he had to perform the Long Down in two inches of water. Some of our students competed in an outdoor show during a blustery rainstorm. The stewards and judges were wearing ponchos to keep dry, and the wind kept whipping the tails of their garments around. A good many dogs disqualified because they were intimidated and frightened by the flapping rain gear while doing the Figure 8 around the stewards.

Build up your dog's resistance to distraction *gradually:* do not suddenly toss him from the idyllic circumstances of his back yard or basement into a tempest to try his mettle. Practice in or near a schoolyard while children are playing and shouting, for instance, or in a large parking lot near traffic noises, or any strange new place where tempting odors and animal scents of diverse and exotic nature attract his attention as much as a command from his master.

Simulating Show Conditions

It is important to train during Week 9 with an assistant who will act out the role of both judge and steward. With a good sales pitch, you can persuade your assistant to read this section of Week 9 training to get an idea of judgelike behavior. To approximate more closely the kinds of circumstances you will confront in an actual show, it would be a good idea to conduct your training in a regulation-size practice ring (fig. II-118). You can use your rake handles or broomsticks as corner posts, and your training.ropes as boundaries for the ring. Select a suitable park, neighbor's yard, or golf course for your training area.

In Open competition, you should enter the show ring with your dog on lead and the dumbbell in your hand. You will normally halt as soon as you step into the ring (spot A in fig. II-118) and wait for the judge to instruct you, with your dog sitting in the proper heeling position. Very likely the steward, your assistant in this case, will ask you how high your dog jumps in the Retrieve over High Jump and how far he jumps in the Broad Jump. If your dog jumps less than thirty-six inches for the High Jump, the judge or steward will measure him at the withers to determine precisely what he must jump (fig. II-68 shows how this is done). If the judge tells you that he wants to measure your dog, put him into a stand and give him the command "Stay!" You are not being judged at this point, so you can use double signals if necessary and your dog can be on lead. When the judge or steward asks you for your lead, unsnap it and hand it to him, along with the dumbbell.

Have your assistant measure your dog (or merely go through the motions of measuring him) just to accustom the dog to show procedure.

Heel Free and Figure 8. After measuring your dog, your assistant will take the lead and dumbbell and instruct you to take your position for the Heel Free exercise.

JUDGE'S COMMANDS TO YOU FOR HEEL FREE
1. Forward
2. Halt
3. Forward
4. Right turn
5. Left turn
6. About turn
7. Slow
8. Normal
9. Fast
10. Normal
11. Halt
12. Exercise finished

JUDGE'S COMMANDS TO YOU FOR FIGURE 8 COMPONENT OF HEEL FREE
1. Forward
2. Halt
3. Forward
4. Halt
5. Exercise finished

On figure II-118, your initial position for this exercise could be point B. Come to a halt facing the opposite end of the ring, with your dog in the normal heeling position. Your assistant will then ask "Are you ready?" You are not officially under judgment until you nod affirmatively or say "Yes." Before you respond, make sure your dog is sitting squarely; if he is not, say "No," give the heel command, make an about turn, and again come to a halt with your dog at your side; you may pat your leg to get him straight, but you may *not* touch his collar or adjust him physically by pushing, pulling, or bumping with your leg. Once you are ready, your assistant gives you the command "Forward!" Give the dog's name and the command "Heel!" * Step off on your left foot without looking at the dog, and walk at a normal pace until the judge says "Halt!" This will usually be after about five or ten paces. Try to come to a gradual halt; if you stop suddenly, your dog may overshoot you and sit too far out in front. The next command will be another "Forward!" As before, give the dog's name and the command "Heel!" The heeling course the judge will ask you to follow from this point on varies from show to show, although the judge will use the same pattern for all contestants. Watch the people who show their dogs before you, therefore, to see what pattern to expect when it is your turn. The usual sequence is (1) right or about turn; (2) slow; (3) normal; (4) fast; (5) normal; and (6) several turns, including left and right. The

* We do not encourage our students to use the dog's name before any "Stay!"

command.

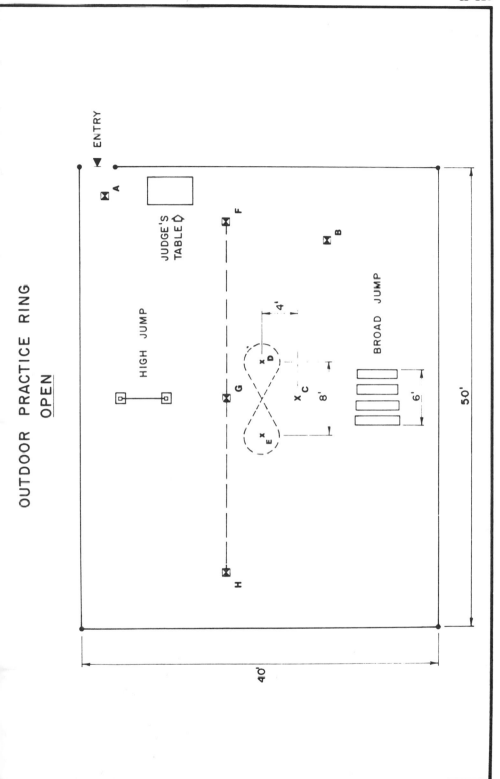

OUTDOOR PRACTICE RING
OPEN

ENTRY

JUDGE'S TABLE

HIGH JUMP

BROAD JUMP

4'

8'

6'

50'

40'

judge normally has you come to your final halt somewhere near the spot where you must do the Figure 8 exercise, usually near point C on figure II-118. When he says "Exercise finished!" you may praise your dog, including a pat on the head or chest. The judge will then call for the stewards to function as the points around which you will perform the Figure 8—they will stand, facing each other, at points D and E on figure II-118. In Open competition you are not allowed to touch the dog or his collar to move him from one exercise to the next. Thus, after the first part of the Heel Free is finished, you may give multiple verbal and leg-pat commands to get your dog into position for the Figure 8, but you may not adjust him physically.

The judge will inform you that you will be doing the Figure 8 exercise and, usually, that you may turn in either direction once you give the initial "Heel!" If he does not so inform you, assume that you may turn in either direction.

Line up your dog so that he is on the center line between the two stewards, and stand in the normal heeling position about four feet away from them (point X on fig. II-118). When the judge has ascertained that you are ready, he will give you the command "Forward!" You will be instructed to come to at least two halts as you execute the Figure 8. Walk at a constant pace throughout the routine, without looking at your dog and without adjusting your pace to fit his. At the second halt, you can expect the judge to tell you that the exercise is finished. You can then praise your dog, but not so much that you get him excited and tempt him to move out of position.

Drop on Recall. In this exercise the judge (your assistant) instructs you to take up a position at one of the extreme ends of the ring (point F or point H on fig. II-118). You will bring your dog into the normal heeling position facing the opposite end of the ring.

JUDGE'S COMMANDS TO YOU FOR DROP ON RECALL
1. Leave your dog
2. Call your dog
3. Drop your dog (or the judge will explain what to do)
4. Call your dog
5. Finish
6. Exercise finished

Either before or after you are positioned, the judge will explain to you where he wants you to drop your dog. ("Drop him opposite the High Jump," for example, or "Drop him when I give you the hand signal to drop him.") The rules regarding this exercise are currently in a state of flux; some judges will inform you that the point they designate is where they want the dog to end up. Others will tell you that they want you to *give the signal* at that spot. You may—and you should—ask the judge what he wants. The present change in judging on this point has to do with the fact that some dogs take a long time to drop, and others go down like a lead shot as soon as they are given the signal. Thus, some handlers have to give a "Down!" to the dog almost im-

II-119. Handler Kathy Olsen heeling
her Labrador, Nemo, in an Open trial
while Judge Charles LeBoutillier in
spects the performance.

II-120. Harry Holmes and his poodle,
Creme Puff, going through a Figure 8
while Judge Carson observes. This
team is tough to beat, and you will see
them frequently in East Coast shows.

211

mediately after he begins his return; other handlers have trained their dogs so well that they will obey immediately on seeing or hearing the down command. The position the judge usually indicates is point G on figure II-118. However, he may choose to have you drop the dog either before or after that point, so pay attention to his instructions.

When you have been informed by the judge about the procedure he wants you to follow, and after he has ascertained that you are ready, the judge will say "Leave your dog!" You may give the simultaneous hand and verbal signal (but not the dog's name). Walk to the opposite end of the ring and turn to face your dog.

The next command from the judge will be "Call your dog!" You may call him with *either* the hand signal *or* the verbal command ("Come!").* Your dog must come swiftly to you in a straight line and show no indication of anticipating the drop signal or command. This is why we emphasized mixing up the straight Recall with the Drop on Recall during your training, and worked on the drop as a separate exercise. You are permitted to give your dog only one signal to go down (verbal or hand). After the dog goes down, the judge will pause a moment and then instruct you, "Call your dog." You may use the verbal command (preceded by the dog's name) or the hand signal. The dog should come briskly in to you, sit squarely at your feet facing you, and neither be so close as to touch you, nor so far away as to cause you to stretch out to touch his head. The judge will then instruct you to "Finish!"; you may use the hand signal (described in the next chapter) or the verbal command "Heel!" When the judge informs you that the "Exercise is finished," praise your dog and be prepared to heel him away, without touching his collar, to the spot where the Retrieve on Flat exercise begins.

Retrieve on Flat. As in the previous exercise, you will be positioned at either point F or point H, facing the opposite end of the ring; the judge (or steward) will hand you your dumbbell as you go to that spot or, occasionally, after you have got there.

JUDGE'S COMMANDS TO YOU FOR RETRIEVE ON FLAT
1. Throw it
2. Send your dog
3. Take it
4. Finish
5. Exercise finished

The judge will determine if you are ready; if you are, he will say "Throw it!" You should have the dumbbell in your right hand at this point, but transfer it to your left as soon as you hear the command. Then give the verbal and hand signals for stay with your right hand, take the dumbbell back into your right hand, and toss it out toward the

* The hand signal to come is taught in Week 7 of Utility training. We mention it here because you may see it being used if you go to shows. Later, when you are competing in Utility, you may also want to be showing your dog in Open B trials. If so, to be consistent, you will probably want to use only the hand signal in the Open B trials as well as in Utility.

II-121. Another excellent team of competitors, Russell Klipple and his golden retriever, Tonka. In this Drop on Recall the handler has given a hand signal for the dog to drop.

II-122. Retrieve on Flat. Tonka is an excellent worker and rarely finishes out of the top four places—and usually winds up with first place.

II-123. The junior author and his shepherd, Gus. Judge Carson carefully observes the Retrieve over High Jump.

opposite end of the ring; try to get it to roll to a stop at a comfortable distance—five to ten feet—from the far barrier. If your dumbbell goes too far or too short to suit the judge, he will walk out, pick it up, and give it back to you. You may give the command "Stay!" a second time if this happens, and then throw the dumbbell. If it lands in a position that is suitable to the judge, he will say "Send your dog!" You then give the command "Take it!" The dog should run straight for the dumbbell, pick it up firmly in his mouth, and run straight back to you without pausing, playing with it, or dropping it. He should sit squarely in front of you, waiting for your next command. The judge will then say "Take it!" Give the command "Out!" and remove the dumbbell from the dog's mouth, using both hands. At this, the judge will say "Finish!" Your response? "Heel!" Then praise.

Retrieve over High Jump. As soon as you have been informed that the previous exercise is finished, you should heel over to about ten feet away from the High Jump and come to a halt with your dog centered on the jump. Get him straight, without touching his collar, and wait for the judge's "Are you ready?"

JUDGE'S COMMANDS TO YOU FOR RETRIEVE OVER HIGH JUMP
1. Throw it
2. Send your dog
3. Take it
4. Finish
5. Exercise finished

When you indicate you are ready, the judge will say "Throw it!" Give the simultaneous hand and verbal stay commands, as you did for the Retrieve on Flat, and throw the dumbbell over the High Jump, trying to have it come to rest about ten feet away from the jump and near the center line. Wait. The judge will then tell you: "Send your dog!" Say "Take it!" and remain motionless until the dog clears the jump, picks up the dumbbell, comes back over the jump, and sits squarely in front of you with the dumbbell between his jaws. When the judge says "Take it!," remove the dumbbell with the command "Out!" The judge's "Finish!" follows, and then the indication that the exercise is over.

The Broad Jump. After you have praised your dog for the Retrieve over High Jump, immediately heel him over to the Broad Jump, coming to the normal heeling position about ten feet from the first obstacle.

JUDGE'S COMMANDS TO YOU FOR BROAD JUMP
1. Leave your dog
2. Send him
3. Finish
4. Exercise finished

When you have indicated that you are ready, the judge will say "Leave your dog!" Give the verbal and hand stay signals and walk over to the side of the Broad Jump, positioning yourself somewhere between the

II-124. AKC judges are often competitors in shows themselves. Here Judge Carson's shepherd clears the Broad Jump straight down the center line. (The 1975 rules do not permit a handler to hold his hands in front of his body.)

II-125. Long Sit, Out of Sight.

II-126. Long Down, Out of Sight. Note that the dogs are all looking toward the area where their handlers have been taken by one of the stewards. Judge LeBoutillier is probably marking "Failed" on his worksheet for the schnauzer that has broken, while Steward Lester Talley stands ready to intercept any other dog that might try to wander away or pester another dog.

215

first and last boards and no more than twenty-four inches away from the line of the jumps. On the judge's command "Send him!," face your dog and give the command "Over!" When the dog is in mid-flight over the jumps, turn 90° to face the opposite end of the jump. The dog must turn on landing, come in to you, and sit squarely at your feet. The next command from the judge will be "Finish!," at which you give the command "Heel!" When he announces that the exercise is over, you can heel out of the ring. As you leave, pick up your lead and dumbbell from the steward. Do not touch your dog's collar until you are out of the ring.

The Group Exercises. At this juncture in an obedience trial you might have to wait for an hour or more for the Group Exercises (Long Sit and Long Down, both with the handlers out of sight) to begin.

JUDGE'S COMMANDS TO YOU FOR GROUP EXERCISES

Long Sit	*Long Down*
1. Sit your dogs	1. Down your dogs
2. Leave your dogs	2. Leave your dogs
3. Back to your dogs	3. Back to your dogs
4. Exercise finished	4. Exercise finished

For your practice sessions this week, you may simply go through the exercises as though they were individual routines, but if you have friends who are training their dogs, you should practice with them. At this time your dog needs fairly rigorous exposure to the temptations he will encounter in competition to break from the Sit and Down. Working with inexperienced dogs, or dogs that are just beginning to learn obedience routines, would be highly desirable—provided their handlers do not allow the Novice dogs to take such advantage of your dog's stoic maintenance of position that he is forced to move in self-defense.

Further Training Hints for Open

Try to work under show conditions, with an assistant to give the commands, at least three times a week from now on—until your dog has earned the C.D.X. degree and begins Utility training. It is important at this time to increase your dog's reliability and selectivity in responding to commands. He is highly trained, and is listening and looking for commands. You will be competing under circumstances where people in the next ring will be giving loud commands to their dogs, and you do not want your dog to respond to them. There are also, of course, the occasional jerks, poor sports, and pranksters in the audience who try to trick your dog into obeying their capricious commands. Your dog might be in a Long Sit when a loud "Down!" is given nearby. To prevent his responding in such a situation, you must work with him and an accomplice: put him into a sit-stay and leave him, walking away about ten feet. Have your assistant say either "Down!" or "Come!," using your dog's name as part of the temptation, from somewhere off to one side or behind you. If the dog responds to the assistant's command, quickly move in to him, correct him smartly, and after bopping his nose, return to your original position. Repeat it until the dog will respond only to *your* command. Praise him enthusiastically if he catches on and obeys your command, ignoring the assistant's. Similarly, try to have your friend tempt your dog to go down during a Long Sit by giving a hand signal. If your dog goes down, correct as before.

A Note About Competition

You are eligible to compete in Open A until you actually receive your C.D.X. degree from the AKC; thus, if you are scheduled to show your dog in five Open A trials and you earn your C.D.X. by qualifying in the first three, you can still go through the next two unless they are months away. After you receive your dog's C.D.X. diploma in the mail, you must then enter him in Open B competition in all subsequent shows. If you wish, you may enter your dog in Open B trials to earn a leg toward the C.D.X. degree (if, for example, the Open A judge in a show you plan to attend also served as judge in a previous Open A trial in which you earned a leg toward the degree). But be advised that the competition is much tougher than in Open A. Even though the exercises are identical to those in Open A, in Open B you will frequently be competing with dogs who have earned the C.D.X. and even the U.D., as well as dogs being handled by AKC judges and professional handlers. That is, the distinction between Open A and Open B is not quite the same as that between Novice A and Novice B, in that dogs may continue indefinitely in Open B after earning the C.D.X. degree.

It is a good idea to continue to compete in Open trials while you are training your dog for Utility competition. This keeps him in condition and keeps you in the proper state of concern to train faithfully and regularly. However, do not begin your training for Utility until your dog has finished the C.D.X. requirements by qualifying in three Open shows.

OPEN WEEK 10

OUTLINE OF TRAINING SCHEDULE
Old Exercises
    Novice
        Straight Recall Combined with Drop on Recall
Modification of Open Exercises
        Continue to work in practice ring, at least three times a week, until you enter your first show
        Concentrate on handler's errors; review Judge's Worksheet as you practice each exercise
Suggested Length of Practice Session: Once daily for Week 10; then every other day until you enter your first show

Eliminating Handler's Errors

By this time you should know whether or not you want to go on to Utility training. If you do, plan ahead as you reach the end of your Open work by obtaining the basic equipment you will need: a set of scent articles and a bar jump.*

While we have given many general instructions during the training in Open exercises regarding proper handling, we have not focused on handling as such. Judging in Open competition is somewhat more rigorous than it is in Novice, and the handler can disqualify himself and the dog quite easily. It is important, therefore, during the final phase of training and touching up, to concentrate on handler tactics and potential errors.

For example, as distinct from Novice competition, a handler in Open *cannot* touch his dog's collar between exercises. When one exercise finishes and another is to begin in a different area of the ring, the handler must merely give the command "Heel!" and walk over to the area designated by the judge, without grabbing the dog's collar. The handler may give the same command twice and may also use both voice and hand signals repetitively to get the dog into a proper and desirable position for the next exercise—but he must not bring the dog over by pulling on the collar. Thus, between exercises, you could get your dog into a straight sit by saying "Heel!" and patting your leg to encourage him to move in closer. It is extremely important to begin each exercise with the dog in the appropriate heeling position—when the judge asks "Are you ready?," the dog must be in the proper starting position if the handler's answer is "Yes!" If the dog is sitting crooked, the judge will subtract points immediately.

During the tenth week and in the time immediately prior to competing in Open, concentrate on the dog's sits and make certain that each exercise is initiated from the proper position. If the dog is not in a satisfactory sit in the show ring, it is legitimate to give a heel command, turn around, and then return to the position previously indicated by the judge. This maneuver must of course be done before you reply affirmatively to the judge's question "Are you ready?" Excessive repetition might be considered as practicing in the ring and constitute grounds for disqualification, but a reasonable judge will warn a handler who does this too often or unnecessarily.

To avoid such pitfalls, you should practice intensively on the heeling exercises during the days immediately prior to a show, putting the dog back on lead if his sits are crooked or if he hesitates to sit when you come to a halt. The dog should be constantly aware of your position; if you move, he must go into an automatic sit—straight—as soon as you come to a standstill. This practice will prevent your having to give double commands in the ring between exercises—and the dog will always look sharp.

* See Appendix II for magazines that advertise ready-made scent articles and bar jumps. Scent articles can sometimes be purchased or ordered at concession stands at the larger dog shows. You may prefer to construct your own bar jump; see Appendix IV for design.

OBEDIENCE JUDGE'S WORKSHEET

For Judge's Use ONLY – Not to be distributed or shown to exhibitors

DATE . . . .   OPEN . . . . . . CLASS   DOG No. . . . .
                                                    (A or B)

SHOW . . . .   BREED . . . . HEIGHT . . . . JUMPS . . . .
                                                                                    At Withers

EXERCISE	NON QUALIFYING		QUALIFYING		Maximum Points	Points Off	NET SCORE
	ZERO	LESS THAN 50%	SUBSTANTIAL	MINOR			
HEEL FREE AND FIGURE 8	Unmanageable ... ☐ Unqualified heeling ☐	Handler continually adapts pace to dog ☐ Leaving handler ... ☐	Heeling Fig. 8 ☐ ... Improper heel position .... ☐ Forging .. ☐ Crowding handler . ☐ Lagging.......... ☐ Sniffing ☐ ....Extra command to heel ..... ☐ Heeling wide ☐ on turns ☐ abouts ☐ No change of pace ☐ fast ☐ slow ☐ ...... No sit ... Poor sits ... ☐ ☐ . Lacks naturalness smoothness ☐		40		
DROP ON RECALL	Does not come on first command or signal .... ☐ Does not drop on first command or signal .... ☐	Extra com. or sig. to stay after handler leaves ... ☐ Moved from place left .... ☐ Anticipated: Recall .... ☐ Drop .... ☐ Come in ...... ☐ Sat out of reach ☐	☐ Stood or lay down Touching handler ☐ ☐ Extra com. or signal Sat between feet ☐ before leaving Poor sit ☐ ☐ Slow response Poor finish ..... ☐ ☐ Slow return Lack of naturalness ☐ Slow drop smoothness ....☐ ☐ No sit in front ☐ No finish		30		
RETRIEVE ON FLAT	Fails to go out on first command or signal .... ☐ Fails to retrieve . ☐	Goes before command or signal ... ☐ Extra command or signal .... ☐ Sat out of reach ☐	. Slow ... ☐ Going ... ☐ Returning . ☐ ....Mouthing or Playing .... ☐ Dropping dumbbell Touching handler ☐ Poor delivery Sat between feet ☐ No sit in front Poor sit ☐ No finish Poor finish ..... ☐ Handler error		20		
RETRIEVE OVER HIGH JUMP	Fails to go out on first command or signal .... ☐ Fails to jump going and returning .... ☐ Fails to retrieve . ☐	Goes before command or signal ... ☐ Jumps only one direction .... ☐ Sat out of reach .. ☐ Extra command or signal .... ☐	Slow ....☐ Going ... ☐ Returning ... ☐ .... Mouthing or Playing .... ☐ Dropping dumbbell Touching handler .. ☐ Poor delivery Sat between feet .. ☐ Climbing jump Poor sit ☐ No sit in front Poor finish .... ☐ No finish Handler error		30		
BROAD JUMP	Refuses to jump on first command or signal .... ☐ Walks over any part ☐	Goes before command or signal ... ☐ Does not clear jump ☐ Sat out of reach ... ☐	Minor jump touch Touching handler .. ☐ Poor return Sat between feet .. ☐ No sit in front Poor sit ... ☐ No finish Poor finish .... ☐		20		
				MAX. SUB-TOTAL ➡	150		
LONG SIT (3 Minutes)	Did not remain in place .... ☐ Goes to another dog .... ☐	Stood or lay down before handler returns .... ☐ Repeated whines or barks .... ☐	☐ Forced into position Minor move after ☐ Minor move before handler returns handler returns to heel position .. ☐ ☐ Minor whine or bark Handler error .... ☐		30		
LONG DOWN (5 Minutes)	Did not remain in place .... ☐ Goes to another dog .... ☐	Stood or sat before handler returns ,, ☐ Repeated whines or barks .... ☐	☐ Forced into position Minor move after ☐ Minor move before handler returns handler returns to heel position.. ☐ ☐ Minor whine or bark Handler error .... ☐		30		
				MAXIMUM POINTS ➡	200		

☐ H. Disciplining ☐ Shows fear ☐ Fouling ring ☐ Disqualified ☐ Expelled ☐ Excused   Less Penalty for ➡
 Unusual Behavior

TOTAL NET SCORE ➡

II-128. Gus, ready for a runoff in
Open A competition. He won it in
the first "Halt!" given by the judge
—he sat down slightly faster than
his competition. One contributing
factor to your success in Open competition could be your dog's skill in
a runoff. Be sure to sharpen up his
heeling especially; in the event you
must break a tie, the runoff will
always be a Heel Free exercise.

In Week 10 of Novice, we discussed a number of common handler's errors and judge's miscalculations; it would be a good idea to review that material also before showing your dog in Open competition.

Common Handler's Errors in the Open Show Ring Finger snapping to keep the dog's attention focused on the handler is a habit that many inexperienced (and often experienced) handlers fall into as they train. This is a disqualifying handler's error. Concentrate on eliminating it if you catch yourself doing it during practice sessions.

In fact, any kind of peculiar, unnecessary, or unconscious body movement on the part of the handler can be—and frequently is—inter-preted by the judge as a signal to the dog. For example, you have put the dog into a sit-stay for the Drop on Recall and you walk to the other end of the ring. A fly lands on your ear and you unconsciously shake your head or raise your hand to brush it away. You could be disquali-fied for that. Or, if you elect to call the dog by using a hand signal for the Recall portion and *lean forward* slightly as you give it, you would be penalized. Finishes are also fraught with possibilities for unconscious handler's errors. On giving the dog the command "Heel!," many handlers unconsciously turn or jerk their heads in the direction they expect the dog to move as he finishes. This is a double signal

Common forms of body English that tend to become unconscious habits for some people are flexing at the knees as the dog is clearing a jump, adjusting to the dog's position during heeling or sitting exercises, moving one's head in the direction the dog is supposed to be moving, and unconsciously clenching and opening one's hands.

Because a handler is often completely unaware of his own behavior, it is good practice to have a friend observe carefully and critically as you work your dog during the last week or two of preparation for competition. You can make a list of handler's errors for the friend, concentrating on those you suspect you are guilty of.

During training, some handlers fall into the habit of talking to their dogs. Under the strain of an AKC show, this habit has an unsettling tendency to surface, and judges could easily interpret your mumbling to yourself or your dog as giving a double signal.

The most instructive way to make yourself aware of point-losing handler's errors is to review carefully the Judge's Worksheet for Open (fig. II-127). Note also the kinds of errors that the *dog* can make in each of the exercises. In short, as you brush up your dog and your handling prior to entering an Open show, pay careful attention to the items listed in the Worksheet for each exercise.

Scoring principles are the same in Open as in Novice trials: your dog must earn at least 170 points to qualify, with more than 50 per cent of the score for each individual exercise. Our students usually move on to Utility very quickly, since most of them take their dogs through the C.D.X. degree in three to five shows. If you have trained properly, your dog should do as well.

III
THE
UTILITY
EXERCISES

Toward the Ph.D. Degree:
Utility Dog

UTILITY WEEK 1

OUTLINE OF TRAINING SCHEDULE
Old Exercises
    Novice
        Long Stand (to be incorporated into Utility training)
    Open. Practice all in show sequence.
        Advanced Heeling: Concentrate on improving side steps and
            pivots in place—essentials for Utility directed retrieve
New Exercises
    The Seek Back (to preadapt for scent discrimination)
    Signal Exercise: Finish
    Pivots to Left and Right in a 360° Arc
Suggested Practice Session: Once daily

Note. It is difficult to recommend an ideal length of time at this level of obedience. If you continue to show your dog in Open B trials, you must keep him in show form *and* train him for Utility, which could easily add up to an hour a day. We suggest that you eliminate the long sit and long down of Open as you train for Utility, unless you have Open B shows scheduled. Utility training could easily take twenty to thirty minutes each session.

Utility competition leads, after three successful shows, to the Utility Dog (U.D.) degree. It is the most difficult obedience degree to attain— very few dogs do so in the theoretical minimum of three shows. The exercises are sufficiently demanding and complicated that a dog can easily make a disqualifying error. The judging is more rigorous: slight handler's errors that may have been overlooked by judges in Novice or Open competition are rarely overlooked in Utility. The Utility judge expects a high-quality performance from both dog and handler. Your training sessions should be undertaken at the outset with these facts firmly in mind.

You should not begin your formal Utility training program until your dog has successfully finished his last leg in Open competition. If you are moving swiftly through the sequence of AKC degrees, the addition of new routines and exercises at a time when the dog is still competing for a degree might interfere with his success in the Open competition. However, after your dog has attained a C.D.X. degree, the risks of his disqualifying at an Open B trial are outweighed by the possible advantage of earning a Highest Scoring Dog in Trial.

While there is some continuation and extension of the general skills acquired during Novice and Open, most of the Utility exercises are totally new. The fact that there is an overlap makes it wise and prudent to practice the basics of Open and Novice while you are training for Utility, especially the Novice and Open heeling exercises and the Open jumping. You should, in short, regularly practice the complete Novice routine and the complete Open routine to keep your dog in
224   good form for these previously acquired skills—the weekly outlines will

draw your attention to this. You will probably find that your dog will do the Novice and Open exercises much more proficiently than he did earlier, and his proficiency, rewarded by your praise, will add to his confidence as he learns the new Utility routines.

The exercises for Utility competition can be briefly described, in proper show sequence, as follows.

1. *Signal Exercises.* Your dog will have to do a heeling routine on hand signals only, it is done absolutely silently. The dog must heel on command, stand on command, lie down on command, sit up on command, come to you on command, and finish on command. The commands, we repeat, are all hand signals.

2. *Scent Discrimination.* Your dog will be expected to find an article that you touched with your hand out of a set of similar articles, ten in all. Five are made of leather and five of metal. If you have not already ordered these, as we suggested in Week 10 of Open training, you should do so now (see Appendix II). One type of scent article is shown in figure III-1.

3. *Directed Retrieve.* Your dog will have to retrieve one of three cotton work gloves that have been placed by the official in both corners and the middle of the narrow end of the ring. You and your dog will be located between the two jumps, somewhere near the middle of the ring (fig. III-2) initially with your back to the gloves. The judge will instruct you to send your dog to retrieve one of the three gloves—it could be any one of the three. Ordinary white cotton gloves are used; they can be obtained at any hardware store.

4. *Directed Jumping.* Your dog must jump, in turn, two obstacles: the solid high jump, used during the Open exercises, and a new jump called the bar jump (fig. III-2).* These are located about midway along the long axis of the ring. You and your dog are at one end, facing the jumps; the dog must run to the opposite end of the ring between the jumps ("Go out!"), turn, sit facing you, and, on your command, jump the obstacle that you point to. Before you give the jump command, the judge will tell you which object he wants the dog to jump first. Since this will usually be the one that is least favorably situated with respect to the dog, your dog will be much better off if he is in the middle, and sitting straight. When the dog has jumped, returned to you and finished, the judge will indicate that he must clear the second obstacle, whereupon you will repeat the above procedure.

5. *The Group Examination.* This is the only group exercise in Utility competition and it is always done last. No less than six or more than fifteen dogs are called into the ring. You stand (or pose) your dog somewhere near the center line of the ring, on a line indicated by the judge, and leave him at the judge's instruction, walking to the opposite side of the ring. The dog must remain standing for a minimum of three minutes, but it could be as long as five or six minutes. As the judge examines each in turn, the dogs must not show resentment, growl, move their feet, or sit down (fig. III-3 shows a group stand practice session).

* See Appendix II for magazines that advertise ready-made bar jumps. See Appendix IV for the jump plans, if you prefer to construct it yourself.

III-1. Scent discrimination. Your dog must find one article of leather and one of metal from a total of ten similar articles. A pair of canning tongs is useful in your training, for you can handle the articles without putting your scent on them. Generally, they will be placed between the two jumps in an AKC show.

Although these exercises might seem simple as you read them, they are actually highly complicated, precise forms of behavior. The training is tougher than anything you have done in Open, and it depends on a firm grasp of all previous work. Unless you have followed our program closely, you might find yourself having to go back to the Open or Novice section; those of you who used a different method to train your dogs through Open should definitely read chapters I and II of this book thoroughly before attempting to jump into chapter III.

We are presenting the Utility training program in a ten-week sequence, but many dogs require a longer period to develop the consistency of performance called for in competition. There is no simple way to provide a fixed schedule for Utility training, since we cannot predict when a dog will master the new and complicated exercises. There are too many variables: the effectiveness with which you trained your dog in the basics; the amount of time you devote to practice; the kind of relationship you have with your dog; and, to a minor extent, his trainability both as an individual and as a breed representative. At an obedience trial there are noticeably more breeds represented in Novice competition than in Utility; two breeds that regularly appear in Utility competition are German shepherds and poodles. This is not to say that they are the most desirable dogs for this kind of competition, merely that they are very heavily represented. Table 3 is a summary of performance in obedience trials by several breeds of dogs.

TABLE 3

A. Top 10 Breeds in Utility by Frequency of U.D. Titles Awarded in 1973, Compared with Frequency of C.D.X. and C.D. Titles

Breed	U.D.	C.D.X.	C.D.
1. German Shepherd	116	313	1276
2. Poodle	77	194	607
3. Shetland Sheep Dog	39	187	602
4. Golden Retriever	30	94	411
5. Doberman Pinscher	15	90	451
6. Irish Setter	14	65	372
7. Miniature Schnauzer	11	45	131
8. Labrador Retriever	10	47	226
9. Welsh Corgi (Pembroke)	9	20	71
10. English Springer Spaniel	8	31	111

B. Frequency of U.D., C.D.X. and C.D. Titles Awarded Among All Breeds for 1971, 1972 and 1973

	1973	1972	1971
U.D.	443	384	319
C.D.X.	1546	1337	1218
C.D.	6930	5955	5599

By Maureen Setter, from *Off-Lead*, 1974, no. 7, pp. 16–17.

III-2. The directed retrieve begins between the two jumps, on the center line of the ring. The three cotton gloves are at the end of the ring, behind the handler, one to the left, one in the center, and one to the right. The judge will designate which glove your dog must retrieve by the commands "Number 1" (the one on your left after you pivot around to face the gloves), or "Number 2," or "Number 3."

III-3. The group examination is the only group exercise in Utility competition. Appendix III shows the Judge's Worksheet used in scoring dogs during this exercise—examine it carefully. The dogs must stand motionless while being examined, in turn. Theoretically, the minimum time is three minutes, but it could last longer. The handlers are at the edge of the ring, facing their dogs; the dogs are positioned somewhere near the center of the ring.

Thus, as you enter Utility training you are entering a rigorous and demanding enterprise. You will need some additional equipment:

- A set of scent articles and canning tongs (fig. III-1)
- A new jump—the bar jump
- Three cotton gloves (white work gloves), and one old leather glove
- A hundred-foot length of rope, and a fifty-foot length of lighter-weight rope
- One simple pulley attached to a stake (or auger-type dog anchor) that is driven into the ground
- An auger-type dog anchor, or stake (fig. II-74)

One final point. You may continue to show your dog in Open B, *not* Open A, after he has earned the C.D.X. degree. Thus you can maintain an active show schedule, if you wish, while you are preparing your dog for Utility competition. We recommend, however, that you refrain from this as your training in Utility comes to a close; there will be quite enough to concentrate on in perfecting the new material.

The Seek Back

The seek back used to be a required Utility exercise, but in 1969 the AKC replaced it with the *directed retrieve*. Essentially, the seek-back exercise required that the handler go through a heeling routine, on the judge's commands, and drop a dark leather glove partly behind an obstacle in such a way that it would not be easily visible to the dog when the heeling exercise was finished. Occasionally it was dropped within the dog's vision. The judge would then give the handler a command to send his dog after the glove. The object of the exercise was that the dog should use his nose to find a lost article. It turned out that the exercise was so simple for the dogs, since they could use both sight and scent, that it was deemed not challenging enough for Utility.

However, we have continued to use the seek back in early Utility training because we find it extremely useful in preparing for the scent discrimination exercises—indeed, we consider it a prerequisite. It is also essential to training for the Tracking degree. Besides, it is a great deal of fun and can be practiced anywhere outdoors—when you take a walk in the woods with your dog, for instance.

The seek-back exercise should be made fairly easy during Week 1 of Utility: the dog should be allowed to both see and smell the article (an old leather glove). You can do this initial training either indoors or outdoors. Once the dog catches on, however, you will start to build up to a point where the object you send him for is out of sight and at a considerable distance. It will then be necessary to practice outside— irrespective of the inclemency of the weather—and in an area where neither his nor your scent is to be found. Thus, you should *plan* to take walks with your dog to places that neither of you have had occasion to visit recently. This might mean a supermarket parking lot, a farmer's field, New York's Central Park, or the Allegheny National Forest—the location is quite irrelevant; the size of the place and its freedom from your scent and your dog's are more critical.

229

To begin the seek-back training, put the dog into the proper heeling position, on lead. Have the leather glove in your right hand. Go out, at a normal heeling rate, for about thirty feet, do an about turn, and, as you complete the turn, drop the glove inconspicuously; continue heeling back toward your starting position. Do another about turn when you reach the original starting point and come to a halt, facing in the direction of the glove. The glove will probably be within the dog's vision, but it is also along the line of march—and therefore along the current of scent—that you and your dog just laid. At this point you want to begin teaching the dog about working with scent. Cup your right hand over his nose, gently (fig. III-4). Allow him to smell your hand; then give an exaggerated outward thrust with your hand (fig. III-5), "throwing" it conspicuously in the direction of the glove, and at the same time the command "Find it!" Run out with the dog to the glove. He should enthusiastically and smartly go out and pick it up; after all, this is just a modification of the retrieve on flat. The major differences are that you do not *throw* the object out in front of the dog, and (for the first few days) that you run toward the object to be fetched with the dog on lead. The commands vary only slightly: "Find it!" for a seek back and "Take it!" for the retrieve on flat. When the dog has the glove in his mouth, run back to your starting position with him, and quickly get in front of him so that he will be sitting in front of and facing you when you stop. Remove the glove on the command "Out!" and praise him before finishing.

Figure III-6 shows two practice courses for the seek-back exercise for Week 1; course A is short and can be used indoors, on lead, if your basement or recreation room is at least thirty feet long. Otherwise, you must work outside—in the snow if necessary.

Use A for the first several days; by the middle of the week, begin to follow pattern B in figure III-6: add a slight turn to the right or left so that your dog gradually becomes conditioned to looking for a lost object and is aware that the object can lie somewhere off the scent track he most recently followed. At this stage, take the dog off lead. Put him in a sit-stay and lay out the course while he watches. After you return to him (following your original path as closely as possible), resume your position, give him your scent, and send him.

If he cannot do course B off lead, keep him on lead and on the simpler course until he catches on. When you begin work on course B, be careful not to make too abrupt a turn: certainly not 90°. However, if there is a building intercepting the dog's vision and preventing him from cutting corners, it *is* appropriate to make a sharper turn as you go past the building. Where there is no obstacle, the dog will probably rely more on vision than nose and, despite whatever turns you make, simply run directly to the object if he can see it. Making your turns less than 90° (fig. III-6) will discourage him from cutting corners and will unconsciously preadapt him to running along the line where the scent should be the heaviest; even though he is working largely by sight at this stage, he is unconsciously learning to follow the scent. As the course becomes more complicated, he will rely more and more on the scent pattern and less on vision.

One of the reasons for working outdoors is the wind, which causes scent drift; when you train in medium to heavy wind, pay particular attention to laying out your seek-back course in such a way that the dog is working into the wind. You should avoid strong wind when you are first training your dog, however; try to condition him to the seek back during fairly calm days. He will gradually be able to handle the more rigorous and difficult assignment of working in heavy wind as he gets more experience.

Therefore, for the first week, you should concentrate on getting the dog to fetch the lost article when it is not far away and within visual range. He should go after it and, once he finds it, complete the exercise as if it were the retrieve on flat. Work on a simple course, such as A in figure III-6. This initial work can be done both indoors and outdoors. If, however, you are training outdoors, it is possible to modify the scent course by introducing the slight turn (B in fig. III-6) by the middle of the week. The major objective, we repeat, is to get the dog to retrieve the article, on command, by going after it along the trail where the scent pattern is richest. The dog may not be aware that he is using his nose at first, but as the exercises become more complicated in later weeks, he will unconsciously rely more and more on his nose—provided that your seek-back course is initially set up in such a way that he must use both his nose and his eyes to find the object.

Signal Exercise: Finish

During Novice Week 5, you trained your dog to *finish* by giving the command "Heel!" *and* by guiding him into the sit by putting pressure on the lead and making a sweeping motion with your left hand. This sweeping motion was, essentially, the hand signal to finish. You will begin your signal training with this exercise.

Teaching Hand Signal for Finish Put the dog on lead and in a sitting position in front of you. When he is sitting, give the command "Heel!" and make a sweeping motion with your left hand (figs. III-7–8). When the dog has finished and is sitting squarely, step out in front of him again and face him. You may have to repeat the exercise several times until your dog has relearned the association of hand signal and verbal command for finish.

Heel the dog away to a new area, on lead, and put him in a sit-stay again, step out in front of him, turn, and stand facing him. This time do not give a vocal finish command, but merely a sweeping motion with your left hand, touching the loose lead with your fingers to remind him that he is to move in the direction of your hand signal. You can expect him to hesitate briefly—in which case, correct him by taking the lead into your left hand and, *without* a verbal command, putting him into the finish motion. Praise him when he goes into the sit. Heel away again and repeat the exercise, using a somewhat exaggerated sweeping motion with your left hand. After several repetitions, the dog should finish on a 231

III-4.

III-5.

III-4. To teach your dog to take scent for both the modified seek back and scent-discrimination exercises, cup your hand and place it around the dog's nose. (Later, when you work with the scent articles, you will give your scent with your palm open.)

III-5. When he has taken your scent, simultaneously throw your hand outward and say "Find it!" Later you will drop the arm motion when you send the dog for a scent article—and the article will be behind you.

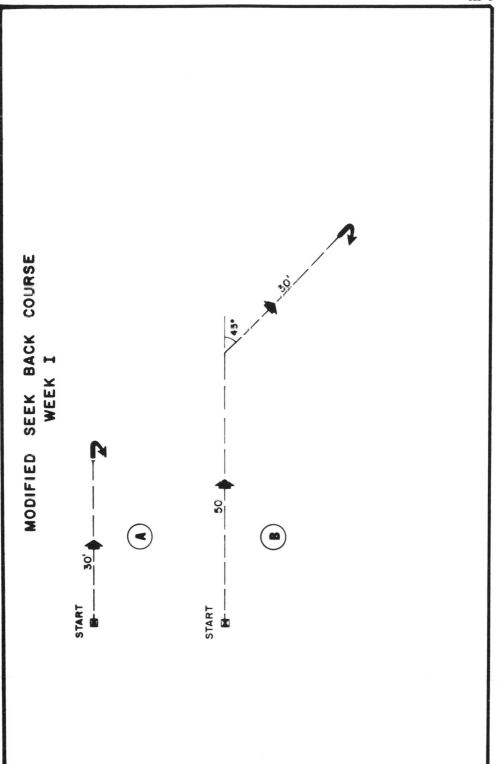

MODIFIED SEEK BACK COURSE
WEEK I

START

30'

(A)

START

50

45°

30'

(B)

III-7–8: Teaching the Hand Signal for Finish. **III-7.** This movement should be familiar to you from Novice training. Your left arm described an arc as you corrected the dog into a finish. The same motion will become your hand signal when you remove the leather lead.

III-8. Off lead, your left hand describes a backward arc. At first, make the motion long and graceful. After the dog begins to respond quickly, make your hand signal less emphatic, until a flick of your wrist is enough to make the dog finish.

hand signal alone. Mix up the training routine after he begins to catch on: periodically walk around him—return to him—instead of giving the finish signal. This will cut down on his tendency to anticipate.

This routine should be done in every practice session throughout Utility training to reinforce his signal knowledge. You should gradually make your hand signal less exaggerated, until you are giving only a slight hand motion, moving only the lower part of your arm and turning your hand at the wrist. Though more motion than this would be acceptable, we are trying to get you to concentrate on eliminating excessive body movement—the less your arm moves, the less your body moves. A word of caution is in order here: it is very tempting for the handler to inadvertently turn his head to look at the dog as he executes the finish; make a concentrated effort to give the hand signal without turning your head.

Pivots to Left and Right in a 360° Arc

You have been practicing back steps and pivots to the right and left to sharpen your dog's awareness of the slightest change you take in direction. To further increase his awareness, you will train your dog to pivot in a complete circle to the left. We are working toward the *directed retrieve* exercise, in which your dog must be able to adjust to your position, no matter how large or small a turn you make.

Let us briefly describe what you must train your dog to do for the directed retrieve in Utility competition. Assume that there are three objects behind both of you, about twenty feet away from you and twenty feet away from one another as well. Your dog will not know where they are, but the judge will tell *you:* one directly behind you; the other two in the corners of the ring. *If* you were *facing* the objects (gloves), the one on your left would be the number-1 glove, the one in front of you the number-2 glove, and the one to your right the number-3 glove. (Try to keep that fixed in your mind.) Your dog will be sitting at your side in the proper heeling position. The judge will tell you by number which glove your dog is to retrieve. You must then turn in place and face the designated glove. As soon as you halt after your turn, your dog must come to a sit, squarely at your side. You point to the glove and send your dog to fetch it with the command "Take it!" The judge makes no further commands after designating the glove—everything else is up to you.

You are permitted to turn to either the right or the left when the judge tells you which glove your dog is to retrieve. It is probably most efficient to pivot to the right, a movement that your dog will associate with being sent out for the *scent discrimination* and the *modified seek back*. However, unlike these exercises, the directed retrieve requires that the dog come to a sit after the pivot.

To reduce the chances of your dog's thinking he no longer has to sit after a pivot, practice the pivot in place as part of the advanced heeling routine you used all during Open training, turning to both the left and the right. Indeed, if your dog confuses the directed-retrieve pivots with the scent-discrimination or seek-back pivots (where he is *not* 235

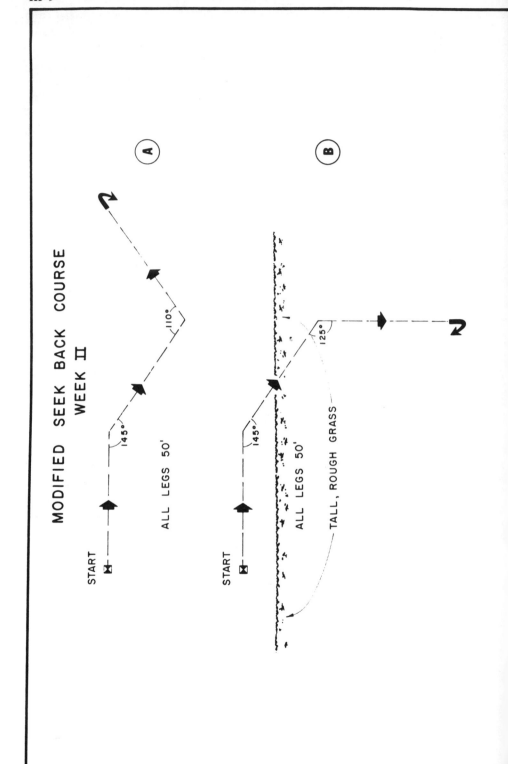

MODIFIED SEEK BACK COURSE
WEEK II

START

ALL LEGS 50'

145°

110°

A

START

ALL LEGS 50'

145°

125°

TALL, ROUGH GRASS

B

expected to come to a sit before going after the article), you might find that by pivoting to the left in a 180° arc you remind him that this is a totally different kind of exercise, and giving the command "Heel!" as you pivot also underscores this fact.

The important thing is to keep your dog aware that you can pivot in any direction and at any angle you wish—and that he must remain constantly in the proper heel position. So practice your pivots randomly: give the heel command and turn counterclockwise in place for 45°, 60°, 90°, 135°, et cetera, until your dog can remain in the proper position no matter where you stop your pivot. Then do the same thing to the right—clockwise—until your dog can confidently pivot in a complete 360° arc in either direction and go into an immediate automatic sit wherever you stop along that arc.

UTILITY WEEK 2

OUTLINE OF TRAINING SCHEDULE
Old Exercises
    Open
        Practice all daily, in show sequence.
        Advanced Heeling: Pivots to the right and left; back steps
    Utility
        Modified Seek Back
        Signal Exercise: Stand and Finish
Modifications of Utility Exercise
    Seek Back: Greater distance, more turns
New Exercises
    Signal Exercise
        Heel and Stay
        Stand and Stay, on Lead
        Stand and Stay, off Lead
    Introduction to Scent Discrimination: Taking articles and carrying
        them
    Introduction to Directed Jumping: The "Go out!"
Suggested Practice Session: Once daily

Seek Back Modified

Do the final seek-back exercise of Utility Week 1 to reinforce your dog's seek-back training. He must go out for the lost object on a single command, pick it up, and return to you with it—without playing with it—and he must sit squarely in front of you, holding the glove in his 237 mouth until given the command "Out!," at which time you remove the glove from his mouth and give the command "Heel!" If the dog is sluggish in his performance, revert to a simple straight-line course of about thirty feet. Put the dog back on lead after you drop the glove and return to him. If he hesitates when you give the command "Find it!," run toward the object swiftly, repeatedly correcting him off balance as you go, give him the command "Take it!" when he gets to the glove, and then correct him in the same fashion on the way back. Then repeat the exercise, but off lead. Should he hesitate again, put him back on lead and repeat the exercise, applying the necessary corrections. One or two such corrective measures will make him quite enthusiastic about going swiftly to the object, picking it up, and returning to you with it.

You are now prepared to complicate the course somewhat and to lengthen it considerably. Quite obviously, you *must* work outdoors at this point. If you want a superb, classy, and enthusiastic dog, you must be prepared to sustain some inconvenience yourself. Outside you must go—in any weather. Now you must look for longer grass or, in the winter, snow. The glove will be so placed that the dog must actually rely on his nose, not his eyes, to find it, and he will have to look for it at some considerable distance from you.

Lay a seek-back trail of the kind shown in A of figure III-9. It should be about one hundred and fifty feet long at first, and, more important, on terrain where the dog has never worked before. That is, you must leave your back yard or your basement at this juncture. A golf course is convenient, or a wooded park where the grass is longish in places. Your dog will enjoy the work, because of the opportunity to be outdoors and run free. By this time, you should have enough control over him when he is off lead so that he will return to you on command. Do a sit-stay or a drop on recall for any would-be complainers who watch you and your dog. They will politely withdraw after they see your dog's performance. Incidentally, you should remember that when your dog is working, he is not free to relieve himself at any convenient location; that should be taken care of either before or after the work—and correct him if he tries to do it while at work. He must realize that there is a time to work and a time to relax. Practice the seek-back A course (fig. III-9) for a day or two, until your dog can find the glove on every try. Then complicate the practice by going to course B.

Let's assume you have chosen a local golf course as the area in which you will practice the B course of the seek back. Put the dog in a sit-stay and walk out along the edge of the rough, on the fairway; make a slight right-hand turn toward the rough, proceed fifty feet or so, and then turn slightly toward deeper rough (fig. III-9). Go into the taller grass of the rough and make an about turn. As you do, drop the leather glove inconspicuously, then proceed back to your starting place, trying to follow the trail you came on. When you reach the starting point, return around your dog to face your original position of march and halt. Give the dog your scent (place your open-palmed hand over his nose) and send him with the command "Find it!" He should have no difficulty

III-10–11: Teaching the Hand Signal for Heel. **III-10.** Your left hand makes a sweeping motion over the dog's head and taps the lead. At first, give the verbal heel command as well.

III-11. When you have conditioned the dog to look for your sweeping hand motion over his head, you can then take him off lead and work him on the hand signal for heel without giving a verbal command. Note that you step off on your left foot as you give the signal.

239

III-12. The hand signal for stay should be familiar to
you from Novice training and your experience in both
Novice and Open competition. It can be given to the
dog from any position, but in Utility competition, you
will be expected to give a silent stay signal while the
dog is standing.

locating the glove and returning with it; but if he does, correct as indicated earlier.

If he retrieves the glove as he should, continue along the fairway
and lay out another seek-back course, increasing the distance this time.
Execute the exercise as above, applying corrections as needed.

Figure III-9 is meant to show only the general shape that your
seek-back course should have during the second week of Utility training. Increase the distance as your dog improves, until, by the end of
the week, the course is at least one hundred yards long; then work with
him at that distance until he is proficient at the seek back under varying
terrain, angle, and distance conditions. Make sure that you modify the
course in such a way that the dog must go both to the left and to the
right of your starting point to find the glove—indeed, you should occasionally drop it in short grass to discourage him from assuming that the
glove will always be in the long grass. By the end of Week 3 he should
definitely be using his nose to find the glove; he might not "know" it,
but he is gradually relying more and more on his nose.

Signal Exercise

Heel and Stay Your dog has already been preadapted to the hand signals we have covered. The *hand signal for heel* will be the first new signal exercise that you and your dog will learn; it is one of the simplest, and Novice and Open training have preadapted both of you for learning it. In the earlier heeling exercises we emphasized the importance of always stepping off on your left foot to begin a heeling routine. At this juncture, it is virtually a signal to your dog. To sharpen his understanding of this exercise into a simple, automatic routine, three modifications will be introduced in sequence: tapping the lead with your left hand as you give the command "Heel!" and step off on your left foot; dropping the verbal portion of the routine, and merely tapping the lead with your left hand in a sweeping motion over the dog's head; removing the lead, so that your left hand will be empty as you make the sweeping motion over the dog's head. When you reach the third modification, your dog will be doing the heel with a hand signal only. The first two modifications are shown in figure III-10, the third in figure III-11.

The training routine to teach the dog to heel on a hand signal is very simple: Put him into the proper heeling position, on lead; as you give the command "Heel!," swing your left hand out and strike the leather lead with your palm, brushing the lead in such a way that it tugs on the dog's collar and continuing to move hand and lead around in front of the dog's face so he can see the motion of the arc. Drop your left hand back to your side after completing the motion. As you make the arc and give the verbal command, step off on your left foot; then heel away for a few yards and come to a halt. After the dog sits, proceed forward with the combined hand, voice, and foot signal. After four or five repetitions, drop the verbal command, making sure that your moving left arm gently taps the leather lead and comes into the dog's visual field as you step off on your left foot (fig. III-10). Repeat this exercise three or four times, making an occasional turn to the left or right to keep the dog from becoming bored.

The final step is to remove the lead entirely and give only the hand signal—a sweeping motion over the dog's head (fig. III-11)—and the left-foot-forward signal. Your dog should heel on hand signal the first time you try it.

After you are convinced that the dog understands the exercise and does it consistently, never again give the verbal signal for heel when you are working on hand signals—even if he remains sitting or hesitates as you start to heel after giving him the hand signal. The remedy for that is to snap his lead back immediately and show him that he must pay attention to your hand movements.

Lack of attention is a major problem in all the signal exercises. It is for this reason that you must never use a verbal command after you have taught the hand signal, no matter how tempting it may be. By following this rule you will reinforce his attention span and make him constantly aware of your signals. A good many dogs disqualify during this portion of the AKC Utility trial merely because they were gazing elsewhere when a hand signal was given.

The *hand signal for stay* should be a breeze for your dog at this point—he has been given the proper hand signal from early Novice training on. Every time you gave the vocal stay command, you reinforced it with the hand signal by sweeping your right arm in an arc toward the dog, finishing with your flat palm in front of his face. The only modification required at this point is simply to drop the verbal portion of the command, telling him to stay with the motion of your arm only (fig. III-12).

Practice the hand signal for stay by heeling your dog on lead. Every time you come to a halt, give him the hand signal only (bringing your open palm up to his face in a long swing), step off on your *right* foot, and walk out to the end of the lead. Return to the dog, being careful not to apply tension to his collar with the lead, just as you did when you taught the sit-stay exercise (see fig. I-45). Heel away with the proper hand and foot (left foot forward) signals, and halt again. At first you will need to exaggerate the motion by slowing it down and taking a rather long step with your *right* foot. After a few stops and starts like this, your dog should be operating on the heel and stay hand signals as if he were a certified Utility dog. If any problems arise on the stay signal, revert to the verbal, hand, and right-foot-forward combination, but make the hand portion of the signal the most conspicuous to the dog. Gradually drop the verbal portion and resume training.

Stand and Stay, on Lead   In Novice training, you learned to heel with the dog and, on a hand signal, to bring him to a standing halt at your side. At that time, you merely stood there a few moments and then heeled away, your dog resuming his march from a standing position. Go back to Novice Weeks 7 and 8 and review this exercise. Practice the stand on hand signal a few times, heeling away after every successful completion of it. Use the verbal heel command to get your dog to move from the standing position. After he seems confident of his expected performance and does it unflinchingly, modify it in the following fashion. After you stand him with just the hand signal, pause a few moments and then give the hand signal for stay. (Because he is on lead, you can quickly correct him if he fails to remain standing. The correction does not actually require the use of the lead, but by this time the dog associates it with learning and will probably be more alert and expectant when it is attached; the mere fact that he is on lead reinforces the over-all situation—he is tipped off that he is subject to correction, which he will probably wish to avoid by paying careful attention to you.) Say absolutely nothing when giving the stay hand signal. Simply make a slow, exaggerated sweep with your right hand, bringing your palm up to the dog's face (fig. III-12). As you finish the signal, step off conspicuously on your right foot, keeping enough balance to jump back and enforce the stand should your dog try to sit or heel forward. If he remains standing, as he probably will, walk out to the end of the lead and turn to face him. Stay there for a few moments before returning around him to the proper heeling position. The dog should remain in the standing position until you give another command, so pause a moment, after you have returned to his side. The idea is to build up his ability to remain standing *after* you have returned; in a show, you might have to wait for ten or fifteen seconds. Therefore, be prepared to correct the dog if he tries to sit down after you have returned to his side. If he does not sit or move, release him from the position by giving the command "Heel!" and stepping forward, *left* foot first, and taking two steps before coming to a halt. The dog should go into the automatic sit at this point, and you should praise him for his performance.

Stand and Stay, off Lead At this point, you will begin preparing the dog for show conditions. The hand signal to stay can be given (without any supplementary vocal command) when the dog is sitting, standing, lying down, or standing on his head (if he can do it). In competition, however, he will have to stay on just the hand signal from a standing position only—and he will have been put into the standing position also by hand signal only.

To prepare him for competition, you will work on the actual exercise to be expected of him. The best training for this is to heel your dog through a typical off-lead pattern of the kind described in Novice Week 9 or of the kind you used in Open competition. Do all turns and all speeds. As you come out of the about turn, give the hand signal for stand and come to a gradual halt (fig. III-13). The dog should stand near your left leg, as if he were in the heeling position. Pause a moment and then, without saying a word, give him the hand signal for stay by sweeping your right hand around in an arc that terminates with your open palm in front of his face (fig. III-14). As you finish the arc, step off on your right foot, walk out about ten or fifteen feet, turn, and face the dog. Remain standing there a few moments, and then return to the dog by circling around behind him, as you did for the *stand for examination* in Novice. Pause a moment, give the hand signal for heel, and take two steps forward—leading off with your *left* foot as you initiate your heeling motion. Come to a halt; the dog should go into an automatic sit. Praise him when he does.

Teaching the dog to stand while coming out of the about turn puts him at maximum learning advantage: he is probably slightly behind you as you complete the turn, and so can most easily see your hand signal. After he understands that he might be given such a signal while coming out of a turn, you can move on to the hand signal out of a right turn. When he has mastered that, you should then give him the hand signal when coming out of a left turn. Finally, you should occasionally give him the hand signal for stand while heeling in a straight line.

After the dog has caught on to standing on hand signal without a vocal command, you should vary his training by making him do the exercise from any speed and out of any kind of turn. This will keep him alert and will sharpen his attentiveness—he will now constantly expect a signal of some sort as he is heeling. Any time that you give the stand-signal, you can and should practice the stay portion of the AKC hand-signal routine. You should also work the heel signal into your routine as you practice the heel off lead. That is, after you have put the   243

III-13. Teaching the dog to stand on hand signal as you come out of an about turn. You will not be permitted to touch your dog in this exercise, but your Novice training prepared you to stand your dog on hand signal from any heeling speed and out of any turn. When the dog has come to a stand, pause a moment and give the hand signal for stay.

III-14. The hand signal for stay while the dog is standing. Be sure to step off with your right foot first as you leave the dog and walk to the opposite side of the ring. Do not look back, and do not back away as you leave the dog.

dog into the stand position, leave him by giving the hand signal for stay, walk out to a minimum of twenty-five feet, pause a few moments, and return. Make sure that you pause after you return and finish the exercise by giving the hand signal for heel and taking two steps forward.

Gradually build up distance and duration while you practice the hand signals: go farther and farther away from the dog as he becomes more proficient and confident, and wait for increasingly longer periods of time while he remains in the perfectly motionless standing position. Your distance should ultimately be about forty feet from the dog; the length of time that you remain standing should vary from five seconds to sixty seconds to keep the dog's attention focused on you. Work initially with five to fifteen seconds of standing. Remember that you are working toward the level of patience required for the group examination—which might last up to five minutes.

As you work with your dog on this exercise, bear in mind that during a show there will be a judge somewhere within your field of vision giving *you* the signals, which you must, in turn, transmit to the dog. The judge's commands will be hand signals, so concentrate on your peripheral vision as you look in the direction of the dog. You must remain motionless; any movement you make could be interpreted as a signal to the dog. Therefore, you will have to roll your eyes to see a judge off to one side, giving you commands to transmit to the dog by pointing his fingers this way and that (see Utility Week 9 for a complete description of judge's signals to handlers).

During the training for stand on hand signal, the dog should not sit down, lie down, move his feet, or scratch himself (see Utility Week 9 for additional discussion of prohibitions). Such actions will disqualify a dog in a show. Nor is it desirable that the dog look around at other dogs or turn his head: in competition, you will be expected to give the dog a hand signal for down while he is in the stand position; you only get one chance to do it, and you must give the signal soon after the judge indicates to you that you should. If, on seeing the judge's signal you notice that your dog is not paying attention to you, pause until your dog is looking at you—then give the proper hand signal.

The best way to discourage these kinds of behavior is to vary your pause time radically—five seconds before returning in one lesson, fifteen seconds in another. This keeps the dog alert and waiting for the next command. In a show, he will be expected to stand only a few seconds during the hand-signal exercise.

Introduction to Scent Discrimination

Late in Open training we suggested that you order (or make) a set of scent articles. At this point it is necessary to use one of the metal articles to begin teaching your dog scent discrimination. A complete set usually includes ten articles for use in shows and two practice articles, one metal and one leather. The *AKC Obedience Regulations* specifies only that the articles must be no longer than six inches and identical to each other (the leather articles should all be alike and the metal articles likewise), and that only enough non-leather construction material be visible on the leather objects to hold them together. You can use household objects for the scent discrimination, but most handlers use dumbbell-shaped articles of the kind shown in figure III-1. We know of several people who decided it would be cheaper to make their own; they ended up paying several times more for the materials and labor than the price of a good commercial set (about twenty dollars). The most practical and convenient way to obtain your scent articles is to order them from somebody who makes them specifically for Utility training and competition (see Appendix II).

You should also obtain an inexpensive attaché case or plastic container for your scent articles. This will keep them clean and reduce the amount of handling that they receive—handling that can leave your scent on them at a time when you wish to keep them free of scent. You should also have a pair of ordinary canning tongs (fig. III-1), to use 245

III-15. In a show, the eight unscented articles will be placed on the ground, behind you and the dog. One metal and one leather article will be given to you. You may take either one of them and rub it with your hands until the judge requests it from you— usually by holding out his clipboard.

III-16. As soon as the judge indicates that he wants the article, place it on his clipboard. He cannot touch the article with his hands. While your back and the dog's are turned, the judge will place the scented article somewhere among the eight unscented ones and then tell you: "Send your dog!"

III-17. When you hear the judge's command to send your dog, give the dog your scent with the palm of your hand. Then drop your hand back to your side and, pivoting clockwise toward the articles, give the command "Find it!" The dog should rise up, pivot around with you, and head for the articles.

III-18. As in the retrieve on flat, the dog must go quickly to the article, pick it up, and return to you quickly, sitting at your feet as he presents the article to you. Unlike the retrieve on flat, he must find the one that has your scent on it. When your dog is sitting like this, the judge will tell you "Take it!" and then, after you remove it (with the verbal command "Out!"), "Finish."

III–17

III–18

both during training and in AKC trials. (In a show, the judge will occasionally use your tongs to handle the articles; he is *not allowed* to touch the two selected for the exercise, either before or after you have put your scent on them, until the exercise on each article is over.)

In Utility competition, the scent discrimination is the second exercise you do in the ring. You hand your briefcase containing the articles and your tongs to a steward or to the judge either before or as you enter the ring, and he removes two articles, using the tongs, one leather and one metal. The steward or judge then places the other eight articles (4 meal, 4 leather) randomly, usually between the jumps but occasionally in a corner of the ring. The steward *must touch* the eight articles, and you may watch as he places them. When the articles are placed and/or on the judge's instruction, you must turn your back on the articles, with your dog in the normal heeling position, so that his back will also be to the articles. The judge will then place the two remaining articles (one metal, one leather) before you—either on the floor, on a chair, or on his clipboard. Neither he nor the steward has touched these articles. At that point you have your choice of which article (metal or leather) you want your dog to find first. The judge then gives you the object and allows you to rub it with your hands (fig. III-15); your back is still toward the remaining eight articles on the floor, and the tenth article will probably have been placed on a chair in front of you. When the judge requests the article from you, you must immediately set it on his clipboard. He then places it in the midst of the articles on the floor behind you and your dog (fig. III-16) and gives you the command "Send your dog!" At this point you may hold your open-palmed (right) hand silently in front of the dog's nose—even touch it lightly—to give your scent to the dog (fig. III-17), but you must drop your hand back to your side before you give the command "Find it!" After your hand has come back to its normal position at the side of your leg, you simultaneously pivot to the right to face the articles and give the command "Find it!" The dog must go directly and briskly to the articles and find the one that has your scent on it. A good dog will smell all of the articles, including the one with your scent on it, before picking up the right one; some dogs will pick up the right article as soon as they locate it. Whatever your dog does, he must be working continuously, looking for the article. If he stops and just stands there, looking confused and puzzled, he is disqualified. We have seen some dogs circle the scent articles for as long as five minutes before actually looking for the scented article. These dogs qualify, but they look pretty unprofessional. In sharp performance, the dog would go quickly to the articles, sniff them in turn, pick up the right one, return smartly and directly to the handler, and come to a square sit facing him (fig. III-18). On the judge's command "Take it!," say "Out!" to the dog and remove the object from his mouth with both hands. When the judge tells you to finish, give the command "Heel!" You are allowed to give praise after your dog finishes, but, as in all the Utility exercises, only a minimum amount—a pat on the head and a reassuring "Good dog!" You should then turn around,

III-19. Most dogs dislike taking metal objects in their mouths, so work with the metal article from the outset. Put the dog on lead and in the proper heeling position. Present the article to the dog with your right hand and apply slight upward tension on the lead with your left. As you present the article, give the command "Take it!" When he takes it, relax the tension, praise him, and heel away while he holds the article in his mouth.

put the now-used article on the chair, and take up the second article to give it your scent. The exercise is repeated exactly as before.

The seek-back exercise will have preadapted your dog for working briskly and using his nose to find a lost article; continue practicing it this week. In addition, the work you have done on the retrieve on flat and retrieve over high jump will help in training your dog for the scent-article exercise. The main objective during the first week of training with the scent articles is to accustom the dog to something totally new: a metal object. For the time being, he will not be trained to do anything except pick it up, carry it, and allow you to remove it from his mouth. Most dogs do not like to pick up a metal object—it is cold and unpleasant to them—and some are therefore difficult to train with it. Thus it is a good idea to start with the metal article.

Number all of your scent articles (if they have not already been numbered by the manufacturer) in two groups, each group from one to five, so that there are two with number 1 on them (one leather and one metal), two with 2, and so on (a felt-tip pen works well). Use the un-numbered articles for practice.*

Begin your first practice session by putting the unnumbered metal article into the dog's mouth, giving the command "Take it!" as you do

* When you begin showing two days in a row in Utility, you will want to use the unnumbered articles as replacements on the second day. Your scent would still be on the articles used the previous day, which might be confusing to your dog. At that time you can number your practice articles, to make a complete set, using soluble ink so that you can easily renumber for subsequent shows.

III–20

III–21

III–22

III–23

III–24

III-20–25: Directed Jumping. **III-20.** You and your dog are at one end of the ring, on the center line between the two jumps. You must send your dog to the opposite end of the ring on the command "Go out!" accompanied by a hand signal indicating his direction of march. The dog must run in a straight line to the opposite end of the ring and stop when you call his name; he should be as far from the jumps on his side of the ring as you are on yours, and as near to the center line as possible.

III-21. As soon as you give the dog's name, he should stop, turn, and face you. By the time he gets turned around, you should have given, without additional instructions from the judge, the command "Sit!" The dog remains sitting until you give him another command. Your next command will depend on the judge; he will tell you which obstacle he wants your dog to jump, and he will pick the one that is most disadvantageously situated for the dog. So train in such a way that the dog remains near the center line of the ring and sits squarely. That way, neither of the jumps will be badly situated—provided the dog is at the far end of the ring.

III-22. The judge has designated the bar; on hearing this, you point toward the bar jump, your arm fully extended, and give the command "Over!"

III-23. When the dog is in mid-air, turn in place and try to line yourself up in such a way that after he lands and makes his turn, he can come in to you straight.

III-24. The dog must come to a straight sit at your feet. Wait until the judge gives you the next command: "Finish!"

III-25. You may give either the verbal heel command to your dog, or the hand signal for finish. When the dog has completed the finish, the judge will tell you that the exercise is finished. Give just a bit of praise and pivot in place to line up on the center line again—for you must repeat the exercise. This time, the judge must tell you to send your dog over the remaining jump, no matter how favorably or unfavorably it is situated from the dog's vantage.

so (fig. III-19). When he takes it, heel with him and be prepared to correct him if he tries to spit it out; even well-trained C.D.X. dogs tend to reject the metal object at first. Give the dog every opportunity to spit it out during this initial week of training in scent discrimination, when he is working on only one article and will thus understand exactly what the correcton is for. If you have to correct for this later, when he is attempting to learn something more complicated, he might confuse the correction with one for poor performance in search or retrieving. An instructive routine at this stage would be to make him heel, do a few sit-stays, and even recalls, for a few minutes each day with the metal article in his mouth.

Near the end of the week, modify the training routine by doing a few retrieves on flat, using the metal scent article. Make sure that you are in a position to correct the dog easily the first time you do this: do not throw the metal object farther than about six feet. If the dog does it proficiently and enthusiastically, you can start to throw it farther away.

When the dog is consistent in carrying the metal object and does not try to spit it out, you can substitute the leather object, training with that in the same fashion: heeling, recall, retrieve, et cetera. This will familiarize him with the scent articles and accustom him to taking both leather and metal into his mouth.

Introduction to Directed Jumping

The *directed jumping* exercise is one of the most complicated obedience routines your dog will learn. It contains several components, which, we feel, should be taught individually and then combined as the final AKC exercise.

Your dog must go over, in turn, a bar jump and a solid jump—the order is determined by the judge. The jumps are approximately in the middle of the ring, eighteen to twenty feet apart (fig. III-20), one on the handler's left and the other on his right. You stand about twenty feet from the line of the jumps, approximately midway between them, with your dog in the normal heeling position. On the judge's command "Send your dog!" you give the command "Go out!" and point your left arm straight ahead—without bending at the knees (fig. III-20). The dog must run out in a straight line between the jumps and continue running until he has gone a distance past the line of the jumps that is equal to your distance from them. Then you may give his name and the command "Sit!" On hearing his name, the dog should turn to face you and, on the command, sit squarely. Ideally, he should be sitting exactly on an imaginary line that runs between you and him, each of you equidistant from the jumps (fig. III-21).

The judge then decides which of the obstacles he wants you to command the dog to jump first. If he elects the bar jump, you point to it and give your dog the command "Over!" (fig. III-22). The dog must run directly to the jump and clear it without touching it. While he is in mid-air, you may turn to face the approximate direction that your dog will be coming from as he lands (fig. III-23), turns, and comes back to a full sit, facing you (fig. III-24). The judge then tells you to "finish," and you give the command "Heel!" (fig. III-25). After the judge informs you that the exercise is finished, turn, line your dog up again, and repeat the exercise, following the judge's instructions. If he designated the bar jump as your first jump, then he *must* give you the high jump next, and vice versa.

We will break this exercise down into several components. One of the most difficult portions is training the dog to run straight away from you on one command and, on a second command—his *name* followed by "Sit!"—come to a halt, turn, and sit facing you. We will begin with this component—the "Go out!"—and treat it as a separate exercise.

This is the first time in his formal obedience career that your dog will hear "Sit!" as a *command*—if you have followed our training recommendations carefully.

One reason that the go-out portion is somewhat difficult to teach the dog is that it will be puzzling for him: he must run directly away from you into a vast, open space and not be expected to jump or retrieve anything. His first reaction might be: "This guy is crazy! What is out there for me to do?" We therefore urge you to be very patient. He will need some time to realize that you simply want him to run straight out, away from you, and turn and sit when he hears his name and the command "Sit!"

To teach this component you will need two ropes—one one hundred feet long and the other, of lighter weight, fifty feet long—a pulley, and an auger-type dog anchor of the kind used in your Open training (see fig. II-74). Most good hardware stores and pet shops stock the anchors, but you can also use a wooden stake about two inches square, painted white to be clearly visible to the dog, driven firmly into the ground. Attach the pulley to the stake with a heavy screw, bolt, or combination of eyebolt and wire. It is best to attach the pulley on one side of the stake so that you can pound it into the ground in different areas of the yard without having to work around the pulley as you hammer. Leave about eight inches of stake sticking up out of the ground. For the first week, only the long piece of rope that you used for Open training will be required; we mention the other equipment now so that you can be shopping for it during the next week or two.

It should be obvious from the description of the whole exercise that you will need a bar jump, which consists of two four-foot uprights, similar to the high-jump uprights but possibly of lighter construction, and a six-foot bar approximately 2½ inches square. We find that a dowel about two inches in diameter is suitable for training. The bar should be painted with three-inch-wide stripes of alternating black and white. The two uprights for the bar jump are set five feet apart (see Appendix IV for jump dimensions and plans for constructing them).

For the first week of the go-out training, you will simply run with the dog along the length of the rope—for about fifty feet in a single direction—and train him to stop quickly and turn when his name is given, and come to a sit on your verbal command. This exercise also 253

III-26–27: Introducing the "Go Out!" Portion of Directed Jumping. **III-26.** Lay out your guide rope and put your dog on the leather lead at one end of the ring. The dog is centered on the rope, sitting in the normal heeling position. Give the dog's name and the command "Go out!," simultaneously striking the lead with your left hand to condition him to the hand signal. Run with him to the other end of the ring at the pace you want him to maintain—a fairly healthy trot.

III-27. When you reach the spot at which you want the dog to turn, give his name loudly and come to a sudden stop, spinning the dog around toward you in this fashion. As soon as he is turned around, give the command "Sit!" and enforce it by pulling up on the lead with your right hand and pushing down on his rump with your left. Then give him a good deal of praise before heeling back to repeat the exercise. A few dogs can learn the go-out portion of directed jumping with just this technique. Most dogs, however, require more intensive training.

accustoms the dog to following the rope guide and to associating the movement of your left hand with running out, away from you.

Lay the rope out in a straight line, making sure you have about fifty feet of it as a guide. It is important to work at about fifty feet, since this conditions the dog to run a great distance from you. In most cases, dogs stop too short of the desired distance in the AKC Utility trials, maximizing their chances to disqualify, lose substantial points for that portion of the exercise, or be in a very poor position to clear the designated jump. Remember, the judge usually tells you to send your dog to the jump that is located most disadvantageously for him, so the farther away from the jumps the dog is, the greater his chances of clearing either of them. Therefore, work on getting your dog to go farther past the jumps than would be minimally required in the show ring. He should, if trained properly on this simple exercise, continue running out from you until he hears you shout his name.

After the rope is laid out in a straight line, put your dog on lead, heel up to the beginning of the rope, and halt. The dog should be centered on the rope. Pause a moment, then give his name and the command "Go out!," simultaneously moving your left hand swiftly along your side and striking the leather lead with it. Continue your hand motion outward, in front of the dog (fig. III-26). This will condition him to the fact that your swiftly moving left arm is a signal to run away from you in the direction that your arm points. Both you and your dog should then move swiftly out, following the rope, and maintain a fast trot until you reach the end of the rope.

Now comes an important part of the lesson: teaching the dog to stop quickly, turn about, and come to an instant, straight sit. The most effective way to do this is to halt suddenly, spin him around toward you (fig. III-27)—giving his name loudly as you do—and, as soon as he has turned, give him the command "Sit!," enforcing it by pushing down on his rump as you pull up on the lead.

Practice this several times each day, but make the dog stop and turn at a different spot every time—you do not want him to think that he should stop automatically at the end of the rope. Run past the end occasionally or stop short of it five or ten feet. You want the dog to learn that his name means "Stop, turn, and expect the sit command to follow immediately."

About the middle of the week you should start doing this exercise in both directions and in different areas of your yard. Try to run your dog out along the rope toward objects or areas—trees, bushes, the side of a building—that vary in shape and distance from the end of the rope. This will accustom him to running at full tilt no matter what lies in his line of march; he should run as quickly toward a brick wall as he would toward a distant field full of grazing pussycats.

It is highly desirable in AKC Utility trials to have a rapidly moving dog on this exercise. To work toward that *you* will have to run quite fast, since the dog has been trained to keep pace with you.

UTILITY WEEK 3

OUTLINE OF TRAINING SCHEDULE
Old Exercises
    Open
        Practice all daily, in show sequence.
        Advanced Heeling: Pivots to the right and left; back steps
    Utility
        Signal Exercises (while heeling off lead): Stay, heel, finish, stand
        Group Examination (Long Stand): Two minutes
Modifications of Utility Exercises
    Seek Back: Sending dog when his back is to the course
    Scent Discrimination: Retrieving metal scent article at five feet
    Directed Jumping: The go out alone and at greater distance; adding
        the bar-jump component
New Exercises
    None
Suggested Practice Session: Once daily

Seek Back Further Modified

Begin the first day of Week 3 with the seek-back improvements of Week 2, giving the dog a chance to review something he has already mastered, as well as preparing him for four additional modifications.

Replacing the original training glove with one that he has never smelled before—or with your wallet, an old shoe that has your scent on it, or even a small article of your clothing—is the first modification. Make sure it has your hand scent on it. Very few people realize how sensitive a dog's sense of smell really is—all you have to do is touch an article for a moment and you have impregnated it indelibly with your unique body scent. It is a fallacy that you must refrain from washing your hands for hours and hours before working your dog on scent discrimination; the only thing you might gain thereby is the ire of your human comrades. Your canine acquaintances can smell you even after you've washed your hands, because your scent, like your fingerprints, is very difficult to alter or conceal.

The second modification is that you will work in short grass so that the dog can find the object readily when he is near it; this will give him every advantage initially in learning what is expected of him when he is sent out to find a lost object.

Also to increase his confidence, you will revert to a short, thirty-foot course; but the dog will be facing in the *opposite* direction as you lay it out. This complication will compensate for the shortening of the course. In fact, the dog will begin the exercise at a considerable disadvantage: he will not have seen you lay the course out; nor will he know where you have dropped the object. The short grass and thirty-foot

256

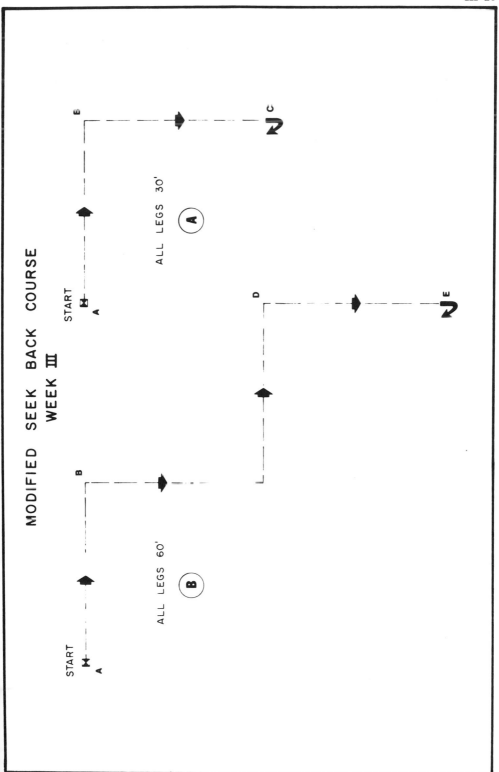

MODIFIED SEEK BACK COURSE
WEEK III

ALL LEGS 30' (A)

ALL LEGS 60' (B)

course will help him find the object easily the first few times you exercise him on this routine. His success and your praising him for it will stimulate him, as the course is lengthened and then complicated with additional turns, to look patiently for something that is not so easily found.

As the final modification for the new work you will add a 90° angle to the course. This creates another pitfall: the dog will have to use his nose to find the lost article, since the right-angle turn will require that he drop back to find the trail. Course A in figure III-28 is ideal for the first few days of training on the seek back during Utility Week 3.

Begin the exercise by taking your dog to an area he has not recently worked in, preferably an open field with nothing visible to interrupt the course. Heel the dog toward a "clean" (unscented) area and come to a halt. Make an about turn in place by pivoting around on your right foot, giving the command "Heel!" as you do so. Then put the dog into a sit-stay with the proper verbal and hand signals, and step off *behind* the dog to lay out your trail. Go out about fifteen feet and make a right turn; go an additional fifteen feet, make an about turn, drop the article, and return to the dog on approximately the same trail. On the dog's right side, pause a moment, put your open-palmed hand over his nose, bring your hand back to your side, and give the command "Find it!" pivoting to the right 180° as you say "Find it!" The dog should turn about and go out along the trail you laid in the short grass, using both nose and eyes to find the new lost article. If he balks, immediately snap the lead onto his collar and apply a series of short corrections to knock him off balance, gradually bringing him to the object, which he

III-29–32: Teaching Retrieve of Scent Article at Five Feet, on Lead. III-29. For those of you who merely wish to teach your dog scent discrimination, any article will do — a wallet, as shown here. For those who plan to compete in AKC Utility trials, it is better to work with the metal scent article. Begin with the dog in the proper heeling position. Place the article out in front of the dog, about five feet away.

III-30. When you are back in the normal heeling position, pivot in a clockwise direction and wait for the dog to sit squarely. The scent article will now be behind you and the dog.

III-31. Give your scent to the dog with your right hand, presenting it in this fashion. Put the lead back into your right hand after you have given him the scent.

III-32. Give the command "Find it!" and pivot around toward the scent article, in a clockwise arc. Make sure you give a smart tug on the lead as you pivot, for you want the dog to move swiftly as you turn. Step toward the article with the dog to give him enough slack to find it, pick it up, and return to you with it. He should bring it back as if he were doing the retrieve on flat.

will undoubtedly take as soon as he sees it—since he knows the retrieve on flat. As an alternative to this correction, you can allow him to watch you lay the course out, by putting him initially in a sit-stay *facing* the modified seek-back course, and allow him to see the new object or even smell it, before you turn him around, opposite your direction of march. If you do choose this alternative, let him have only one chance at it, then immediately move to a new area, where neither your scent nor his is present, and make him find the new object from the turnabout position.

If the dog can execute the basic short course shown as A in figure III-28, you should gradually lengthen both legs of the course until he is going about sixty feet in one direction before hitting the turn. Make sure you turn both right and left as you lay out successive courses so that your dog is not being conditioned to veer immediately in one direction only. You can now modify the course further by working in taller grass, but do not place the object behind anything; having it concealed in the tall grass will be enough of an obstacle for your dog at this point. By the end of the week, you should complicate the course by adding two additional 90° turns (course B in fig. III-28). Work with the dog in fairly calm wind with this course. After several practice sessions, he should be tracking well and finding the object that you dropped.

This exercise is usually so much fun for the dog that it becomes difficult to make the course complicated enough for him. If the dog has become proficient on the B course in figure III-28, he is ready for his initial work in actual scent discrimination as described in Week 4. You may stop complicating the modified seek-back courses at this point and merely continue to work the B course in figure III-28. However, if your dog enjoys the seek-back work, you can, for the fun of it, continue to increase the distance of his search up to several hundred yards (safety conditions permitting).

It may seem unusual to teach a dog something that is no longer required in AKC competition, but there are some very good reasons for doing so. First, the modified seek back is fun for both dog and handler. Second, skill in this exercise will be absolutely essential to your dog if you eventually decide to train him for the Tracking degree. The third reason would alone justify your taking the time to teach the modified seek back: no other exercise does quite so much to facilitate your dog's learning scent discrimination.

Scent Discrimination Modified

The object this week is to teach your dog to do the following: take your scent when you put your hand on his nose, remain sitting while you bring your hand back to your side, and turn with you as you pivot and give the command "Find it!" You will use only one article at a time this week; use the metal article more often than the leather to continue to expose the dog to the more unpleasant of the two.

Begin the first day of practice with the dog in the normal heeling position on the six-foot leather lead. You should have the metal scent article in your right hand, along with the end of the lead. Transfer both the article and the lead to your left hand, give the dog the command

III-33. Most dogs cannot be taught to go out if the handler merely runs with them to the opposite end of the ring; additional aids are required. Place the auger and pulley about twenty feet away, and pass the rope through the pulley. Fasten one end to the dog's collar and take up the other end in your hand. The dog should be sitting slightly askew so that a tug on the rope will knock him a little off balance and forward.

"Stay!," step away, and place the scent article on the ground about five feet from him (fig. III-29). Return to your dog and take up the normal heeling position by walking around behind him so that the article is continuously in his sight. Give the command "Heel!" and turn 180° in place, coming to a halt with the scent article directly behind you (fig. III-30). Transfer the leather lead to your left hand and give the dog your scent with your right hand, allowing him to sniff it (fig. III-31). Then drop your arm back to the normal position, pause a moment after taking the lead back into your right hand, and give the command "Find it!" as you pivot around to the right, in place. As you pivot, give a moderately hard tug on the lead to knock the dog slightly off balance and get him into the 180° turn—close to your body—and moving toward the scent article (fig. III-32). In this week's seek-back training, you taught him this turn. But now, instead of finding a leather glove off lead, he will go out only about five feet, on lead, and retrieve a metal scent article. He should bring it directly back to you without hesitating and come to a straight sit at your feet, facing you.

The dog is kept on lead for this exercise because it is basically new and will become very complicated very rapidly. The lead makes it easier to correct him at this stage, while the work is fairly simple, instead of later, when he must be doing several things at once.

The rest of the week should be spent practicing the scent-article   261 retrieve in exactly this fashion, occasionally using the leather object instead of the metal one. The dog must be proficient at this by the end of the week; the work quickly becomes complicated, and you will not want to have to correct for spitting the article out (very likely with the metal one), or for slowness in his going after it, his return to you with it, or his sits. Be extremely demanding in getting the dog to do this portion of the scent discrimination flawlessly—but also give bountiful praise when he does the exercise well.

Directed Jumping Modified

The Go Out Alone This week you will begin to teach your dog to go out, turn, and sit without your running alongside him. This will require the equipment already described in Utility Week 2: the auger-type anchor or wood stake with the attached pulley and the one-hundred-foot rope with a swivel snap attached. The rope will run through the pulley and back to the dog's collar; the loose end will be used to pull the dog.

Some dogs are extremely precocious and catch on quickly. Before resorting to the rope aids described here, test your dog to see if he needs them in the first place: lay out the guide rope as a center line and start at one end with the dog in the normal heeling position, on lead. Give the command "Go out!" and run out with him, turning him around when you reach the other end of the ring. Repeat this several times, and then try it off lead, being sure to give his name as you reach the spot at which you want him to turn and sit. If he does it off lead while you run with him, try it without running with him. If he is able to do this, you can eliminate the rope aids for this exercise.

Otherwise lay out the hundred-foot rope, pass it through the pulley at the auger (or stake), and double it back so that the distance between you and the stake is about fifteen or twenty feet. Coil up the rest of the rope and lay it on the ground behind the dog. The major objective is to get the dog running at a healthy clip toward the pulley anchor on the command "Go out!" Your practice in Week 2 should have indicated to him the speed that was expected of him.

Bring the dog up to the coiled rope and the swivel snap—about fifteen or twenty feet from the anchor. Have him sit slightly askew of his eventual line of march—that is, in such a way that he will be tugged off balance when you pull on the rope (fig. III-33).

After you have the dog positioned correctly, attach the swivel snap to his collar and pick up the other end of the rope. Make sure the collar is placed high on the dog's neck to maximize the effectiveness of the corrections you make when you pull on the rope.

You are now ready to begin the practice session. Your job will be to give the command "Go out!" and then run backward, tugging on the rope to pull the dog toward the anchor. The first time you do this exercise, you might have to take a step forward to get him in motion, as you did last week when you ran the length of the rope with the dog on lead.

A measure of common sense is required. You do not have to pull hard or run too far if your dog is small—a miniature poodle or a Shetland sheep dog, for instance. Needless to say, if you run too far and apply too much pressure, you may drag your dog into the anchor. A larger dog, such as a pointer, setter, or shepherd, might require more effort on your part. An assistant for this exercise would be a big help, but is not absolutely necessary.

Let us repeat the description of the procedure in more detail now. Your dog is at heel, slightly askew to the left, with the swivel end of the longer rope attached to his collar. The anchor and pulley are about fifteen or twenty feet away. You are standing with the loose end of the rope in your right hand. Give the command "Go out!" as you swiftly move your left hand out in front of you to give the hand signal. You should then quickly grab the rope with your extended left hand and begin running backward to get the dog in rapid motion. As he approaches the anchor, come to a halt, release the tension on the rope, and give his name loudly, followed immediately by the command "Sit!" The dog should stop, turn, and come to a sit. Drop the rope, walk up to the dog, and praise him. Take up the swivel end of the rope, near his collar, and heel him back to the starting area.

If the dog fails to sit, quickly correct him, repeating "Sit!" as you do, and follow with praise.* The major objective this week is to get him to go out on command, so your corrections for a failure to sit should not be harsh at this time.

The second time you do the exercise, go out to twenty-five feet. It is important to build up a long distance very rapidly in this exercise and get out to the full AKC-required distance as soon as possible; actually, we want the dog to go out *farther* than he would in an AKC show. By the end of this week, he should be running out fifty feet (this means that your training area must be at least one hundred feet long, since you will be running in the opposite direction for an equal distance). He should also be anticipating your "Go out!" slightly leaning toward the anchor as he is set up to start the exercise, waiting for your command and the inevitable tug on the rope as you start running backward. You can correct for the anticipation later; the important thing now is to have him enthusiastic about going out.

Bar Jump Some of you may have already familiarized your dog with bar-jump preliminaries during Open Week 3, when you taught him to clear the broad jump—at that time, it was suggested that you place a black-and-white-striped bar on the number-2 jump.

You should by now have made the uprights for the bar jump and have the bar painted as described in Utility Week 2. Place the bar on the uprights about eight inches to twelve inches from the ground. The dog must go over the bar, not under it; so if your dog is small, put the bar lower rather than higher for now.

---

* This is one of few times you repeat a verbal command during Utility training. The major reasons in this case are that the command is a new one, the exercise is complicated, and you are at a great distance when the dog makes the error. 263

III-34. As you practice the Open retrieve over high jump, modify it in such a way that you condition your dog to jumping over the bar. Begin with the bar set at the dog's maximum jump height and take one board out. In the next weeks continue to remove boards, but only after you are certain that the dog knows he must go *over* the bar, not between the bar and the boards.

The first two or three days of introduction to the bar jump involves a heeling-on-lead routine during which you and the dog run to and over the jump. Your dog should do this easily, since he is already trained to clear an obstacle. As you jump, give the command "Over!" As soon as you land, quickly get in front of the dog so that he can come to you and sit facing you, just as you did when you trained your dog to clear the eight-inch board of the high jump in Open. Finish as in previous exercises and praise the dog.

Beginning this week, when you practice the Open retrieve over high jump you should attach the striped bar to the jump. You can do this easily by nailing two spikes into the uprights at your dog's proper jumping height and placing the bar on the spikes. This will gradually condition the dog to seeing the bar at maximum jumping height (fig. III-34). Begin by jumping the dog with the bar and all boards in the jump. Gradually, in the next two weeks, remove some of the boards, but leave the bar at regulation height.

Practice the bar jump introduction as described—running to the obstacle and clearing it with your dog on the command "Over!"—for two or three days. Then, after the dog has mastered this initial routine, modify the exercise in the following fashion. Put the dog in a sit-stay (on lead) about three feet from the bar jump and carefully step over the jump. Give the command "Over!" and, if necessary, tug the dog toward you to get him in motion. The bar should still be at the height you used for the preliminary jumping—eight to twelve inches above-ground. When the dog has cleared the jump, bring him in to you with the lead and make him come to a straight sit. Praise him and then give the command "Heel!" Work on this modification for the remainder of the week.

UTILITY WEEK 4

OUTLINE OF TRAINING SCHEDULE
Old Exercises
    Open
        Practice all daily, except the long sit and long down, in proper show sequence.
        Advanced Heeling: Pivots to right and left (components of the directed-retrieve exercise, introduced this week)
        Retrieve over High Jump: More boards removed, bar at full jump height
    Utility
        Signal Exercises (while heeling off lead): Stay, heel, finish, stand
        Seek Back: Practice as described in Week 3 for one day only.
        Group Examination (Long Stand): 2 minutes
Modification of Utility Exercise
    Directed Jumping: Perfecting the turn and sit (an assistant will be required); adding distance and hand signal to the bar jump
New Exercises
    Signal Exercise: Sit
    Scent Discrimination with Articles
    Directed Retrieve
Suggested Practice Session: Once daily

Directed Jumping Further Modified

Perfecting the Turn and Sit   This week we will concentrate more on the dog's turn and sit by applying a correction with a second rope. This phase of training will be greatly facilitated if you have an assistant to manipulate the one-hundred-foot rope—to get the dog out near the anchor—while you work with a shorter rope to correct the dog into turning and sitting.

    Most dogs will not turn and sit immediately when they reach the anchor until they are shown that their name means "Stop suddenly, turn, and expect the command 'Sit!' to follow immediately." By the end of last week your dog should have begun to anticipate the command "Go out!" and probably did not require much assistance from the rope to   265 be set in motion out to the area of the anchor. For the first day of this week, practice the go out with the dog on the one-hundred-foot rope to make sure he knows that he must run all the way out to the anchor before stopping. Unless he does, you cannot proceed with the next step.

When you feel confident that your dog has mastered this procedure, give him a momentary rest while you measure off the fifty-foot rope and tie a knot near one end. The knot will be your handle to stop the dog when he reaches the spot at which you give his name and command him to sit. This spot must be somewhat short of the pulley anchor. The most certain way to determine where you should tie the knot is to attach the swivel end of the rope to the dog's collar and take him out near the anchor. Then lay the rope out, back toward the spot from which you will begin the training; if you have an assistant, he can help you by tying the knot in the rope at that spot (fig. III-35). Bring your dog back to the starting point, and coil up the rope so that it will play out easily when the dog runs out. The coil of rope should be on your right side, since you will have it running through your right hand as the dog goes out. When the knot comes into your hand, you know that the dog has reached the proper spot, and it is time to say his name loudly as you tighten your grip on the knot and spin him off balance, back toward you.

Bring the dog to the starting area and attach both ropes to his collar (fig. III-36). When you send him out with "Go out!" and the proper hand signal, remain at the starting point. This means that if your dog still needs encouragement to run out, your assistant will have to move in the opposite direction to pull him.

When you are ready to start the training, have the fifty-foot rope coiled up at your right and free to run through your right hand. As soon as you give the command "Go out!," your assistant should run in the direction opposite to the dog's line of march, applying tension to the rope as needed (fig. III-37). A major objective is to have the dog maintain a steady, fairly rapid pace out to the anchor. The fifty-foot rope should be passing through your hand freely, adding very little drag on the dog's collar from behind. Your right hand should be extended out behind you so that you can feel the knot slightly in advance (fig. III-38); when you feel it, quickly tighten your grip around it, allow your hand to move forward at the same pace that the dog is running, and give his name loudly (fig. III-39). Your assistant should *drop* his rope at this instant. As you shout the dog's name, pull the cord back toward you with enough force to knock him off balance, spinning him around toward you. Give the command "Sit!" as soon as he has turned. If he sits, walk up to him, giving verbal praise as you approach him and more praise when you reach him. Take up your heeling position and grab both ropes near his collar to heel him back to the starting area. (See figs. III-35–40 for the entire sequence.)

It is important to remember that the dog must *hear* the command before or at the instant he feels the correction. It is not a good idea to pull on the fifty-foot rope and *then* give his name. By keeping your right hand extended behind you, you will feel the knot enough in advance to be able to time your verbal command correctly and apply the necessary tension on the rope to spin the dog around toward you.

Your practice on the go out for the remainder of the week will consist of this exercise without any further modifications—unless he needs no asistance to go out to the anchor, in which case you can eliminate your assistant. By the end of the week your dog should be running out quickly and turning around smartly as soon as he hears his name. In fact, at the end of the week try the exercise without pulling on the fifty-foot rope to stop him. If he has caught on to the vocal signal, the correction will be unnecessary; give verbal praise instead. Also by the end of the week, your assistant will probably not have to apply corrections while running with the hundred-foot rope. Indeed, your dog should be able to outdistance your assistant easily; so encourage the assistant to be alert and avoid accidentally applying tension on the rope when the dog has been commanded to stop.

Adding Distance and Hand Signal to the Bar Jump For the bar-jump training this week, you will put the dog in a sit-stay at a greater distance from the jump; you will also walk out an equally increased distance on the opposite side of the jump. The bar should be kept low to the ground—no more than a foot high. The training will again be on lead—but you will substitute a rope for the leather lead so that you can increase the distance. Place the bar on the approach side of the uprights to minimize the chances that the rope, dragging behind the dog, will knock the bar off as he clears the jump.

Attach the rope lead (either the one-hundred-foot rope or the fifty) to the dog's collar and put him in a sit-stay about six feet from the jump. Walk around the jump and stand facing the dog about six feet from the bar, with the rope draped over it (fig. III-41). Make certain you are centered on the bar and that your rope lead provides an appropriate guide for the dog's jump. Give the command "Over!" and, only if necessary, tug the rope to get the dog in motion toward the jump. When he has cleared the jump, make sure he comes in to you and sits squarely at your feet, facing you. Take up all the excess rope and be certain the dog can finish without getting entangled in it. When you are ready, give him the command "Heel!" and praise him.

Work the dog on this exercise for several days, adding distance each time; he should be about ten feet away from the jump by the middle of the week. At that point, you will modify the exercise further by introducing the dog to the hand signal (you will need an assistant for this). The bar should still be about a foot off the ground. When you have finally reached a distance of twenty feet from the dog and he is performing acceptably, gradually begin to position yourself toward one side of the bar jump when you move around opposite the dog and about the same distance away from the bar jump as he is. The dog, remember, is still on the rope lead. Make your transition to the askew position gradually (fig. III-42). The first time you do the exercise from twenty feet, have your assistant hold the centered rope while you take a single side step, remaining within the two uprights. Then give the com-

III–36

III-35–40: Perfecting the Turn and Sit. **III-35.** Use two rope aids. One of them must be measured in this fashion: take the dog out to the spot at which you want him to stop and turn and have an assistant tie a knot in the other end of the rope. The knot will be at the spot from which you will give the dog's name, followed by the command "Sit!"

III-36. Put your dog in the heeling position. Your assistant will pull the rope that passes through the pulley and back to the dog's collar. The other rope, coiled up at your right side, will pass through your hand as the dog goes out. When you feel the knot reach your hand, give his name loudly, and tighten your grip on the knot.

III–37

III-37. Simultaneously give the hand signal and the command "Go out!" The snap of the rope will set the dog into motion quickly. Your assistant should run in the opposite direction, applying tension to the rope *if*

the dog hesitates or does not run. Your practice in the previous week indicated to your dog the rate at which you wanted him to run out; most dogs will easily outdistance any assistant.

III-38. As the dog runs out toward the pulley anchor, allow the rope to pass through your right hand, but keep your hand behind you so you can feel the knot coming and have time to give the dog's name to spin him around toward you.

III-39. When you feel the knot reach your hand, give the dog's name loudly and tighten your grip on the knot to stop the dog at that point. When he has stopped and turned, give him the verbal sit command.

III-40. Give your dog praise as you approach him, to encourage him to remain sitting in this fashion. Take up the ropes near his collar and heel back to the starting point to repeat the exercise.

269

III-41. Line up on the center line and give your dog the command "Over!," enforcing it, if necessary, by tugging on the rope. Note that the bar is on the side of the uprights closer to the dog. This makes it less likely that the rope will accidentally pull the bar off when the dog clears it. Later, when the jump is at maximum height and the dog is jumping off lead, you should have the bar on the other side of the uprights.

III-42. Move out to the askew position gradually, while the bar is still low. The rope should be draped over the bar, both to define the dog's jump path and to serve as a correction rope if he hesitates to jump on the first command. Here, the handler is giving the hand signal with his left hand, after having taken a long side step off to the right.

mand "Over!" but now, as you say it, point your hand toward the jump (fig. III-42). The dog will see your hand signal—a definite pointing motion—and hear the command simultaneously. Work with him on that exercise several times the first day you try it, not going more than one step away from the center line and keeping the dog jumping in the same direction each time.

On the second day, remain at the twenty-foot distance and repeat the exercise. This time, after he clears the jump, comes to you, sits, and finishes, put him in a sit-stay on that side of the jump, drape the rope over the bar, and go across to the opposite side, out a distance equal to the distance that the dog is sitting from the bar. This time you must make a side step in the other direction. Remain, as before, within the two uprights, but askew of the dog's center line of jump. When you give the command "Over!," point to the jump with your other hand (fig. III-43).

Toward the end of the week you will be able to add a further step in your progress by moving farther away from the dog's center line of jump. Make sure, however, that your assistant continues to hold the rope in a straight center line down the middle of the jump. Put the dog in a sit-stay, walk around the jump, make sure the rope is draped over the bar at the center line, and then go out about ten feet in a direct line. After you turn to face the dog, take a long side step to the left and come to a halt where you can see the dog along the outside edge of the innermost upright; he now must jump in a straight line down the center, as defined by the guide rope, but you will be off to one side. As you give the command "Over!," point to the jump with your right hand. When the dog is in mid-air, turn in place to face the spot at which he will land and rapidly bring him in to you with verbal encouragement so that he comes to a straight sit at your feet, facing you. Make sure that your assistant has provided enough slack in the rope to allow the dog to move toward you without getting tangled in it. Praise your dog, and then give the command "Heel!"

Heel the dog to the center line on your side of the jump and go over to the opposite side. Readjust the ropes. This time, step over to the *right* so that you must give the dog a hand signal with your *left* hand. Repeat the exercise.

Work on this routine for the remainder of the week. The object is to condition your dog to expecting your hand signal from either direction. Since he is still on the rope lead, which defines his center line over the bar jump, he will learn simultaneously to jump down the center line and pay attention to your hand signal.

If the dog is having difficulty learning this exercise, keep him at the twenty-foot distance but adjust your own distance so that you are closer to the jump on your side—perhaps as close as five feet. As the dog clears the jump, back up quickly to the ten-foot distance on your side and bring him straight in to you with the rope.

Remember to practice the retrieve over high jump with the bar placed at your dog's maximum jumping height. You can remove more boards at this point.

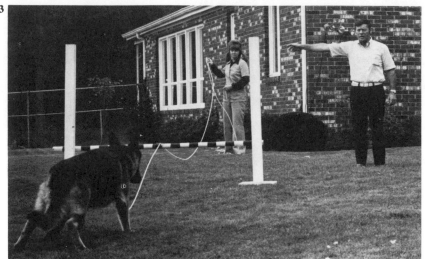

III-43. To show the dog that the hand signal can be given with either hand—that he must be prepared to move in either direction—reverse your position. Here, the handler has taken a long side step to the left of the jump's center line, and is giving the signal with his right hand as he says "Over!"

Signal Exercise: Sit

This may be one of the most difficult AKC obedience exercises that you will try to teach. We will take the next four weeks to build up to AKC requirements. Here is what must happen: The dog is lying down, facing you. You must give a hand signal to make him rise and sit—without creeping forward. You have one chance—one command—to make him do it. If he does not see it, you are disqualified. If he sees it and does not rise, you are disqualified. The signal is a smooth upward motion of the right arm, hand open; the arm stops somewhere between the waist and head, although a higher command is legal, and as soon as it does, it must be dropped smoothly to the side of the body. Posing the arm at the high point of the motion would be considered giving a double signal.

In a show, this routine is part of a heeling exercise; the judge tells you to "stand your dog!," which you do, on hand signal only. Then he gives *you* a verbal signal to leave your dog, at which time you give the dog the *hand* signal only (no verbal reinforcement) for stay, walk away from the dog without looking back, and proceed to the end of the ring. When you have turned to face your dog, the judge will give you a hand signal to drop your dog. After the dog drops, the judge gives you the hand signal to sit your dog; it is this signal—the smooth upward right-arm motion—that you will now try to teach the dog (figs. III-44–46).

III-44–46: The Hand Signal for Sit. **III-44.** Keep your arm slightly out, away from your body, and raise it upward in a fairly swift —but smooth—motion.

III-45. The hand signal should terminate somewhere between your waist and your head. This is an ideal position to stop the upward motion. Begin with a somewhat slow, exaggerated hand signal and gradually work for more speed.

III-46. The dog will be given the sit hand signal when he is lying down. He must come up into a sitting position immediately, without moving forward. He can push himself up with his front feet or lean on his front feet and push his body up with his back feet, or a combination of both. But he must not move forward excessively to do it.

The rate at which most dogs move into the sitting position reflects the speed of the hand signal they are given. Thus, if you want your dog to go into the sit quickly, make your signal a swift—but smooth—motion. This is the most desirable kind of performance for the sit hand signal. If you give a slower, more deliberate signal, the dog will tend to come up equally slowly.

One important point: your hand signal should be obvious to the dog. Two kinds of obstacles present themselves to him when you give a signal to sit. One is that your arm motion is in line with your body and is therefore somewhat obscure from his perspective. Try to make your upward hand sweep away from your body slightly so that your arm's silhouette is clear to the dog. The second obstacle is the blending in of your clothing with the background, which reduces the sharpness of the signal even though you make it slightly away from your body. The best way to guarantee a visible hand signal is to wear a long-sleeve shirt that is full of light and dark patterns of a large size, so that no matter what the background is, it will contrast with the shirt.

Training for the Sit Hand Signal   Begin the training with the dog on lead and in the proper heeling position. Part of the initial training for the sit hand signal is the verbal command "Sit!" This command will be dropped when the dog has learned to associate your arm motion with the sit exercise. (The word "sit" is a very specific command in dog handling and should be used only when it is "legal" and desirable. The main problem is that it is also commonly used by noncompetitors to encourage their dogs to sit down. One habit that people fall into as they enter training is to assume that the dog will sit only when he hears the English word. Because it has so specific a usage in dog training, we have avoided using it until Utility.)

When the dog is in the proper heeling position, give him the command "Down!" so that he drops to a lying position at your feet. Wait several seconds so that the dog is convinced he is in fact on a command and is about to receive another one. The object is to get the dog to rise up to a sitting position without moving forward a single inch. You are to remain standing in the same position. To do this, you must execute the same kind of motion you used when you taught the dog the automatic sit: raise your right hand up over the dog's head so as to put slight upward tension on his lead and collar, and move your left hand around to just above his back so that you can correct him into the sitting position if he attempts to move forward.

Just as you begin raising your right hand upward to apply a quick bit of tension to his collar, give the verbal sit command; he will hear it at about the time that the lead snaps tight on his collar and begins to pull him up. He should rise quickly to avoid what should be a sharp correction. If he tries to move forward when you give the command and put tension on the lead, be prepared to push his rump down quickly, as in the automatic sit.

Practice this simple routine in every training session this week; you are teaching your dog one of the most difficult of all AKC exercises.

Be sure to enforce the *full* upward sit when you give the command. Some dogs seem to catch on quickly, but they rise only about three quarters of the required height on the command "Sit!" You want your dog to come up all the way, and quickly. Therefore, be prepared to correct him into the full upright position as soon as you give the command. If he is slow or comes up only partially, correct him sharply to remind him that he must be both quick and complete in his motion. You are to work this week for performance on command *and* speed of performance. We will expand the exercise in the following weeks, so do not deviate from the pattern we have outlined; it is intrinsically related to what will follow.

Scent Discrimination with Articles

You will now begin to complicate the scent-discrimination work by accustoming the dog to finding one article out of a set of identical articles, using his nose to do so. We want to avoid harsh corrections in this phase, and the best way to accomplish this is to let the dog correct himself when he makes a mistake; he can try to pick up the wrong article but, because it will be securely fastened to a large board with a piece of wire, he will not be able to; he must continue looking for the right article—the only loose one on the board and the only one that has fresh scent on it.

The size of board you use depends on both the size of the dog and the size of his scent articles. For the best results, the board should be larger than it has to be; if the dog is large and powerful and the board is too small, he might just return to you with the entire board hanging out of his mouth, holding firmly on to the wrong dumbbell. The board should be large enough to ensure that the dog step onto it to make his search for the right dumbbell. We find that pegboard or hardboard is the best material to use. Both come in standard-size sheets at lumber yards, and most lumber yards will cut them to order. A good size for medium to large dogs would be about three feet by four feet. You might even want to hinge two pieces together for easy storage and transportation. A further advantage to pegboard is that it already has holes in it, so that you can conveniently move the articles around and wire them down.

For the first two days of training, you will merely put the metal practice article on the board and send the dog for it. Some dogs seem to shy away from the practice board if they are suddenly confronted with several articles and a strange board. You want to get your dog used to walking on and around the board to take the article. Continue practicing with the single metal article until the dog is confident about walking on and around the board; you can then modify the exercise by adding three more articles, all metal and all firmly wired down so that the dog cannot retrieve the wrong one. Arrange the three new articles on the board in a random fashion, keeping at least fifteen to eighteen inches between them (fig. III-47). One of the three articles should be at a considerable distance from the other two—at an extreme end of 275

III-47. After the dog is confident about walking on the board to take a single scent article, wire three metal articles to the board. Place the scented article among them, but vary the configuration each time so that he must search for the scented article.

the board. If *you* wire the articles to the board, you will have to let them air out overnight so as to allow your scent to dissipate. If someone else wires them down, you can begin working immediately; the dog is to find the article that has *your* scent on it.

Put the dog in a sit-stay, on lead, with his back to the board and about ten feet away from it; in later weeks, you will work at the regulation distance of fifteen feet. Give the dog the command "Stay!," place his lead on the ground, and walk out to the board, rubbing your metal article. Place it somewhere in the middle of the board, away from the other objects. Return to the dog, take up your lead, and give him your scent. As you give him the command "Find it!," pivot around and step toward the board so that he has enough lead to work comfortably around it.

This will be the first time your dog must choose from among several identical-looking articles. They may all look alike, but one of them is very different: it has your scent on it. He might look puzzled temporarily, but most dogs, as soon as they smell their handler's scent, will simply pick up the correct article and bring it back. If your dog does this, give him a good deal of praise—before you finish but *after* you remove the article from his mouth with the command "Out!"

If the dog does not pick up the article—or if he refuses even to look for it—move up close to him and apply a series of moderate (*not* harsh) tugs on his collar, knocking him slightly off balance each time and gradually bringing him to the correct article. When he picks it up, quickly back up to your original starting position with the dog following you and carrying the article in his mouth. When he sits squarely, remove it from his mouth as you give the command "Out!," and then praise him before making him finish. The corrections at this stage of training, we repeat, should not be harsh, for they will confuse the dog and discourage him from working. But they should be firm enough to get the dog to pick up the article. Each handler will have to exercise his own judgment about the optimum degree of force his dog will tolerate and still work enthusiastically.

If the dog tries to pick up one of the wired-down objects, he will discover that it will not move. If he then looks for and finds the scented article, allow him to bring it to you, praise him, as above, and repeat the exercise. He may have discovered, on this first mistake, that the scented article is the only one that will come off the board, and he will then deliberately search for the scented article, as he is supposed to. If, however, after several repetitions, he still tries to get one of the wired articles, move in and correct him toward the proper one. It is extremely unlikely that a dog with this much training and preparation will fail to catch on, but if he persists in trying to pick up the first article that he comes to, you might have to encourage him to take the proper one by putting your hand on it or moving it slightly with your fingers as it lies on the board. However, he should now be working with his nose; unless he does so very soon, you may have to take a hard look at your rate of training. Some people exceed their dog's learning capacity by working too rapidly, pushing the dog along too fast. If your dog has trouble with the scent articles and you have followed the rate and sequence of our training schedule, it might be a good idea to give him a rest for several days and not work on obedience exercises at all.

If your dog has caught on to the scent articles rapidly, as most do, you can gradually begin to complicate the exercise at the end of the first week: instead of placing the practice metal article on the board, substitute the leather one. This will tip off your dog to the fact that the correct article can be either leather or metal. Most dogs, when transferred to the leather article, make a qualitative leap in their understanding of and enthusiasm for the scent-discrimination exercise. They seem to enjoy finding the leather object, and along with that enjoyment comes a new and keener interest in the work.

Thus, the end of the week should find you and your dog working with both the leather and the metal articles. The board should still have the three metal articles wired to it, and the dog should still be working on lead. Do not repeat the exercise more than two or three times each session.

Directed Retrieve

The directed retrieve in Utility competition requires that the dog retrieve a glove that has been placed somewhere along the narrow end of the show ring. The judge (or steward) puts three gloves out, one in each corner of the ring and one in the center. While he is doing this, the handler stands in the middle of the ring, his back to the judge, the dog at heel, and in between and in line with the bar and high jumps (fig. III-48).

After the judge lays out the gloves, he will step out of the area and give the handler—you—*one* of three possible commands: "One," "Two," or "Three." Let us assume he designates glove number 3. You are allowed to give your dog's name and the command "Heel!" ("Gus! 277

III-48–52: Preview of the Directed Retrieve. **III-48.** At first, you allow the dog to watch the "judge" place the gloves, but in an AKC Utility trial, your back must be turned.

III-49. The judge will indicate to the handler which glove he wants the dog to retrieve . . . here it is glove number 3. On hearing this, the handler gives the command "Heel!" and pivots to face the glove on the right. The dog must pivot with him and come to an immediate sit. Without any further instructions from the judge, the handler sends his dog for the glove.

III-50. The handler is permitted to squat down and point his arm toward the glove. The dog must remain sitting while he does this. When the handler is confident that the dog is looking at the correct glove, he sends him with the command "Take it!," and then stands up while the dog goes for the glove.

III-51. The dog must run swiftly and directly to the glove, pick it up, and run straight back to the handler, without playing with or dropping the glove.

III-52. When the dog returns, he must sit squarely at the handler's feet and hold the glove in his mouth. The judge then says "Take it!" The glove is removed with both hands *and* the command "Out!" The judge will then tell the handler to finish. The dog is required to retrieve only one glove.

III–49

III–50

III–51

III–52

III-53–56: Teaching Dog to Retrieve One Glove. **III-53.** Put your dog in a sit-stay and place a single glove out in front of him about twenty feet. Return to your dog, give him the command "Stay!," and step out one pace toward the glove. In a show you are not allowed to do this, but while you are training, the extra pace forward will condition your dog to pay attention to your arm, which points to the correct glove.

III-54. When you step out one pace, squat down, point to the glove and, making sure your dog is paying attention to your arm, give the command "Take it!" Stand up as soon as the dog passes you.

III-55. The dog should run directly to the glove and take it; this should be pretty simple for him, since he has been doing the retrieve on flat all through his Open training and competition.

III-56. The dog returns with the glove, just as he did with the dumbbell in the retrieve on flat. Pause a moment before taking the glove with the command "Out!"

Heel!") and you must turn in place, either to the right or to the left. Your dog must turn with you, returning to a sitting position (fig. III-49). Then you are allowed to squat down, point toward the glove with your left arm, and give the command "Take it!" (fig. III-50). As soon as you give the command, the dog must run *directly* to the glove, pick it up, run straight back to you (fig. III-51), sit in front of you, and wait for your next command. At that point, the judge says "Take it!" You then give the command "Out!" and remove the glove from the dog's mouth with both hands (fig. III-52). When the judge tells you to finish, give the command "Heel!" That terminates the directed retrieve.

Some additional complications are discussed at the end of this chapter. For the time being, you may assume that the sequence is identical for the retrieve of gloves number 1, 2 and 3. Thus the essentials of the exercise are as follows: The judge tells you which glove your dog is to retrieve. You then give the command "Heel!" and, once the dog is again sitting, the command "Take it!," without any further instructions from the judge. When the dog is sitting in front of you with the glove in his mouth, you wait for the judge's "Take it!" After you have removed the glove from the dog's mouth, the judge will tell you to finish. You are required to send your dog for just one of the gloves, and the judge must alternate the gloves as he sends each contestant.

Training for Directed Retrieve   Needless to say, you will need three gloves to do this exercise. It is very difficult to buy three gloves at most hardware stores, so if you have a friend who is also training a dog at this level the two of you should buy three pairs and divide them. Ordinary white cotton work gloves are suitable; the size is irrelevant, but you should attempt to match them with your dog's size—do not buy extra-large gloves for a dachshund or small ones for a Great Dane.

From the dog's point of view, there are two major components to this exercise, one familiar and one not. He knows that on the command "Take it!" he must go out and pick something up in his mouth— this is old glove to him. The unfamiliar part of the exercise is the hand signal that designates the direction he must travel to pick up whatever it is he is sent for. Thus, you will concentrate on this new portion, working to make the dog aware of the hand signal.

The best way to accomplish this is to train with just one of the gloves. Place it somewhere in the training area with your dog in a sit-stay or down at some random point from which he can watch you place the glove. (Initially, you will train with the dog facing the glove; later, you will introduce the pivots.) Be sure to have your dog in a different position each day while you place the glove; otherwise he might later assume that when he is near the rosebush (or elm tree, or picnic table), he must go after "the one on the left." He should not be in the starting point of the exercise while you are placing the glove.

After you have placed the glove, return to your dog and heel away with him to the position you plan to start from. At first, work as if you wanted the dog to take glove number 2. This means that you heel him to about twenty feet from the glove and come to a halt. The dog should assume the sitting position automatically. Give him both the vocal and hand-signal commands for stay, and step forward one pace (fig. III-53). Squat slowly to your knees and extend your left hand slowly out in the direction of the glove. When you are fully squatted and your left arm is fully extended (fig. III-54), give the command "Take it!" Because of your dog's training in the Open retrieve on flat, he should immediately go after the glove (fig. III-55), pick it up, and return with it firmly in his mouth (fig. III-56). When he has done so, pause a moment, then give the command "Out!" and remove the glove from his mouth with both hands. Praise him at this point. Then give him the finish command and heel away to another part of the ring.

The reason for making the step forward in training—it is not allowed in a show—before sending the dog is to emphasize the hand-signal portion of the exercise. Imagine it from the dog's point of view when there are *three* gloves out there in front of him, not all that far apart, from which he must choose one to retrieve for you. Any one of them will seem like fair game unless he has learned to pay attention to your hand signal. Taking a step out in front of the dog eliminates from his vision anything on the right side of your arm (if you are sending him to the left or center), and also gives him a clue to his direction of march.

In your work this week on a single glove, with the dog heeled up to within twenty feet of the glove and going for what amounts to glove number 2, you will not make a pivot before sending him for it. Rather, you will give him the familiar command "Stay!" and, with your one pace forward, indicate his direction of march. Your slow, deliberate squat and extended arm will attract his attention, for this is a new form of behavior on your part. He has only one choice: the single, white, and very visible glove in front of him. A week on this simple exercise will fix a new routine into his behavior. He should be confident of it by the end of the week, and aware that your extended arm means something.

Be sure to continue your practice on advanced heeling routines—pivots to the right, left, and in a 360° arc—for you will need them for this exercise soon.

UTILITY WEEK 5

OUTLINE OF TRAINING SCHEDULE
Old Exercises
    Open
        Practice all daily, except the long sit and long down, in proper show sequence.
        Advanced Heeling: Pivots to right and left (incorporated into directed-retrieve practice from now on); back steps

Retrieve over High Jump: Several boards removed, bar at full
jump height
Utility
Signal Exercise (while heeling off lead): Stay, heel, finish, stand
Group Examination (Long Stand) (2½ minutes)
Modifications of Utility Exercises
Directed Jumping: Increasing the dog's speed on the go out; regu-
lation-height bar jump, off lead
Signal Exercise: Sit on hand signal alone
Scent Discrimination: Six articles, off lead
Directed Retrieve: Three gloves
New Exercises
None
Suggested Practice Session: Once daily

Directed Jumping Further Modified

Increasing Speed on the Go Out   During the training this week you will
build up the dog's initial speed so that he leaps forward as soon as he
hears "Go out!" and sees the hand signal; also, the technique you use
to accomplish this will take you one step closer to working with the dog
completely off lead and off the training ropes. One minor modification
for the week will be to start the exercise with the dog sitting perfectly
straight, on the center line of his direction of march, instead of askew
of it. By this time he should understand that he must go out; any correction you have to make will be a small one. Finally, you will begin to
approximate show conditions by training with the dog between the bar
and high jumps. This will accustom him to running between the jumps
and prevent errors later, when he is off lead and exposed to the jumps.
You will need an assistant for this week again.

Both ropes will be used and attached to the dog's collar as before.
The assistant will apply considerable tension to the one-hundred-foot
rope by pulling on it from behind you. You will hold the swivel-snap
end of the rope in your left hand, about a foot from the dog's collar,
resisting the tension with your body weight and arm (fig. III-57). It is
important for your assistant to apply as much tension to the rope as
you can comfortably resist. The dog will be aware of the taut rope,
because it will no longer be lying on the ground. As soon as you give the
command "Go out!," you must release the rope and let the tension
snap the dog forward. Your left hand should remain out in front to give
the hand signal. After two or three attempts at this, your dog should be
anticipating the sudden snap of the guide rope, watching for your hand
to release it. He will literally leap forward as soon as he sees the tension
released and hears the command "Go out!" Your assistant should run
back to be in a position to apply additional corrections only if the dog
slows down before reaching the proper spot.

If your dog is particularly large, he will require somewhat more

III-57. To build up the dog's initial speed on the
go out, have your assistant put as much tension on
the rope as you can comfortably resist with your
left hand. You might tie a knot in the rope about
fifteen inches from the swivel and hold on to this
to resist the tension. As soon as you give the command "Go out!," let go of the rope and allow
your left hand to shoot forward with it. The
suddenly relaxed resistance will put an immediate
sharp tug on the dog's collar and get him into
motion quickly. By this time, your dog should go
out without any additional assistance from the
rope, and your assistant will usually be running
hard to keep up with the dog.

tension to get him moving rapidly—you might tie a knot in the one-
hundred-foot rope about twelve or eighteen inches from the swivel end.
This will give you additional leverage and enable you to resist somewhat more tension.

The Bar Jump off Lead   By the end of Week 4, your dog was clearing the bar jump, following the rope. You were standing off to one
side of the jump to accustom him to seeing you in a peculiar position
with respect to his line of march. In addition, you were using a hand
signal to point to the jump and had the option of moving closer to it
should the dog have difficulty learning the exercise.

This week you will make a number of fairly ambitious modifications to the bar-jump training. First, you will put the dog on the center
line of the training area, as he would be in an AKC show, with the bar
jump located about ten feet off this center line. The dog will be at least
twenty feet away from the jump. The guide rope will still be draped
over the bar, defining the dog's direction of march. You will need an   285

assistant again this week, to apply, if necessary, a tug on the rope to set the dog in motion after your "Over!" Keep the bar at a low height. If a correction is required, the rope can easily knock the bar off; the closer it is to the ground the less startling the noise of its fall will be for the dog. The major objective this week is to move the angle of the jump to 90° from the center line of the practice ring. Early in the week the dog will be jumping the bar when it is about 60° off the center line (Step I in fig. III-58), and by the end of the week he will be jumping it while it is 90° off the center line—as in an AKC trial (Step III of fig. III-58). The move from 60° to 90° should be gradual, to condition the dog to jumping over the bar at the center. Keeping the dog at the full twenty-foot distance will also help: the farther away from the jump he is, the greater the likelihood that he will select an approach that enables him to clear it over the center, even when it is turned 90° from the ring center line.

Begin the first session this week with the dog on the center line of the practice ring with the hundred-foot rope attached to his collar. Drape the rope over the bar and continue it out to where your assistant is standing. Turn the bar jump 60° from center line, facing the dog. The bar should be only about twelve inches above the ground; it would be a good idea to place it on the side of the uprights that is facing the dog, thus reducing the likelihood that it will be accidentally knocked off by the rope as the rope is dragged along behind the dog or tugged by the assistant. You should have the free end of the rope at your side, defining the dog's line of march from the assistant to you after he has cleared the jump. The rope goes from the dog, across the bar, to the assistant and then to you. It is unlikely that you will be able to take up the rope fast enough to use it for a correction; if the dog makes a mistake after clearing the jump and does not come directly to you, quickly move toward him, take the rope near his collar, and apply a series of side-to-side corrections while moving rapidly back to the correct position. When the dog is sitting squarely, the command for finish can be given, followed by praise.

Alternate your position and the dog's position so that he is jumping to both the right and the left of the ring's center line, and you are giving the hand signal with first one hand and then the other. Begin to pay more attention to your handling techniques as you simultaneously give the command "Over!" and the hand signal; avoid body English and bending at the knees. Your hand signal should be a smooth motion, pointing in the direction of the bar jump.

As soon as the dog is performing the exercise smoothly, you can disconnect the rope from his collar, but continue to allow it to define the appropriate line of march for the dog. As soon as the rope is disconnected, you can begin moving the bar to a higher position. Determine the height that your dog is required to jump and subtract twelve inches from it. Divide the remainder by four since you will move up to maximum height in four increments. If your dog must jump thirty-six inches in an AKC trial, for example, subtract twelve, which gives twenty-four, and divide by four: six. Each day you will then move the bar up six

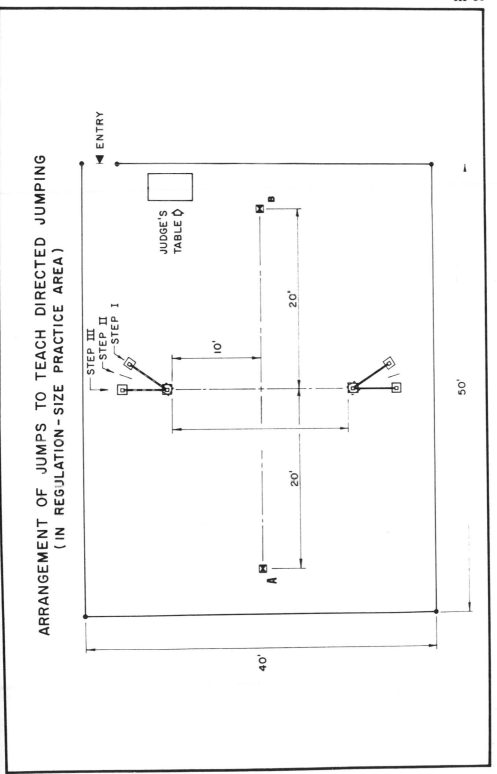

ARRANGEMENT OF JUMPS TO TEACH DIRECTED JUMPING
(IN REGULATION-SIZE PRACTICE AREA)

inches; by the end of the week, your dog will be jumping the full thirty-six inches. As you add height, be certain to place the bar on the side of the uprights *not* facing the dog's starting position, so that if he hits it while trying to jump over, it will fall off the pegs easily. Of course, when you alternate sides you will have to turn your uprights around.

It is impossible to give a precise schedule for this week, since each handler/dog team varies in its skills and proficiency. In general, however, by the end of the week the dog should be clearing the full jump height, and the bar jump should be placed at 90° to the practice-ring center line (Step III in fig. III-58). Ideally, as soon as the bar has been moved up two increments and the dog is jumping it easily, the rope guide should be removed. However, you may continue to use the rope this week, even when the bar is at thirty-six inches. If you do, be sure that it hangs down to the ground directly under the bar and does not constitute an obstacle to the dog's jump (see fig. III-59).

Sit Hand Signal Modified

You will introduce a number of modifications for the sit hand signal this week; but, before you do, practice what you accomplished in Week 4: give the dog, simultaneously, the command "Sit!" *and* the smooth upward correction on the leather lead with your right hand. This correction reinforces the fact that ignoring the verbal command will bring about a penalty: a sharp upward correction. What you taught the dog in Week 4 was that the verbal command was associated with an upward tug on the lead—if the dog hesitated, he was physically reminded that he had to sit up. From the dog's-eye view, assuming he has made this intellectual equation, "Sit!" means to come up from the lying-down position to a full sit, fast and without moving forward—or else get a very sharp tug on the leather lead.

This week, the idea is to move gradually—a little each day—in a slow arc out of the heel position, until you are out in front of the dog (figs. III-60–63). Each day, you will give the verbal sit command, simultaneously applying an upward tug on the leather lead to enforce it—but you will be applying the upward tension on the lead with your right hand, instead of your left, and will also be giving the dog the hand signal for sit with your right hand. That is, the upward hand motion as you grasp the lead gradually becomes the hand signal for sit.

As you move around to the front of and away from the dog, he will sit on hand signal alone, with no other commands required. However, it is important for him always to remember that the hand signal you give contains a potential correction—upward tension on the leather lead.

For practice this week, put the dog in the proper heeling position and give the command "Down!" followed by the command "Stay!" Step off on your right foot, so as to be facing the dog 90° away from your original position (fig. III-60). Pause a moment. Transfer the lead to your left hand. Now quickly give your dog the hand-signal command for sit, simultaneously with the verbal sit command, by definitively

III-59. Your dog can jump the bar with the guide rope draped over it; let it hang straight up and down so that it does not constitute an obstacle to the dog as you increase the height of the bar.

raising your open-palmed *right* hand and grabbing the lead with it (figs. III-60–61).

Practice this routine for several days, until the dog is anticipating the command slightly—as soon as he sees your right hand beginning to move up to make the signal, he should be rising to the sit position. If the dog is beginning to rely on the signal from your hand, *periodically* eliminate the verbal sit command. But, since he is still learning, you should not eliminate it entirely, at least not for a few days. The ultimate objective is, of course, to eliminate the verbal component of the command, but only after the dog has *indelibly* associated sit with the hand signal.

For now, continue to "hit" the lead with your right hand when you give the hand signal: scoop it into your hand as you make the upward motion (fig. III-61).

Toward the middle of the week, instead of stopping at a 90° angle from the dog after you have given him the down command, go an additional 45°. Go through the same routine from this position. If the dog continues to show progress, then move to a full 180°. You will then be facing the dog, standing directly in front of him (fig. III-62). If he performs properly from this position as you give the verbal and hand signals for sit, then gradually move out to about three feet (fig. III-63). Work with him at the three-foot distance; if the dog continues to do the exercise properly, gradually back farther away from him.

A word of caution: the moment you begin adding distance, your position is such that any correction you make will pull the dog *toward you* unless you step toward him as you make the correction; for instance, if the dog fails to sit on command and you correct from three feet away, you are actually pulling him toward you and encouraging him to move forward to come into the sit position. This is wrong. Therefore, if you must correct him from a three-foot (or greater) distance, take a long step *in,* toward the dog, and make the correction above him so that he does not have to move forward (figs. III-63–64).

In most training programs, the dog learns to sit on hand signal only if the handler is directly in front of him. Our method is designed to teach the dog to sit on hand signal no matter what position you are in—in front, to the side, et cetera. If you follow the training sequence just outlined, all your dog needs is a clear line of vision to you in order to rise from the down position on your hand signal.

Scent Discrimination Further Modified

The first session for scent discrimination this week will be a repeat of the last day's work from Week 4: the dog will be on lead, the three metal articles will be wired down, and the leather practice article will be alternated with the metal one. The dog should be sent for each article twice, alternating the article each time. This will reinforce what he has learned up to this point and provide an opportunity for additional praise on the eve of a new complication.

After you have finished this first session, wire three metal articles

III-60–63: Modifying the Hand Signal for Sit. **III-60.** Put the dog in a down position and step 90° to the side. Pause a moment, then give the command "Sit!" and grasp the lead with a conspicuous upward motion, applying a quick tug up as you say "Sit!"

III-61. Continue to practice the two simultaneous sit commands—"Sit!" and the upward sweep of the hand. Remember to apply upward tension *as* you say "Sit!" and make your hand sweep visible to the dog. Gradually work for more speed.

III-62. The objective is to get out in front of the dog and give the verbal and hand-signal sit commands from there. Make sure the dog is proficient at sitting while you are directly in front of him—that is, do not increase your distance away from the dog too rapidly.

III-63. When the dog is anticipating your hand and verbal commands for sit and is sitting proficiently while you stand in front of him, move out to about three feet. Convince him that he must not move forward when you give the sit command; enforce this by stepping in to him as you give the command.

III-64. When you are giving the hand signal for sit from a distance of several feet, any correction you make might pull the dog forward. If you must make a correction, step toward the dog so that you can apply the correction in a vertical direction. You want the dog to come up to a sit without moving forward.

in new locations on the board and add three leather articles to the board, also wired firmly. The articles should be kept a good distance away from one another so that when you add the loose practice article, there will always be six inches between any two articles on the board. The leather and metal articles should be randomly assorted on the board.

Allow the board and articles to air out well overnight to remove your scent. When you begin practice on the second day, proceed as you did when there were only three articles on the board: Put the dog in a sit-stay, on lead, about ten feet from the board and with his back to it. Place the scented practice article somewhere near the center of the board, and, after returning to the dog, give him your scent, pivot, and send him to find the article, going with him toward the board to provide him enough slack to make the search. He should now begin examining more of the articles as he searches and consistently finding the scented article without trying to pick up one of the wired-down, unscented ones. Give him a good deal of praise when he picks up the correct article— but *after* you remove it from his mouth with both hands on the command "Out!" Give him the finish command ("Heel!") after the praise, then repeat the exercise, remembering to alternate the loose metal with the loose leather article.

From the third day on, you can begin modifying the exercise and making it a bit more difficult for the dog—but only if he is consistently and enthusiastically looking for the scented article.

One modification is to place the scented article in odd positions—set it first on one side of the board, then on the other, in the front, in the back. Occasionally you can move it off the board entirely, but no farther away than six inches. Another modification is to turn the board to a new position after each successful find—as you place a new article down, rotate the board 90°, using tongs. Work with these two modifications until the end of the week. In each practice session, send your dog for the scented article at least twice, but no more than four times, alternating the metal with the leather. If you make the dog do the exercise more than four times, it becomes boring for him.

At the end of the week, you can introduce another modification: remove the leather lead from the dog's collar and put on the short knotted rope, this time with one more knot in it so that it is short enough not to dangle down and touch the scent articles as the dog examines them. The rope will be used only if a correction is needed. Remember, a correction at this point should be relatively mild. Do not use any vocal reprimands if the dog tries to pick up the wrong article; its being wired down is sufficient notification to the dog that he has made a mistake.

Thus, on the last workout this week, proceed as follows: Put the dog in a sit-stay, with his back facing the board. Remove the lead and put the short rope on the dog. Go through the routine of the previous days, but this time remain in place when the dog goes for the scented article. Let him find it of his own accord and return with it to you. When he has come to a sit, give the command "Out!," and then praise him before giving the command "Heel!" and proceeding with the next article.

Pay attention to the dog's speed as he returns. If he creeps and is sluggish, now is the time to make a correction: go out, take him by the knotted rope, and correct him in to you quickly, verbally encouraging him to come faster. If he drops the article, make him pick it up by himself and continue back to your starting position. The reason that this correction should be made now is that the dog might, on his next attempt, try to take the first article he comes to, just to please you. If you wait to correct for a slow return or for dropping until later, when the articles are no longer wired down, your correction will lead automatically to a second and a more serious error: picking up the wrong article and bringing it back to you. You should concentrate on speed and precision in your dog's work when all the odds are in your favor, so be prepared to be rigorous while the scent articles are still wired to the board.

Directed Retrieve Modified

This week, you will use all three gloves in the directed retrieve. Two will be fastened to a peg with a piece of strong cord; one will be free. Select a training area that is at least forty feet wide and fifty feet long. 293

Place the two outside gloves about forty feet apart, and the remaining glove halfway between them. Drive two pegs into the ground, one near the glove on the left (glove number 1) and one near the glove in the middle (glove number 2), and, using strong cord, firmly tie each glove to its peg (monofilament fishing line, about number 20 test, would work well). The glove on the right remains free.

Put the dog in a sit-stay or down somewhere away from the training area before you lay the gloves out as indicated. Heel him up to about twenty feet from the center glove (glove number 2), and come to a halt facing it. Be sure that the free glove is the one to your right. Give the dog's name and the command "Heel!," and pivot to the right, as you have been practicing since Open training. The dog should pivot to the right with you and come to a sit parallel to your new direction of march, and both of you should be facing the glove to the right (number 3). Give the stay command (verbally and by hand signal) and step forward one pace. Without turning back to look at the dog, squat down to your knees and extend your left arm out, pointing to glove number 3 (on the right). Pause a moment, your arm still pointing at the glove, then give the command "Take it!" The dog should run directly out to the glove on the right, pick it up, turn, and return with it to you. The remainder of the exercise should be obvious to you: take the glove with the command "Out!," pause, give the finish command, and take two steps forward to end the exercise. Be sure to keep your arms at your sides when you stand up after sending the dog.

Let us assume that the dog decides to retrieve the glove in the center (or the one on the left, which is less likely). If you can see that he is going after the wrong glove, let him try to pick it up. Then give the command "No!," quickly go to him, grab the short cord on his collar, and correct him back to the starting position. Your "No!," as well as the string on the glove, will convince him that he has made an error. After he is back at the starting position, facing the correct glove (number 3, on the right), do not give another vocal command, but, by an application of short, sharp corrections on the knotted rope, take him out quickly to glove number 3 and allow him to pick it up. Back up to your original position, applying short left-to-right corrections until he has come to the starting point and assumed a straight sit facing you, with the glove in his mouth. Remove the glove on the command "Out!" and praise him *before* finishing.

The next thing to do is test the dog to see how much he has learned from the correction. Heel with him to the starting position, coming to a halt facing the number-2 (center) glove. This time, increase your right pivot by 10° (overshoot the target). Give the command "Stay!," step out a pace, and send the dog with the command "Take it!" He should do it right this time. If he does, give him a good deal of praise, after you remove the glove from his mouth but before you finish.

Heel the dog to the opposite side of the training area and face the gloves again. This time the glove to your left (number 1) will be the free glove. After giving his name and the heel command, give the command "Stay!" and step out a full pace before squatting and indicating, with your left arm, the direction he must go to retrieve the glove. On your command "Take it!," he should run directly out to the glove on the left, number 1, and fetch it. If he does not, correct him as you did before.

For the remainder of the week practice the directed retrieve in exactly this fashion. If the dog tries to get the wrong glove, be sure to allow him to try to pick it up before you give him the command "No!"; this will reinforce the built-in correction of the tied-down glove. Remember to send him from both directions so that he must do both right and left pivots before fetching the correct glove.

UTILITY WEEK 6

OUTLINE OF TRAINING SCHEDULE

Note. Unless you are showing your dog in Open B, you can eliminate practicing the Open exercises and concentrate on Utility training. Your dog is rapidly approaching show form.

Old Exercises
> Utility
>> Signal Exercise (while heeling off lead): Stay, heel, finish, stand, and, by the end of the week, sit
>> Group Examination (Long Stand) (3 minutes)

Modifications of Utility Exercises
> Signal Exercise: Adding distance and gradually eliminating aids in the sit on hand signal
> Scent Discrimination: All the articles
> Directed Retrieve: Eliminating the forward step before sending dog
> Directed Jumping: Removing rope aids on the go out; sending the dog over both the high jump and the bar jump, and from a greater distance

New Exercises
> None

Suggested Practice Session: Once daily

Sit Hand Signal Further Modified

By this time, your dog should be sitting on hand signal from a distance varying between three and ten feet. At six feet, he is close enough that you can rapidly step in to him and make a straight upward correction should he hesitate or fail to sit on signal. (Figs. III-65–67 show what your dog should be doing as you move into Week 6.)

The maximum distance between you and the dog that can be re-   295

III-65

III-66

III-67

III-65–67: Where Your Dog Should Be in the Hand Signal for Sit by Week 6. **III-65.** Put him on lead and move out to about six feet.

III-66. Give him the sit hand signal without any verbal reinforcement. He should come up quickly, without moving forward.

III-67. He remains alert, waiting for the next command. In an AKC Utility trial, you will give him the hand signal for come after he has got up into his sit (Week 7).

quired for this exercise, as defined in the AKC rule book, is the length of the ring—about forty feet. That distance will be your goal this week.

The trick, if there is one, to achieving this distance lies in the correction procedure you use once you get beyond the three-foot distance. We find the most effective to be a pulley arrangement. Select a tree with a fairly low branch in your regular training area (or use the ceiling of your basement or garage) and fasten an ordinary hardware-store pulley to it; run the long rope with the swivel snap attached through the pulley.

When you have the dog in a sit-stay directly under the pulley, replace his leather lead with the rope. Lay out the free end of the rope about thirty or forty feet in your direction of march. Give the dog the command "Down!," leave him (stepping off on your right foot), and go out about ten feet. Pick up the end of the rope and pause a moment. Give him only the hand signal for sit; if he hesitates, give a slight tug on the rope—the pulley should transmit your correction directly to the dog, tugging him slightly upward. He should then rise to a sit.

Work with the dog on this exercise for a few days, giving him a great deal of praise when he rises without any encouragement from the pulley contraption. If he rises on hand signal alone, go on to another exercise: walk in to him happily to give him enthusiastic praise, clandestinely remove the swivel snap from his collar, and heel away.

Toward the middle of the week, if the dog is beginning to rise consistently with no correction from the rope, go out forty feet, the complete distance, and work as you did at ten feet. If he continues to show progress and rises on the first hand-signal command, you are ready for the next two—and final—steps toward the full show sequence. If he is inconsistent, come in to the ten-foot distance, or even to the three-foot distance if you think it necessary, and go back to the leather lead. Whatever you do, you should not try to exceed the dog's ability at this point—if he does not rise up definitively and completely on your hand signal at least nine times out of ten from the full forty-foot distance, you are not ready to move on.

The next and penultimate step begins with putting the cord *behind* the dog, still attached to his collar and still passing through the overhead pulley; he will thus not be able to see the rope that can correct him, and will possibly assume that he is therefore in an uncorrectable position. How wrong he is! For you will have cleverly persuaded a helpful friend to hold on to the rope behind the dog and out of sight, and he will make the correction if the dog fails to rise on your hand signal. At this point, concentrate on the precision of your handling: make your hand signal clearly visible to the dog—a smooth, rapid upward motion slightly off from your body so that your arm does not blend into your body. Also concentrate on moving only your arm as you give the signal: body English of any kind should be eliminated.

Put the dog into a sit-stay with his collar attached to the rope-pulley contraption. Lay the rope out behind the dog's line of march so that he cannot see it, and have your confederate take up his position without attracting the dog's attention. Give the dog the command "Down!" and walk out (right foot first) to the forty-foot distance. Be certain not to turn back to look at the dog; you could be penalized in a trial for doing that. When you are about forty feet out, turn around and face the dog. Stand there until you are sure your attendant is ready and the dog's attention is fixed on you; then give the hand signal for sit. If he comes up, give verbal praise from where you are, then walk in to him, praising him more. Release the rope, heel away—continuing the praise—and go to the next exercise, scent discrimination.

At the end of the week, if the dog is rising on hand signal consistently, eliminate the cord completely but continue to put him into the down in the customary working area, underneath the pulley. If he does it off lead and without the rope, he has mastered the exercise. The test is to put him into a down in a different area of the yard or basement, one without any overhead stimulus. Walk out the full forty feet, turn, and pause before giving the hand signal. If he does it under those circumstances, he is nearly ready for the show ring—at least on *that* exercise. Continue to work with him each day on it, but vary both the distance and, occasionally, the angle from which you give him the hand signal. Return to the dog every time he rises, praise him, and heel away for at least two steps before going on to another exercise. Gradually cut down on the praise, and when he has caught on, refrain from giving it until after the two-steps-forward heeling routine.

If the dog is inconsistent or hesitates and acts confused, put him back on the rope and gradually build his confidence back up until he rises on hand signal consistently.

Scent Discrimination Further Modified

When you begin the scent-discrimination work this week, the board should have six articles wired to it: three metal, three leather. Work off lead, keeping the knotted cord on the dog's collar in case a correction is required (the exercise will be getting more complicated, giving the dog more opportunities to make mistakes). You will gradually add the remaining articles to the board but without wiring them down, so that you will have six loose articles, of which two are the practice articles.

Begin by diagnosing your dog's progress. The first day, work with only the six wired-down articles on the board as you put down the scented article. When you send the dog, watch carefully to see if he is nudging the wired-down articles to find out if they move. If not, then he is clearly working with his nose, and you can proceed as follows in your next practice session: In addition to placing the article that has your scent on it, take one of the loose articles from your attaché case, using the tongs, and place that article somewhere on the board. Send your dog to find the article with your scent; if he retrieves it, continue practicing the remainder of the session with the one loose article on the board.

The next practice day, put two loose articles on the board: one leather, one metal. Your board will have six wired-down articles and two loose. If the dog continues to progress, add an article a day until all the articles are on the board: six will still be wired down and four will be loose. Continue to use the same practice articles for the exercise, putting your scent on those only. Remember to alternate the position of the scent articles, and to vary the exercise by using first the metal object, then the leather.

Thus, at the end of the week your dog will be finding the one article with your scent on it from among eleven articles. In a show, your dog must choose one article out of nine (the AKC regulation number of articles in a set is ten articles, only nine of which are on the ground at any time).

Directed Retrieve Further Modified

If your dog did the pivots correctly during Week 5, and consistently went after and retrieved the gloves to the left and the right respectively, numbers 1 and 3 respectively, you can move on now to the center glove, number 2.

For the first two days, therefore, tie down the two end gloves and leave the center glove free. Arrange your training area just as you did last week (if it was satisfactory last week!).

Even though you will be sending your dog for only glove number 2 this week, you should do it from both directions. The best way to make your dog consistent and reliable is to vary the exercises as much as you can, so that he will be able to do the essential portions of the routine under any circumstances.

At the end of two training sessions on the center glove (number 2), you should know if your dog can retrieve all three with equal facility when he is facing them and can see them all. Most dogs will do all three with about the same—usually very high—level of reliability at this stage in their training.

In a show, the handler may not take a step forward toward the proper glove. We will now modify the exercise again to eliminate this step. In order to show the dog that he must follow your *hand* signal— the extended arm pointing to the proper glove—revert to tying down one of the end gloves and the center glove. You should work toward the proper show performance gradually. Begin by stepping out less than a full pace before indicating the proper glove with your extended arm; out of the corner of your eye, watch the dog's eyes. If he is looking down your arm at the correct glove, you can send him with "Take it!" If he does not appear to be looking in the correct direction, spend more time on the exercise still taking a full pace out from the dog.

Ideally, by the end of this week, you should not have to take a step forward to indicate the proper glove with your left arm; after the dog has come to a sit (pivoting to the right or left), you should need only to squat in place, point to the glove, and say "Take it!" (figs. III-68–69).

Directed Jumping Further Modified

Removing Rope Aid on the Go Out   The training for the go out this   299

III-68–69: Eliminating the One Step Forward from Directed Retrieve. **III-68.** Merely drop down to a squatting position at the dog's side and point toward the glove with your left arm.

III-69. When you are confident that the dog is looking at the correct glove, give the command "Take it!" After the dog is in motion, stand up.

week will involve a *gradual* removal of the rope aids—that is, you want to eliminate them in such a way that the dog is never really aware that he has made the transition to off-lead work. Work between the jumps this week.

The first day of go-out practice will consist of a repetition of the routine from the previous week: your assistant applies tension on the hundred-foot rope, and the fifty-foot rope is still used to spin the dog around when the stop command (the dog's name) is given. If the dog performs this exercise correctly, do it the second time without the fifty-foot rope. Work with only the hundred-foot rope for the next day or two, paying careful attention to the dog's turns. If he continues to turn well and sit squarely, you will not have to use the fifty-foot rope again—unless, of course, he suffers a lapse of memory and requires some additional training. Your assistant should continue to work with you this week, applying tension to the hundred-foot rope.

On about the third day, begin the exercise as before, but surreptitiously remove the hundred-foot rope from the dog's collar. Take up the rope and have your assistant apply the tension as before; give the command "Go out!," releasing the rope at the same time. The assistant should still run and keep the rope in motion. The dog should run along the rope and come to a halt when you say his name. If he does the entire exercise properly, praise him. If he errs, it should be obvious what you must do to correct him. There are only two major errors he could make: failure to go out and failure to turn and sit. The solution for these is to put the dog back on the proper rope aid and continue working on the ropes until you feel confident enough about his performance to take them off again.

Continue to practice the go out in this fashion for the remainder of the week, going through all the motions as if the dog were attached to the ropes. It is important that your assistant apply the tension as before—this conditions the dog to pay attention to your hand movement.

The last day of the week can be used to diagnose any problems in your dog's skill and understanding. Begin the exercise as before, but without an assistant. Remove the hundred-foot rope from the dog's collar and lay it on the ground next to him. This time, give the "Go out!" command and hand signal simultaneously. If the dog runs out quickly, halts when you give his name, turns, and sits facing you, he has essentially mastered the go-out portion of the directed-jumping exercise. If he makes mistakes, put him back on the ropes and train with them until he is proficient enough to work off lead, with the hundred-foot rope used only as a guide for his direction of march.

Sending the Dog over Both Jumps, and from a Greater Distance This week you will begin to combine some of the components of AKC directed jumping in their proper sequence. You will still not have everything together, but you are gradually approaching show form.

Set up a practice ring with the bar jump and high jump approximately in the middle and about twenty feet apart. They should be at   301 full regulation height for your dog. You will be practicing along the long axis of the ring.

Heel the dog to one end of the ring, with the leather lead in your hip pocket. Sit the dog, facing toward the other end of the ring, on the center line. Give him the command "Stay!" and walk down the center line until you are about five feet past the jumps. Turn and face the dog. You are now going to put him to a test. He has never been commanded to jump over the high jump while he is sitting at the opposite end of the ring from you. However, he has been jumping the high jump all through Open, and you have been training him to go over the bar jump on a combined verbal and hand signal from the opposite side of the jump. You are now going to see if the dog can combine several components of his training and jump over the high jump on your verbal and hand-signal commands. To make things a bit easier for him, step toward the high jump as you give the signal.

Let's assume that the high jump (the solid jump) is on your right as you initiate the command. Take a long step toward it as you say "Over!" and point your arm to your right. The dog should unhesitatingly run to the jump, clear it, come to you, and sit.

If he balks at your command to go over the high jump, quickly move in to him and put him back in his original position; without saying a word, attach his leather lead and run with him toward the high jump, applying a series of sharp left and right corrections, keeping him off balance until you get near the jump. He should clear it without another verbal command; when he does, quickly bring him up, make him sit in front of you, and give him praise. Heel him back to his initial position at the end of the ring, put him in a stay, and walk out again about five feet past the jumps. This time stand somewhat closer to the high jump than you did previously, tipping him off that you want him to jump to that side. Pause a moment, then give both the hand signal and the command "Over!," pointing at and stepping toward the high jump. He should do it this time.

When he comes in to you and sits, give him the command "Heel!," and praise him only after he has sat squarely. Heel him back to the same starting point and repeat the exercise, but this time make him jump the bar. If he errs on this, use the correction described for the high jump error.

Now heel the dog to the opposite end of the ring and face him toward his initial position. This time the obstacles will be reversed in position—the dog should not be allowed to get it into his mind that the bar jump is always to his left (or right).

For the remainder of the week, jump your dog only four times each day, twice from each end of the ring. Jumping is fairly strenuous work for many dogs, and, if the dog has mastered the hand signals, he will become bored by having to repeat a known exercise unnecessarily often.

Toward the middle of the week, begin to increase your distance past the jumps until, by the end of the week, you are all the way back to the end of the ring and there is nearly fifty feet between you and the dog. Also by midweek, begin to reduce your hints to the dog as you

III-70. By the end of this week you should be forty feet from the dog, the maximum distance you would be expected to work from during an AKC Utility trial. Begin to concentrate on eliminating your body-English hints as you give your hand signals for the dog to jump.

III-71. Make certain you begin paying attention to the dog's landing point and the distance he travels before turning toward you. Try to turn in place when he is clearing the jump, and face his characteristic return path so that he comes in to you straight.

give the hand signal to jump: instead of the long side step toward the jump you used at the beginning of the week, take smaller steps, and then gradually cut down your body motion until, by the last day of training this week, you are merely pointing your arm to the jump you want the dog to clear (see figs. III-70–71).

By the end of the week, begin to put your handling techniques into more professional order. In an AKC trial, you are expected to pivot in place as the dog is clearing the jump (fig. III-71), so that he can come back in to you and sit squarely at your feet. This means that you must begin paying attention both to where your dog lands after he clears the jump and to how much distance he usually travels to reduce his momentum and make his turn back to you. The idea is to face the spot at which he completes his turn. For a large dog, this might be five feet beyond his landing spot; for very small dogs, it might be only a few inches. But each dog develops his own style as he becomes a proficient jumper, so it is not possible to give a fixed rule of thumb for particular breeds or even within one breed. Our experience with shepherds, for instance, has been that some are very lightfooted jumpers and can turn on a dime as soon as they land, and that others (the junior author's Gus, for example) rumble on like tanks, taking a lot of distance to make the turn and return to the handler.

UTILITY WEEK 7

OUTLINE OF TRAINING SCHEDULE
Old Exercises
    Signal Exercise (while heeling off lead): Stay, heel, finish, stand,
        sit
    Group Examination (Long Stand) (3½ minutes)
Modifications of Utility Exercises
    Directed Jumping: Combining the go out with the jumping
    Scent Discrimination: Eliminating the board
    Directed Retrieve: Working with all the gloves free
New Exercise
    Signal Exercise: Come
Suggested Practice Session: Once daily

Directed Jumping Further Modified
By the end of this week, you will have combined the go-out exercise
with the jumping. You will also be rapidly eliminating all rope aids from

the go-out position; but to remind the dog that he is always correctable, leave the anchor and pulley in the ground and have the ropes handy.

The first day of training will require the hundred-foot rope and the anchor pulley. Lay the rope out between the jumps (which are about twenty feet apart) and pass it through the pulley. Start the exercise at the proper distance from the jumps—about twenty feet. The anchor should be located about twenty five feet beyond them, on the other end of the training area. When you give the command "Go out!" and the hand signal, pay attention to your handling technique: do not bend at the knees or lean. The dog should be off lead; the rope, at this time, serves only as a guideline.

You will also begin to correct your dog if he anticipates the signal. If he is jumpy and too anxious to go out, attach the short knotted rope to his collar and place the rings of the collar on the back of his neck. This will enable you to grab the correction rope easily if the dog tries to leave you before the command.

If the dog does the go out, turn, and sit proficiently, you can then eliminate the guide rope completely; but leave the anchor at the end of the training area in case the dog begins to make errors and you have to use the ropes again. Practice the go out as a separate exercise until the end of the week.

At the end of the week, you can combine the go out with the jumping. The jumps should be set up in the proper show arrangement: about twenty feet apart and midway between the ends of the practice area. Lay the long rope down the center of the ring the first time you combine the two exercises, and put the dog into the proper heeling position at one end of it. Reach down and adjust the rope, as if you were going to attach it to the dog's collar, and then adjust his collar—he will think that he has been attached to the rope and that the pulley tug-and-grunt routine is back again. Come back up to a perfectly straight stand and pause, then give the hand signal and the command "Go out!," being careful not to bend at the knees or lean forward. When the dog gets nearly to the end of the rope, say his name to turn him; as he comes out of his turn, give the command "Sit!" Pause a moment and then, without stepping toward the jump you want him to clear, give the hand signal and the command "Over!" Turn in place to be in line with the dog's return direction. When he comes up to you and sits, pause a moment, give the command "Heel!," and, after he has come to a square sit, give him a pat on the head and a reassuring "Good dog!" At this point in your dog's training you must begin to modify your praise. Too much might make him leap up jubilantly and put his paws on you, or do some fantastic spin, panting happily and wagging his tail. This might be nice during training, but in AKC Utility trials it is considered "uncontrollable" behavior and is penalized by the judge.

The dog has been trained to do the go out and jumping separately and ought now to be proficient at the combination. If so, you can eliminate the final aid: remove the guide rope that was defining his center line and practice without it from now on. Your dog is now doing the AKC regulation directed jumping: the jumps are at regulation height, 305 you and the dog are properly positioned (the dog should go out past the jumps a distance approximately equal to your distance from the jumps), and your handling techniques are correct.

Scent Discrimination Further Modified

At the end of Week 6, you were working with all the articles on the board; six were wired down and four were lying loose. Begin this week's work with the same arrangement. If the dog retrieves the two scented articles, you can begin to make some modifications—gradually getting the articles off the board, and then eliminating the board entirely.

The first step toward this is to remove four of the loose articles from the board with the tongs and place them on the ground, near the board (fig. III-72). Place the scented article somewhere in the middle of the arrangement and go through the proper routine: giving your scent, pivoting, sending the dog, taking the article from his mouth, praising him, and finishing. You should now cut down on the praise; give it only after the dog has finished and has come to a square sit at your side.

The second day of practice, your scent-article arrangement should still resemble figure III-72, but with five articles off the board. Go through the proper routine, remembering to reduce the praise a bit more.

On the third day, you will have to unwire all but two of the articles and arrange the loose ones on the ground next to the board. Go through the practice routine with the scented articles, but start from about twelve feet away.

On the fourth day, put all the articles on the ground next to the board (fig. III-73). Begin the exercise the full fifteen feet from the articles.

Finally, on the fifth day of practice, you can eliminate the board. Let the dog retrieve at least one article with the board present; after he has returned, let him watch you remove the board. From this point on, he should not have to work on the board.

Your dog is now actually doing more than is required in an AKC trial: he is finding one article out of eleven loose ones.

Be sure to allow the scent articles to air out for one full day after you touch them. This means that if you remove the wire from an article with your own hands, you will have to do it the day before you plan to work. The best solution is to have someone else remove the wire for you, or, if that is not possible, to cut the wire with snips while you hold the article with your tongs.

Directed Retrieve Further Modified

This week, you will work in the same training area and in essentially the same fashion as before, except that all the gloves will be free (you may leave the pegs in the ground near the gloves).

In the first part of the week, show the dog that he might have to retrieve any one of the three gloves by sending him for a different one each day. Delay praise until after the dog has completed his finish. Do

III-72. Removing the wired-down scent articles from the board is a gradual, day-by-day process. Begin by removing four; place them on the ground near the board.

III-73. By the fourth day, you should have all the articles off the board. Leave the board where it is the first time you work with all the articles off. The next time you work, you can dispense with the board entirely.

not do the exercise more than two or three times each session, and never send him for a particular glove more than once in a session—unless he is weak on that one. In that case, peg the two other gloves and work on the one he is missing consistently.

By midweek you will need an assistant to act as judge and place the gloves for you. For the first half of the week, allow the dog to face the assistant while the gloves are being placed. This means that you must heel the dog to about the center of an imaginary ring and face the narrow end. If your jumps are set up—and they should be—you will be standing between them and in line with them. Your dog is at heel. The assistant walks to the end of the ring and conspicuously places the gloves—one in one corner, one in the middle, one in the opposite corner. By "conspicuously" we mean that the assistant shakes the glove to fluff it up and places it so that it is plainly visible to the dog and the handler. When all three have been placed, and when your assistant has got out of the dog's way, pivot in place 180° so that you and your dog

will have your backs to the gloves. Your assistant should then tell you which glove to have your dog retrieve: "Number 1," "Number 2," or "Number 3."

You could, of course, practice without an assistant. Give the dog a stay command in the appropriate starting position, walk out and place the gloves yourself, return to the dog, walk around him, and then turn around to begin the exercise with the gloves behind you.

Since you have the option of pivoting either to the right or to the left when the judge designates the glove, practice *both;* then select the one that seems most comfortable for your dog, the one that he seems to do best. It might be that a clockwise pivot (to the right) works best for gloves 1 and 2, but a counterclockwise (to the left) pivot is best for number 3. Experiment until you arrive at the best combination.

This completes the training for the directed retrieve. By the end of the week, the gloves should be placed while the dog has his back turned to them, as in an AKC Utility show. Practice this way for the remainder of the Utility course.

Signal Exercise: Come

This week you will add all but one of the components to the signal-exercise routine; next week you will combine all the signals in proper show sequence.

To make the proper *hand signal for come* sweep your right arm out to the side and up to shoulder level, then bend your elbow in toward

III-74–76: The Hand Signal for Come.
III-74. Your right arm describes a smooth arc, rising until it is at shoulder height.

III-75. From shoulder height, continue the arc smoothly, reaching outward from this point and then in, across your chest.

III-76. The hand signal terminates in this position, at which time you drop your arm back to your side.

your body, finishing with your hand near your chest (figs. III-74–76). The gesture should be a single smooth motion, without any pauses. Only your arm should move while the signal is given, not your body. Any such extra body movement could be interpreted as an additional signal in a show. We recommend that you practice the hand signal in front of a mirror a few times before springing it on the dog. Have a critic watch while you try to make it without moving your body.*

This week, you will teach the signal portion while the dog is in a sitting position—that is, as if you were doing a straight recall. Heel the dog out, make an about turn, halt; when the dog goes into an automatic sit, give the stay signal and leave him. Walk out about twenty feet and turn to face him. After a brief pause, give his name and the command "Come!" As you begin the vocal signal, simultaneously make the come hand motion. When the dog comes in to you, do not finish. Praise him for coming, and then give him a verbal stay command. Walk around him, pause, and repeat the exercise.

The reasons for not finishing are to prevent the dog's anticipating the finish signal, and to ensure that he associates the praise he gets with having come to you on hand signal. Your dog is sufficiently well trained

* We once heard about a student who attempted to train her dog using a book in which the photographic illustrations, not to mention the text itself, were somewhat less than clear. The come hand-signal photograph (just one) showed a man who had just finished making the complete hand signal and seemed to have his hand on his chest. The student thought that to get the dog to come on hand signal, all she had to do was to put her hand on her chest: the dog would intuitively know it was a hand signal to come.

III-77–81: Teaching the Dog to Come on Hand Signal. **III-77.** Put him on the rope, in a sit-stay, and walk out about twenty feet. If you have an assistant, he should be behind you to give a slight tug on the rope as soon as you give the hand signal to the dog.

III-78. You can perform the exercise without an assistant, but if the dog fails to come when you give the hand signal, your correction will be delayed slightly—you will have to bend down, pick up the rope, and tug it, *post factum.*

III-79. Do not give a vocal come signal when you give the hand signal, not even the first time. This is a very simple exercise, and your dog must learn to keep his eyes focused on you. If he fails to see the signal or does not come to you immediately, apply a smart tug on the rope.

III-80. The tug should get him in motion toward you.

III-81. After he comes and sits, praise him.

by now so that if you practice a recall combined with the finish five or six times, he is not likely to wait for your signal to finish on the seventh repetition. Therefore, train him with repetitive practice in the hand signal for come, and without any additional exercise that would require him to move to a new position. Thus he will be concentrating only on the new portion of an otherwise old routine—and getting praise for it.

Practice this routine for several days only; it is essentially Novice work and the dog will soon get bored with it.

At the end of the week, drop the vocal command. When you do so, modify the routine by adding a long rope. You should have an assistant help you for the first two or three sessions. Lay the long rope out in a straight line and heel the dog to the swivel end, putting him into an automatic sit facing down the length of the rope. Attach the swivel snap to his collar. Leave him with the proper stay signal and go out about twenty feet, turn, and straddle the rope (fig. III-77). Your assistant should be behind you, prepared to give a slight tug on the rope the moment you give the hand signal. Do *not* give a vocal signal even the first time you practice this modification.

If you do not have an assistant, you can of course work alone, but to correct the dog, should he not come on hand signal, you must bend over, take up the rope, and tug it—which will be quite some time after the hand signal. However, the dog should catch on after a few corrections of this sort. Figures III-77 through 81 show how to work on this exercise without an assistant.

Practice this routine for the remainder of the week, but only two or three times per training session, and do not combine it with the finish. If the dog does come on hand signal, give him a goodly amount of praise, but do not remove the rope; premature short cuts have a way of coming back to haunt you when the chips are down. We can hear you complaining to your show peers after you disqualify: "But he always comes at home!" He will always come, anywhere, if he is given a fair opportunity now to make a mistake—and be corrected.

UTILITY WEEK 8

OUTLINE OF TRAINING SCHEDULE
Old Exercises
    Signal Exercise (while heeling off lead): Stay, heel, sit, finish, stand
    Group Examination (Long Stand): Five minutes
    Directed Jumping: Go out combined with jumping
    Directed Retrieve
Modifications of Utility Exercises
    Signal Exercise: Improving the come and combining it with the
    finish

Scent Discrimination: Using only the ten regulation articles
Directed Jumping: The go out under adverse conditions
New Exercises
   None
Suggested Practice Session: Once daily, or once every other day

Hand Signal for Come Modified

By now, the dog should be moving toward you immediately after you give the come hand signal, without being tugged by the rope. (If he is not coming on hand signal alone, continue to practice precisely as you did in Week 7.)

Lay out the rope and heel the dog to the swivel end; do not attach the rope to his collar—it will serve only as a guideline at this point. The short knotted cord will be sufficient in case you must make a correction. Leave the dog and go out to the familiar twenty-foot distance. Face him, pause, and give the hand signal for come. This time, if the dog does come, give him the hand signal for finish, and mete out the praise after he finishes.

You could make a very serious mistake here. If the dog does not come on hand signal, the temptation is overwhelming to give a vocal command. If you did so, the dog would be justified in thinking something like this: If I don't see the hand signal, my master will give me a vocal command anyway, so I can allow my mind to wander and not pay attention. The proper correction is to move in to him quickly, *without saying a word,* and apply a series of timed, sharp, side-to-side corrections on the short rope all the way out to the twenty-foot position. After you get him into a straight sit, walk around him to the heeling position instead of finishing and heel him back to his original place at the swivel end of the rope. Repeat the exercise; this time he should keep his eyes glued to you.

Practice the come hand signal for several days, giving the dog the hand signal for finish as part of the exercise each time he does the come portion properly. When he is giving a consistent performance in the come-finish combination (by midweek for most dogs), remove the rope guideline. However, keep the short knotted cord on him for the remainder of the week.

When the dog is doing extremely well, periodically (about one time in five) replace the finish portion with your walk-around routine; this will keep him honest and alert, and therefore discourage anticipation of the finish command.

At the point when you stop using the rope, you are ready to add more distance to the routine. Gradually build it up to about forty feet, the approximate distance used for this exercise in the show ring. You should also modify the training by practicing with the dog in new places and by reversing direction in your regular training area (after the dog has come and finished on hand signals, let him sit while you walk out in the direction he has just come from; turn and repeat the exercise).   313

III-82. To encourage your dog to search systematically among all the articles, lay them out the first day this week in a linear pattern.

III-83. On the second day of scent discrimination for Week 8, modify the straight line to an arc. On each remaining day of the week, draw the ends closer to each other until, on day 5, you have a circle (fig. III-84).

III-84. By the end of the week, the arc has become a circle.

Scent Discrimination Further Modified

The scent-discrimination practice for this week will require the use of only the ten regulation articles. Put the practice articles away for the week (unless your dog needs work on the board or some other earlier step in the training). You will vary the arrangement of the articles, starting with all of them in a perfectly straight line and about a foot apart from one another, metal alternating with leather (fig. III-82). Place only one scented article among the unscented ones each time you practice. Select a different pair of articles every day so that you use any given article about as often as any other. Try to keep track of the numbers as you work: Mondays use the 1's, Tuesdays the 2's, Wednesdays the 3's, et cetera. The purpose of the linear arrangement is to encourage the dog to search for the scented article, either going from one object to the next until he has found and taken the scented one, or searching the whole line and coming back to take the one he likes best—the one with your scent on it.

You will work on lead during this week. Begin the exercise about six or eight feet away from the articles, stepping toward them when you send the dog, and moving along with him to give him slack. When he picks up the article, you should back up to your original position and allow the dog to come in to you to sit and present the article. Complete the exercise as in previous weeks; then repeat it with the other article you have selected for the day's training. For the remainder of the week, send the dog just two times each session, as in a show: once for metal, once for leather. When you finish each practice session, walk over to the line of objects and pick each one up with your hand, not your tongs. This is to teach your dog to go for the freshest scent. You will allow your articles to air out overnight, of course, but when you begin the exercise the next day, all of them will still carry some latent scent. Only one will have fresh scent, and your dog will quickly learn that he must retrieve that one. This complication makes for a more thorough search pattern and reduces the possibility that the dog will take the wrong article in a competitive situation.

For the second practice session of the week, arrange the articles in a broad arc (fig. III-83), using the tongs. Remember to keep the two articles with number 2 on them for the exercise, and, when you alternate them, be sure you use a different spot. Again, give your dog plenty of slack in the lead so he can make his search, and remember to pick up the articles with your hands at the end of practice and air them before using them again.

On each of the remaining days this week, close the arc somewhat until, on the fifth day, you have a small circle (fig. III-84).

Directed Jumping Further Modified

This week you will make the directed jumping a bit more trying for your dog to condition him to adverse show circumstances. For instance, some show rings have cement walls, and you might wind up having to send your dog directly toward such a wall in the go out. To condition　315 him not to be fazed by forbidding-looking obstacles, practice sending him toward fences, sides of buildings, hedges—and also a vast, wide-open space defined only by a thin, suspended piece of rope. Thus you will have to begin to work on directed jumping in new areas. Whenever possible, set up a practice ring that is defined on all sides by your training ropes (you should have accumulated by now something like a hundred and fifty feet). Setting up a practice ring is not absolutely necessary this week in your new practice areas, but you should set one up in your back yard, as you did for Novice and Open, defined by stakes and ropes.

UTILITY WEEK 9

OUTLINE OF TRAINING SCHEDULE
New Exercises
    Signal Exercise: Drop
    Simulating Show Conditions
Suggested Practice Session: Once daily, or once every other day

We are now rapidly approaching completion of the Utility exercises at a level of performance that would qualify in an AKC Utility trial; by the middle of this week, in fact, you will have accomplished all of the formal "course work." From then on, the practice sessions are geared toward perfecting already known sequences of behavior while simultaneously approaching show conditions.

Signal Exercise: Drop
We have saved the simplest signal—for drop—until now for a good reason. On seeing their dogs progress, many people attempt to put everything into a package too quickly, before the dog has the fundamental components reasonably fixed into his behavior. Such prematurity can lead to serious setbacks and the expenditure of more time and effort than would have been necessary had the learning sequence been followed accurately and at the right rate from the outset. This is not to say that it takes a minimum of nine or ten weeks to teach a dog to do the AKC hand-signal exercises. In our classes, we can train dogs much more quickly than this; but we assume that you are working pretty much alone and do not have ready access to training help from somebody whose experience could substantially speed up your training.

In addition to adding the final hand signal, you will combine all the hand signals (into the Signal Exercise) from the very first day of this week.

Remember that in Open you taught your dog the Drop on Recall with the help of your leather lead wrapped in a white sock; this will come in handy now for teaching the down (from a stand) hand signal. This time, the dog will not be moving toward you.

Put the wrapped-up leather lead in your pocket, and attach the short knotted cord to the dog's collar. Do a heeling routine with him, using only hand signals to get him in motion. Go through all turns and speeds, and make at least one complete halt. As you come out of a right (or an about) turn, give the dog the hand signal for stand, pause a moment, and then give the hand signal for stay, using no verbal commands whatsoever.

Walk out about ten or fifteen feet, turn to face the dog, and pause a moment, taking the wrapped-up lead out of your pocket. When you give the hand signal for drop the first time, reinforce it with the command "Down!" The dog has never been expected to drop from a standing position, and he might be a little confused without the supplementary vocal command. You might also have to throw the lead-sock in his direction as you give both the verbal command and the hand signal. The dog should drop in place and go into a lying position. If he does, give him vocal praise but do not move toward him. Put the lead-sock back in your pocket (if you have not thrown it toward him) and, after a slight pause, give him the hand signal for sit. He should move, in place, to a full sitting position, facing you. Pause a moment and then give him the hand signal for come. When he sits in front of you, give the hand signal for finish. If he does the whole routine, he has essentially performed the AKC regulation Signal Exercise. All that remains is for you to eliminate the one vocal command ("Down!") and build up your distance to about forty feet when you leave him in the stand.

Practice the drop signal in this fashion for the first half of the week, building up the distance between you and the dog for the recall portion (come on hand signal). Concentrate on your handling techniques (no body English) as you work. By midweek you can eliminate the command "Down!" and give only the hand signal. You will then be ready to incorporate the exercise into the complete AKC regulation Signal Exercise, described below.

Simulating Show Conditions

We are now reaching the crest of the hill and beginning formal preparation for an AKC obedience trial in Utility. From midweek on, you must attempt to simulate actual show conditions during your training periods and work toward regulation handling techniques.

Regulation Ring and Assistant as Judge   The first step is to set up a regulation-size practice ring of the shape and dimensions given in figure III-85. You may use the training ropes as ring boundaries and the old rake handles and broomsticks left over from the similar practice routines at the end of your Novice and Open training. This week set up the ring in your regular training area to accustom your dog, in familiar surroundings, to boundaries and regulation jump arrangements peculiar to Utility   317 trial conditions. Next week you will move to new training areas to work your dog, in order to get him to feel at home in the practice show ring, no matter where it is.

The second step in simulating show conditions is to have an assistant act as judge during your training routine in the regulation practice ring, just as you did for Novice and Open. By this time, your assistant is probably familiar with the judge's commands and the AKC regulations and knows how to act out the role tolerably well, with a semblance of authority and aplomb.

After you have your ring set up and your assistant prepared and in the ring, pick up your attaché case containing the scent articles, gloves, and tongs and walk to the entrance with your dog on lead. Remove the lead as soon as you enter the ring.

Your assistant must play two roles: judge and steward. As steward, he now invites you into the ring. Come to a halt when you get inside; your dog should go into an automatic sit. Hand over the lead and attaché case to the steward. When the judge is prepared to begin judging you, the steward hands him the case. The judge will usually ask you how high your dog jumps; if it is less than the maximum thirty-six inches, he must measure your dog. Be certain to condition your dog to having strangers approach him with a folding rule or measuring stick; you can lose points during the measuring if your dog shies away or shows resentment.

Practicing Exercises in Proper Show Sequence   After the judge advises you that the first exercise will begin—the Signal Exercise—he will indicate to what part of the ring you must go and in what direction to face.

Signal Exercise. This is a silent, heeling-off-lead routine. During the first part of the exercise, the judge gives you verbal commands for forward, slow, fast, normal, left turn, et cetera—and you essentially go through the Open Heel Free routine, except that you do not have to do the Figure 8 and your commands to the dog are all hand signals (after the judge says "Forward!"). As you come out of an about turn, the judge says "Stand your dog!" At this, give the hand signal for stand and wait at the dog's side for the next command from the judge. By this time, the judge is usually in a position such that his signals to you cannot be seen by the dog. He now says "Leave your dog!"—this is his last verbal signal to you. You give the hand signal for stay and, stepping off on your right foot, walk away from the dog to the opposite end of the ring, without looking back. When you approach the end of the ring, turn to face the dog, but keep your eye on the judge as well. Make sure you are in a position at which your dog can finish without any inconvenience—not flush against the back barricade of the ring, for instance.

At this point, the judge silently gives you hand signals, which he will probably have explained to you beforehand. They are usually finger modifications of the regular hand signals and are given in such a way that the dog will not be able to see the judge's hands move (figs. III-86–89), although normally the judge is behind the dog anyway.

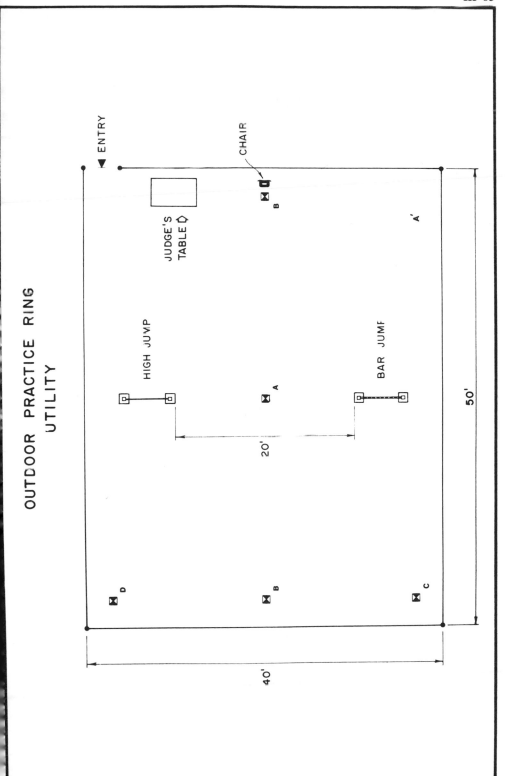

OUTDOOR PRACTICE RING
UTILITY

ENTRY

CHAIR

JUDGE'S TABLE

HIGH JUMP

BAR JUMF

A

B

A'

D

B

C

20'

50'

40'

Make *certain* that you can see both the dog and the judge before you give a signal; this could mean that you will have to look in one direction to see the judge, and in another to see the dog. If you are over-anxious, you might begin to give your hand signals before you have determined that the dog is actually watching you. It is very tempting to give the hand signal as soon as you know what the judge wants—without checking first to see if your dog is looking at you. By the time your hand is in motion for the drop, you realize, to your horror, that your dog is actually looking over at some attractive poodle in the next ring and has not seen your signal. Since you can only give it once, you are done. Thus, once you recognize the judge's signal, turn your eyes toward the dog and pause—only slightly—before giving him the signal. If your dog is not paying attention to you, wait until he is before giving a hand signal.

JUDGE'S SILENT COMMANDS TO YOU FOR THE SIGNAL EXERCISE
1. Down
2. Sit
3. Come
4. Finish (after dog is sitting at your feet)

Everything, bear in mind, is done silently. Even the heel commands begin with a hand signal only. Keep your lips pursed so that the judge cannot possibly suspect you of whispering encouragements, especially during the heeling routine.

III-86–89: Signal Exercise, Down Through Finish. III-86. Your assistant should act as judge and give you the signals that you would see in the ring—the judge is normally behind your dog. Here is a typical down signal.

III-87. After your dog is down, the judge will indicate, usually with a slight upward hand motion, that you are to sit your dog. Note that the dog is focusing intently on his handler and cannot see the judge.

III-88. When you have got your dog to sit on your hand signal, the judge will motion to you to call your dog, usually by pointing his finger toward you.

III-89. After your dog is sitting at your feet, the judge will give you the signal to finish by a twist of the wrist, with or without making one of his fingers conspicuous.

Scent Discrimination. After you complete the Signal Exercise, the judge indicates to you where the next exercise—Scent Discrimination—will begin. Normally, this is position B on figure III-85. Heel your dog to that spot and wait while the judge brings you the two articles to be used and the steward places the remaining articles on the ground. (If you have a show the following day, ask the judge and steward to keep the two scented articles you use on this day separate from those you will use the next day. Unless you do this, you increase the possibility of your dog's making an error in the next show: the scented articles might contaminate the unscented ones, or the following day's judge might pick two different articles, so that there would be four with various degrees of scent concentration. In the next day's show, you will be able to substitute your practice articles—which you have numbered with water-soluble ink for just such a contingency—by removing their numbers and replacing them with the numbers of the articles kept separate.) After you take one metal and one leather article from the judge, the steward takes the remaining articles over to the area between the upright jumps (point A on fig. III-85) or, occasionally, to a different area of the ring—near one of the corners, perhaps. He places them on the ground, about six inches apart from one another and more or less randomly distributed. The steward *must* touch each article with his hand. The judge records on his Worksheet the number of each of the articles your dog is to retrieve.

From here on, procedure for the Scent Discrimination is the same as it was in practice. You and your dog may observe the steward placing the articles on the ground. When they are placed, you and your dog turn about to face away from them, the dog assuming the normal heeling position (fig. III-90). The judge usually allows you to choose which article you want to use first. Since he must not touch the articles, he either presents them to you now on his clipboard, or has allowed you to select them earlier from the attaché case. You may rub the article for as long as the judge permits—usually about five or ten seconds—but when he extends his clipboard toward you for it, you must place it on the board immediately (fig. III-91).

The rest of the exercise is old hat to you. After the judge puts the article among the others, he backs away and gives you the command "Send your dog!" You give the dog your scent (fig. III-92), return your arm to your side, and pivot to the right to face the articles, simultaneously giving the command "Find it!" (fig. III-93). The dog must rise, turn, go immediately to the articles, and find the right one (fig. III-94). After he returns with it and sits squarely at your feet, the judge says "Take it!" and, when you have done so, "Finish!"—at which time you give either the verbal heel command *or* the hand signal (but not both). Praise your dog when the judge declares "Exercise finished!," but not excessively. A pat on the head and a quiet "Good girl!" is all you should do. Then pivot around to your original position, put the old article on the chair, take the new article to put your scent on it, and proceed as before.

When that exercise is finished, you are ready for the Directed Retrieve. In between, however, your dog must remain absolutely under control—he must not jump up enthusiastically, lick your face, or otherwise break from the normal heeling position. This would be considered "uncontrollable behavior" by the judge, and penalized. So scale down your praise and make your dog behave as though he were under a command all the time you are in the performance ring.

Directed Retrieve. After declaring the Scent Discrimination exercise finished, the judge tells you to bring your dog to the center of the ring (point A of fig. III-85) and come to a halt, facing one end (fig. III-95). You should be located immediately between the two jumps with your dog on the center line of the long axis of the ring. You then pivot in place so that your back—and your dog's—will be to the steward as he places the three gloves at the opposite end of the ring: one in each corner and one in the middle of the ring, all in a straight line. The steward usually shakes the gloves to puff them up before setting them on the ground.

While your back is still to the gloves, the judge asks "Are you ready?" Check to see that your dog is sitting perfectly straight before replying affirmatively; if he is crooked, say "No!" and adjust his position by verbal commands or, if necessary, a slight pivot and the command "Heel!"

The next word from the judge is a number: "One!" or "Two!" or "Three!" As soon as you hear it, give the command "Heel!" and simultaneously pivot around toward the appropriate glove. Remember, when you are *facing* the gloves, the one on your left is 1, the one in the middle 2, and the one to your right 3. You know which pivot your dog is better at—clockwise or counterclockwise—and that is the one to use now. Probably you will be pivoting to the right (clockwise) since two other Utility exercises require that pivot, but you do have a choice. As soon as you are facing the glove, send your dog; there is no further command or instruction from the judge to wait for. In your practice this week, continue to correct your dog immediately if he fails to sit.

Your hand signal to indicate the glove should be a single, smooth motion with your left hand and arm. You may squat to give it, and then, if the dog is alert and looking at the proper glove, say "Take it!" and stand up perfectly straight. Keep your hands at your sides. The dog should run directly to the glove, pick it up, run directly back to you, and sit at your feet, holding the glove in his mouth. The judge then says "Take it!," and you remove the glove from the dog's mouth with both hands while giving the command "Out!" On the judge's next instruction, "Finish!," give the command "Heel!" and wait for him to tell you that the exercise is over.

Directed Jumping. After you have been told that the Directed Retrieve exercise is finished, go to one end of the ring for the Directed Jumping (from observing the previous contestants, you will automatically know which end; if you are the first contestant, the judge will explain where you should position yourself). Most judges tell every contestant where he should begin the exercise, but co-operating by moving without further instruction usually makes a favorable impression on the 323

III-90–94: Scent Discrimination. **III-90.** The steward will place the articles on the ground with you and the dog facing them. This gives the dog an opportunity to see what it is that is coming up next. When the articles have been placed, the judge instructs the handler to turn around so that his back and the dog's are to the articles. Here, handler David Boyer prepares to send his poodle, while the judge, Mrs. Oliver James Hart, checks her Worksheet.

III-91. You must surrender the scent article to the judge as soon as he requests it (it really doesn't take much time to put your scent on it). Dan Barker places his leather article on Judge Max McCammon's clipboard. Whereas the steward *must* handle the other articles as he places them, the judge *must not* handle the scented articles.

III-92. When you give the dog your scent with the palm of your right hand, you may touch his nose gently. Make certain that you allow your hand to drop back to your side before sending the dog.

III-93. Pivot in place toward the articles after giving your scent to the dog, and give the command "Find it!" Your dog must go directly to the articles and look for the scented one.

III-94. He may take his time looking for the article, but he must keep working all the time. Most dogs will sniff several of the articles before hitting the right one, sniff back and forth between it and the others, and then pick up the correct one and bring it back. Some dogs will immediately pick up the right one as soon as they hit it.

III-95. The Directed Retrieve begins between the two jumps. The gloves are placed behind the handler by the steward. You may pivot in either direction when the judge designates which glove your dog is supposed to retrieve. Your dog must retrieve only one glove, and the judge must alternate gloves as he sends each handler/dog team.

weary judge, who is thereby exonerated from explaining for the umpteenth time where a handler should go next.

The judge asks if you are ready. When you indicate you are, the judge will say "Send your dog!" You must not put any body English into your signal; merely point to the opposite end of the ring and say "Go out!" (fig. III-96). When the dog has got as far as you want him to go, give his name loudly (but not screechingly) and then say "Sit!" He should spin on hearing his name, turn, and come to a sit, facing you and right on center line. The dog will probably not be disqualified if he fails to sit—provided he is somewhere near the proper position. The judge gives the next instruction: "The bar!" This means that you must make your dog clear the bar jump. Give the hand signal and the command "Over!" (fig. III-97). When the dog is in mid-air, turn and face his most probable direction of return, and remain there until he comes in to you and sits. The judge then says "Finish!" and, after that is completed, informs you that the exercise is over. Resume your original position with the dog in the proper heeling position facing down the center line of the ring. The judge again asks if you are ready; on your affirmative, he says "Send your dog!"; you immediately give the simultaneous verbal and hand-signal go-out commands, pointing, without bending over, to the opposite end of the ring. This time, after your dog

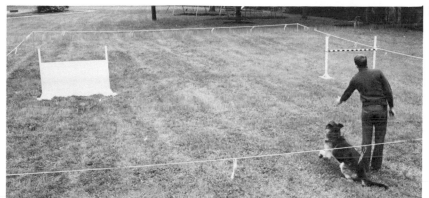

III-96. The Directed Jumping can begin at either end of the ring. After ascertaining that you are ready, the judge says "Send your dog!" On hearing this, you may give a hand signal simultaneously with the command "Go out!" Technically, this handler could lose half a point or so because of his bit of body English while giving the hand signal. It is not obligatory to give the hand signal; if you tend toward body English and if your dog will go out properly without the hand signal, you can send him with merely the verbal "Go out!"

III-97. Handler Edward Hamm gives the hand signal and "Over!" to his shepherd in the Directed Jumping exercise. Note that, in giving the signal for the solid jump, he avoids body English—a perfect signal and part of the reason that Hamm consistently wins.

327

III-98. Group Examination. Judge Hart approaches each dog in turn and examines it physically. The dogs must not show any resentment or shyness—in fact, tail wagging and licking are considered desirable. This can be an excrutiatingly long three minutes for the handlers, as they watch from across the ring, hoping their dogs keep their feet firmly planted.

has come to a sit facing you, expect to send him over the remaining jump; if you did the bar jump the first time, you must be given the solid jump the second time.

The termination of this exercise, as before, is indicated by the judge's statement "Exercise finished."

This ends the individual Utility exercises; you now leave the ring. In Utility competition, it is highly desirable for you to walk out as soon as the judge tells you that you have finished on the second jump. This has to do with "uncontrollable" behavior: in an AKC trial, the gallery will often clap and cheer if your dog performed well, and this could excite him into jumping up on you and licking your face. We once saw an otherwise flawless performance get penalized five or six points when a retriever did a little dance of appreciation of the crowd's generous clapping. Because this happened in the ring, the judge considered it "uncontrollable" behavior, and the penalty knocked the dog's score down so far that he lost the first place he would surely have otherwise taken. So make it a point to get out of the ring as soon as you have finished the second jump of Directed Jumping. If necessary, leave your dog with someone outside and come back into the ring alone to get your scent-article case and your lead.

Group Examination (*Long Stand*). Your practice session for the Group Examination will probably have to be conducted under less than ideal circumstances, since it is unlikely that you know many people who have Utility dogs. Still, you should do the long-stand exercise as part of your training, even if you must do it alone. You probably do have a number of friends who are training their dogs in Novice or Open; it is a good idea to work with them when they practice as a group. During the Open Long Sit and Long Down, you could put your dog in a stand. If your friends are using this course to prepare their dogs for competition, they will be practicing the Utility Group Examination at Open level; it would be to your mutual advantage to work together.

In any event, make your dog stand for at least three minutes and have your assistant examine him. The examination should be more rigorous than what your dog was exposed to in Novice. Your assistant should approach the dog, slowly feel his body, walk around behind the dog, gently push down on the dog's rump, and then return to you (see fig. III-98 for a Group Examination at an AKC trial). Remain standing there until the full three minutes are up, and return to your dog when the judge gives you the instruction to "return." Your dog must remain standing until that time.

This constitutes the proper show sequence. Practice it for the remainder of the week, in your back yard. You will easily spot the exercises that are giving your dog trouble. After going through the complete sequence, rest your dog a few moments, and then work on those exercises that he failed during the more formal practice routine. You should make corrections for major errors (with the short cord your dog is wearing) during the practice session in which your assistant is helping you. However, avoid sharp corrections for minor deficiencies, such as slightly crooked sits; work with the dog on these later, as a separate practice routine, until he does them properly.

UTILITY WEEK 10

OUTLINE OF TRAINING SCHEDULE
Old Exercises
> Resume practicing Open exercises—you can enter your dog in both Open B and Utility in your next show.

Modifications of Utility Exercises
> Simulating the Show Ring
> Practice in regulation ring with assistant as judge and steward. Move to new areas at least three times a week.
> Practice near crowds and noise and occasionally in foul weather. (A common statement on premiums for outdoor shows: "This show will be held outdoors rain or shine.")
> Condition dog to obey only your signals.
> Review Utility Judge's Worksheet for each exercise to improve handling.

Suggested Practice Session: Three times a week in a ring, supplemented by additional work on weak exercises

III-99. The Utility runoff exercise is the Signal Exercise. John Epperly and his Rottweiler start out simultaneously with Daniel Snyder and his shepherd, two excellent handler/dog teams that provide rigorous competition wherever they show.

There are four objectives in this week's training: (1) working your dog in new areas with a regulation-size practice ring; (2) exposing your dog to crowds while working him; (3) conditioning your dog to obeying only *your* signals; and (4) improving your handling techniques and eliminating handler's errors.

Utility training requires the use of a considerable amount of equipment, materials that are bulky and somewhat difficult to pack in your car. Moving the equipment may be an annoying task, but it is absolutely essential to work your dog in new surroundings at this stage. A minimum of three new areas each week prior to entering competition is an acceptable amount of exposure. The days in between can be devoted to perfecting the exercises that need work by practicing in your back yard. Those of you who are especially enthusiastic *aficionados* of obedience training might want to build a lightweight, portable jump set for practice in new areas. There are many lightweight construction materials available. If you are handy with your hands and have a few carpentry tools, you can make a collapsible set of jumps that would be easily transportable. Commercially made sets are advertised in *Dog World* (see Appendix II), which is sold at many pet shops.

The area you select for the new exposure can be just about anywhere. Make sure that it is permissible to take your dog there. If you work in public places, early in the morning or late in the afternoon

OBEDIENCE JUDGE'S WORKSHEET

For Judge's Use ONLY — Not to be distributed or shown to exhibitors

DOG No.

DATE. . . . . UTILITY . . . . . . CLASS
(A or B)

SHOW. . . . .

ARTICLES NO. . . . . BREED . . . . HEIGHT . . . . JUMPS. . . . . .
at withers

EXERCISE	NON QUALIFYING		QUALIFYING		Maximum Points	Points Lost	NET SCORE
	ZERO	LESS THAN 50%	SUBSTANTIAL	MINOR			
SIGNAL EXERCISE	Unmanageable . . . . ☐ Unqualified heeling . ☐	Any audible comm . ☐ Handler adapting self to dog pace . ☐ Failure on first signal to: Stand . . . ☐ Stay . . . . ☐ Drop . . . . ☐ Sit . . . . ☐ Come . . . ☐ Anticipated . . . . ☐ Sat out of reach . . ☐	☐ . . . Forging . . . Crowding handler . ☐ ☐ . . . Lagging . . . Sniffing . . . . ☐ ☐ No change of pace ☐ Fast ☐ Slow ☐ ☐ . Heeling wide — on turns — abouts . ☐ ☐ . Extra signal to heel ☐ . . ☐ Sit . . . ☐ ☐ . . . . . . Holding signals . . . . ☐ Slow response to signal to ☐ . . Stand . . Down . . Sit . . Come . . . ☐ ☐ No sit front - finish Touching handler ☐ ☐ Lack of Sat between feet . ☐ naturalness Poor sits . . . . . ☐ smoothness Poor finish.	40		
SCENT DISCRIMI-NATION	No go out 1st comm. ☐L ☐M	No retrieve ☐L ☐M	Wrong article ☐L ☐M Anticipated . . . . . ☐ Double command . ☐ Sat out of reach: LEATHER . . . . . ☐ METAL . . . . . ☐	L M ☐ ☐ . . Handler roughness . . . ☐ ☐ ☐ . . . . Sat after turn . . . ☐ ☐ ☐ Doesn't work continuously ☐ ☐ ☐ Dropping article on return ☐ Picks up wrong Mouthing . ☐ article then dropped: Touched ☐ ☐ handler . ☐ ☐ ☐ Slow response Sat between ☐ ☐ No sit in front feet . . . ☐ ☐ ☐ No finish Poor sits . . . ☐ ☐ ☐ Handler error Poor finish . ☐	L M LEATHER 30 METAL 30		
DIRECTED RETRIEVE	Does Not: Go out on command ☐ Go directly to glove . . . . ☐ Retrieve right article . . . . ☐ Fails to retrieve . . ☐	Anticipated . . . . . ☐ Sat out of reach . . ☐	☐ . . . . . Touching dog sending . . . . ☐ ☐ . . . . . Excessive signals . . . . . . ☐ ☐ . . . Slow response to command . . . ☐ ☐ . . Mouthing . ☐ Playing . . . ☐ ☐ Dropping article Touching handler . ☐ ☐ Poor delivery . . . Sat between feet . ☐ ☐ No sit in front Poor sit . . . ☐ ☐ No finish Poor finish . . . . . ☐ ☐ Lack of naturalness smoothness . . . . ☐	30		
DIRECTED JUMPING	HIGH JUMP Does Not: Leave on order . . . ☐ Go substantially in right direction . ☐ Stop on command . ☐ Jump as directed . ☐ Climbing jump . . . ☐ ☐ . . . . . . Anticipated	BAR JUMP Does Not: Leave on order . . . ☐ Go substantially in right direction . ☐ Stop on command . ☐ Jump as directed . ☐ Knocking bar off . . ☐ command . . . ☐	☐ . . . . . Holding signals . . . . ☐ ☐ . . . Slow response to directions . . . ☐ ☐ . . . . . Slightly off direction . . . . . ☐ ☐ . . . . . Not back far enough . . . . . ☐ ☐ . . Anticipated ☐ Turn ☐ Stop ☐ Sit ☐ . . . . . Does not sit on command . . . ☐ ☐ No sit in front Touched handler ☐ ☐ No finish Sat between feet ☐ ☐ Lack of naturalness Poor sits . . . ☐ —smoothness Poor finishes . . . ☐	40		
			MAX SUB-TOTAL ➡		165		
GROUP EXAMI-NATION	Substantial move growls or snaps . . . ☐ Goes to another dog . . . . . ☐ Sits or lies down be- fore handler returns ☐	Minor move away . . ☐ Shows shyness . . . ☐ Resentment . . . ☐ Repeated barks or whines . . ☐	☐ . . . Resistance to handler posing . ☐ ☐ . . . . . Moved feet slightly . . . . . . ☐ ☐ . . . . . Minor whine or bark . . . . . . ☐ ☐ Sits or lies down after handler returns to heel position . . . . . . ☐	30		
			MAXIMUM POINTS ➡		200		

☐ H. Disciplining ☐ Shows Fear ☐ Fouling Ring ☐ Disqualified ☐ Expelled ☐ Excused Less Penalty for ➡
Unusual Behavior

EXPLANATION
 OF PENALTY

TOTAL NET SCORE ➡

© Ralston Purina Company 1968

331

would be best, so that you can avoid inconveniencing other patrons. Some of the exercises, such as hand-signal work or Scent Discrimination, require minimal equipment, so it is possible—as well as desirable—to work on those in more crowded areas, such as a ball park during a Little League baseball game or some other place where there are numerous distractions in terms of noise and people moving about. You could heel your dog into such an area and quickly go through Scent Discrimination and the hand-signal routine without bringing along the cumbersome jumps. We have even practiced Scent Discrimination on the public mall of a busy shopping center, a situation that certainly improves a dog's ability to work in the midst of heavy distraction.

It is important to train your dog in such a way that he will obey only your signal while you are handling him. Otherwise he might interpret a movement in the crowd as a signal. Your dog is so highly trained at this point that while you are working the hand-signal routine in competition, he might, unless conditioned not to, take a sudden upward thrust of somebody else's hand to mean a drop signal. Thus, as an extension of the training from Open, work your dog in the hand signals while someone in the distant background tries to tempt him into a premature down by giving a hand signal. If your dog shows any inclination to drop, rush in and correct him smartly; repeat the temptation until he will absolutely ignore a signal from anyone but you.

Do not forget to practice a few runoffs with your friends and their dogs just before you enter a Utility show. The runoff exercise you must do in Utility is the Signal Exercise, which confirms the importance of practicing your hand signals when someone else is giving hand signals nearby. Figure III-99 shows a runoff in Utility competition.

As in Novice and Open, you should conclude your formal training for the competition exercises by carefully reviewing the Judge's Worksheet (fig. III-100). It lists all the exercises and the various aspects of performance scrutinized by the Utility judge as he scores you and your dog. In addition, review the kinds of errors you and your dog might make in the Group Stand for Examination, a worksheet for which is given in Appendix III.

APPENDIX I

AKC Obedience Regulations

Purpose

Obedience trials are a sport and all participants should be guided by the principles of good sportsmanship both in and outside of the ring. The purpose of obedience trials is to demonstrate the usefulness of the pure-bred dog as a companion of man, not merely the dog's ability to follow specified routines in the obedience ring. While all contestants in a class are required to perform the same exercises in substantially the same way so that the relative quality of the various performances may be compared and scored, the basic objective of obedience trials is to produce dogs that have been trained and conditioned always to behave in the home, in public places, and in the presence of other dogs, in a manner that will reflect credit on the sport of obedience. The performances of dog and handler in the ring must be accurate and correct and must conform to the requirements of these regulations. However, it is also essential that the dog demonstrate willingness and enjoyment of its work, and that smoothness and naturalness on the part of the handler be given precedence over a performance based on military precision and peremptory commands.

CHAPTER 1
General Regulations

Section 1. *Obedience Clubs.* An obedience club that meets all the requirements of The American Kennel Club and wishes to hold an Obedience Trial at which qualifying scores toward an obedience title may be awarded, must make application to The American Kennel Club on the form provided for permission to hold such trial. Such a trial, if approved, may be held either in conjunction with a dog show or as a separate event. If the club is not a member of The American Kennel Club it shall pay a license fee for the privilege of holding such trial, the amount of which shall be determined by the Board of Directors of The American Kennel Club. If the club fails to hold its trial at the time and place which have been approved, the amount of the license fee paid will be returned.

Section 2. *Dog Show and Specialty Clubs.* A dog show club may be granted permission to hold a licensed or member obedience trial at its dog show, and a specialty club may also be granted permission to hold a licensed or member obedience trial if, in the opinion of the Board of Directors of The American Kennel Club, such clubs are qualified to do so.

Section 3. *Obedience Classes.* A licensed or member obedience trial need not include all of the regular obedience classes defined in these Regulations, but a club will be approved to hold Open classes only if it also holds Novice classes, and a club will be approved to hold a Utility class only if it also holds Novice and Open classes. A specialty club which has been approved to hold a licensed or member obedience trial, if qualified in the opinion of the Board of Directors of The American Kennel Club, or an obedience club which has been approved to hold a licensed or member obedience trial may, subject to the approval of The American Kennel Club, offer additional nonregular classes for dogs not less than six months of age, provided a clear and complete description of the eligibility requirements and performance requirements for each such class appears in the premium list. However, the nonregular classes defined in these Regulations need not be described in the premium list. Pre-Novice classes will not be approved at licensed or member obedience trials.

Section 4. *Tracking Tests.* A club that has been approved to hold licensed or member obedience trials and that meets the requirements of The American Kennel Club, may also make application to hold a Tracking Test. A club may not hold a tracking test on the same day as its show or obedience trial, but the tracking test may be announced in the premium list for the show or trial, and the tracking test entries may be included in the show or obedience trial catalog. If the entries are not listed in the catalog for the show or obedience trial, the club must provide, at the tracking test, several copies of a sheet, which may be typewritten, giving all the information that would be contained in the catalog for each entered dog. If the tracking test is to be held within 7 days of the obedience trial the entries must be sent to the same person designated to receive the obedience trial entries, and the same closing date should apply. If the tracking test is not to be held within 7 days of the obedience trial the club may name someone else in the premium list to receive the tracking test entries, and may specify a different closing date for entries at least 7 days before the tracking test.

The presence of a veterinarian shall not be required at a tracking test.

Section 5. *Obedience Trial Committee.* If an obedience trial is held by an obedience club, an Obedience Trial Committee must be appointed by the club, and this committee shall exercise all the authority vested in a dog show's Bench Show Committee. If an obedience club holds its obedience trial in conjunction with a dog show, then the Obedience Trial Committee shall have sole jurisdiction only over those dogs entered in the obedience trial and their handlers and owners; provided, however, that if any dog is entered in both obedience and breed classes, then the Obedience Trial Committee shall have jurisdiction over such dog, its owner, and its handler, only in matters pertaining to the Obedience Regulations, and the Bench Show Committee shall have jurisdiction over such dog, its owner and handler, in all other matters.

When an obedience trial is to be held in conjunction with a dog show by the club which has been granted permission to hold the show, the club's Bench Show Committee shall include one person designated as "Obedience Chairman." At such event the Bench Show Committee of the show-giving club shall have sole jurisdiction over all matters which may properly come before it, regardless of whether the matter has to do with the dog show or with the obedience trial.

Section 6. *Sanctioned Matches.* A club may hold an Obedience Match by obtaining the sanction of The American Kennel Club. Sanctioned obedience matches shall be governed by such regulations as may be adopted by the Board of Directors of The American Kennel Club. Scores awarded at such matches will not be entered in the records of The American Kennel Club nor count towards an obedience title.

All of these Obedience Regulations shall also apply to sanctioned matches except for those sections in which it is specified that the provisions apply to licensed or member trials, and except where specifically stated otherwise in the Regulations for Sanctioned Matches.

Section 7. *American Kennel Club Sanction.* American Kennel Club sanction must be obtained by any club that holds American Kennel Club obedience trials, for any type of match for which it solicits or accepts entries from non-members.

Section 8. *Dog Show Rules.* All the Dog Show Rules, were applicable, shall govern the conduct of obedience trials and tracking tests, and shall apply to all persons and dogs participating in them except as these Obedience Regulations may provide otherwise.

Section 9. *Identification.* No badges, club jackets, coats with kennel names thereon or ribbon prizes shall be worn or displayed, nor other visible means of identification used, by an individual when exhibiting a dog in the ring.

Section 10. *Immediate Family.* As used in this chapter, "immediate family" means husband, wife, father, mother, son, daughter, brother, or sister.

Section 11. *Pure-Bred Dogs Only.* As used in these regulations the word "dog" refers to either sex but only to dogs that are pure-bred of a breed eligible for registration in the American Kennel Club stud book or for entry in the Miscellaneous Class at American Kennel Club dog shows, as only such dogs may compete in obedience trials, tracking tests, or sanctioned matches. A judge must report to The American Kennel Club after the trial or tracking test any dog shown under him which in his opinion appears not to be pure-bred.

Section 12. *Unregistered Dogs.* Chapter 16, Section 1 of the Dog Show Rules shall apply to entries in licensed or member obedience trials and tracking tests, except that an eligible unregistered dog for which an ILP number has been issued by The American Kennel Club may be entered indefinitely in such events provided the ILP number is shown on each entry form.

Section 13. *Dogs That May Not Compete.* No dog belonging wholly or in part to a judge or to a Show or Obedience Trial Secretary, Superintendent, or veterinarian, or to any member of such person's immediate family or household, shall be entered in any dog show, obedience trial, or tracking test at which such person officiates or is scheduled to officiate. This applies to both obedience and dog show judges when an obedience trial is held in conjunction with a dog show. However, a tracking test shall be considered a separate event for the purpose of this section.

No dogs shall be entered or shown under a judge at an obedience trial or tracking test if the dog has been owned, sold, held under lease, handled in the ring, boarded, or has been regularly trained or instructed, within one year prior to the date of the obedience trial or tracking test, by the judge or by any member of his immediate family or household, and no such dog shall be eligible to compete. "Trained or instructed" applies equally to judges who train professionally or as amateurs, and to judges who train individual dogs or who train or instruct dogs in classes with or through their handlers.

Section 14. *Qualifying Score.* A qualifying score shall be comprised of scores of more than 50% of the available points in each exercise and a final score of 170 or more points, earned in a single regular or nonregular class at a licensed or member Obedience Trial or Sanctioned Match.

Section 15. *When Titles Are Won.* Where any of the following sections of the regulations excludes from a particular obedience class dogs that have won a particular obedience title, eligibility to enter that class shall be determined as follows: a dog may continue to be shown in such a class after its handler has been notified by three different judges of regular classes in licensed or member trials, that it has received three qualifying scores for such title, but may not be entered or shown in such a class in any obedience trial of which the closing date for entries occurs after the owner has received official notification from The American Kennel Club that the dog has won the particular obedience title.

Where any of the following sections of the regulations require that a dog shall have won a particular obedience title before competing in a particular obedience class, a dog may not be shown in such class at any obedience trial before the owner has received official notification from The American Kennel Club that the dog has won the required title.

Section 16. *Disqualification and Ineligibility.* A dog that is blind or deaf or that has been changed in appearance by artificial means (except for such changes as are customarily approved for its breed) may not compete in any obedience trial or tracking test and must be disqualified. Blind means having useful vision in neither eye. Deaf means without useful hearing.

When a judge finds any of these conditions in any dog he is judging, he   335 shall disqualify the dog marking his book "Disqualified" and stating the reason. He shall not obtain the opinion of the show veterinarian.

The judge must disqualify any dog that attempts to attack any person in the ring. He may excuse a dog that attacks another dog or that appears dangerous to other dogs in the ring. He shall mark the dog disqualified or excused and state the reason in the judge's book, and shall give the Superintendent or Show or Trial Secretary a brief report of the dog's actions which shall be submitted to AKC with the report of the show or trial.

When a dog has been disqualified under this section as being blind or deaf or having been changed in appearance by artificial means or for having attempted to attack a person in the ring, all awards made to the dog at the trial shall be cancelled by The American Kennel Club and the dog may not again compete unless and until, following application by the owner to The American Kennel Club, the owner has received official notification from The American Kennel Club that the dog's eligibility has been reinstated.

Spayed bitches, castrated dogs, monorchid or cryptorchid males, and dogs that have faults which would disqualify them under the standards for their breeds, may compete in obedience trials if otherwise eligible under these regulations.

A dog that is lame in the ring at any obedience trial or at a tracking test may not compete and shall not receive any score at the trial. It shall be the judge's responsibility to determine whether a dog is lame. He shall not obtain the opinion of the show veterinarian. If in the judge's opinion a dog in the ring is lame, he shall not score such dog, and shall promptly excuse it from the ring and mark his book "Excused—lame."

No dog shall be eligible to compete if it is taped or bandaged in any way or if it has anything attached to it for medical or corrective purposes. Such a dog must be immediately excused from the ring, and under no circumstance may it be returned later for judging after the tape, bandage or attachment has been removed.

With the exception of Maltese, Poodles, Shih Tzu and Yorkshire Terriers, which may be shown with the hair over the eyes tied back as they are normally shown in the breed ring, no dog shall be eligible to compete if it appears to have been dyed or colored in any way or if the coat shows evidence of chalk or powder, or if the dog has anything attached to it for protection or adornment. Such a dog may, at the judge's sole discretion, be judged at a later time if the offending condition has been corrected.

An obedience judge is not required to be familiar with the breed standards nor to scrutinize each dog as in dog show judging, but shall be alert for conditions which may require disqualification or exclusion under this section.

Section 17. *Disturbances.* Bitches in season are not permitted to compete. The judge of an obedience trial or tracking test must remove from competition any bitch in season, any dog which its handler cannot control, any handler who interferes willfully with another competitor or his dog, and any handler who abuses his dog in the ring, and may excuse from competition any dog which he considers unfit to compete, or any bitch which appears so attractive to males as to be a disturbing element. If a dog or handler is expelled or excused by a judge, the reason shall be stated in the judge's book or in a separate report.

Section 18. *Obedience Ribbons.* At licensed or member obedience trials the following colors shall be used for prize ribbons or rosettes in all regular classes and for the ribbon or rosette for Highest Scoring Dog in the Regular Classes:

First Prize   Blue
Second Prize   Red
Third Prize   Yellow
Fourth Prize   White

Qualifying Prize   Dark Green
Highest Scoring Dog in the Regular Classes   Blue and Gold
and the following colors shall be used for nonregular classes:
First Prize   Rose
Second Prize   Brown
Third Prize   Light Green
Fourth Prize   Gray

Each ribbon or rosette shall be at least two inches wide and approximately eight inches long, and shall bear on its face a facsimile of the seal of The American Kennel Club, the words "Obedience Trial," the name of the prize, the name of the trial-giving club, the date of the trial, and the name of the city or town where the trial is given.

Section 19. *Match Ribbons.* If ribbons are given at sanctioned obedience matches they shall be of the following colors and shall have the words "Obedience Match" printed on them, but may be of any design or size:

First Prize   Rose
Second Prize   Brown
Third Prize   Light Green
Fourth Prize   Gray
Qualifying Prize   Green with Pink edges

Section 20. *Ribbons and Prizes.* Ribbons for the four official placings and all prizes offered for competition within a single regular or nonregular class at licensed or member trials or at sanctioned matches shall be awarded only to dogs that earn qualifying scores.

Prizes for which dogs in one class compete against dogs in one or more other classes at licensed or member trials or at sanctioned matches shall be awarded only to dogs that earn qualifying scores.

Prizes at a licensed or member obedience trial must be offered to be won outright, with the exception that a prize which requires three wins by the same owner, not necessarily with the same dog, for permanent possession, may be offered for the dog with the highest qualifying scores in one of the regular classes, or the dog with the highest qualifying score in the regular classes, or the dog with the highest combined qualifying scores in the Open B and Utility classes.

Subject to the provisions of paragraphs 1 and 2 of this section, prizes may be offered for the highest scoring dogs of the Groups as defined in Chapter 2 of the Dog Show Rules, or for the highest scoring dogs of any breeds, but not for a breed variety. Show varieties are not recognized for obedience. In accordance with Chapter 2, all Poodles are in the Non-Sporting Group and all Manchester Terriers in the Terrier Group.

Prizes offered only to members of certain clubs or organizations will not be approved for publication in premium lists.

Section 21. *Highest Scoring Dog in the Regular Classes.* The dog receiving the highest qualifying score in the regular classes shall be awarded the ribbon and any prizes offered for this placement, after the announcement of final scores of the last regular class to be judged. The Superintendent or Show or Trial Secretary shall mark the catalog to identify the dog receiving this award.

In case of a tie between dogs receiving the highest qualifying score in two or more regular classes, the dogs shall be tested again by having them perform at the same time some part or parts of the Heel Free exercise. The judge for the run-off shall be designated by the Bench Show or Obedience Trial Committee from among the judges of the obedience trial. When the run-off has been completed, the judge shall record the results on a special sheet which shall identify the dogs taking part in the run-off by catalog number, class and breed. When the judge has marked and signed the sheet, it shall be turned over to the Superintendent or Show or Trial Secretary who   337 shall mark the catalog accordingly and forward the sheet to The American Kennel Club as part of the records of the trial.

Section 22. *Risk.* The owner or agent entering a dog in any obedience trial does so at his own risk and agrees to abide by the rules of The American Kennel Club and the Obedience Regulations.

Section 23. *Decisions.* At the trial the decisions of the judge shall be final in all matters affecting the scoring and the working of the dogs and their handlers. The Obedience Trial Committee, or the Bench Show Committee, if the trial is held by a show-giving club, shall decide all other matters arising at the trial, including protests against dogs made under Chapter 20 of the Dog Show Rules, subject, however, to the rules and regulations of The American Kennel Club.

Section 24. *Dogs Must Compete.* Any dog entered and received at a licensed or member obedience trial must compete in all exercises of all classes in which it is entered unless disqualified, expelled, or excused by the judge or by the Bench Show or Obedience Trial Committee, or unless excused by the official veterinarian to protect the health of the dog or of other dogs at the trial. The excuse of the official veterinarian must be in writing and must be approved by the Superintendent or Show or Trial Secretary, and must be submitted to The American Kennel Club with the report of the trial. The judge must report to The American Kennel Club any dog that is not brought back for the Group exercises.

Section 25. *Judging Program.* Any club holding a licensed or member obedience trial must prepare, after the entries have closed, a program showing the time scheduled for the judging of each of the classes. A copy of this program shall be mailed to the owner of each entered dog and to each judge, and the program shall be printed in the catalog. This program shall be based on the judging of no more than 8 Novice entries, 7 Open entries, or 6 Utility entries, per hour during the time the show or trial will be open as published in the premium list, taking into consideration the starting hour for judging if published in the premium list, and the availability of rings. No judge shall be scheduled to exceed this rate of judging. In addition, one hour for rest or meals must be allowed if, under this formula, it will take more than five hours of actual judging to judge the dogs entered under him. No judge shall be assigned to judge for more than eight hours in one day under this formula, including any breed judging assignment if the obedience trial is held in conjunction with a dog show.

If any nonregular class is to be judged in the same ring as any regular class, or by the judge of any regular class, the nonregular class must be judged after the regular class.

Section 26. *Limitation of Entries.* If a club anticipates an entry in excess of its facilities for a licensed or member trial, it may limit entries in any or all regular classes, but nonregular classes will not be approved if the regular classes are limited. A club may limit entries in any or all regular classes to 64 in a Novice class, 56 in an Open class, or 48 in a Utility class.

Prominent announcement of such limits must appear on the title or cover page of the premium list for an obedience trial or immediately under the obedience heading in the premium list for a dog show, with a statement that entries in one or more specified classes or in the obedience trial will automatically close when a certain limit or limits have been reached, even though the official closing date for entries has not arrived.

Section 27. *Additional Judges, Reassignment, Split Classes.* If when the entries have closed, it is found that the entry under one or more judges exceeds the limit established in Section 25, the club shall immediately secure the approval of The American Kennel Club for the appointment of one or more additional judges, or for reassignment of its advertised judges, so that no judge will be required to exceed the limit.

338   If a judge with an excessive entry was advertised to judge more than

one class, one or more of his classes shall be assigned to another judge. The class or classes selected for reassignment shall first be any nonregular classes for which he was advertised, and shall then be either the regular class or classes with the minimum number of entries, or those with the minimum scheduled time, which will bring the advertised judge's schedule within, and as close as possible to, the maximum limit. If a judge with an excessive entry was advertised to judge only one class, the Superintendent, Show Secretary, or Obedience Trial Secretary, shall divide the entry as evenly as possible between the advertised judge and the other judge by drawing lots.

The club shall promptly mail to the owner of each entry affected, a notification of any change of judge. The owner shall be permitted to withdraw such entry at any time prior to the day of the show, and the entry fee shall then be refunded. If the entry in any one class is split in this manner, the advertised judge shall judge the run-off of any tie scores that may develop between the two divisions of the class, after each judge has first run off any ties resulting from his own judging.

Section 28. *Split Classes in Premium List.* A club may choose to announce two or more judges for any class in its premium list. In such case the entries shall be divided by lots as provided above. The identification slips and judging program shall be made up so that the owner of each dog will know the division, and the judge of the division, in which his dog is entered, but no owner shall be entitled to a refund of entry fee. In such case the premium list shall also specify the judge for the run-off of any tie scores which may develop between the dogs in the different divisions, after each judge has first run off any ties resulting from his own judging.

Section 29. *Split Classes, Official Ribbons, Prizes.* A club which holds a split class, whether the split is announced in the premium list or made after entries close, shall not award American Kennel Club official ribbons in either division. The four dogs with the highest qualifying scores in the class, regardless of the division or divisions in which such scores were made, shall be called back into the ring and awarded the four American Kennel Club official ribbons by one of the judges of the class. This judge shall be responsible for recording the entry numbers of the four placed dogs in one of the judges' books.

If a split class is announced in the premium list, duplicate placement prizes may be offered in each division. If prizes have been offered for placements in a class that must be split after entries close, duplicate prizes or prizes of equal value may be offered in the additional division of the class.

Section 30. *Stewards.* The judge is in sole charge of his ring until his assignment is completed. Stewards are provided to assist him, but they may act only on the judge's instructions. Stewards shall not give information or instructions to owners and handlers except as specifically instructed by the judge, and then only in such a manner that it is clear that the instructions are those of the judge.

Section 31. *Ring Conditions.* If the judging takes place indoors the ring should be rectangular and should be about 35′ wide and 50′ long for all obedience classes. In no case shall the ring for a Utility class be less than 35′ by 50′, and in no case shall the ring for a Novice or Open class be less than 30′ by 40′. The floor shall have a surface or covering that provides firm footing for the largest dogs, and rubber or similar non-slip material must be laid for the take off and landing at all jumps unless the surface, in the judge's opinion, is such as not to require it. At an outdoor show or trial the rings shall be about 40′ wide and 50′ long. The ground shall be clean and level, and the grass, if any, shall be cut short. The Club and Superintendent are responsible for providing, for the Open classes, an appropriate place approved by the judge, for the handlers to go completely out of sight of their dogs. If inclement weather at an outdoor trial necessitates the judging of obedience under shelter, the requirements as to ring size may be waived.

Section 32. *Obedience Rings at Dog Shows.* At an outdoor dog show a separate ring or rings shall be provided for obedience, and a sign forbidding anyone to permit any dog to use the ring, except when being judged, shall be set up in each such ring by the Superintendent or Show Secretary. It shall be his duty as well as that of the Show Committee to enforce this regulation. At an indoor show where limited space does not permit the exclusive use of any ring for obedience, the same regulation will apply after the obedience rings have been set up. At a dog show the material used for enclosing the obedience rings shall be at least equal to the material used for enclosing the breed rings. The ring must be thoroughly cleaned before the obedience judging starts if it has previously been used for breed judging.

Section 33. *Judge's Report on Ring and Equipment.* The Superintendent and the officials of the club holding the obedience trial are responsible for providing rings and equipment which meet the requirements of these regulations. However, the judge must check the ring and equipment provided for his use before starting to judge, and must report to The American Kennel Club after the trial any undesirable ring conditions or deficiencies that have not been promptly corrected at his request.

CHAPTER 2
Regulations for Performance and Judging

Section 1. *Standardized Judging.* Standardized judging is of paramount importance. Judges are not permitted to inject their own variations into the exercises, but must see that each handler and dog executes the various exercises exactly as described in these regulations. A handler who is familiar with these regulations should be able to enter the ring under any judge without having to inquire how the particular judge wishes to have any exercise performed, and without being confronted with some unexpected requirement.

Section 2. *Standard of Perfection.* The judge must carry a mental picture of the theoretically perfect performance in each exercise and score each dog and handler against this visualized standard which shall combine the utmost in willingness, enjoyment and precision on the part of the dog, and naturalness, gentleness, and smoothness in handling. Lack of willingness or enjoyment on the part of the dog must be penalized, as must lack of precision in the dog's performance, roughness in handling, military precision or peremptory commands by the handler. There shall be no penalty of less than ½ point or multiple of ½ point.

Section 3. *Qualifying Performance.* A judge's certification in his judge's book of a qualifying score for any particular dog constitutes his certification to The American Kennel Club that the dog on this particular occasion has performed all of the required exercises at least in accordance with the minimum standards and that its performance on this occasion would justify the awarding of the obedience title associated with the particular class. A qualifying score must never be awarded to a dog whose performance has not met the minimum requirements, nor to a dog that shows fear or resentment, or that relieves itself at any time while in an indoor ring for judging, or that relieves itself while performing any exercise in an outdoor ring, nor to a dog whose handler disciplines or abuses it in the ring, or carries or offers food in the ring.

In deciding whether a faulty performance of a particular exercise by a particular dog warrants a qualifying score, the judge shall consider whether the awarding of an obedience title would be justified if all dogs in the class performed the exercise in a similar manner. The judge must not give a qualifying score for the exercise if he decides that it would be contrary to the best interests of the sport if all dogs in the class were to perform in the same way.

Section 4. *Judge's Directions.* The judge's orders and signals should be given to the handlers in a clear and understandable manner, but in such a way that the work of the dog is not disturbed. Before starting each exercise, the judge shall ask "Are you ready?" At the end of each exercise the judge shall say "Exercise finished." Each contestant must be worked and judged separately except for the Group exercises, and in running off a tie.

Section 5. *No Added Requirements.* No judge shall require any dog or handler to do anything, nor penalize a dog or handler for failing to do anything, that is not required by these regulations.

Section 6. *A and B Classes and Different Breeds.* The same methods and standards must be used for judging and scoring the A and B Classes, and in judging and scoring the work of dogs of different breeds.

Section 7. *Interference and Double Handling.* A judge who is aware of any assistance, interference, or attempts to control a dog from outside the ring, must act promptly to stop any such double handling or interference, and shall penalize the dog substantially or, if in the judge's opinion the circumstances warrant, shall give the dog a score of zero for the exercise during which the aid was received.

Section 8. *Rejudging.* If a dog has failed in a particular part of an exercise, it shall not ordinarily be rejudged nor given a second chance; but if in the judge's opinion the dog's performance was prejudiced by peculiar and unusual conditions, the judge may at his own discretion rejudge the dog on the entire exercise.

Section 9. *Ties.* In case of a tie any prize in a Novice or Open class, the dogs shall be tested again by having them perform at the same time all or some part of the Heel Free exercise. In the Utility class the dogs shall perform at the same time all or some part of the Signal exercise. The original scores shall not be changed.

Section 10. *Judge's Book and Score Sheets.* The judge must enter the scores and sub-total score of each dog in the official judge's book immediately after each dog has been judged on the individual exercises and before judging the next dog. Scores for the group exercises and total scores must be entered in the official judge's book immediately after each group of dogs has been judged. No score may be changed except to correct an arithmetical error or if a score has been entered in the wrong column. All final scores must be entered in the judge's book before prizes are awarded. No person other than the judge may make any entry in the judge's book. Judges may use separate score sheets for their own purposes, but shall not give out nor allow exhibitors to see such sheets, nor give out any other written scores, nor permit anyone else to distribute score sheets or cards prepared by the judge. Carbon copies of the sheets in the official judge's book shall be made available through the Superintendent or Show or Trial Secretary for examination by owners and handlers immediately after the prizes have been awarded in each class. If score cards are distributed by a club after the prizes are awarded they must contain no more information than is shown in the judge's book and must be marked "unofficial score."

Section 11. *Announcement of Scores.* The judge shall not disclose any score or partial score to contestants or spectators until he has completed the judging of the entire class or, in case of a split class, until he has completed the judging of his division; nor shall he permit anyone else to do so. After all the scores are recorded for the class, or for the division in case of a split class, the judge shall call for all available dogs that have won qualifying scores to be brought into the ring. Before awarding the prizes, the judge shall inform the spectators as to the maximum number of points for a perfect score, and shall then announce the score of each prize winner, and announce to the handler the score of each dog that has won a qualifying score.

Section 12. *Explanations and Errors.* The judge is not required to explain his scoring, and need not enter into any discussion with any contestant who appears to be dissatisfied. Any interested person who thinks that there may have been an arithmetical error or an error in identifying a dog may report the facts to one of the stewards or to the Superintendent or Show or Trial Secretary so that the matter may be checked.

Section 13. *Compliance with Regulations and Standards.* In accordance with the certification on the entry form, the handler of each dog and the person signing each entry form must be familiar with the Obedience Regulations applicable to the class in which the dog is entered.

Section 14. *Handicapped Handlers.* Judges may modify the specific requirements of these regulations for handlers to the extent necessary to permit physically handicapped handlers to compete, provided such handlers can move about the ring without physical assistance or guidance from another person, except for guidance from the judge or from the handler of a competing dog in the ring for the Group exercises.

Dogs handled by such handlers shall be required to perform all parts of all exercises as described in these regulations, and shall be penalized for failure to perform any part of an exercise.

Section 15. *Catalog Order.* Dogs should be judged in catalog order to the extent that it is practicable to do so without holding up the judging in any ring.

Judges are not required to wait for dogs for either the individual exercises or the group exercises. It is the responsibility of each handler to be ready with his dog at ringside when required, without being called. The judge's first consideration should be the convenience of those exhibitors who are at ringside with their dogs when scheduled, and who ask no favors.

A judge may agree, on request in advance of the scheduled starting time of the class, to judge a dog earlier or later than the time scheduled by catalog order. However, a judge should not hesitate to mark absent and to refuse to judge any dog and handler that are not at ringside ready to be judged in catalog order if no arrangement has been made in advance.

Section 16. *Use of Leash.* All dogs shall be kept on leash except when in the obedience ring or exercise ring. Dogs should be brought into the ring and taken out of the ring on leash. Dogs may be kept on leash in the ring when brought in to receive awards, and when waiting in the ring before and after the Group exercises. The leash shall be left on the judge's table or other designated place, between the individual exercises, and during all exercises except the Heel on Leash and Group exercises. The leash may be of fabric or leather and, in the Novice classes, need be only of sufficient length to provide adequate slack in the Heel on Leash exercise.

Section 17. *Collars.* Dogs in the obedience ring must wear well-fitting plain buckle or slip collars. Slip collars of an appropriate single length of leather, fabric or chain with two rings, one on each end are acceptable. Fancy collars, or special training collars, or collars that are either too tight or so large that they hang down unreasonably in front of the dogs, are not permitted. There shall not be anything hanging from the collars.

Section 18. *Heel Position.* The heel position as used in these regulations, whether the dog is sitting, standing, or moving at heel, means that the dog shall be straight in line with the direction in which the handler is facing, at the handler's left side, and as close as practicable to the handler's left leg without crowding, permitting the handler freedom of motion at all times. The area from the dog's head to shoulder shall be in line with the handler's left hip.

Section 19. *Hands.* In all exercises in which the dog is required to come to or return to the handler and sit in front, the handler's arms and hands shall hang naturally at his sides while the dog is coming in and until the dog has sat in front. A substantial deduction shall be made if a handler's arms and hands are not hanging naturally at his sides.

Section 20. *Commands and Signals.* Whenever a command or signal is mentioned in these regulations, a single command or signal only may be given by the handler, and any extra commands or signals must be penalized; except that whenever the regulations specify "command and/or signal" the handler may give either one or the other or both command and signal simultaneously. When a signal is permitted and given, it must be a single gesture with one arm and hand only, and the arm must immediately be returned to a natural position. Delay in following a judge's order to give a command or signal must be penalized, unless the delay is directed by the judge because of some distraction or interference.

The signal for downing a dog may be given either with the arm raised or with a down swing of the arm, but any pause in holding the arm upright followed by a down swing of the arm will be considered an additional signal.

Signaling correction to a dog is forbidden and must be penalized. Signals must be inaudible and the handler must not touch the dog. Any unusual noise or motion may be considered to be a signal. Movements of the body that aid the dog shall be considered additional signals except that a handler may bend as far as necessary to bring his hand on a level with the dog's eyes in giving a signal to a dog in the heel position, and that in the Directed Retrieve exercise the body and knees may be bent to the extent necessary to give the direction to the dog. Whistling or the use of a whistle is prohibited.

The dog's name may be used once immediately before any verbal command or before a verbal command and signal when these regulations permit command and/or signal. The name shall not be used with any signal not given simultaneously with a verbal command. The dog's name, when given immediately before a verbal command, shall not be considered as an additional command, but a dog that responds to its name without waiting for the verbal command shall be scored as having anticipated the command. The dog should never anticipate the handler's directions, but must wait for the appropriate commands and/or signals. Moving forward at heel without any command or signal other than the natural movement of the handler's left leg, shall not be considered as anticipation.

Loud commands by handlers to their dogs create a poor impression of obedience and should be avoided. Shouting is not necessary even in a noisy place if the dog is properly trained to respond to a normal tone of voice. Commands which in the judge's opinion are excessively loud will be penalized.

Section 21. *Additional Commands or Signals.* If a handler gives an additional command or signal not permitted by these regulations, either when no command or signal is permitted, or simultaneously with or following a permitted command or signal, or if he uses the dog's name with a permitted signal but without a permitted command, the dog shall be scored as though it had failed completely to perform that particular part of the exercise.

Section 22. *Praise.* Praise and petting are allowed between and after exercises, but points must be deducted from the total score for a dog that is not under reasonable control while being praised. A handler shall not carry or offer food in the ring. There shall be a substantial penalty for any dog that is picked up or carried at any time in the obedience ring.

Section 23. *Handling between Exercises.* In the Novice classes the dog may be guided gently by the collar between exercises and get it into proper position for an exercise. No other physical guidance, such as placing the dog in position with the hands or straightening the dog with the knees or feet, is permitted and shall be substantially penalized even if occurring before or between the exercises.

In the Open and Utility classes there shall be a substantial penalty for any dog that is physically guided at any time or that is not readily controllable.

Posing for examination and holding for measurement are permitted. Imperfections in heeling between exercises will not be judged. Minor penalties shall be imposed for a dog that does not respond promptly to its handler's commands or signals before or between exercises in the Open and Utility classes.

Section 24. *Orders and Minimum Penalties.* The orders for the exercises and the standards for judging are set forth in the following chapters. The lists of faults are not intended to be complete but minimum penalties are specified for most of the more common and serious faults. There is no maximum limit on penalties. A dog which makes none of the errors listed may still fail to qualify or may be scored zero for other reasons.

Section 25. *Misbehavior.* Any disciplining by the handler in the ring, any display of fear or nervousness by the dog, or any uncontrolled behavior of the dog such as snapping, barking, relieving itself while in the ring for judging, or running away from its handler, whether it occurs during an exercise, between exercises, or before or after judging, must be penalized according to the seriousness of the misbehavior, and the judge may expel or excuse the dog from further competition in the class. If such behavior occurs during an exercise, the penalty must first be applied to the score for that exercise. Should the penalty be greater than the value of the exercise during which it is incurred, the additional points shall be deducted from the total score under Misbehavior. If such behavior occurs before or after the judging or between exercises, the entire penalty shall be deducted from the total score.

The judge must disqualify any dog that attempts to attack any person in the ring. He may excuse a dog that attacks another dog or that appears dangerous to other dogs in the ring.

Section 26. *Training on the Grounds.* There shall be no drilling nor intensive or abusive training of dogs on the grounds or premises at a licensed or member obedience trial or at a sanctioned match. No practice rings or areas shall be permitted at such events. All dogs shall be kept on leash except when in the obedience ring or exercise ring. Special training collars shall not be used on the grounds or premises at an obedience trial or match. These requirements shall not be interpreted as preventing a handler from moving normally about the grounds or premises with his dog at heel on leash, nor from giving such signals or such commands in a normal tone, as are necessary and usual in everyday life in heeling a dog or making it stay, but physical or verbal disciplining of dogs shall not be permitted except to a reasonable extent in the case of an attack on a person or another dog. The Superintendent, or Show or Trial Secretary, and the members of the Bench Show or Obedience Trial Committee, shall be responsible for compliance with this section, and shall investigate any reports of infractions.

Section 27. *Training and Disciplining in the Ring.* The judge shall not permit any handler to train his dog nor to practice any exercise in the ring either before or after he is judged, and shall deduct points from the total score of any dog whose handler does this. A dog whose handler disciplines it in the ring must not receive a qualifying score. The penalty shall be deducted from the points available for the exercise during which the disciplining may occur, and additional points may be deducted from the total score if necessary. If the disciplining does not occur during an exercise the penalty shall be deducted from the total score. Any abuse of a dog in the ring must be immediately reported by the judge to the Bench Show or Obedience Trial Committee for action under Chapter 2, Section 29.

Section 28. *Abuse of Dogs.* The Bench Show or Obedience Trial Committee shall investigate any reports of abuse of dogs or severe disciplining of dogs on the grounds or premises of a show, trial or match. Any person who, at a licensed or member obedience trial, conducts himself in such manner or in any other manner prejudicial to the best interests of the sport, or who fails to comply with the requirements of Chapter 2, Section 26, shall be dealt with promptly, during the trial if possible, after the offender has been notified of the specific charges against him, and has been given an opportunity to be heard in his own defense in accordance with Chapter 2, Section 29.

Any abuse of a dog in the ring must be immediately reported by the judge to the Bench Show or Obedience Trial Committee for action under Chapter 2, Section 29.

Article XII Section 2 of the Constitution By-Laws of The American Kennel Club Provides:

Section 29. *Discipline.* The Bench Show, Obedience Trial or Field Trial Committee of a club or association shall have the right to suspend any person from the privileges of The American Kennel Club for conduct prejudicial to the best interests of pure-bred dogs, dog shows, obedience trials, field trials or The American Kennel Club, alleged to have occurred in connection with or during the progress of its show, obedience trial or field trial, after the alleged offender has been given an opportunity to be heard.

Notice in writing must be sent promptly by registered mail by the Bench Show, Obedience Trial or Field Trial Committee to the person suspended and a duplicate notice giving the name and address of the person suspended and full details as to the reasons for the suspension must be forwarded to The American Kennel Club within seven days.

An appeal may be taken from a decision of a Bench Show, Obedience Trial or Field Trial Committee. Notice in writing claiming such appeal together with a deposit of five ($5.00) dollars must be sent to The American Kennel Club within thirty days after the date of suspension. The Board of Directors may itself hear said appeal or may refer it to a committee of the Board, or to a Trial Board to be heard. The deposit shall become the property of The American Kennel Club if the decision is confirmed, or shall be returned to the appellant if the decision is not confirmed.

(See Guide for Bench Show and Obedience Trial Committees in Dealing with Misconduct at Dog Shows and Obedience Trials for proper procedure at licensed or member obedience trials.)

(The Committee at a Sanctioned event does not have this power of suspension, but must investigate any allegation of such conduct and forward a complete and detailed report of any such incident to The American Kennel Club.)

CHAPTER 3
Novice

Section 1. *Novice A Class.* The Novice A class shall be for dogs not less than six months of age that have not won the title C.D. A dog that is owned or co-owned by a person who has previously handled or regularly trained a dog that has won a C.D. title may not be entered in the Novice A class, nor may a dog be handled in this class by such person.

Each dog in this class must have a different handler who shall be its owner or co-owner or a member of the immediate family of the owner or co-owner, provided that such member has not previously handled or regularly trained a C.D. dog. The same person must handle the same dog in all exercises. No person may handle more than one dog in the Novice A class.

Section 2. *Novice B Class.* The Novice B class shall be for dogs not less than six months of age that have not won the title C.D. Dogs in this class may be handled by the owner or any other person. A person may handle more than one dog in this class, but each dog must have a separate handler for the Long Sit and Long Down exercises when judged in the same group. No dog may be entered in both Novice A and Novice B classes at any one trial.

Section 3. *Novice Exercises and Scores.* The exercises and maximum scores in the Novice classes are:

1. Heel on Leash	40 points
2. Stand for Examination	30 points
3. Heel Free	40 points
4. Recall	30 points
5. Long Sit	30 points
6. Long Down	30 points
Maximum Total Score	200 points

Section 4. *C.D. Title.* The American Kennel Club will issue a Companion Dog certificate for each registered dog, and will permit the use of the letters "C.D." after the name of each dog that has been certified by three different judges to have received qualifying scores in Novice classes at three licensed or member obedience trials, provided the sum total of dogs that actually competed in the regular Novice classes at each trial is not less than six.

Section 5. *Heel on Leash & Figure Eight.* The principal feature of this exercise is the ability of the dog and handler to work as a team.

Orders for the exercise are "Forward," "Halt," "Right turn," "Left turn," "About turn," "Slow," "Normal" and "Fast." "Fast" signifies that the handler must run, handler and dog moving forward at noticeably accelerated speed. In executing the About turn, the handler will always do a Right About turn.

The orders may be given in any sequence and may be repeated as necessary, but the judge shall attempt to standardize the heeling pattern for all dogs in any class.

The leash may be held in either hand or in both hands, provided the hands are in a natural position. However, any tightening or jerking of the leash or any act, signal or command which in the judge's opinion gives the dog assistance shall be penalized.

The handler shall enter the ring with his dog on a loose leash and stand with the dog sitting in the Heel Position. The judge shall ask if the handler is ready before giving the order, "Forward." The handler may give a command or signal to Heel, and shall walk briskly and in a natural manner with his dog on a loose leash. The dog shall walk close to the left side of the handler without swinging wide, lagging, forging or crowding. Whether heeling or sitting, the dog must not interfere with the handler's freedom of motion at any time. At each order to Halt, the handler will stop and his dog shall sit straight and promptly in the Heel Position without command or signal, and shall not move until the handler again moves forward on order from the judge. It is permissible after each Halt, before moving again, for the handler to give a command or signal to Heel. The judge shall say, "Exercise finished" after this portion of the exercise.

Before starting the Figure Eight the judge shall ask if the handler is ready. Figure Eight signifies that on specific orders from the judge to Forward and Halt, the handler and dog, from a starting position midway between two stewards and facing the judge, shall walk briskly twice completely around and between the two stewards, who shall stand 8 feet apart. The Figure Eight in the Novice classes shall be done on leash. The handler may choose to go in either direction. There shall be no About turn or Fast or Slow in the Figure Eight, but the judge must order at least one Halt during and another Halt at the end of this portion of the exercise.

Section 6. *Heel on Leash & Figure Eight Scoring.* If a dog is unmanageable, or if its handler constantly controls its performance by tugging on the leash or adapts pace to that of the dog, the dog must be scored zero.

Substantial deductions shall be made for additional commands or signals to Heel and for failure of dog or handler to change pace noticeably for Slow and Fast.

Substantial or minor deductions shall be made for such things as lagging, heeling wide, poor sits, handler failing to walk at a brisk pace, occasional guidance with leash and other imperfections in heeling.

In scoring this exercise the judge shall accompany the handler at a discreet distance so that he can observe any signals or commands given by the handler to the dog. The judge must do so without interfering with either dog or handler.

Section 7. *Stand for Examination.* The principal features of this exercise are that the dog stand in position before and during the examination, and that the dog display neither shyness nor resentment.

Orders are "Stand your dog and leave when you are ready," "Back to your dog" and "Exercise finished." There will be no further command from the judge to the handler to leave the dog.

The handler shall take his dog on leash to a place indicated by the judge, where the handler shall remove the leash and give it to a steward who shall place it on the judge's table or other designated place.

On judge's order the handler will stand and/or pose his dog off leash by the method of his choice, taking any reasonable time if he chooses to pose the dog as in the show ring. When he is ready, the handler will give his command and/or signal to the dog to Stay, walk forward about six feet in front of the dog, turn around and stand facing the dog.

The judge shall approach the dog from the front, and shall touch only the dog's head, body and hindquarters, using the fingers and palm of one hand only. He shall then order, "Back to your dog," whereupon the handler shall walk around behind his dog and return to the Heel Position. The dog must remain standing until after the judge has said, "Exercise finished."

Second 8. *Stand for Examination, Scoring.* The scoring of this exercise will not start until the handler has given the command and/or signal to Stay, except for such things as rough treatment of the dog by its handler or active resistance by the dog to its handler's attempts to make it stand. Either of these shall be penalized substantially.

A dog that displays any shyness or resentment or growls or snaps at any time shall be scored zero, as shall a dog that sits before or during the examination or a dog that moves away before or during the examination from the place where it was left.

Minor or substantial deduction, depending on the circumstance, shall be made for a dog that moves its feet at any time or sits or moves away after the examination has been completed.

Section 9. *Heel Free, Performance and Scoring.* This exercise shall be executed in the same manner as Heel on Leash & Figure Eight except that the dog shall be off leash and that there shall be no Figure Eight. Orders and scoring shall also be the same.

Section 10. *Recall.* The principal features of this exercise are that the dog stay where left until called by its handler, and that the dog respond promptly to the handler's command or signal to Come.

Orders are "Leave your dog," "Call your dog" and "Finish."

On order from the judge, the handler may give command and/or signal to the dog to Stay in the sit position while the handler walks forward about 35 feet to the other end of the ring, where he shall turn and stand in a natural manner facing his dog. On judge's order or signal, the handler will give command or signal for the dog to Come. The dog must come straight in at a brisk pace and sit straight, centered immediately in front of the handler's feet, close enough that the handler could readily touch its head without moving either foot or having to stretch forward. The dog must not touch the handler or sit between his feet.

On judge's order the handler will give command or signal to Finish and   347 the dog must go smartly to the Heel Position and sit. The manner in which the dog finishes shall be optional with the handler provided that it is prompt and that the dog sit straight at heel.

Section 11. *Recall, Scoring.* A dog must receive a score of zero for the following: not staying without additional command or signal, failure to come on the first command or signal, moving from the place where left before being called or signalled, not sitting close enough in front that the handler could readily touch its head without moving either foot or stretching forward.

Substantial deductions shall be made for a slow response to the Come, varying with the extent of the slowness; for extra command or signal to Stay if given before the handler leaves the dog; for the dog's standing or lying down instead of waiting in the sit position; for extra command or signal to Finish and for failure to Sit or Finish.

Minor deductions shall be made for slow or poor Sits or Finishes, for touching the handler on coming in or while finishing, and for sitting between the handler's feet.

Section 12. *Group Exercises.* The principal feature of these exercises is that the dog remain in the sitting or down position, whichever is required by the particular exercise.

Orders are "Sit your dogs" or "Down your dogs," "Leave your dogs" and "Back to your dogs."

All the competing dogs in the class take these exercises together, except that if there are 12 or more dogs they shall, at the judge's option, be judged in groups of not less than 6 nor more than 15 dogs. When the same judge does both Novice A and Novice B, the two classes may be combined provided that there are not more than 15 dogs competing in the combined classes. The dogs that are in the ring shall be lined up in catalog order along one of the four sides of the ring. Handlers' armbands, weighted with leashes or other articles if necessary, shall be placed behind the dogs.

For the Long Sit the handlers shall, on order from the judge, command and/or signal their dogs to Sit if they are not already sitting. On further order from the judge to leave their dogs, the handlers shall give a command and/or signal to Stay and immediately leave their dogs. The handlers will go to the opposite side of the ring, turn and stand facing their respective dogs.

If a dog gets up and starts to roam or follows its handler, or if a dog moves so as to interfere with another dog, the judge shall promptly instruct the handler or one of the stewards to take the dog out of the ring or to keep it away from the other dogs.

After one minute from the time he has ordered the handlers to leave their dogs, the judge will give the order to return, whereupon the handlers must promptly go back to their dogs, each walking around and in back of his own dog to the Heel Position. The dogs must not move from the sitting position until after the judge has said, "Exercise finished." The judge shall not give the order "Exercise finished" until the handlers have returned to the Heel Position.

Before starting the Long Down the judge shall ask if the handlers are ready. The Long Down is done in the same manner as the Long Sit except that instead of sitting their dogs the handlers shall, on order from the judge, down their dogs without touching either the dogs or their collars, and except further that the judge will order the handlers to return after three minutes. The dogs must not move from the down position until after the judge has said, "Exercise finished."

The dogs shall not be required to sit at the end of the Down exercise.

Section 13. *Group Exercises, Scoring.* During these exercises the judge shall stand in such position that all of the dogs are in his line of vision, and where he can see all the handlers in the ring without having to turn around. Scoring of the exercises will not start until after the judge has ordered the handlers to leave their dogs, except for such things as rough treatment of a dog by its handler or active resistance by a dog to its handler's attempts to make it Sit or lie Down. These shall be penalized substantially; in extreme cases the dog may be excused.

A score of zero is required for the following: the dog's moving at any time during either exercise a substantial distance away from the place where it was left, or going over to any other dog, or staying on the spot where it was left but not remaining in whichever position is required by the particular exercise until the handler has returned to the Heel Position, or repeatedly barking or whining.

A substantial deduction shall be made for a dog that moves even a minor distance away from the place where it was left or that barks or whines only once or twice. Depending on the circumstance, a substantial or minor deduction shall be made for touching the dog or its collar in getting the dog into the Down position.

There shall be a minor deduction if a dog changes position after the handler has returned to the Heel Position but before the judge has said, "Exercise finished." The judge shall not give the order "Exercise finished" until the handlers have returned to the Heel Position.

CHAPTER 4
Open

Section 1. *Open A Class.* The Open A Class shall be for dogs that have won the C.D. title but have not won the title C.D.X. Obedience judges and licensed handlers may not enter or handle dogs in this class. Each dog must be handled by its owner or by a member of his immediate family. Owners may enter more than one dog in this class but the same person who handled each dog in the first five exercises must handle the same dog in the Long Sit and Long Down exercises, except that if a person has handled more than one dog in the first five exercises he must have an additional handler, who must be the owner or a member of his immediate family, for each additional dog, when more than one dog that he has handled in the first five exercises is judged in the same group for the Long Sit and Long Down.

Section 2. *Open B Class.* The Open B class will be for dogs that have won the title C.D. or C.D.X. A dog may continue to compete in this class after it has won the title U.D. Dogs in this class may be handled by the owner or any other person. Owners may enter more than one dog in this class but the same person who handled each dog in the first five exercises must handle each dog in the Long Sit and Long Down exercises, except that if a person has handled more than one dog in the first five exercises he must have an additional handler for each additional dog, when more than one dog that he has handled in the first five exercises is judged in the same group for the Long Sit and Long Down. No dog may be entered in both Open A and Open B classes at any one trial.

Section 3. *Open Exercises and Scores.* The exercises and maximum scores in the Open classes are:

1. Heel Free	40 points
2. Drop on Recall	30 points
3. Retrieve on Flat	20 points
4. Retrieve over High Jump	30 points
5. Broad Jump	20 points
6. Long Sit	30 points
7. Long Down	30 points
Maximum Total Score	200 points

Section 4. *C.D.X. Title.* The American Kennel Club will issue a Companion Dog Excellent certificate for each registered dog, and will permit the use of the letters "C.D.X." after the name of each dog that has been certified by three different judges of obedience trials to have received qualifying scores in Open classes at three licensed or member obedience trials, provided the sum total of dogs that actually competed in the regular Open classes at each trial is not less than six.

Section 5. *Heel Free, Performance and Scoring.* This exercise shall be executed in the same manner as the Novice Heel on Leash and Figure Eight exercise, except that the dog is off leash. Orders and scoring are the same as in Heel on Leash and Figure Eight.

Section 6. *Drop on Recall.* The principal features of this exercise, in addition to those listed under the Novice Recall, are the dog's prompt response to the handler's command or signal to Drop, and the dog's remaining in the Down position until again called or signalled to Come. The dog will be judged on the promptness of its response to command or signal and not on its proximity to a designated point.

Orders for the exercise are "Leave your dog," "Call your dog," an order or signal to Drop the dog, another "Call your dog" and "Finish." The judge may designate in advance a point at which, as the dog is coming in, the handler shall give his command or signal to the dog to Drop. The judge's signal or designated point must be clear to the handler but not obvious or distracting to the dog.

On order from the judge, the handler may give command and/or signal for the dog to Stay in the sit position while the handler walks forward about 35 feet to the other end of the ring, where he shall turn and stand in a natural manner facing his dog. On judge's order or signal, the handler shall give command or signal to Come and the dog must start straight in at a brisk pace. On judge's order or signal, or at a point designated in advance by the judge, the handler shall give command or signal to Drop, and the dog must immediately drop completely to the down position, where he must remain until, on judge's order or signal, the handler again gives command or signal to Come. The dog must come straight in at a brisk pace and sit straight, centered immediately in front of the handler's feet, close enough that the handler could readily touch the dog's head without moving either foot or having to stretch forward. The dog must not touch the handler nor sit between his feet.

The Finish shall be executed as in the Novice Recall.

Section 7. *Drop on Recall, Scoring.* All applicable penalties listed under the Novice Recall as requiring a score of zero shall apply. In addition, a zero score is required for a dog that does not drop completely to the down position on a single command or signal, and for a dog that drops but does not remain down until called or signalled.

Substantial deductions, varying with the extent, shall be made for delayed or slow response to the handler's command or signal to Drop, for slow response to either of the Comes, for extra command or signal to Stay if given before the handler leaves the dog, for the dog's standing or lying down instead of waiting where left in a sit position, for extra command or signal to Finish and for failure to finish.

Minor deductions shall be made for slow or poor sits or finishes, for touching the handler on coming in or while finishing, or for sitting between the handler's feet.

Section 8. *Retrieve on the Flat.* The principal feature of this exercise is that the dog retrieve promptly.

Orders are "Throw it," "Send your dog," "Take it" and "Finish."

The handler shall stand with his dog sitting in the Heel Position in a place designated by the judge. On order, "Throw it," the handler shall give command and/or signal to Stay, which signal may not be given with the hand that is holding the dumbbell, and throw the dumbbell. On order to send his dog, the handler shall give command or signal to retrieve. The retrieve shall be executed at a fast trot or gallop, the dog going directly to the dumbbell and retrieving it without unnecessary mouthing or playing with the dumbbell. The dog must sit straight to deliver, centered immediately in front of the handler's feet, close enough that the handler can readily take the dumbbell without moving either foot or having to stretch forward. The dog must not touch the handler nor sit between his feet. On order from the judge to take it, the handler shall give command or signal and take the dumbbell.

The finish shall be executed as in the Novice Recall.

The dumbbell, which must be approved by the judge, shall be made of one or more solid pieces of one of the heavy hardwoods, which shall not be hollowed out. It may be unfinished, or coated with a clear finish, or painted white. It shall have no decorations or attachments but may bear an inconspicuous mark for identification. The size of the dumbbell shall be proportionate to the size of the dog. The judge shall require the dumbbell to be thrown again before the dog is sent if, in his opinion, it is thrown too short a distance, or too far to one side, or too close to the ringside.

Section 9. *Retrieve on the Flat, Scoring.* A dog that fails to go out on the first command or signal, or goes to retrieve before the command or signal is given, or fails to retrieve, or does not return with the dumbbell sufficiently close that the handler can easily take the dumbbell as described above, must be scored zero.

Substantial deductions, depending on the extent, shall be made for slowness in going out or returning or in picking up the dumbbell, for not going directly to the dumbbell, for mouthing or playing with or dropping the dumbbell, for reluctance or refusal to release the dumbbell to the handler, for extra command or signal to finish and for failure to sit or finish.

Substantial or minor deductions shall be made for slow or poor sits or finishes, for touching the handler on coming in or while finishing, or for sitting between the handler's feet.

Section 10. *Retrieve over High Jump.* The principal features of this exercise are that the dog go out over the jump, pick up the dumbbell and promptly return with it over the jump.

Orders are "Throw it," "Send your dog," "Take it" and "Finish."

This exercise shall be executed in the same manner as the Retrieve on the Flat, except that the dog must clear the High Jump both going and coming. The handler must stand at least eight feet, or any reasonable distance beyond 8 feet, from the jump but must remain in the same spot throughout the exercise.

The jump shall be as nearly as possible one and one-half times the height of the dog at the withers, as determined by the judge, with a minimum height of 8 inches and a maximum height of 36 inches. This applies to all breeds with the following exceptions:

The jump shall be once the height of the dog at the withers or 36 inches, whichever is less, for the following breeds—

    Bloodhounds
    Bullmastiffs
    Great Danes
    Great Pyrenees
    Mastiffs
    Newfoundlands
    St. Bernards

The jump shall be once the height of the dog at the withers or 8 inches, whichever is greater, for the following breeds—

    Spaniels (Clumber)
    Spaniels (Sussex)
    Basset Hounds

Dachshunds
Welsh Corgis (Cardigan)
Welsh Corgis (Pembroke)
Australian Terriers
Cairn Terriers
Dandie Dinmont Terriers
Norwich Terriers
Scottish Terriers
Sealyham Terriers
Skye Terriers
West Highland White Terriers
Maltese
Pekingese
Bulldogs
French Bulldogs

The jumps may be preset by the stewards based on the handler's advice as to the dog's height. The judge must make certain that the jump is set at the required height for each dog. He shall verify in the ring with an ordinary folding rule or steel tape to the nearest one-half inch, the height at the withers of each dog that jumps less than 36 inches. He shall not base his decision as to the height of the jump on the handler's advice.

The side posts of the High Jump shall be 4 feet high and the jump shall be 5 feet wide and shall be so constructed as to provide adjustment for each 2 inches from 8 inches to 36 inches. It is suggested that the jump have a bottom board 8 inches wide including the space from the bottom of the board to the ground or floor, together with three other 8 inch boards, one 4 inch board, and one 2 inch board. A 6 inch board may also be provided. The jump shall be painted a flat white. The width in inches, and nothing else, shall be painted on each side of each board in black 2 inch figures, the figure on the bottom board representing the distance from the ground or floor to the top of the board.

Section 11. *Retrieve over High Jump, Scoring.* Scoring of this exercise shall be as in Retrieve on the Flat. In addition, a dog that fails, either going or returning, to go over the jump, or that climbs or uses the jump for aid in going over, must be scored zero. Touching the jump in going over is added to the substantial and minor penalties listed under Retrieve on the Flat.

Section 12. *Broad Jump.* The principal features of this exercise are that the dog stay sitting until directed to jump and that the dog clear the jump on a single command or signal.

Orders are "Leave your dog," "Send your dog" and "Finish."

The handler will stand with his dog sitting in the Heel Position in front of and at least 8 feet from the jump. On order from the judge to "Leave your dog," the handler will give his dog the command and/or signal to Stay and go to a position facing the right side of the jump, with his toes about 2 feet from the jump, and anywhere between the lowest edge of the first hurdle and the highest edge of the last hurdle.

On order from the judge the handler shall give the command or signal to jump and the dog shall clear the entire distance of the Broad Jump without touching and, without further command or signal, return to a sitting position immediately in front of the handler as in the Recall. The handler shall change his position by executing a right angle turn while the dog is in mid-air, but shall remain in the same spot. The dog must sit and finish as in the Novice Recall.

The Broad Jump shall consist of four hurdles, built to telescope for convenience, made of boards about 8 inches wide, the largest measuring about 5 feet in length and 6 inches high at the highest point, all painted a flat white. When set up they shall be arranged in order of size and shall be evenly spaced so as to cover a distance equal to twice the height of the High

Jump as set for the particular dog, with the low side of each hurdle and the lowest hurdle nearest the dog. The four hurdles shall be used for a jump of 52" to 72", three for a jump of 32" to 48", and two for a jump of 16" to 28". The highest hurdles shall be removed first. It is the judge's responsibility to see that the distance jumped is that required by these Regulations for the particular dog.

Section 13. *Broad Jump, Scoring.* A dog that fails to stay until directed to jump, or refuses the jump on the first command or signal, or walks over any part of the jump, or fails to clear the full distance, with its forelegs, must be scored zero. Minor or substantial deductions, depending on the specific circumstances in each case, shall be made for a dog that touches the jump in going over or that does not return directly to the handler. All other applicable penalties listed under the Recall shall apply.

Section 14. *Open Group Exercises, Performance and Scoring.* During Long Sit and the Long Down exercises the judge shall stand in such a position that all of the dogs are in his line of vision, and where he can see all the handlers in the ring, or leaving and returning to the ring, without having to turn around.

These exercises in the Open classes are performed in the same manner as in the Novice classes except that after leaving their dogs the handlers must cross to the opposite side of the ring, and then leave the ring in single file as directed by the judge and go to a place designated by the judge, completely out of sight of their dogs, where they must remain until called by the judge after the expiration of the time limit of three minutes in the Long Sit and five minutes in the Long Down, from the time the judge gave the order to "Leave your dogs." On order from the judge the handlers shall return to the ring in single file in reverse order, lining up facing their dogs at the opposite side of the ring, and returning to their dogs on order from the judge.

Orders and scoring are the same as in the Novice Group exercises.

CHAPTER 5
Utility

Section 1. *Utility Class.* The Utility class shall be for dogs that have won the title C.D.X. Dogs that have won the title U.D. may continue to compete in this class. Dogs in this class may be handled by the owner or any other person. Owners may enter more than one dog in this class, but each dog must have a separate handler for the Group Examination when judged in the same group.

Section 2. *Division of Utility Class.* A club may choose to divide the Utility class into Utility A and Utility B classes, provided such division is approved by The American Kennel Club and is announced in the premium list. When this is done the Utility A class shall be for dogs which have won the title C.D.X. and have not won the title U.D. Obedience judges and licensed handlers may not enter or handle dogs in this class. Owners may enter more than one dog in this class but the same person who handled each dog in the first five exercises must handle the same dog in the Group Examination, except that if a person has handled more than one dog in the first five exercises he must have an additional handler, who must be the owner or a member of his immediate family, for each additional dog, when more than one dog he has handled in the first five exercises is judged in the same group for the Group Examination. All other dogs that are eligible for the Utility class but not eligible for the Utility A class may be entered only in the Utility B class to which the conditions listed in Chapter 5, Section 1 shall apply. No dog may be entered in both Utility A and Utility B classes at any one trial.

Section 3. *Utility Exercises and Scores.* The exercises, maximum scores and order of judging in the Utility classes are:

1. Signal Exercise	40 points
2. Scent Discrimination Article No. 1	30 points
3. Scent Discrimination Article No. 2	30 points
4. Directed Retrieve	30 points
5. Directed Jumping	40 points
6. Group Examination	30 points
Maximum Total Score	200 points

Section 4. *U.D. Title.* The American Kennel Club will issue a Utility Dog certificate for each registered dog, and will permit the use of the letters "U.D." after the name of each dog that has been certified by three different judges of obedience trials to have received qualifying scores in Utility classes at three licensed or member obedience trials in each of which three or more dogs actually competed in the Utility class or classes.

Section 5. *Signal Exercise.* The principal features of this exercise are the ability of dog and handler to work as a team while heeling, and the dog's correct responses to the signals to Stand, Stay, Drop, Sit and Come.

Orders are the same as in Heel on Leash and Figure Eight, with the additions of "Stand your dog," which shall be given only when dog and handler are walking at normal pace, and "Leave your dog." The judge must use signals for directing the handler to signal the dog to Drop, to Sit and to Come, in that sequence, and to finish.

Heeling in the Signal Exercise shall be done in the same manner as in Heel Free, except that throughout the entire exercise the handler shall use signals only and must not speak to his dog at any time. On order from the judge, "Forward," the handler may signal his dog to walk at heel, and on specific order from the judge in each case, shall execute a "Left turn," "Right turn," "About turn," "Halt," "Slow," "Normal" and "Fast." These orders may be given in any sequence and may be repeated as necessary, but the judge shall attempt to standardize the heeling pattern for all dogs in the class.

On order from the judge, and while the dog is walking at heel, the handler shall signal his dog to Stand in the heel position near one end of the ring. On further order, "Leave your dog," the handler shall signal his dog to Stay, go to the other end of the ring and turn to face his dog. On separate and specific signals from the judge, the handler shall give his signals to Drop, to Sit, to Come and to Finish as in the Recall. During the heeling part of this exercise the handler may not give any signal except when a command or signal is permitted in the Heeling exercises.

Section 6. *Signal Exercise, Scoring.* A dog that fails, on a single signal from the handler, to stand or remain standing where left, or to drop, or to sit and stay, or to come, or that receives a command or audible signal from the handler to do any of these parts of the exercise, shall be scored zero.

Minor or substantial deductions depending on the specific circumstances in each case, shall be made for a dog that walks forward on the Stand, Drop or Sit portions of the exercise.

A substantial deduction shall be made for any audible command during the Heeling or Finish portions of the exercise.

All the penalties listed under the Heel on Leash and Figure Eight and the Recall exercises shall also apply.

Section 7. *Scent Discrimination.* The principal features of these exercises are the selection of the handler's article from among the other articles by scent alone, and the prompt delivery of the right article to the handler.

Orders are "Send your dog," "Take it" and "Finish."

In each of these two exercises the dog must select by scent alone and retrieve an article which has been handled by its handler. The articles shall be provided by the handler and shall consist of two sets, each comprised of five identical objects not more than six inches in length, which may be items of everyday use. One set shall be made entirely of rigid metal, and one of leather of such design that nothing but leather is visible except for the minimum amount of thread or metal necessary to hold the object together. The articles in each set must be legibly numbered, each with a different number and must be approved by the judge.

The handler shall present all 10 articles to the judge, who shall designate one from each set and make written note of the numbers of the two articles he has selected. These two handler's articles shall be placed on a table or chair within the ring until picked up by the handler, who shall hold in his hand only one article at a time. The judge or steward will handle each of the remaining 8 articles as he places them on the floor or ground about 15 feet in front of the handler and dog, at random about 6 inches apart. The judge must make sure that the articles are properly separated before the dog is sent, so that there may be no confusion of scent between the articles.

Handler and dog shall turn around after watching the judge or steward spread the articles, and shall remain facing away from those articles until the judge has taken the handler's scented article and given the order, "Send your dog."

The handler may use either article first, but must relinquish each one immediately when ordered by the judge. The judge shall make certain that the handler imparts his scent to each article only with his hands and that, between the time the handler picks up each article and the time he gives it to the judge, the article is held continuously in the handler's hands which must remain in plain sight.

On order from the judge, the handler will immediately place his article on the judge's book or work sheet. The judge, without touching the article with his hands, will place it among those on the ground or floor.

On order from the judge to "Send your dog," the handler may give the command to Heel before turning, and will execute a Right about Turn, stopping to face the articles, the dog in the Heel Position. The handler shall then give the command or signal to retrieve. Handlers may at their discretion on orders from the judge to "Send your dog," execute with their dog a Right about Turn to face the articles, simultaneously giving the command or signal to retrieve. In this instance the dog shall not assume a sitting position, but shall go directly to the articles. The handler may give his scent to the dog by gently touching the dog's nose with the palm of one open hand, but this may only be done while the dog and handler have their backs to the articles and the arm and hand must be returned to a natural position before handler and dog turn to face the articles.

The dog shall go at a brisk pace to the articles. It may take any reasonable time to select the right article, but only provided it works continuously. After picking up the right article the dog shall return at a brisk pace and complete the exercise as in the Retrieve on the Flat.

These procedures shall be followed for both articles. Should a dog retrieve a wrong article in the first exercise, that article shall be placed on the table or chair. The correct article must be removed, and the second exercise shall be conducted with one less article on the ground or floor.

Section 8. *Scent Discrimination, Scoring.* Deductions shall be the same as in the Retrieve on the Flat. In addition, a dog that fails to go out to the group of articles, or retrieves a wrong article, or fails to bring the right article to the handler, must be scored zero for the particular exercise.

Substantial deductions shall be made for a dog that picks up a wrong article, even though he puts it down again immediately, for any roughness by the handler in imparting his scent to the dog, and for any excessive motions by the handler in turning to face the articles.

Minor or substantial deductions, depending on the circumstances in each case, shall be made for a dog that is slow or inattentive, or that does not work continuously. There shall be no penalty for a dog that takes a reasonably long time examining the articles provided the dog works smartly and continuously.

Section 9. *Directed Retrieve.* The principal features of the exercise are that the dog stay until directed to retrieve, that it go directly to the designated glove, and that it retrieve promply. The orders for the exercise are "One," "Two" or "Three," "Take it" and "Finish." In this exercise the handler will provide three predominantly white, cotton work gloves, which must be open and must be approved by the judge. The handler will stand with his back to the unobstructed end of the ring with his dog sitting in the Heel Position mid-way between and in line with the two jumps. The judge or steward will then drop the three gloves across the end of the ring, while the handler and dog are facing the opposite direction, one glove in each corner and one in the center, about 3 feet from the end of the ring and for the corner gloves about 3 feet from the side of the ring. All three gloves will be clearly visible to the dog and handler, when the handler turns to face the glove designated by the judge. There shall be no table or chair at this end of the ring.

The gloves shall be designated "One", "Two" or "Three" reading from left to right when the handler turns and faces the gloves. The judge will give the order "One," or "Two" or "Three." The handler then must give the command to Heel and turn in place, right or left to face the designated glove. The handler will come to a halt with the dog sitting in the Heel Position. The handler shall not touch the dog to get it in position. The handler will then give his dog the direction to the designated glove with a single motion of his left hand and arm along the right side of the dog, and will give the command to retrieve either simultaneously with or immediately following the giving of the direction. The dog shall then go directly to the glove at a brisk pace and retrieve it without unnecessary mouthing or playing with it, completing the exercise as in the Retrieve on the Flat.

The handler may bend his knees and body in giving the direction to the dog, after which the handler will stand erect in a natural position with his arms at his sides.

The exercise shall consist of a single retrieve, but the judge shall designate different glove numbers for successive dogs.

Section 10. *Directed Retrieve, Scoring.* A dog must receive a score of zero for the following: not going out on a single command, not going directly to the designated glove, not retrieving the glove, anticipating the handler's command to retrieve, not returning promptly and sufficiently close so that the handler can readily take the glove without moving either foot or stretching forward.

Depending on the extent, substantial or minor deductions shall be made for a handler who over-turns, or touches the dog or uses excessive motions to get the dog in position.

All other deductions listed under Retrieve on the Flat shall also apply.

Section 11. *Directed Jumping.* The principal features of this exercise are that the dog go away from the handler in the direction indicated, stop when commanded, jump as directed and return as in the Recall.

The orders are "Send your dog," the designation of which jump is to be taken, and "Finish."

The jumps shall be placed midway in the ring at right angles to the sides of the ring and 18 to 20 feet apart, the Bar Jump on one side, the High Jump on the other. The judge must make certain that the jumps are set at the required height for each dog by following the procedure described in Retrieve over the High Jump.

The handler, from a position on the center line of the ring and about 20 feet from the line of the jumps, shall stand with his dog sitting in the Heel Position and on order from the judge shall command and/or signal his dog to go forward at a brisk pace to a point about 20 feet beyond the jumps and in the approximate center. When the dog has reached this point the handler shall give a command to Sit; the dog must stop and sit with his attention on the handler but need not sit squarely.

The judge will designate which jump is to be taken first by the dog, and the handler shall command and/or signal the dog to return to him over the designated jump. While the dog is in mid-air the handler may turn so as to be facing the dog as it returns. The dog shall sit in front of the handler and, on order from the judge, finish as in the Recall. The judge will say "Exercise finished" after the dog has returned to the Heel Position.

When the dog is again sitting in the Heel Position the judge shall ask, "Are you ready?" before giving the order to send the dog for the second part of the exercise. The same procedure shall be followed for the second jump.

It is optional with the judge which jump is taken first, but both jumps must be taken to complete the exercise and the judge must not designate the jump until the dog is at the far end of the ring. The dog shall clear the jumps without touching them.

The height of the jumps shall be the same as required in the Open classes. The High Jump shall be the same as that used in the Open classes, and the Bar Jump shall consist of a bar between 2 and 2½ inches square with the four edges rounded sufficiently to remove any sharpness. The bar shall be painted a flat black and white in alternate sections of about 3 inches each. The bar shall be supported by two unconnected 4 foot upright posts about 5 feet apart. The bar shall be adjustable for each 2 inches of height from 8 inches to 36 inches, and the jump shall be so constructed and positioned that the bar can be knocked off without disturbing the uprights.

Section 12. *Directed Jumping, Scoring.* A dog must receive a score of zero for the following: anticipating the handler's command and/or signal to go out, not leaving the handler, not going out between the jumps, not going at least 10 feet beyond the jumps, not stopping on command, anticipating the handler's command and/or signal to jump, not jumping as directed, knocking the bar off the uprights, climbing or using the top of the High Jump for aid in going over.

Substantial deductions shall be made for a dog that does not stop in the approximate center of the ring; for a dog that turns, stops or sits before the handler's command to Sit, and for a dog that fails to sit.

Substantial or minor deductions, depending on the extent, shall be made for slowness in going out or for touching the jumps. All of the penalties listed under Recall shall also apply.

Section 13. *Group Examination.* The principal features of this exercise are that the dog stand and stay, and show no shyness or resentment.

All the competing dogs take this exercise together, except that if there are 12 or more dogs, they shall be judged in groups of not less than 6 nor more than 15 dogs, at the judge's option. The handlers and dogs that are in the ring shall line up in catalog order, side by side down the center of the ring, with the dogs sitting in the Heel Position. Each handler shall place his armband, weighted with leash or other article if necessary, behind his dog. The judge must instruct one or more stewards to watch the other dogs while he conducts the individual examinations, and to call any faults to his attention.

On order from the judge, "Stand your dogs," all the handlers will stand or pose their dogs and on further order, "Leave your dogs," will give command and/or signal to Stay and walk forward to the side of the ring where they shall turn and stand facing their respective dogs. The judge will approach each dog in turn from the front and examine it, going over the dog with his hands as in dog show judging except that under no circumstance shall the examination include the dog's mouth or testicles.

When all dogs have been examined and after the handlers have been away from their dogs for at least three minutes, the judge will promptly order the handlers, "Back to your dogs," and the handlers will return, each walking around and in back of his own dog to the Heel Position, after which the judge will say, "Exercise finished." Each dog must remain standing at its position in the line from the time its handler leaves it until the end of the exercise, and must show no shyness or resentment. The dogs are not required to sit at the end of this exercise.

Section 14. *Group Examination, Scoring.* There should be no attempt to judge the dogs or handlers on the manner in which the dogs are made to stand. The scoring will not start until after the judge has given the order to leave the dogs, except for such general things as rough treatment of a dog by its handler, or active resistance by a dog to its handler's attempts to make it stand. Immediately after examining each dog the judge must make a written record of any necessary deductions, subject to further deductions for subsequent faults.

A dog must be scored zero for the following: displaying shyness or resentment, moving a minor distance from the place where it was left, going over to any other dog, sitting or lying down before the handler has returned to the Heel Position, growling or snapping at any time during the exercise, repeatedly barking or whining.

Substantial or minor deductions, depending on the circumstance, must be made for a dog that moves its feet at any time during the exercise, or sits or lies down after the handler has returned to the Heel Position.

CHAPTER 6
Tracking

Section 1. *Tracking Test.* This test shall be for dogs not less than six months of age, and must be judged by two judges. With each entry form for a licensed or member tracking test for a dog that has not passed an AKC tracking test there must be filed an original written statement, dated within six months of the date the test is to be held, signed by a person who has been approved by The American Kennel Club to judge tracking tests, certifying that the dog is considered by him to be ready for such a test. These original statements cannot be used again and must be submitted to The American Kennel Club with the entry forms. Written permission to waive or modify this requirement may be granted by The American Kennel Club in unusual circumstances. Tracking tests are open to all dogs that are otherwise eligible under these Regulations.

This test cannot be given at a dog show or obedience trial. The duration of this test may be one day or more within a 15 day period after the original date in the event of an unusually large entry or other unforeseen emergency, provided that the change of date is satisfactory to the exhibitors affected.

Section 2. *T.D. Title.* The American Kennel Club will issue a Tracking Dog certificate to a registered dog, and will permit the use of the letters "T.D." after the name of each dog which has been certified by the two judges to have passed a licensed or member tracking test in which at least three dogs actually participated.

The owner of a dog holding both the U.D. and T.D. titles may use the letters "U.D.T." after the name of the dog, signifying "Utility Dog Tracker."

Section 3. *Tracking.* The tracking test must be performed with the dog
on leash, the length of the track to be not less than 440 yards nor more than

500 yards, the scent to be not less than one half hour nor more than two hours old and that of a stranger who will leave an inconspicuous glove or wallet, dark in color, at the end of the track where it must be found by the dog and picked up by the dog or handler. The article must be approved in advance by the judges. The tracklayer will follow the track which has been staked out with flags a day or more earlier, collecting all the flags on the way with the exception of one flag at the start of the track and one flag about 30 yards from the start of the track to indicate the direction of the track; then deposit the article at the end of the track and leave the course, proceeding straight ahead at least 50 feet. The tracklayer must wear his own shoes which, if not having leather soles, must have uppers of fabric or leather. The dog shall wear a harness to which is attached a leash between 20 and 40 feet in length. The handler shall follow the dog at a distance of not less than 20 feet, and the dog shall not be guided by the handler. The dog may be restrained by the handler, but any leading or guiding of the dog constitutes grounds for calling the handler off and marking the dog "Failed." A dog may, at the handler's option, be given one, and only one, second chance to take the scent between the two flags, provided it has not passed the second flag.

Section 4. *Tracking Tests.* A person who is qualified to judge Obedience Trials is not necessarily capable of judging a tracking test. Tracking judges must be familiar with the various conditions that may exist when a dog is required to work a scent trail. Scent conditions, weather, lay of the land, ground cover, and wind, must be taken into consideration, and a thorough knowledge of this work is necessary.

One or both of the judges must personally lay out each track, a day or so before the test, so as to be completely familiar with the location of the track, landmarks and ground conditions. At least two of the right angle turns shall be well out in the open where there are no fences or other boundaries to guide the dog. No part of any track shall follow along any fence or boundary within 15 yards of such boundary. The track shall include at least two right angle turns and should include more than two such turns so that the dog may be observed working in different wind directions. Acute angle turns should be avoided whenever possible. No conflicting tracks shall be laid. No track shall cross any body of water. No part of any track shall be laid within 75 yards of any other track. In the case of two tracks going in opposite directions, however, the first flags of these tracks may be as close as 50 yards from each other. The judges shall make sure that the track is no less than 440 yards nor more than 500 yards and that the tracklayer is a stranger to the dog in each case. It is the judges' responsibility to instruct the tracklayer to insure that each track is properly laid and that each tracklayer carries a copy of the chart with him in laying the track. The judges must approve the article to be left at the end of each track, must make sure that it is thoroughly impregnated with the tracklayer's scent, and must see that the tracklayer's shoes meet the requirements of these regulations.

There is no time limit provided the dog is working, but a dog that is off the track and is clearly not working should not be given any minimum time, but should be marked Failed. The handler may not be given any assistance by the judges or anyone else. If a dog is not tracking it shall not be marked Passed even though it may have found the article. In case of unforeseen circumstances, the judges may in rare cases, at their own discretion, give a handler and his dog a second chance on a new track. A track for each dog entered shall be plotted on the ground by one or both judges not less than one day before the test, the track being marked by flags which the tracklayer can follow readily on the day of the test. A chart of each track shall be made up in duplicate, showing the approximate length in yards of each leg, and major landmarks and boundaries, if any. Both of these charts shall be marked at the time the dog is tracking, one by each of the judges, so as to show the approximate course followed by the dog. The judges shall sign their charts and show on each whether the dog "Passed" or "Failed," the time the tracklayer started, the time the dog started and finished tracking, a brief description of ground, wind and weather conditions, the wind direction, and a note of any steep hills or valleys.

The Club or Tracking Test Secretary, after a licensed or member tracking test, shall forward the two copies of the judges' marked charts, the entry forms with certifications attached, and a marked and certified copy of the catalog pages or sheets listing the dogs entered in the tracking test, to The American Kennel Club so as to reach its office within seven days after the close of the test.

CHAPTER 7
Nonregular Classes

Section 1. *Graduate Novice Class.* The Graduate Novice class shall be for C.D. dogs that have not been certified by a judge to have received a qualifying score toward a C.D.X. title prior to the closing of entries. Dogs in this class may be handled by the owner or any other person. A person may handle more than one dog in this class, but each dog must have a separate handler for the Long Sit and Long Down exercises when judged in the same group. Dogs entered in Graduate Novice may also be entered in one of the Open classes.

Performances and judging shall be as in the Regular classes, except that the Figure 8 is omitted from the Heel on Leash exercise. The exercises, maximum scores and order of judging in the Graduate Novice class are:

1. Heel on Leash (no Figure 8)	30
2. Stand for Examination	30
3. Open Heel Free	40
4. Open Drop on Recall	40
5. Open Long Sit	30
6. Open Long Down	30
Maximum Total Score	200

Section 2. *Brace Class.* The Brace class shall be for braces of dogs of the same breed that are eligible under these Regulations and capable of performing the Novice exercises. The dogs need not be owned by the same person, but must be handled by one handler. Dogs may be shown unattached or coupled, the coupling device to be not less than six inches over-all length; whichever method is used must be continued throughout all exercises. A separate Official Entry Form must be completed in full for each dog entered.

Exercises, performances and judging shall be as in the Novice class. The brace should work in unison at all times. Either or both dogs in a brace may be entered in another class or classes at the same trial.

Section 3. *Veterans Class.* The Veterans class shall be for dogs that have an obedience title and are eight or more years old prior to the closing of entries. The exercises shall be performed and judged as in the Novice class. Dogs entered in the Veterans class may not be entered in any Regular class.

Section 4. *Versatility Class.* The Versatility class shall be for dogs that are eligible under these Regulations and capable of performing the Utility exercises. Owners may enter more than one dog. Dogs in this class may be handled by the owner or any other person, and may be entered in another class or classes at the same trial.

Six exercises will be performed, two each from the Novice, Open and

Utility classes, except that there will be no Group exercises. The exercises will be performed and judged as in the Regular classes. The exercises to be performed by each dog will be determined by the handlers drawing one of a set of cards listing combinations of the six exercises totaling 200 points. These cards will be furnished by the trial-giving clubs. Each handler shall provide a dumbbell, Scent Discrimination articles and Directed Retrieve gloves.

Novice	exercise No. 1.	25
Novice	exercise No. 2.	25
Open	exercise No. 1.	35
Open	exercise No. 2.	35
Utility	exercise No. 1.	40
Utility	exercise No. 2.	40
	Maximum Total Score	200

Section 5. *Team Class.* The Team class shall be for teams of any four dogs that are eligible under these Regulations. Five dogs may be entered, one to be considered an alternate for which no entry fee shall be required. However, the same four dogs must perform all exercises. Dogs need not be owner-handled, need not be entered in another class at the same trial, and need not have obedience titles. A separate Official Entry Form must be completed in full for each dog entered.

There shall be two judges, one of whom will call commands while the other scores the teams' performances. The teams will be judged one at a time, except for the Long Sit and Long Down exercises which shall be done with no more than four teams (16 dogs) in the ring.

The dogs on a team will perform the exercises simultaneously and will be judged as specified for the Novice class, except that a Drop on Recall will be used in place of the Recall exercise. In all exercises except the Drop on Recall, the teams have the option of executing the judge's commands on the team captain's repeat of the command.

In the Figure Eight portion of the Heel on Leash exercise, five stewards will be used. The stewards shall stand eight feet apart in a straight line. One dog and his handler shall stand between two stewards, all members of the team facing in the same direction. On orders from the judge, the team shall perform the Figure Eight, each handler starting around the steward on his left and circling only the two stewards between whom he had been standing.

In the Drop on Recall exercise, the handlers will leave their dogs simultaneously on command of the judge. The dogs shall be called or signalled in one at a time on a separate command from the judge to each handler. The handler shall, without any additional command from the judge, command or signal his dog to drop at a spot mid-way between the line of dogs and the handlers. Each dog shall remain in the Down position until all four have been called and dropped, whereupon the judge shall give the command to call the dogs, which shall be called or signalled simultaneously. The finish shall be done in unison on command from the judge.

Section 6. *Team Class, Scoring.* Scoring of the Team class shall be based on the performance of the dogs and handlers individually plus team precision and coordination. Each dog and handler will be scored against the customary maximum, for a team total of 800 maximum available points. Individual dog's scores need not be recorded. The exercises and maximum scores are:

1.	Heel on Leash	160
2.	Stand for Examination	120
3.	Heel Free	160
4.	Drop on Recall	120
5.	Long Sit	120
6.	Long Down	120
	Maximum Total Score	800

APPENDIX II

Where to Obtain Show Information

Several monthly publications list upcoming shows and obedience trials. The most complete listing is to be found in the *AKC Gazette,* which can be obtained from the American Kennel Club, 51 Madison Avenue, New York, New York 10010.

In addition, the following three magazines are available at most good pet shops, and contain relatively complete listings of upcoming shows all over the country:

Dog World
Judy-Berner Publishing Company
10060 West Roosevelt Road
Westchester, Illinois 60153

Front and Finish
P.O. Box 333
Galesburg, Illinois 61401

Off-Lead
8140 Coronado Lane
Rome, New York 13440

Once you have decided on the shows you wish to enter, you can write for premium listings to the trial secretary of that show, if it is being locally sponsored, or to the company that is holding the show on behalf of the particular kennel club. The following are licensed superintendents and companies that regularly hold obedience trials:

Mrs. Bernice Behrendt
470 38th Avenue
San Francisco, California, 94121

Bow Dog Show Organization
9999 Broadstreet
Detroit, Michigan, 48204

Jack Bradshaw III
727 Venice Boulevard
Los Angeles, California, 90015

Norman E. Brown
Route 2, Box 256
Spokane, Washington, 99207

Foley Dog Show Organization
2009 Ranstead Street
Philadelphia, Pennsylvania, 19103

Roy J. Jones
P. O. Box 307
Garrett, Indiana, 46738

Lewis C. Keller
P. O. Box 11
Mohnton, Pennsylvania, 19540

Moss Dog Shows
P. O. Box 20205
Greensboro, N.C., 27420

Jack Onofrio
P. O. Box 25764
Oklahoma City, Oklahoma, 73125

Jack Thomsen Dog Shows
2573 W. Main Street
Littleton, Colorado, 80120

Webb Dog Shows
500 West North Street
P. O. Box 546
Auburn, Indiana, 46706

APPENDIX III

Obedience Judge's Worksheets:
Graduate Novice Class and Long Sit, Long Down,
Group Examination Chart

OBEDIENCE TRIAL SCORE BREAKDOWN

For Judge's Use ONLY — Not to be distributed or shown to exhibitors
GRADUATE NOVICE CLASS

SHOW.......................................   Dog No.............

DATE.......................................   BREED ....

EXERCISE	NON-QUALIFYING ZERO	NON-QUALIFYING LESS THAN 50%	QUALIFYING (OVER 50%) SUBSTANTIAL ... MINOR	MAXIMUM POINTS	SCORE
HEEL ON LEASH	Unmanageable....... ☐ Unqualified Heeling ☐	Handler continually adapts pace to dog.. ☐ Constant tight leash, or guiding............. ☐	☐ ....Dog interferes with handler........ ☐ ....Extra commands or signals......... ☐ ....Sluggish.................. ☐ ....Sniffing................ ☐ ....Lagging................ ☐ ....Forging................ ☐ ....Heeling wide-turns-abouts......... ☐ ....Poor sits.............. ☐ Handler error...................	**30**	
STAND FOR EXAMINATION OFF LEAD	Sits before or during examination.......... ☐ Growls or snaps.... ☐	Moves away before or during examination............ ☐ Shows shyness or resentment........... ☐	☐ ....Extra command or signal........... ☐ ....Moving feet.............. ☐ ....Moves after examination completed. ☐ ....Sits as handler returns.............. ☐ Handler error...............	**30**	
HEEL FREE AND FIGURE 8	Unmanageable....... ☐ Unqualified heeling ☐	Handler continually adapts pace to dog.. ☐ Leaving handler...... ☐	Heeling Fig. 8 ☐ ...Extra commands or signals........ ☐ ☐ ☐ ...Forging...................... ☐ ☐ ☐ ...Crowding handler.............. ☐ ☐ ☐ ...Sniffing..................... ☐ ☐ ☐ ...Lagging...................... ☐ ☐ ☐ . Heeling wide - on turns - abouts.. ☐ ☐ ☐ ..Poor sits.................... ☐ ☐ ☐ Handler error .... ☐ ☐	**40**	
DROP ON RECALL	Does not come on first command or signal .... ☐ Does not drop on first command or signal .... ☐	Extra com. or sig. to stay after handler leaves........ ☐ Moved from place left...................... ☐ Anticipated: Recall................. ☐ Drop .... ☐ Come in .... ☐ Sat out of reach ...... ☐	☐ Stood or lay down Touching Handler ☐ ☐ Extra com. or sig. Sat between feet ☐ ☐ Before leaving ☐ Finish Poor sit ☐ ☐ Slow response Poor finish........... ☐ ☐ Slow return Lack of naturalness ☐ Slow drop smoothness.......... ☐ ☐ No sit in front ☐ No finish	**40**	
			MAX. SUB-TOTAL	**140**	
LONG SIT (3 MINUTES) Handler out of sight	Did not remain in place................. ☐ Disturbed other dog ☐	Stood or lay down before handler returns to heel position............ ☐	☐ Minor move before Minor move after handler returns to handler returns heel position to heel position..... ☐	**30**	
LONG DOWN (5 MINUTES) Handler out of sight	Did not remain in place................. ☐ Disturbed other dog ☐	Sat or stood before handler returns to heel position................. ☐	☐ Minor move before Minor move after handler returns to handler returns heel position to heel position..... ☐	**30**	
Total Score			**MAX. POINTS ▶**	**200**	

Less Penalty for Un-controlled Behavior   ☐ H. Disciplining   ☐ Shows fear   ☐ Fouling ring   ☐ Disqualified   ☐ Expelled   ☐ Excused   ☐ Other*

COMMENTS*   TOTAL NET SCORE ▶

Several nonregular classes can be given at obedience trials (see Appendix I, chap. 7), one of the most frequent being Graduate Novice. Figure A-1 shows the obedience judge's score sheet for this class. Before entering, read the AKC regulations for Graduate Novice (Appendix I) and consult the premium announcement for the show you decide on.

The Graduate Novice class is designed to enable your dog to compete in obedience trials after he has earned a C.D. degree, but is not quite ready to enter Open competition and work toward the C.D.X. degree. However, some Open training is presupposed in the exercises—that is, your dog must be in some stage of training toward Open competition.

No titles are awarded in Graduate Novice (or in any of the non-regular classes); it is just for fun. Often there are handsome prizes offered for dogs who score highly in this class.

Figure A-2 is the Obedience Judge's Worksheet used to score dogs in the regular Novice, Open, and Utility classes for the group exercises. We have included it here because it covers all three regular classes.

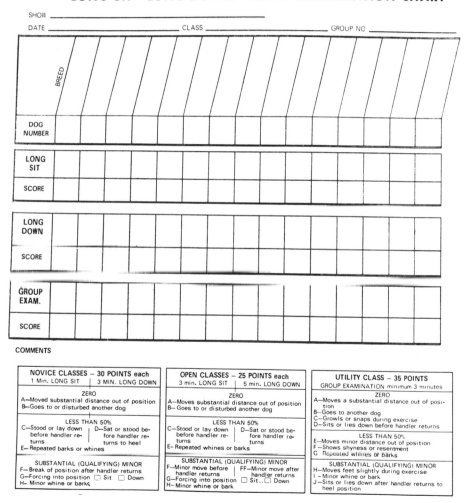

OBEDIENCE JUDGE'S WORKSHEET — not to be distributed
LONG SIT • LONG DOWN • GROUP EXAMINATION CHART

SHOW _____

DATE _____ CLASS _____ GROUP NO _____

NOVICE CLASSES – 30 POINTS each	OPEN CLASSES – 25 POINTS each	UTILITY CLASS – 35 POINTS
1 Min. LONG SIT	3 MIN. LONG DOWN	3 min. LONG SIT	5 min. LONG DOWN	GROUP EXAMINATION minimum 3 minutes

NOVICE CLASSES – 30 POINTS each
1 Min. LONG SIT | 3 MIN. LONG DOWN
ZERO
A—Moved substantial distance out of position
B—Goes to or disturbed another dog
LESS THAN 50%
C—Stood or lay down before handler returns | D—Sat or stood before handler returns to heel
E—Repeated barks or whines
SUBSTANTIAL (QUALIFYING) MINOR
F—Break of position after handler returns
G—Forcing into position ☐ Sit ☐ Down
H—Minor whine or barks

OPEN CLASSES – 25 POINTS each
3 min. LONG SIT | 5 min. LONG DOWN
ZERO
A—Moves substantial distance out of position
B—Goes to or disturbed another dog
LESS THAN 50%
C—Stood or lay down before handler returns | D—Sat or stood before handler returns
E—Repeated whines or barks
SUBSTANTIAL (QUALIFYING) MINOR
F—Minor move before handler returns | FF—Minor move after handler returns
G—Forcing into position ☐ Sit ☐ Down
H—Minor whine or bark

UTILITY CLASS – 35 POINTS
GROUP EXAMINATION minimum 3 minutes
ZERO
A—Moves a substantial distance out of position
B—Goes to another dog
C—Growls or snaps during exercise
D—Sits or lies down before handler returns
LESS THAN 50%
E—Moves minor distance out of position
F—Shows shyness or resentment
G Repeated whines or barks
SUBSTANTIAL (QUALIFYING) MINOR
H—Moves feet slightly during exercise
I – Minor whine or bark
J—Sits or lies down after handler returns to heel position

365

APPENDIX IV

Plans for Constructing Broad Jump and High Jump Used in Open and Utility Training

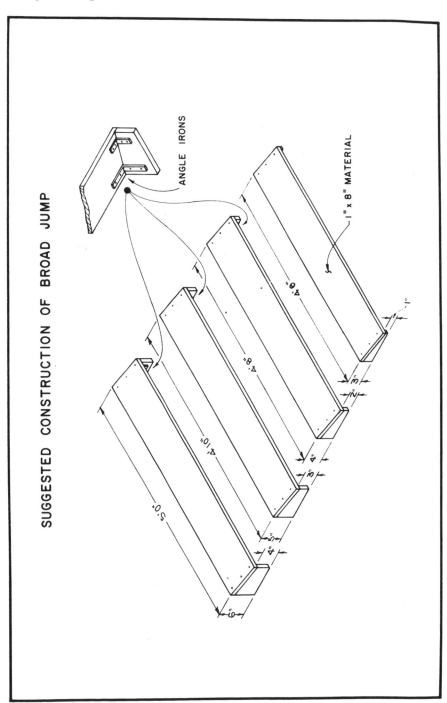

SUGGESTED CONSTRUCTION OF BROAD JUMP

ANGLE IRONS

1" x 8" MATERIAL